The School Superintendent: Theory, Practice, and Cases

Theodore J. Kowalski
Ball State University

Pearson
Education

Merrill,
an imprint of Prentice Hall
Upper Saddle River, New Jersey   *Columbus, Ohio*

Library of Congress Cataloging-in-Publication Data

Kowalski, Theodore J.
    The school superintendent : theory, practice, and cases / Theodore J. Kowalski.
      p. cm.
    Includes bibliographical references and indexes.
    ISBN 0-13-462953-1
    1. School superintendents—United States. 2. School management and organiza-
tion—United States. 3. School superintendents—United States—Case studies. 4. School
management and organization—United States—Case studies.   I. Title.
    LB2831.72.K69   1999   98-6237
                                                          CIP

Cover art: © Diana Ong/SuperStock
Editor: Debra A. Stollenwerk
Production Editor: Linda Hillis Bayma
Design Coordinator: Karrie M. Converse
Text Designer: STELLARViSIONs
Cover Designer: Rod Harris
Production Manager: Pamela D. Bennett
Electronic Text Management: Marilyn Wilson Phelps, David Snyder, Karen L. Bretz, Tracey
    B. Ward
Illustrations: Tom Kennedy
Director of Marketing: Kevin Flanagan
Marketing Manager: Suzanne Stanton
Advertising/Marketing Coordinator: Krista Groshong

This book was set in Leawood Book by Prentice Hall and was printed and bound by R.R.
Donnelley & Sons Company. The cover was printed by Phoenix Color Corp.

 © 1999 by Prentice-Hall, Inc.
Simon & Schuster/A Viacom Company
Upper Saddle River, New Jersey 07458

Printed in the United States of America

10 9 8 7 6 5 4 3 2 1

ISBN: 0-13-462953-1

Prentice-Hall International (UK) Limited, *London*
Prentice-Hall of Australia Pty. Limited, *Sydney*
Prentice-Hall of Canada, Inc., *Toronto*
Prentice-Hall Hispanoamericana, S. A., *Mexico*
Prentice-Hall of India Private Limited, *New Delhi*
Prentice-Hall of Japan, Inc., *Tokyo*
Simon & Schuster Asia Pte. Ltd., *Singapore*
Editora Prentice-Hall do Brasil, Ltda., *Rio de Janeiro*

To the thousands of dedicated school district superintendents
who devote their service to our nation's youth.

Preface

INTRODUCTION

Throughout the history of American public education, there have been recurring cycles during which critics expressed their displeasure with schools and demanded improvements. In part, these periods of unrest reflect the fact that this country's citizens have never reached consensus regarding the purposes of public education. The current quest for educational excellence, however, has several distinct characteristics that make it unique. First, the spotlight of public interest has been on public schools for an inordinately long time; at least since the early 1980s, there have been myriad written reports calling for school reform. Second, policymakers appear to have learned that liberty, equity, efficiency, and excellence in schools need to be balanced; failed policy initiatives spanning the past two decades remind us that many legal, social, economic, and political circumstances prevent narrow, centralized agendas for school reform from succeeding. Third, this era of reform has been evolutionary: Current efforts have shifted from tinkering with programs and people and are now concentrating on reshaping institutional culture and structure. And fourth, the contemporary context of school reform presents intricate challenges: Political instability, demographic change, and social uncertainty exemplify conditions that make school improvement both more necessary and more difficult. Collectively, these developments have produced new opportunities and challenges for local districts and schools—and they also have created unfamiliar role expectations for school administrators.

The current context of practice has increased the demand for highly qualified educational leaders. In addition to traditional management roles, school superintendents are now being called upon to be visionary leaders, capable of bringing communities and educators together so that all can engage in meaningful discussions about school and society and use democratic procedures to chart a course for the future. While arguably a daunting task, it is also an extraordinary opportunity. The leadership of superintendents in the next few decades may well shape the nature of education for much of the 21st century. However, at a time when the need for leadership has never been greater, there appears to be a diminishing interest among administrators in this key position. Many school boards, especially in the most troubled districts, report dwindling pools of applicants. Women, who constitute approximately two thirds of the educational profession, and minorities, who constitute the fastest-growing segments of the population, are grossly underrepresented in the superintendency. Among the many causes for these conditions is the reality that the superintendency remains one of least understood and least studied positions in education.

ABOUT THIS BOOK

This book is about professional practice in the superintendency. It is intended for educators who are studying school administration, practicing superintendents, and others who have an interest in school district governance. The primary intent is to provide both theoretical and practical insights into the evolving responsibilities associated with being the chief executive officer of a local school system. As such, school administration is treated as a science and a craft involving professional artistry. The position is examined in relation to challenges and potential rewards, frustrations and accomplishments. Each chapter concludes with a brief case study that addresses a major topic and attempts to engage you in reflective thinking. By relating the content of the chapter to your own rich experiences in life and in the profession, you should expand your professional knowledge base and gain a better understanding of yourself as a practitioner.

Many individuals contributed to this book. First, I want to recognize the five outstanding practitioners who served as an editorial panel for the case studies: Michael Benway, Superintendent, Valparaiso, Indiana; Philip McDaniel, Superintendent, Rock Hill, South Carolina; Douglas Otto, Superintendent, Plano, Texas; Wendy Robinson, Deputy Superintendent, Fort Wayne, Indiana; and C. Steven Snider, Superintendent, Maine Township High School District 207, Park Ridge, Illinois. Their comments and recommendations were invaluable, and I am truly grateful for their assistance.

Appreciation also is expressed to professional colleagues at other universities who served as reviewers: Carol J. Carter, Central Connecticut State University; Gary M. Crow, University of Utah; Glen I. Earthman, Virginia Polytechnic Institute and State University; and Beverly Geltner, Eastern Michigan University. Their insights were not only helpful but also encouraging and constructive.

I am especially grateful to my editor at Merrill/Prentice-Hall, Debbie Stollenwerk. She provided counsel throughout the writing of the book, and she is an excellent teacher. On a day-to-day basis, my work was facilitated by my graduate assistants, Michelle Springer, Melissa Peraino, and Shilo Cowles. Special assistance and encouragement were contributed by faculty colleagues and students in my doctoral seminar at Ball State University. Many practicing superintendents also contributed by sharing their thoughts about their profession and their work. To all of these individuals and to my wife, Mary Anne, and my four children, I express deep appreciation.

Brief Contents

Contents

6 ✧ Policy Statements: Purpose, Analysis, and Implementation   161

7 ✧ Four Conceptions of the Superintendency   183

8 ✧ Leadership in the School District   209

9 ✧ Management of the School District   245

10 ✧ Being an Effective Communicator   281

11 ✧ Leadership in the Larger Community   313

12 ✧ Work Lives, Stress, and Adjustments   343

13 ✧ Personal Development: Decision-Making Skills and Ongoing Professional Growth   369

14 ✦ Becoming a Superintendent   401

Chapter 1

The Superintendent: Yesterday and Today

Key Concepts

- ✧ The evolution of the superintendency in education
- ✧ Early influences on practice
- ✧ Changing ideas about the position of superintendent
- ✧ Common roles and responsibilities
- ✧ Professional knowledge and skills
- ✧ Licensure
- ✧ Quality-of-life considerations
- ✧ Career paths to the superintendency
- ✧ Unique issues facing women and minorities

In November 1907, the cover of the *School Board Journal* exhibited a cartoon that showed a vacancy notice for a superintendent of schools posted on the front door of the office of a board of education. The notice stated that the board was seeking an individual who would please everybody, from ultraconservatives to radical progressives. This almost-century-old cartoon illustrates that even in the formative years of public education and city government in the United States, larger public school systems expected superintendents to appease groups holding divergent values and beliefs. Democratic pluralism, however, is but one factor that has made the superintendency a challenging, complex position of public trust.

This chapter looks back over the period of history in the United States when the school superintendency was created, tracing the role as it was shaped by a myriad of social, economic, and political factors. The purpose of the overview is to provide a foundation for understanding present conditions of practice, especially those involving qualifications, role expectations, and rewards of school superintendents. Also explored is the topic of access: that is, how do educators typically become superintendents? In the discussion of access, a special focus is placed on barriers faced by women and minorities.

HISTORY OF THE POSITION

Although most readily identified with local school districts, superintendency actually exists at three levels in a state: local, statewide, and regional or intermediate. In addition to local district superintendents, states have either a commissioner or a superintendent of public instruction (commonly called state superintendents). State superintendents serve as the chief executive officer of a state's department of education and typically report to a state board of education. In many states, there are also superintendents who administer intermediate districts, that is, regional entities that serve as middle units of government between the state and local districts. Directly or indirectly, the position of superintendent evolved at all three of these levels for essentially the same reason—those charged with operating state government recognized the need to develop and coordinate state systems of public elementary and secondary education.

Development of State Agencies

The period of 1830 to 1850 is recognized as the era of the common school movement—that is, the quest to build a state system of public elementary and secondary education. Joel Spring (1994) identified three distinctive aspects of this movement that separated it from previous educational developments. They were (1) an emphasis on educating all children in a common schoolhouse, (2) the idea of using schools as an instrument of government policy, and (3) the creation of state agencies to control local schools (p. 63). Superintendency developed in conjunction with this movement. The first state superintendency was established in 1812 in New York, and the duties assigned to the position included developing a plan for a common school system, reporting the management of public funds, and providing school-related information for the state legislature (Butts & Cremin, 1953).

Between 1830 and 1850, every northern state and some southern states created an office of state superintendent. In several states, however, the establishment of this office merely entailed adding specific educational responsibilities to state officials already employed in other positions. By 1880, 24 states had also established a state presence in public education by enacting legislation establishing state boards of education (Butts & Cremin, 1953). State departments of education—agencies of control under the jurisdiction of state superintendents and state boards—provided a hierarchical system of control necessary to implement a common system of public elementary and secondary education in a state (Spring, 1994). Thus, responsibility for education in the state typically was consolidated in the superintendent, board of education, and department of public instruction. This setup was designed to ensure that students across a given state would receive a relatively uniform curriculum and relatively similar educational experiences.

Development of Intermediate School Districts

Perhaps intermediate school districts are best described as confederations of local districts established to facilitate communication and decision making between local school systems and state government. The word *confederation* connotes that member local districts usually have substantial control over the scope of activities to be executed by the intermediate districts (Knezevich, 1984). Often the governance board of an intermediate district is composed of superintendents from the member local districts, but in some instances, school board members from affiliated districts also serve in this capacity.

Often associated with intermediate districts is the position of *county superintendent*. This administrative office typically served in the past as a liaison between small rural districts and the state department of education. Its primary responsibilities were to provide management and collective services for schools that had neither a district superintendent nor a school board (many of these schools operated under the jurisdiction of township trustees). It was not unusual for county superintendents to be elected by popular vote, and in some instances, they were elected on partisan ballots. However, as states moved to reorganize and consolidate local school districts, the position of county superintendent became less common.

Both the form and scope of services provided by intermediate districts differ substantially among the states in which they are found. This is to be expected since "each of the thirty-nine states with intermediate units of school administration has a somewhat unique history of the unit's development" (Campbell, Cunningham, Nystrand, & Usdan, 1990, p. 133). Today, intermediate units often provide a range of services such as cooperative purchasing, cooperative media libraries, and technology repair services—services made less expensive because of higher volumes of transactions. The chief administrator in an intermediate district is not always called a superintendent; some have the title of executive director or director.

Development of Local School Districts

The establishment of local school districts is unique to the United States, and the decision to create this system was rooted in the nation's cherished principles of liberty and equity. In colonial America, public education was governed through town meetings, and subsequently it was placed under the control of town select-men (that is, elected representatives). This system of control was carried over into the new American republic (Russo, 1992). Thus, long before the creation of state departments of education, communities determined both the type and scope of education provided. While self-determination was perceived by many citizens to fit in with the philosophy of an emerging democracy, astute state government officials realized that total local control would likely result in at least some inadequate schools that provided less than equal opportunities to students. Even in the earliest years in the history of the nation, inequities in the quantity and quality of education among communities were apparent. Some state leaders realized that problems relating to the adequacy and equity of public education would not resolve themselves; solving them would require the intervention of state government. Actively involving the state in matters of public elementary and secondary education, though, would undoubtedly be a distasteful act to most local officials, who would see their freedom of action limited.

Faced with this dilemma, state officials sought a compromise that would reasonably balance the principles of adequacy and equity in education with liberty. Their solution was to simultaneously establish state control and reaffirm local control. This seemingly contradictory approach was accomplished by creating state agencies to oversee public education, while delegating select policy powers to local school boards. The strategy effectively made local school boards legal extensions of state government. It was within this context that state officials achieved the compromise between seeking adequacy and efficiency through a state system of public education and the provision of liberty through local boards of education (Butts & Cremin, 1953).

In its early days, the United States was predominantly rural. A lack of transportation meant that schools had to be dispersed so that students could readily reach them on foot. This resulted in many relatively small schools and school districts. In the numerous sparsely populated areas of the nation, local school districts consisted of only one school. As the United States urbanized and industrialized, this situation gradually changed, and local districts became larger in area, in the number of schools operated, and in student enrollment. Following World War II, large cities spilled into suburbs, and the new communities created additional school districts. In rural areas and smaller towns, economic realities and educational goals encouraged states to enact school consolidation laws that led to fewer but larger school districts. Collectively, these trends reduced the number of school districts in the United States from approximately 130,000 in 1930 to 15,500 in 1990 (Lunenburg & Ornstein, 1991).

Powers vested in school boards are specified in state constitutions and statutes. Commonly, these powers include the ability to raise money through taxes, expend public funds, enter into legal contracts, and otherwise function as a legal entity. Generally speaking, boards have three primary responsibilities: (1) ensure that state laws, rules, and regulations are followed; (2) establish policy in areas not covered by state laws, rules, and regulations; and (3) employ a superintendent to serve as chief executive officer.

From an organizational perspective, local school districts were far more complex than most observers realized. Campbell et al. (1990) described local districts as the most common but diverse agencies of local government. They wrote, "Their diversity illustrates the tenaciousness with which Americans hold to these remnants of localism and grassroots expression of the public will" (p. 107). From their inception, local districts have been political entities (subdivisions of the state that serve to balance centralization and decentralization), legal entities (quasi-municipal corporations), geographic entities (defined by specific boundaries), social institutions (engaged in symbiotic relationships with their communities), and educational entities (agencies with specific responsibilities for transmitting knowledge and skills) (Knezevich, 1984).

While the specific scope of responsibility and authority granted to local boards has varied among the states, these subdivisions of state government generally have been given the duties of establishing schools, erecting buildings, employing a superintendent, establishing policy and rules necessary to govern the schools, and raising and expending public funds (Campbell et al., 1990). But despite a similar base of authority that gives them broad discretion in action, local school boards have exhibited significant differences in the way they exercise their power, especially in the arena of formulating effective policy. To a very large extent, the variation can be explained by two critical factors that form the parameters for any analysis of local school boards:

- The extent to which members of the local boards of education represent the population of the schools
- The actual amount of power wielded by boards of education in relation to the professional staffs of schools (Spring, 1985)

Even within a given state, the efficacy of local school boards varies markedly.

Evolution of the Superintendency

The position of local school superintendent emerged in the mid-1800s. Between 1837 and 1850, 13 districts (all urban) established the position; by 1890, most major cities had followed this lead. However, efforts to establish the post often generated substantial conflict. For instance, a number of political bosses feared that school superintendents would amass their own power and be able to stand apart from the entangled mechanisms of big-city government. The fact that some cities disestablished and then reestablished the post shows the ambivalence with which the office was regarded (Knezevich, 1984). Even in these formative years, it was evident that politics was on a collision course with the professional role of school superintendents. Political bosses were suspicious of government officials who sought independence, and they became extremely distrustful of school superintendents who were trying to use professionalism as a shield against political machines.

In large measure, the evolution of the superintendency paralleled the development of schools that were divided into grades. Previously most schools had one room and were operated by a single educator who acted as teacher, principal, and at times, even custodian; in fact, many who held this position were called head teachers (Brubacher, 1966). As the one-room schoolhouse was replaced with graded schools organized into local districts, one of the major responsibilities of the superintendent was to write a uniform course of study that could be implemented in all schools in the system. Spring (1994) wrote:

> The development of the role of the superintendent was important in the evolution of the hierarchical educational organization. The primary reason for creating the position was to have a person work full-time at supervising classroom instruction and assuring uniformity in the curriculum. (p. 119)

As previously noted, the common school reform movement contributed substantially to the need for both state and local district superintendents. The superintendent's role was key in communicating the elements of the common curriculum and in providing the supervision to ensure its implementation.

Prompted primarily by political fears, powerful individuals in the community often exerted influence to ensure that the very first superintendents were relegated to doing menial assignments and detail work. The status of the superintendents was purposely reduced so that they would act as servants to, rather than leaders of, the school board. Apprehensions regarding the power of superintendents also resulted from a lack of confidence by school board members in the ability of the people in the position, mostly former teachers, to manage money and other resources (Knezevich, 1984). Most men who were appointed to this position in the formative years, especially during the 19th century, were teachers who had no specific training in managing finance, people, or other material resources. Kowalski and Reitzug (1993) noted:

> Some were elevated to administration because they were perceived by school trustees, or others legally in control of the school, as possessing the qualities of a leader; some were selected because they were effective teachers; others were advanced because of political connections; and still others were promoted simply because they were men. (p. 9)

Around 1910, a number of critical circumstances pushed the superintendency toward a preoccupation with management. Some of the more important ones are summarized in Table 1–1. These included the growing influence of scientific management, the increasing size of school districts, the quest for standardization,

Table 1–1
Examples of factors that encouraged a managerial role for the superintendency (approximately 1910 to 1930)

Factor	Explanation
Principles of scientific management	Practices deemed successful in industry were applied to schools.
Casting schools as agencies of control	Close supervision was necessary to ensure that the goals of the common school effort would be attained.
Separating teaching from administration	Management was deemed to be a male responsibility; teaching was cast as a subordinate role to be performed largely by women.
Establishing bureaucratic-like structures	Efficiency would be achieved if administrators carefully managed material and human resources; teachers and other employees required supervision to ensure that they did their work in accordance with policies and rules.
Quest for identity and prestige	School administration most likely would be recognized as a responsibility separate from, and superior to, teaching if it was viewed by the public as a managerial responsibility.
Demarcation between policy development and policy administration	School boards would be responsible for determining what should be done, and administrators would be responsible for determining how things would get done.

and the emergence of school administration as a specialization within the education profession. Leading figures in school administration wanted to separate themselves from teachers (largely because teachers were not generally held in high esteem nor were they paid reasonable salaries). Gradually they succeeded: in the eyes of the public, principals and superintendents became managers, and teachers were relegated to a subordinate role.

William Eaton (1990) defined professionalism as a concerted effort, over time, to create a distinct occupational role and then persuading others to accept this role as the standard. According to him, both actual skills and preferred behaviors are involved. He wrote, "In exchange for systematic training and endorsement of a code of ethics, the professional demands autonomy in the process of exercising judgment over practice" (p. 33). There were multiple reasons superintendents sought this standing. In addition to the obvious desire to gain status, at least three other motivations were evident:

- The economic and social successes of industrial management were viewed positively by the general public, and, thus, the idea of being classified as professional managers was appealing to many school administrators.
- Professionalism almost always bestowed additional powers on individuals in offices that attained that status.

- Breaking free of the big-city bureaucracies made it more likely that key decisions relating to schools could be made on the basis of educational rather than political considerations.

The quest for professionalism was also abetted by those professors who saw an opportunity to establish educational administration as a respected specialization, one equal to management in the private sector (Callahan, 1962).

Before 1900, only a few courses in school administration were offered at universities; Columbia University granted the first two doctorates in this specialization in 1905 (Cooper & Boyd, 1987). From approximately 1900 to 1920, professors of education expanded course offerings in administration, especially in areas such as business management, finance, and efficiency techniques. Momentum toward separate degree programs kept building. By 1927, the catalog of Columbia University described the superintendent of schools as the manager of the entire school system, a claim designed to affirm that the position had become comparable to ones in the business profession (Callahan, 1962).

Most historians agree that the role of the urban superintendency as it developed during the Industrial Revolution influenced practice in all types of school districts for much of the 20th century. Keep in mind that big-city districts were the models to follow at the end of the 19th century; they were at the forefront of educational reform. Many of the practices of urban districts, especially those involving specialization and uniform curricula, were ultimately emulated by smaller districts; education professors often presented urban superintendents to their students as role models. Even more relevant, the accomplishments of big-city school districts were usually ascribed to the successful implementation of bureaucratic structure and scientific management—features that had become institutionalized in most big-city districts by the mid-1920s (Kowalski, 1995). Thus, standardized programming, the principles of scientific management, and perceptions of urban superintendents as ideal practitioners intertwined to create an image of superintendent as manager.

Over the past 5 decades, several scholars have studied the work lives of early urban superintendents in an effort to identify their motivations and long-term influence on the practice of school administration. Among these studies, the one that has unquestionably received the most attention was done by Raymond Callahan. In his book *Education and the Cult of Efficiency* (1962), Callahan described the thesis of vulnerability. Studying the development of urban schools during and immediately following the Industrial Revolution, the noted historian concluded that early urban superintendents were the political pawns of the rich and powerful. He argued that urban superintendents, especially during the period between 1910 and 1930, were often intimidated by strong-willed and persuasive school board members who advocated the wholesale infusion of scientific management into public education.

Since the mid-1960s, however, a number of scholars have questioned the accuracy of Callahan's conclusion that superintendents at the time were merely dupes manipulated by the rich and powerful. For example, some writers have argued that rather than being political weaklings, many superintendents during that era were actually cunning, intelligent leaders who skillfully worked within existing political realities (e.g., Burroughs, 1974; Tyack, 1972). Others concluded that the superintendents embraced bureaucracy, not because of fear and intimidation, but as a means to amass and protect personal power (e.g., Thomas & Moran, 1992). Despite differing conclusions about motivations, scholars generally agree that school administrators during this era had embraced the principles of industrial management.

While the managerial responsibilities of the superintendency have remained prominent in job descriptions ever since the early 1900s, opinions about the ideal role for this position have changed over time. A few years after the publication of *Education and the Cult of Efficiency*, Raymond Callahan (1966) authored a historical analysis of ideas about the role of the superintendent between 1865 and 1966. Again focusing on big-city districts, he identified four stages in development of the position, each resulting in an emphasis on a new and different aspect of the ideal role for the superintendent.

1. The first aspect, beginning after the Civil War and continuing to approximately 1910, was the *superintendent as scholarly leader*. From this perspective, the men in the position (the position was at first exclusively for males) saw themselves as teachers of teachers, and they discussed their jobs primarily in educational journals and at professional meetings. Their interests centered on educational needs, problems, and innovations of the day.

2. *Superintendent as business manager* constituted the second aspect (and the focal point of Callahan's previously mentioned book published in 1962).

3. The third aspect was that of *superintendent as educational leader in democratic schools*. In part, this shift was engendered by critics who attacked the viewpoint that school superintendents should be primarily managers. At least in formal discussions of ideal roles, professors and leading practitioners advocated that instructional leadership in democratic institutions was the most important responsibility of a superintendent. In the literature in the field, from roughly 1930 to 1954, a dominant theme was advocacy for the superintendent to be an educational leader.

4. The *superintendent as applied social scientist* constituted Callahan's fourth and final aspect. This stage, from approximately 1955 to 1966, was reflected in a shift in the literature from discussions about what superintendents ought to do to discourse about the realities of practice. Authors argued that economic and political realities required superintendents to understand and apply social science principles in school administration.

Those who occupied the superintendency almost always recognized differences between how they spent their time and energy and what their textbooks had encouraged them to do. In essence, they took for granted that there was a gap between theory and practice. Larry Cuban (1976) studied the actual work lives of three prominent urban superintendents who held office in the late 1960s.

He used as a framework for his study three aspects of the role of the superintendent similar to those developed by Callahan:

- *Teacher-scholar* (the education professional, the instructional leader)
- *Administrative chief* (the authoritarian manager, the specialist in scientific management)
- *Negotiator-statesman* (the person generating support from diverse groups, the one who resolves conflict)

Cuban concluded that superintendents were expected to assume each of these roles at varying times with different publics. Superintendents' success, and even survival, often depended on their ability to make successful transitions among these three distinct roles. To achieve this goal, they not only required an understanding of these roles, they also had to possess the personal flexibility to make appropriate adjustments.

GENERAL CONDITIONS OF PRACTICE

While the literature provides general descriptions of the superintendency, there is surprisingly little information about the actual work lives of the people holding this office. In large measure, this fact is attributable to two circumstances. First, there are many personal variables and situational variables (that is, those related to community and school district) connected with the role of a superintendent—a condition that often diminishes the reliability and validity of research and makes it difficult to formulate generalizations (Kowalski, 1995). Second, the demands of the position make many superintendents reluctant to allocate the time necessary to participate in formal studies. Hence, the superintendency is often discussed in a broad context and within a normative frame of reference.

Role Expectations and Responsibilities

Regardless of the size of a school district, most formal job descriptions for superintendents are long and expansive. They typically include a wide range of managerial duties, instructional leadership responsibilities, and analytical tasks (e.g., planning). Uniformly the job descriptions identify the superintendent as the highest-ranking administrator and the person responsible for reporting directly to the school board. Recently a report approved by a joint committee consisting of representatives from the American Association of School Administrators (AASA) and the National School Boards Association (NSBA) identified the following specific responsibilities for superintendents:

- To serve as the school board's chief executive officer and preeminent educational adviser in all efforts of the board to fulfill its school system governance role

- To serve as the primary educational leader for the school system and chief administrative officer of the entire school district's professional and support staff, including staff members assigned to provide support service to the board
- To serve as a catalyst for the school system's administrative leadership team in proposing and implementing policy changes
- To propose and institute a process for long-range and strategic planning that will engage the board and the community in positioning the school district for success in ensuing years
- To keep all board members informed about school operations and programs
- To interpret the needs of the school system to the board
- To present policy options along with specific recommendations to the board when circumstances require the board to adopt new policies or review existing policies
- To develop and inform the board of administrative procedures needed to implement board policy
- To develop a sound program of school/community relations in concert with the board
- To oversee management of the district's day-to-day operations
- To develop a description for the board of what constitutes effective leadership and management of public schools, taking into account that effective leadership and management are the result of effective governance and effective administration combined
- To develop and carry out a plan for keeping the total professional and support staff informed about the mission, goals, and strategies of the school system and about the important roles all staff members play in realizing them
- To ensure that professional development opportunities are available to all school system employees
- To collaborate with other administrators through national and state professional associations to inform state legislators, members of Congress, and all other appropriate state and federal officials of local concerns and issues
- To ensure that the school system provides equal opportunity for all students
- To evaluate personnel performance in harmony with district policy and to keep the board informed about such evaluations
- To provide all board members with complete background information and a recommendation for school board action on each agenda item well in advance of each board meeting
- To develop and implement a continuing plan for working with the news media[1]

Statements of responsibility that cover all superintendencies obviously must be rather general; however, actual job descriptions approved at the local district level are often equally unspecific. Containing about a dozen sweeping statements of responsibility, job descriptions often convey the message that the superintendent is responsible for all phases of the school district's operations. Therefore, these documents also fail to provide detailed information about the real work lives of superintendents.

---

[1] From *Roles and Relationships: School Boards and Superintendents* by the American Association of School Administrators, 1994, pp. 11–12. Arlington, VA: Author. Printed by permission.

The enrollment and complexity of a school district often are key factors in determining what superintendents actually do on a daily basis. In large districts, for instance, specialization has become quite common. That is to say, superintendents in these settings are able to concentrate on one or two key areas because their other official responsibilities (those listed in the job description) can be relegated to subordinates. At times, school boards in larger districts purposely seek candidates who have established reputations as specialists (e.g., in community relations or in strategic planning). By contrast, superintendents in small-enrollment districts are far more likely to be generalists; that is, they directly engage in all facets of administration. This is especially true in districts where the superintendent is the only professional staff member in central administration. However, despite the obvious differences in the actual work of superintendents in large versus small districts, school boards across all local districts generally continue to emphasize three areas when seeking a new superintendent: (1) curriculum, (2) finance, and (3) public relations (Chand, 1987).

Changing Priorities

Studying the behavior of superintendents in the late 1970s, Jon Morris (1979) found that these administrators tended to have contact networks oriented inward, toward interactions with subordinates, rather than outward, toward interactions outside the school system. This profile was in contrast to the contact networks of top-level managers in business, which look outward. The apparent insulation of the superintendent from other government agencies and civic leaders became a primary reform issue for those who judged school officials to be insensitive to community needs and impervious to changing economic, political, and social conditions.

Expectations that superintendents maintain an ongoing dialogue with the wider community are stronger today than ever before. In large measure, this is because the public increasingly expects superintendents to be builders rather than caretakers. Writing about a new generation of administrators, Susan Moore Johnson (1996) observed, "New superintendents are expected to diagnose local educational needs and recommend strategies for improvement" (p. 276). This means that they must be transformational leaders, individuals who can guide others to rebuild organizational cultures and climates. Perhaps most notable, they must pursue these complex and difficult tasks in a context of democratic decision making and shared authority. Specific initiatives—such as teacher empowerment, community involvement in governance, and deregulation—are reshaping the ideal and the actual role of the superintendent. Facilitation, planning, and effective communication are becoming at least as important in the position as traditional management functions.

One highly visible example of this transition is found in Kentucky, a state in which massive restructuring efforts were initiated with the passage of the Kentucky Education Reform Act of 1990 (commonly called KERA). Ruling that existing laws, policies, and regulations were invalid, the courts ordered a complete reconstruction of governance, curriculum, and financing in the state's system of public elementary and secondary education. This strategy of totally rebuilding a public institution gave local district superintendents little choice but to rethink their roles. Joseph Murphy (1994) made the following observation about local district superintendents in that state: "They saw themselves as managing more by consensus than by command and as facilitating rather than controlling" (p. 27). Generally, the Kentucky reform effort has produced at least three emerging themes for the school district superintendency: (1) a redefining of leadership expectations (e.g., a greater emphasis on the facilitating role), (2) an emphasis on the superintendent's role in community development (e.g., rebuilding a symbiotic relationship between the school and its wider environment), and (3) an expectation of providing support and direction to individual schools as they experience substantive change (Murphy, 1994).

Attempts to redefine the superintendency also are evident in scholarly pursuits and the activities of national organizations. For instance, researchers are beginning to examine superintendent behaviors in relation to effective schools and effective student performance in those schools (e.g., Griffin & Chance, 1994). In past decades, scholars in educational administration concentrated on social psychological processes in organizations, and they basically assumed that effective practices led to desirable outcomes (Boyd, 1992). Now, however, there are strong demands for evidence regarding the effects of superintendent behavior and organizational structure on school effectiveness.

What leadership styles are most effective in redesigned school districts? What mix of centralization and decentralization produces the most favorable outcomes? Questions such as these prompted the primary professional organization for school superintendents, the American Association of School Administrators (AASA), to develop revised standards for practice. Looking at contemporary conditions, the commission charged with this responsibility declared:

> Recent research on the superintendency makes one point amply clear—top-down bureaucratic management is being replaced by bottom-up executive leadership that encourages shared decision making among school staff, community, business, and other stakeholders. (Hoyle, 1993, p. 3)

After obtaining input from practitioners, school board members, professors of educational leadership, and other interested parties in the early 1990s, the AASA embraced eight standards that broadly define practice. An outline of these standards is presented in Table 1–2. John Hoyle (1994), chairman of the AASA Commission on Standards for the Superintendency, declared that these standards provide benchmarks for improving the selection, preparation, and development of superintendents. He additionally asserted that they reflect an environment in which superintendents will be expected to perform as decentralized enablers rather than centralized controllers.

While the AASA standards are useful guidelines for practice, some analysts have questioned whether they address what may be the most relevant issue of the day—the demand to establish links between effective leadership and school outcomes. Larry Cuban (1994) observed the following about the standards:

Table 1–2
General professional standards for the superintendency developed by the
American Association of School Administrators (1993)

Standard	Foci
Leadership and district culture	Developing a collective vision; shaping school culture and climate; providing purpose and direction for individuals and groups; demonstrating an understanding of international issues affecting education; formulating strategic plans, goals, and change efforts with staff and community; setting priorities in the context of community, student, and staff needs; serving as an articulate spokesperson for the welfare of all students in a multicultural context
Policy and governance	Developing procedures for working with the board of education that define mutual expectations, working relationships, and strategies for formulating district policy for external and internal programs; adjusting local policy to state and federal requirements and constitutional provisions, standards, and regulatory applications; recognizing and applying standards involving civil and criminal liabilities
Communications and community relations	Articulating district purpose and priorities to the community and mass media; requesting and responding to community feedback; demonstrating consensus building and conflict mediation; identifying, tracking, and dealing with issues; formulating and executing plans for internal and external communications; exhibiting an understanding of school districts as political systems and applying communication skills to strengthen community support; aligning constituencies in support of district priorities; building coalitions to gain financial and programmatic support; formulating democratic strategies for referenda; relating political initiatives to the welfare of children
Organizational management	Exhibiting an understanding of the school district as a system by defining processes of gathering, analyzing, and using data for decision making; managing the data flow; framing and solving problems; developing priorities and formulating solutions; assisting others to form reasoned opinions; reaching logical conclusions and making quality decisions to meet internal and external expectations; planning and scheduling personal and organizational work; establishing procedures to regulate activities and projects; delegating and empowering at appropriate organizational levels; securing and allocating human and material resources; developing and managing the district budget; maintaining accurate fiscal records

I was surprised by the absence of not one single performance indicator that held
superintendents accountable for the academic performance of students, the improvement of teaching, or the performance of principals. (p. 28)

The degree to which the superintendency will change in light of recent trends
and the duration of these new role expectations remains uncertain. For many in

Standard	Foci
Curriculum planning and development	Designing curriculum and a strategic plan that enhance teaching and learning in multiple contexts; providing planning and future methods to anticipate occupational trends and their educational implications; identifying taxonomies of instructional objectives and validation procedures for curricular units, using theories of cognitive development; using valid and reliable performance indicators and testing procedures to measure performance outcomes; describing the proper use of computers and other learning and information technologies
Instructional management	Exhibiting knowledge of instructional management by implementing a system that includes research findings on learning and instructional strategies, instructional time, advanced electronic technologies, and resources to maximize student outcomes; describing and applying research and best practice on integrating curriculum and resources for multicultural sensitivity and assessment strategies to help all students achieve high levels
Human resources management	Developing a staff evaluation and development system to improve the performance of all staff members; selecting appropriate models for supervision based on adult motivation research; identifying alternative employee benefit packages; describing and applying the legal requirements for personnel selection, development, retention, and dismissal
Values and ethics of leadership	Understanding and modeling appropriate value systems, ethics, and moral leadership; knowing the role of education in a democratic society; exhibiting multicultural and ethnic understanding and related behavior; adapting educational programming to the needs of diverse constituencies; balancing complex community demands in the best interest of the student; scanning and monitoring the environment for opportunities for staff and students; responding in an ethical and skillful way to the electronic and printed news media; coordinating social agencies and human services to help each student grow and develop as a caring, informed citizen

Source: From *Professional Standards for the Superintendency* by J. R. Hoyle, 1993, pp. 6–12. Arlington, VA: American Association of School Administrators. Adapted by permission.

the position, true work lives continue to be consumed with conflict, crisis, and surprises. social leadership and facilitation remain distant ideals rather than realities. In reality, they remain heavily focused on the political and managerial aspects of these positions.

As far back as the 1920s, some writers were developing lengthy lists of characteristics deemed to be necessary for a superintendent. These lists included managerial, political, educational, and personal skills. Elwood Cubberley (1922), a noted pioneer in educational administration, observed that superintendents during his day had to possess a sense of honor, the solemnity and dignity of an owl, political skills, a level head, and the ability to avoid political tricks and the latest ideas of wild-eyed reformers. The increased complexity of contemporary practice make these traits and abilities even more relevant. Studying the behavior of school district superintendents, Arthur Blumberg (1985) wrote the following:

> [W]hat we seem to have is a growing insight that the role of the superintendent involves an ever more sophisticated understanding of the community as an organism, of its political structure, of the need to deal with power centers outside of the superintendent's office, and of the wide variety of both human and technical skills needed to create a viable educational organization. (p. 43)

Reconfigured role expectations almost always require practitioners to master an ever-expanding professional knowledge base and to devote more time to applying that knowledge. However, as priorities in education shift and as superintendents inherit more responsibilities, they face the harsh reality that their traditional duties have become no less important.

Changes occurring at the local school district level have contributed to a growing uncertainty about the nature of the superintendency in the future. Many see the role becoming less directive and more facilitative. Rather than exercising traditional forms of authority, future superintendents are likely to be engaged in the following activities:

> . . . developing a wide shared, defensible vision; in the short run, directly assisting members of the school community to overcome obstacles they encounter in striving for the vision; and in the long run, increasing the capacity of the members of the school community to overcome subsequent obstacles more successfully and with greater ease. (Leithwood, ley, & Cousins, 1992, p. 8)

Unfortunately, increased consensus regarding future practice has not necessarily resolved diverse opinions about professional preparation. Consider the significant philosophical divide between those who call for fewer and more demanding programs for preparing school administrators (e.g., Clark, 1989) and those who warn that elitism and the flag of professionalism will widen chasms between administrators and others (e.g., Sergiovanni, 1991). Will our schools be more effective if administrators are required to complete more rigorous professional programs of study? Will student performance on tests improve if graduate schools raise standards for admission, retention, and graduation of students in educational administration programs? Or, is it in the best interest of the profession to prepare future administrators to work in institutions substantially different from those that now exist?

Thomas Sergiovanni (1994) argues that public schools should operate not as organizations, but rather as communities. He contends that at the very root of educational leadership is the duty to connect people morally to each other and to their work. Rather than emphasizing political manipulation and management, he describes educational leadership as a process of developing shared purposes and philosophy, community building, collegiality, and character development. Many practitioners, however, continue to be mired in state mandates, local political battles, collective bargaining, and litigation issues that make it difficult for them to ignore the need to manage and control public resources.

In many respects, the superintendency is at a crossroads because public elementary and secondary education is at a crossroads. One path is guided by concern for equity and social justice. Along this avenue, ideas of collaboration and community are nurtured. The other road is defined by economic-driven principles stressing competition and efficiency. On this avenue would be ideas such as school choice and vouchers (Boyd, 1992). Will America choose one over the other? Or will compromise contribute yet another alternative? The outcomes have obvious consequences for the superintendency.

In the final analysis, the descriptions of the superintendency that have the most significance are those created in local communities. Many of the nearly 14,000 superintendents in the United States are consumed by the realities of their daily work lives, and for them, management and politics remain center stage. The future responsibilities of superintendents are likely to be shaped much as they have been in the past—by the never-ending quest to balance equity, liberty, adequacy, and efficiency in public policy.

Professional Knowledge and Skills

Giving individual schools greater autonomy is not the only apparent reform trend in public elementary and secondary education. At the very time when decentralization is being touted as necessary, political figures are exerting ever-higher levels of pressure to develop national goals and standards (Danzberger, Kirst, & Usdan, 1992). And even though centralization and decentralization are opposite concepts, there is growing evidence that future policy and administrative decisions will be an intricate mix of the two. For instance, states are likely to set outcome policies, such as exit examinations from high school, while simultaneously reducing regulations on schools so that programming adjustments are more likely to be based on the needs and wants of local communities or even neighborhoods. This tactic of concurrently emphasizing centralization and decentralization is quite evident in the Kentucky reform law. Expectedly, this strategy has generated fundamental questions about the future role of local school boards and superintendents in that state. Studying the reactions of Kentucky superintendents, Murphy (1994) wrote, "Nearly all the leaders in these school districts are frustrated. They feel disempowered, yet they believe they remain on the point of the march toward greater accountability" (p. 30). The decision to set general policy at the state level raises questions about the role of superintendents and the knowledge and skills their jobs will require.

Inquiries into the professional preparation of school administrators have produced a long list of perceived faults. Some of the more notable examples are presented in Table 1–3. In an analysis of such criticisms, several key points should be weighed:

- There is no national curriculum for preparing school superintendents; both curricula among universities and licensing requirements among states vary.
- Nearly 500 colleges and universities offer some courses in educational administration; some programs consist of only a handful of courses taught

Table 1–3
Examples of recurring criticisms of preparation for superintendents

Issue	Criticism
Dominance of management courses	Emphasis on management perpetuates industrial-based practices inappropriate for schools. Administrators are socialized to outdated practices that relegate teachers to subordinate roles.
Too much emphasis on theory	Students learn abstract theories that are not linked to contemporary problems faced by practitioners. Too little time is devoted to field-based learning experiences (e.g., internships).
Scope of theory covered	Traditional organizational and leadership theories predicated on assumptions of rationality dominate the curriculum; too little attention is given to alternative explanations of behavior in schools (e.g., chaos theory).
Faculty out of touch with practice	Many professors of educational administration either have never been practitioners or have not maintained an active involvement with schools. Hence, much of their teaching is abstract and unrelated to contemporary practice.
Political orientations to decision making	Students are taught to focus on compromise in allocating scarce resources; too little emphasis is placed on the ethical and moral dimensions of practice.
Androcentric bias	Even though women constitute a majority of the education profession and doctoral students in educational administration, much of what is taught often ignores the female perspective of life in schools.
Focus on managerial behavior	Management is far more important than leadership; administrators are not being prepared to be visionaries, risk takers, and motivators.
Schools as agencies of control	Rather than being prepared to be change agents in an increasingly heterogeneous and democratic society, administrators are taught to focus on control mechanisms that deter change.

by adjunct faculty, while other programs offer multiple degrees under the instruction of as many as 10 or more full-time faculty members.

- The quantity and quality of clinical and field-based experiences differ markedly across institutions.
- The needs of new administrators can be divided into three categories:
  - Technical skills related to new roles (What do I do?)
  - Socialization skills (What am I supposed to look like and act like?)
  - Self awareness skills (What do I look like?).

Not all universities give equal weight to these needs (Daresh & Playko, 1995).

In addition, professional preparation for one administrator may mean as many as 2 to 3 years of full-time graduate study, but for another it may mean 6 or 7 years of part-time study. Largely for these reasons, criticisms of professional preparation are appropriately considered on a university-by-university basis.

The absence of a national curriculum, recurring criticisms of professional study, and the growing uncertainty about future practice apparently have failed to devalue graduate study. The trend continues to be one of employing more highly educated school superintendents. Data collected in 1990 indicated that approximately 36% of the superintendents in the United States had completed a doctoral degree; less than 1% had completed only a bachelor's degree. This same study found that about 27% of the superintendents rated their graduate program as *excellent*; 47% said it was *good*; 26% said it was *fair* or *poor* (Glass, 1992). Yet those who have denounced their academic preparation for supposedly being too theoretical and disconnected from practice have been given an inordinate amount of attention in the literature.

While there are arguably several courses that should be added to the professional preparation curriculum, conflict arises when faculty try to determine which courses should be displaced. The area of management studies offers an excellent example. While practitioners and professors often debate the extent to which management courses are included in professional preparation, they uniformly recognize that superintendents require a firm grounding in responsibilities such as finance, law, facility planning, and personnel administration. They also recognize, however, that contemporary conditions nurture expectations that superintendents are adequately prepared in areas such as communication, multiculturalism, shared decision making, democratic institutions, policy development and analysis, and child development. Rather than simply allowing the curriculum for professional preparation to expand, forward-thinking professors are seeking ways to connect the content of existing courses to contemporary needs (e.g., infusing technology and communication into courses on community relations). There also is an effort to establish a more precise nexus between academic courses and field experiences.

Further complicating discussions of the professional knowledge base needed by superintendents is the fact that the practice of school administration is both an art and a science. The study of research and theory provides a foundation for entering practice, but equally important to the administrator is craft knowledge, that is, the body of information accumulated through practice and transmitted from one administrator to another. Two resulting questions set the parameters for professional study:

- What knowledge and skills are essential before entering practice?
- What knowledge and skills are best learned in graduate school?

As you consider your career in school administration, realize that no degree program or set of university experiences can provide sufficient knowledge and skills for an entire career. Effective leadership requires both a commitment to lifelong learning and a dedication to reflective practice—issues that will be discussed later in this book.

Licensing and Certification

The words *licensing* and *certification* are used synonymously in education. Each of the 50 states, the District of Columbia, and territories of the United States (e.g., Puerto Rico) control the licensing of educators in their jurisdictions, and licensing criteria among these jurisdictions are less than uniform. A professional license issued by a governmental board or agency is not a property right (Hessong & Weeks, 1991). In other words, it is not a contract between the holder (e.g., a school administrator) and the issuer (e.g., state). This fact allows the issuer to change conditions of licensure without concern for violating the holder's property rights. State legislatures and licensing boards, however, usually grant exemptions to license holders, commonly called "grandfathering"; these protect current licensees from being adversely affected by new requirements (Kowalski & Reitzug, 1993). In addition, many states have compacts with each other providing reciprocity. Where such compacts exist, an administrator holding a license in one state is virtually assured of obtaining a license to practice in a cooperating state.

Not only do licensing criteria vary across the United States, the magnitude of the differences has increased as a result of reforms initiated over the past 2 decades. While all states issue licenses to teachers, not all do so for the school superintendency. In the early 1990s, 39 states had some special requirements for superintendents: 23 states required superintendents to have a superintendent's license, and 16 states required them to have a superintendent's endorsement on a general administrative license. All but 2 states required superintendents to have at least a master's degree (Ashbaugh & Kasten, 1992). In addition to specific academic degrees, common criteria include experience in teaching and administration, course work, and internships. Eleven states require a clinical component for first licensure, and 10 states require applicants to pass an administrative examination (a number of other states require applicants to pass a teacher's examination, and the teaching license is a prerequisite for administrative licensing). Regional and professional accreditation of degree-granting institutions is another criterion some states have adopted (that is, applicants are required to have degrees from accredited universities). In recognition of the need to engage in lifelong learning, states have moved away from issuing life licenses (Ashbaugh & Kasten, 1992). Where this has occurred, administrators are typically required to complete a specific number of continuing education credits for license renewal.

In recent years, efforts have been made to provide national certification for educators. The intent is not to replace state licensure, but rather to provide an additional credential similar to board certification in the practice of medicine. Professional associations, such as the Association of School Business Officials (ASBO), already offer several professional certificates of competence. The National Board for Professional Teaching Standards, a group dedicated to providing national certification for educators, has pursued a trilateral agenda for certificates of competence that includes (1) rigorous assessment, (2) extended courses of professional study, and (3) practica. To date, however, there is little evidence that national certification will have a dramatic impact on either state licensing or the employment of school superintendents.

Quality-of-Life Considerations

There are many reasons some educators aspire to become school superintendents. Clearly, compensation is often one of them. Superintendents have the highest average salary of any employee group in public elementary and secondary education; in many communities, the school superintendent is the highest-paid public official. A 1994–95 school-year study found that the average salary for a school superintendent in the United States was just over $90,000. In districts with 25,000 or more students, the average salary was about $112,000 (ERS Report, 1995). In considering these averages, several factors need to be taken into account. First, salaries vary considerably from one region of the country to another. For instance, superintendents in suburban New York City have significantly higher salaries than do superintendents in rural South Dakota. Second, demographic variables such as size of school district, academic degrees, and professional experience almost always influence salaries.

Because administrative salaries are public information, they are often the subject of controversy. Taxpayers may object simply because they think the salaries are excessive; or they may object specifically to the superintendent's salary because it is much higher than a teacher's salary. Unfortunately these critics overlook a number of critical issues affecting compensation. Consider these three:

- In many communities, the school system operates the largest food service and largest transportation program. So, in addition to the obvious responsibility of being the top educational leader, the superintendent is responsible for a number of auxiliary services. However, taxpayers are not inclined to view the responsibilities of superintendents as comparable to top-level executives in the private sector—individuals who command much higher salaries.

- Criticisms of administrative salaries rarely take into account daily time commitments, scope of responsibilities, and the number of days worked in a year. For example, the average teacher in America is employed for 186 days per year, while the average superintendent is employed for 241 days per year (ERS Report, 1995).
- Critics are far more likely to see superintendents as public servants than as highly educated professionals. Little consideration is given to the time and financial investment required in most states to become a superintendent.

In many school districts, superintendents receive fringe benefit packages that exceed those provided to other employee groups. Community affluence and culture often shape both a superintendent's salary and fringe benefits. For example, school board members in affluent suburbs are usually more inclined to provide fringe benefits similar to those given to executives in the private sector. Depending on culture and past practices, superintendents may receive a combination of the following in addition to salary:

- Tax-sheltered annuities
- Payment of personal retirement contributions
- An automobile (in some instances for personal use as well as business purposes)
- Payment of professional dues
- Allowances for routine expenses and travel
- An individualized insurance program (that is, with benefits greater than those in the employee group program)

The scope of benefits provided and length of contract may be subject to statutory limitations. Several states have specific restrictions on the scope and type of benefits that can be given to any public employee. In Minnesota, for example, the salaries of public employees are capped by indexing them to the governor's salary.

While salary and fringe benefits often are positives for the position of superintendent, job security frequently is viewed as a negative aspect. Overall, superintendents remain in office in a single district for about 6 years (Glass, 1992; Renchler, 1992). However, this picture changes markedly when only the large school districts are considered. Studies of larger school districts (typically considered to be those with more than 25,000 students) conducted in the 1990s have consistently found that the average is only about 2.5 years (Glass, 1992; Kowalski, 1995; Renchler, 1992). Perhaps most noteworthy is the fact that the average tenure for superintendents is still declining. This pattern may be attributable to many circumstances, including the following:

- School superintendents often accept mobility as part of their career: that is, they realize that they may have to relocate several times to advance their careers.

- Public dissatisfaction with public schools often initiates a pattern of instability that begins with the school board and ends with the superintendent.
- Especially in larger districts, where massive change is extremely difficult, new superintendents often have unrealistic expectations placed on them (Kowalski, 1995).
- Dwindling applicant pools often make it easier for veteran superintendents to change jobs. When problems arise (e.g., facing a teachers' strike, having to close schools), some practitioners simply prefer to relocate.

In addition to salary and job security, a multitude of factors affect the quality of life experienced by a superintendent. One relates to a loss of privacy, which many superintendents experience as public officials. Blumberg (1985) found that many superintendents believed that their communities treated them as if they were public property. He described two aspects of this condition:

> The first is the public perception that he is and ought to be accessible, regardless of time, place, or occasion. The second is that somehow, because of both the publicness of his position and his position as chief among the educators of the community's children, his personal life should be above reproach. (p. 156)

Despite the negative aspects of the public servant syndrome, many superintendents are admired and respected and have high status in their communities.

Many bright, energetic educators are drawn to the superintendency because of the professional freedoms the position may allow. Consider the following:

- Compared with other educators, superintendents typically have greater latitude in allocating personal time.
- Superintendents usually can influence major decisions that have a long-term effect on school systems.
- Superintendents often have access to community and state leaders; hence, compared with other educators, they usually have greater influence on critical economic and political decisions.
- Superintendents can lead other professionals to make decisions benefiting large numbers of young people; some practitioners find this to be intrinsically rewarding.

In the past, the job of the superintendent was more predictable and routine because schools were cast as agencies of control rather than as agencies of change. Many who succeeded in the job 50, 25, or 10 years ago would find today's challenges intolerable and excessively stressful. A myriad of social, economic, and political conditions require superintendents to adapt constantly. Yet for some educators, the opportunity to provide leadership in such a context remains exciting, invigorating, and enticing.

ACCESS TO THE SUPERINTENDENCY

How does one become a superintendent? Do most school boards employ an administrator already working in the school district? These questions are more difficult to answer today than they were just 20 or 30 years ago. Consider several reasons why this is true:

- The quantity and quality of applicants for the superintendency vary substantially across school districts. Some districts receive over 100 applications, while other districts get just 3 or 4.
- There is less uniformity today in what school board members seek in a superintendent. While some may want a manager, others may want a skilled change agent. It is not uncommon for members of the same board to have significantly different expectations for an administrator's performance.
- A growing number of administrators do not aspire to become superintendents; they are content being principals, directors, or assistant superintendents.
- Many school superintendents no longer automatically equate movement to bigger school districts and higher-paying jobs with career advancement. Personal satisfaction, family needs, and pragmatic issues of quality of life are receiving greater consideration.
- Candidates in any given applicant pool vary markedly; not only do they differ with regard to age, gender, race, and professional experience, they also are likely to have different educational backgrounds.

A better understanding of access to the superintendency can be provided through reviewing two especially relevant topics: career paths and the special challenges facing women and minorities.

Career Paths

Surveys over the past hundred years give a rather consistent profile of the public school superintendent. Superintendents traditionally were virtually all white males who were married, highly experienced in education, and members of Protestant churches (Kowalski, 1995). Scholars theorize that both the ambiguity and diffuseness of goals for the job and the difficulty of determining the real success of schools reinforced the significance of "maleness, mature age, 'proper' ethnicity, acceptable church membership, and appearance (not surprisingly, superintendents were taller than average, giving people someone to look up to)" (Tyack & Hansot, 1982, p. 170). A dominant career path for men was assistant high school principal to high school principal to superintendent (Gaertner, 1981). This path was particularly common in smaller school districts.

In his national study of school superintendents, Thomas Glass (1992) identified the following career patterns for superintendents:

- Teacher Only   5.9%
- Principal Only   4.0%
- Central Office Only   2.0%
- Teacher & Principal   36.4%
- Teacher & Central Office   10.3%
- Principal & Central Office   3.7%
- Teacher, Principal, & Central Office   37.7% (p. 23)

Clearly, the prevalent career path is one in which individuals have had both teaching and administrative experience. And this pattern is more true when one examines superintendents in districts with the largest enrollment. A number of states require that applicants have both teaching and administrative experience to obtain a superintendent's license or endorsement.

Data also show that superintendents are twice as likely to be appointed from outside the school district than from within. When districts are examined on basis of enrollment, the figures are even more significant. In very small districts (that is, those with 300 or fewer students), only about 16% of the superintendents received "internal promotions." By contrast, about 43% of the superintendents in large districts (25,000 students or greater) fall into this category (Glass, 1992). This pattern is partially explained by the fact that large districts have more administrative employees who aspire to, and hold the required license for, the superintendency. When a vacancy occurs, these "insiders" may already have the support of certain groups and key individuals making the decision of who will be hired.

Both sponsorship and mentoring have been critical aspects in career paths in school administration, especially for those who ultimately reach the superintendency. Sponsorship involves being assisted or promoted by others who have influence and power in the arena of job placement. Studies (e.g., Maienza, 1986) have identified three common sources of sponsorship: (1) university professors, (2) coalitions of practitioners operating on a regional or state level, and (3) search consultants. Recently, the use of consultants (often called "headhunters") to assist school boards with superintendent searches has been growing, making this form of sponsorship more common than in the past. Mentoring entails the opportunity to work with an influential practitioner who both shares craft knowledge and directly assists with career advancement. Whereas sponsorship often has political connotations, mentoring is usually described as a professional relationship.

Whether traditional career paths to the superintendency will continue is uncertain. Growing frustrations with public education have led some reformers to question the value of both licensing and graduate study in educational administration. Yet it is unlikely that teaching and administrative experience in elementary and secondary education will be devalued. The vast majority of school districts in the United States have fewer than 3,000 students; in these organizations, a broad base of experience remains essential. In large urban districts, there appears to be a greater willingness to experiment. In the early 1990s, for example, Milwaukee and Minneapolis broke with tradition and employed superintendents who had neither previous experience nor academic preparation in education (Jones, 1994).

While there are arguably dozens of forces that could change the traditional career paths for school superintendents, the most powerful appears to be the reform strategy of increased state authority coupled with the decentralization of authority within school districts. As noted earlier, this trend raises serious questions about the future role and power of both school boards and superintendents. To date though, efforts to redesign school governance have not resulted in new, unique career paths to the superintendency.

Issues for Women and Minorities

Both women and members of racial and ethnic minority groups constitute a small portion of the nation's school superintendents, and, therefore, the issue of access is especially significant for them. Their underrepresentation persists even though many communities have substantial and growing minority populations; it persists even though two thirds of the licensed professionals in public education are women; and it persists even though women now constitute a majority of the doctoral students in educational administration (Kowalski & Reitzug, 1993). Numerous studies (e.g., Cunanan, 1994) have shown that the increase of women in school administration preparation programs has not been paralleled by an increase in job placements—especially in the superintendency. There is, however, some hope that barriers to access are becoming less insurmountable. In 1974–75, a mere 1% of the nation's superintendents were women (Paddock, 1981); by 1990, this figure increased to about 6% (Jones & Montenegro, 1990); and in 1992, it was reported to be 6.7% (Glass, 1992). In 1990, only 12.5% of all school administrators and 3.4% of the superintendents were members of racial or ethnic minority groups (Jones & Montenegro, 1990); in 1992, the number of minorities in the superintendency had risen only slightly, to 3.9% (Glass, 1992).

Interestingly, women and minorities have made their greatest strides in becoming superintendents in some of the very largest school districts; namely, urban school systems. A report issued by the Council of Great City Schools (1992), a consortium of urban districts, indicated that women held 15% and minorities 60% of 47 superintendencies in that organization. While these figures are substantially higher than those for all types of school districts, they need to be weighed in light of current conditions in such school systems. Urban districts, once the models for public education, are now besieged with problems, and they have become the primary targets of education critics. In urban districts, the average tenure of a superintendent is only 2.4 years, and these districts are experiencing dwindling pools of superintendent applicants (Kowalski, 1995). Thus, access for women and minorities has come at a time when urban school districts are engulfed in what seem to be irresolvable social, economic, and political problems. Women and minorities may have greater opportunities because the jobs have become less desirable.

Perhaps the most significant issue surrounding access to the superintendency for women involves gender-related behaviors in administrative positions. More specifically, do female superintendents tend to function differently from men when in positions of power? In recent years, the school administration literature has paid increasing attention to the feminocentric critique—the idea that women see practice differently from men, hold different values, seek different goals, and establish different priorities (Owens, 1998). There is mounting evidence supporting the validity of this perspective. Studies have concluded that women administrators differ from male administrators in key areas such as perceptions of power (e.g., Bruner, 1994; Dunlap & Goldman, 1991), dispositions toward working with people (e.g., Shakeshaft, 1989; Wesson & Grady, 1994), and emphasis on the human dimension of organizations (e.g., Bell & Chase, 1989). What makes these differences particularly important are the current changes occurring in school structure—changes such as decentralized governance, shared decision making, and greater teacher autonomy. These conditions emphasize collaboration—a style more associated with women—rather than control. The feminocentric critique already has spawned reconsiderations of traditional male assumptions about organizational behavior, management, and leadership (Owens, 1998).

Issues related to racial and ethnic minorities accessing the superintendency present additional challenges to the profession. Some critics have charged that insufficient attention has been given to the relationship of social context to the underrepresentation of people of color in educational leadership positions (Banks, 1995). The accusation is supported by studies that have identified obstacles facing minorities who seek to be principals and superintendents. For example, reliance on informal contacts to secure administrative positions (Hudson, 1994) or the simple perpetuation of male-dominated networks to provide encouragement and support to potential administrators (Feistritzer, 1988) often are disadvantageous to racial and ethnic minorities. Overall, women have had greater success accessing the superintendency than have minorities; the greatest gains for minority representation in the superintendency have been in school districts where there is a substantial minority population (Montenegro, 1993).

Unfortunately, school reform efforts alone will not remove the barriers that exist for women and minorities. These barriers are both internal (aspects of personality, values, and attitudes) and external (environmental circumstances that mediate entrance into the superintendency) (Leonard & Papalewis, 1987). As such, they must be attacked on multiple fronts. Examples of needed actions would be addressing androcentric (male-dominant) biases in professional preparation, as well as creating positive socialization opportunities for women and minorities, providing them with enrichment experiences, and facilitating their access to mentors and sponsors. Even more broadly, communities must be willing to change, because societal stereotypes and prejudices still place women and minorities in subordinate roles in all parts of society (Yeakey, Johnston, & Adkison, 1986).

FOR FURTHER REFLECTION

This chapter examined the evolution of school districts and the superintendency. This overview provides a context for understanding the dynamics of contemporary practice in school administration. Detailed treatment was given to these aspects of the position of school superintendent: role expectations, responsibilities, professional knowledge and skills, changing priorities, licensing, and quality-of-life considerations. Access to the superintendency was addressed by looking at traditional career paths and issues presenting particular challenges to women and minorities.

As you consider what you read in this chapter, answer the following questions:

1. Public elementary and secondary schools in the United States were structured as agencies of control. That is to say, one of their primary purposes was to ensure a common school experience stressing the values and beliefs of those who were most influential in society. How has this tradition shaped the role of the school superintendent?

2. Traditionally administration is viewed as separate from teaching. Administration has been largely identified as a male occupation, while teaching has been largely perceived as a female activity. What circumstances led to this separation? What circumstances have sustained this separation?

3. Some superintendents receive salaries that are 200% to 250% greater than those paid to the average teacher in the same school district. Is this equitable? Should the salaries of superintendents be controlled? Give reasons for your opinion.

4. In addition to salary, many superintendents receive fringe benefit packages that are significantly more lucrative than those provided to other employees. Philosophically, do you think that superintendents should or should not receive the same benefits given to top-level professional employees in government or in the private sector? Give reasons for your opinion.

5. The superintendency has often been described as "life in a fishbowl." Clearly, many taxpayers believe that superintendents are public servants whose lives should be open to constant inspection. How does the public perceive the role of superintendent in your school district?

6. Do you think national certification for teachers and administrators is a sound idea? What effect might it have on the stature of education as a profession?

7. There is considerable documentation supporting the fact that women and minorities are underrepresented in the superintendency. What is meant by *underrepresentation*? What would constitute adequate representation?

8. While the population of the United States is becoming more heterogeneous, fewer African Americans and Hispanics are opting to enter the education profession. Logically, fewer minority teachers translates into fewer minority administrators and ultimately, fewer minority superintendents. Some politi-

cal leaders have argued that licensure and certification deter highly qualified minorities from entering the superintendency; hence, they argue for leeway to permit these individuals to become superintendents without traditional credentials. Do you support this position? Why or why not?

9. Do you know of any actions that have been taken in your community or state to reduce the level of underrepresentation of women and minorities in the superintendency? To what extent have these measures been fruitful? What actions, if any, would you recommend to your state legislature?

10. What do you believe will be the most dramatic changes in the superintendency in the next 2 decades? What will drive these changes?

CASE STUDY

Rachel Armstrong was about to complete her second year as superintendent of the Bentbridge School District—a school system with slightly less than 2,000 students located in a southwestern state. Prior to holding this position, she had been a high school principal for 3 years and an English teacher for 15 years. Her passage from the classroom to administration occurred immediately after she completed a doctoral program in school administration.

At the time that Rachel became a principal, only 4 of 312 high school principals in the state were women. She was the only female principal who had a doctoral degree, and she was more active and visible than her female peers in the state principals' association. For example, she was the first woman elected to that organization's interscholastic athletic committee, and she was the first woman appointed to that organization's ethics committee. Rachel was also very successful in her role as principal. The local newspaper did a series of stories praising her leadership in creating a new student discipline program that reduced student suspensions and expulsions.

Rachel's achievement in her profession and in her job reinforced her conviction that she was capable of being a superintendent. Increasingly, she viewed the principalship not as her career, but as a stage of her career. She wanted to become a superintendent as quickly as possible.

When Rachel moved from teaching to the principalship, she encountered few experiences that she did not expect. The same, however, was not true regarding her transition to the superintendency. Her expectations proved to be incorrect in at least two noteworthy ways. First, she quickly discovered that the superintendency required more, not fewer, hours on the job. Duties she performed as a principal such as supervising athletic programs, clubs, and PTA meetings were replaced by school board meetings, community activities, and membership on various committees. Second, she thought she would be able to have greater control of her workday. As a principal, her day was filled with unexpected emergencies that constantly distracted her from her plans, especially those relating to instructional supervision. She thought the superintendency would be more predictable and controllable, allowing her to work closely with principals and teacher committees. This assumption, too, proved to be incorrect.

When Rachel interviewed for the job in Bentbridge, she told the five school board members that her greatest strength was instructional leadership. She said, "I know that budgets, buildings, buses, and managing employees are essential tasks. But much of this can be handled by other employees. If I become your superintendent, I would work closely with principals, teachers, parents, and students on matters most directly affecting teaching and learning." Uniformly the board members responded positively to this philosophy. For years, they had attended conferences where they heard experts say that superintendents should be instructional leaders. Now they had a candidate who truly wanted to fill this role.

The central office staff in Bentbridge includes a superintendent, a business manager, and three full-time secretaries (secretary to the superintendent, secretary to the business manager, and a receptionist). The business manager has responsibility for fiscal records, transportation, food services, and facility management. He is an accountant who came to work for the school district after retiring from military service.

Even in her first year in Bentbridge, Rachel had became concerned that she was not able to devote much time to instructional programs. While she had considerable contact with principals because they reported directly to her, her time with them was largely consumed by management, legal, or political problems. Instructional planning was continually delayed because of unexpected problems demanding administrative attention. It seemed that the entire administrative staff was caught in a cycle where it had little choice but to spend most of its time reacting to crisis after crisis.

Midway through her second year in the superintendency, Rachel concluded that she could not be an effective instructional leader in the school district unless she had additional support staff in the central office. She described this need to the school board. She did so in an executive session during which she also discussed staffing needs for the coming school year: "When you hired me, I promised that I would spend much of my time working to improve instructional programs. While I remain committed to this goal, I must tell you that we do not have sufficient staff in the central office to permit this to occur. Hence, I have developed a recommendation to create a new position, assistant superintendent. This administrator will assist me with the day-to-day management of the school district. Without this assistance, I don't see how I will have the time to be an effective instructional leader."

The board members were surprised by these comments. Rachel had told them in the past that her job was tremendously time-consuming, but they had heard these same words from her predecessor. As the individual members commented on her proposal to employ an assistant superintendent, two points became clear to Rachel: (1) The board members still supported her intention to be a strong instructional leader, but they did not fully understand the demands of this role and (2) The board members were extremely apprehensive about the potential for negative reactions from the community and teachers' union if they approved the recommendation to add an assistant superintendent. Rachel attempted to define what she meant by instructional leadership, and she shared some statistics showing that other districts with similar enrollments in the state had more professional staff in the central office than did Bentbridge. The board members listened courteously, but they were not persuaded. They reaffirmed support for Rachel's goal of being an instructional leader, but they told her it had to be accomplished within the context of the current staffing pattern. The board president noted, "We are all having to learn to do more with less."

Even though Rachel had not expected the board to immediately agree to her recommendation, she did not expect them to dismiss it so abruptly. She left the executive meeting with many doubts. A number of questions ran through her mind: Should I go back to being a principal? Do the school board members really want their superintendent to be an instructional leader? Did I properly present this matter to them? Are they treating me differently because I am a woman? Can I succeed in this job? For the first time in her career, Rachel was questioning her decision of becoming a superintendent.

Issues for Discussion

1. Rachel was a classroom teacher for 15 years before entering administration. Is this typical? Is it typical for females who enter administration? What are typical patterns?

2. Rachel was a high school principal prior to becoming a superintendent (one of only four female principals in her state). Women are most likely to be principals in elementary schools and least likely to be principals in high schools. What are the reasons for this condition? Is the condition changing in your state?

3. Was Rachel prepared to enter the superintendency? Why or why not?

4. Is it common for school boards to expect superintendents to be instructional leaders? What evidence do you have to support your response?

5. What does the literature tell us about differences between male and female administrators with regard to leadership styles and interest in working on instructional matters?

6. Do you believe the school board would have rejected the recommendation to create an assistant superintendency if the superintendent were a male?

7. Do most superintendents face the reality that they must devote most of their time to managing and putting out fires regardless of the size of the school district or the size of the central office staff? Give evidence based on your knowledge and experience.

8. If you were on the school board in Bentbridge, do you think that adding an assistant superintendent would diminish the unpredictable situations that consume Rachel's time? Why or why not?

9. What else could Rachel have done to convince the school board that her request was necessary?

10. Are there other tactics (other than the one suggested in the case—an assistant superintendent) that Rachel could pursue that would allow her to spend more time in the area of instructional leadership?

11. Should Rachel have ascertained how individual board members felt about her recommendation before presenting it to them publicly? How could she have done this?

12. Because the board expresses support for Rachel, should she use this support to seek a compromise on her recommendation? What should her plan of action be?

REFERENCES

American Association of School Administrators (1994). *Roles and relationships: School boards and superintendents.* Arlington, VA: Author.

Ashbaugh, C. R., & Kasten, K. L. (1992). *The licensure of school administrators: Policy and practice.* (ERIC Document Reproduction Service No. ED 347 163)

Banks, C. A. (1995). Gender and race as factors in educational leadership and administration. In J. Banks (Ed.), *Handbook of research on multicultural education* (pp. 65–80). New York: Macmillan.

Bell, C. S., & Chase, S. E. (1989). *Women as educational leaders: Resistance and conformity.* Paper presented at the annual meeting of the American Educational Research Association, San Francisco.

Blumberg, A. (1985). *The school superintendent: Living with conflict.* New York: Teachers College Press.

Boyd, W. L. (1992). The power of paradigms: Reconceptualizing policy and management. *Educational Administration Quarterly, 28*(4), 504–528.

Brubacher, J. S. (1966). *A history of the problems of education* (2nd ed.). New York: McGraw-Hill.

Bruner, C. C. (1994). *Superintendent selection: Lessons from political science.* (ERIC Document Reproduction Service No. ED 373 434)

Burroughs, W. A. (1974). *Cities and schools in the gilded age.* Port Washington, NY: Kennikat.

Butts, R. F., & Cremin, L. A. (1953). *A history of education in American culture.* New York: Henry Holt and Company.

Callahan, R. E. (1962). *Education and the cult of efficiency.* Chicago: University of Chicago Press.

Callahan, R. E. (1966). *The superintendent of schools: A historical analysis.* (ERIC Document Reproduction Service No. ED 0104 410)

Campbell, R. F., Cunningham, L. L., Nystrand, R. O., & Usdan, M. D. (1990). *The organization and control of American schools* (6th ed.). Upper Saddle River, NJ: Merrill/Prentice Hall.

Chand, K. (1987). *A handbook for the school boards in America for the selection of the superintendent of schools.* (ERIC Document Reproduction Service No. ED 277 120)

Clark, D. L. (1989). Time to say enough! *Agenda, 1*(1), 1, 4.

Cooper, B. S., & Boyd, W. L. (1987). The evolution of training for school administrators. In J. Murphy & P. Hallinger (Eds.), *Approaches to administrative training in education* (pp. 3–27). Albany: State University of New York Press.

Council of Great City Schools (1992). *Superintendent characteristics.* Washington, DC: Author.

Cuban, L. (1976). *Urban school chiefs under fire.* Chicago: University of Chicago Press.

Cuban, L. (1994). Muddled reasoning will limit standards' impact. *School Administrator, 51*(7), 28.

Cubberley, E. P. (1922). *Public school administration.* Boston: Houghton Mifflin.

Cunanan, E. S. (1994). *A comparative career profile in 1985–1990 female and male graduates of educational administration from a midwestern research university.* (ERIC Document Reproduction Service No. ED 374 539)

Danzberger, J. P., Kirst, M. W., & Usdan, M. D. (1992). *Governing public schools: New times, new requirements.* Washington, DC: Institute for Educational Leadership.

Daresh, J. C., & Playko, M. A. (1995). *Alternative career formation perspectives: Lessons for educational leadership from law, medicine, and priesthood.* Paper presented at the Annual Meeting of the University Council for Educational Administration, Salt Lake City.

Dunlap, D. M., & Goldman, P. (1991). Rethinking power in schools. *Educational Administration Quarterly, 27*(1), 5–29.

Eaton, W. E. (1990). The vulnerability of school superintendents: The thesis reconsidered. In W. Eaton (Ed.), *Shaping the superintendency: A reexamination of Callahan and the Cult of Efficiency* (pp. 11–35). New York: Teachers College Press.

ERS Report (1995). *Scheduled salaries for professional personnel in public schools: 1994–95* (22nd ed.). Arlington, VA: Educational Research Service.

Feistritzer, C. E. (1988). Point: A good ole boy mentality rules your schools. *Executive Educator, 10*(5), 24–25,37.

Gaertner, K. N. (1981). Administrative careers in public organizations. In P. Schmuck, W. Charters, & R. Carlson (Eds.), *Educational policy and management of sex differentials* (pp. 199–217). New York: Academic Press.

Glass, T. E. (1992). *The 1992 study of the American school superintendency.* Arlington, VA: American Association of School Administrators.

Griffin, G., & Chance, E. W. (1994). Superintendent behaviors and activities linked to school effectiveness: Perceptions of principals and superintendents. *Journal of School Leadership, 4*(1), 69–86.

Hessong, R. F., & Weeks, T. H. (1991). *Introduction to the foundations of education* (2nd ed.). New York: Macmillan.

Hoyle, J. R. (1993). *Professional standards for the superintendency.* Arlington, VA: American Association of School Administrators.

Hoyle, J. R. (1994). What standards for the superintendency promise. *School Administrator, 51*(7), 22–23, 26.

Hudson, M. J. (1994). Women and minorities in school administration: Re-examining the role of informal job contact systems. *Urban Education, 28*(4), 386–397.

Johnson, S. M. (1996). *Leading to change: The challenge of the new superintendency.* San Francisco: Jossey-Bass.

Jones, E. H., & Montenegro, X. P. (1990). *Women and minorities in school administration: Facts and figures 1989–1990.* Arlington, VA: American Association of School Administrators.

Jones, R. (1994). Instant superintendent. *American School Board Journal, 181*(4), 22–26.

Knezevich, S. J. (1984). *Administration of public education: A sourcebook for the leadership and management of educational institutions* (4th ed.). New York: Harper & Row.

Kowalski, T. J. (1995). *Keepers of the flame: Contemporary urban superintendents.* Thousand Oaks, CA: Corwin.

Kowalski, T. J., & Reitzug, U. C. (1993). *Contemporary school administration: An introduction.* New York: Longman.

Leithwood, K., Begley, P. T., & Cousins, J. B. (1992). *Developing expert leadership for future schools.* London: Falmer.

Leonard, P. Y., & Papalewis, R. (1987). The underrepresentation of women and minorities in educational administration: Patterns, issues, and recommendations. *Journal of Educational Equity and Leadership, 7*(3), 188–207.

Lunenburg, F. C., & Ornstein, A. C. (1991). *Educational administration: Concepts and practices.* Belmont, CA: Wadsworth.

Maienza, J. G. (1986). The superintendency: Characteristics of access for men and women. *Educational Administration Quarterly, 22*(4), 59–79.

Montenegro, X. P. (1993). *Women and racial minority representation in school administration.* Arlington, VA: American Association of School Administrators.

Morris, J. R. (1979). Job(s) of the superintendency. *Educational Research Quarterly, 4*(4), 11–24.

Murphy, J. (1994). The changing role of the superintendent in Kentucky's reforms. *School Administrator, 50*(10), 26–30.

Owens, R. G. (1998). *Organizational behavior in education* (6th ed.). Boston: Allyn and Bacon.

Paddock, S. C. (1981). Male and female career paths in school administration. In P. Schmuck, W. Charters, & R. Carlson (Eds.), *Educational policy and management of sex differentials* (pp. 187–198). New York: Academic Press.

Renchler, R. (1992). *Urban superintendent turnover: The need for stability.* (ERIC Document Reproduction Service No. ED 346 546)

Russo, C. J. (1992). The legal status of school boards in the intergovernmental system. In P. First & H. Walberg (Eds.), *School boards: Changing local control* (pp. 3–20). Berkeley, CA: McCutchan.

Sergiovanni, T. J. (1991). The dark side of professionalism in educational administration. *Phi Delta Kappan, 72*(7), 521–526.

Sergiovanni, T. J. (1994). The roots of school leadership. *Principal, 74*(2), 6–7, 9.

Shakeshaft, C. (1989). *Women in educational administration* (2nd ed.). Newbury Park, CA: Sage.

Spring, J. H. (1985). *American education: An introduction to social and political aspects* (3rd ed.). New York: Longman.

Spring, J. H. (1994). *The American school, 1642–1993* (3rd ed.). New York: McGraw-Hill.

Thomas, W. B., & Moran, K. J. (1992). Reconsidering the power of the superintendent in the Progressive Period. *American Educational Research Journal, 29*(1), 22–50.

Tyack, D. (1972). The "One Best System": A historical analysis. In H. Walberg & A. Kopan (Eds.), *Rethinking urban education* (pp. 231–246). San Francisco: Jossey-Bass.

Tyack, D., & Hansot, E. (1982). *Managers of virtue: Public school leadership in America, 1820–1980.* New York: Basic Books.

Wesson, L. H., & Grady, M. L. (1994). An analysis of women urban superintendents: A national study. *Urban Education, 28*(4), 412–424.

Yeakey, C. C., Johnston, G. S., & Adkison, J. A. (1986). In pursuit of equity: A review of research on minorities and women in educational administration. *Educational Administration Quarterly, 22* (3), 110–149.

Chapter 2

Current Conditions of Practice

Key Concepts

◇ Changing size of local districts

◇ Changing social contexts

◇ Changing role of schools

◇ Public dissatisfaction with education

◇ Purposes of education

◇ Differing demands for reform

◇ Influence of technology

While educational change can be initiated from within schools, more often than not the impetus for it is external. That is to say, change typically originates outside local school districts. Prime examples of sources for change include these:

- Federal legislation, e.g., National Defense Education Act, Civil Rights Act
- State legislation, e.g., state mandates for school reform
- Litigation, e.g., *Brown v. Board of Education,* school finance plans
- Changing social conditions, e.g., growing number of one-parent families, teenage pregnancies, crime
- Changing economic conditions, e.g., increased competition for scarce resources, taxpayer revolts

Throughout history, schools have been largely reactionary agencies. They are continuously prodded or coerced to respond to societal needs and wants.

The relationship between public schools and their environments has a major impact on the role of those in educational administration. The nature of the community, prevailing laws, policies, and regulations, the people and groups who constitute the school district, and specific tasks influence administrative behavior. For example, there are obvious differences among local communities in which schools exist, such as rural versus urban settings or affluent versus economically deprived communities. However, context is also shaped by prevailing societal conditions affecting all communities. Examples include demographic trends, economic changes, demands for new knowledge, or significant changes in how we learn, such as using new technologies.

This chapter explores the more significant conditions framing contemporary practice in the superintendency. Three broad categories are addressed: (1) the changing profile of American society, (2) public dissatisfaction with public schools, and (3) the increasing influence of technology in education and administration.

THE CHANGING NATURE OF AMERICAN SOCIETY

The previous chapter included a review of the early years of the superintendency and gave insights as to why certain images of the position continued for so many decades. Before 1960, most taxpayers were satisfied with the superintendent's traditional roles of imparting knowledge and providing structure and discipline. Even the failure of 1 in 3 students to graduate from high school was not particularly alarming because good factory and other blue collar jobs were plentiful in a manufacturing society for people who did not finish high school. In such a society, schools essentially sorted students, culling from the cohort those who did not show academic promise, those who did not have the economic means to continue their education, and those who did not show an interest in education.

Since the 1960s, however, the traditional mission of education—and with it, the role of the superintendent—has been increasingly challenged. A growing concern for equity, higher levels of ethnic and racial diversity in the nation, and a shift to an information-based society are primarily responsible for the educational system's being asked to meet new and different demands.

Philip Schlechty (1990) wrote, "America's educators have had considerable success in running schools where there is value consensus" (p. 28). He suggested that many private and magnet schools experience success today because they demand acceptance of their purposes, values, and practices. These institutions, however, do not represent the world of work as it exists for the average school superintendent. Educators in the typical public school system encounter continuous conflicts over values to pursue, and their attempts to articulate clear purposes and goals are often challenged or resisted. The diversity in communities over values is often evident when issues relating to sex education, teaching evolution, or student discipline are debated. Schlechty (1990) concluded, "If public education is to survive as a vital force in American life, there must be a reformulation of the school's purpose" (p. 31).

During the formative years of public education in the United States, the concept of the common school—in which all children were entitled to receive public education—was widely accepted by policymakers and citizens. However, as the United States opened its doors to immigrants at the end of the 19th century, thoughtful leaders—such as John Dewey (1899)—were already perceiving that increased diversity in American culture would lead to disagreements about the purpose and content of public education. Immigrants from Ireland, for example, were concerned that the public schools would lead their children away from the Catholic religion. Rather than confronting such fears and growing disagreements about the purposes of public education, the power elites of that day became even more resolute in their effort to require the common school experience—a goal that was directly linked to the intention of enculturating immigrant children to values and beliefs of the white, Anglo-Saxon, Protestant majority (Spring, 1990). As a consequence, major policy decisions that were made defined public schools as agencies of control rather than catalysts for building a new social order (Burroughs, 1974).

The fact that public schools were never designed to be agencies of change continues to have a profound influence on school reform initiatives and the challenges faced by contemporary superintendents. To more fully outline these challenges, three important factors relating to schools are discussed in this chapter. The first pertains to the current status of public school districts in the United States; the second deals with issues of social and economic change; and the third addresses the changing role expectations for public schools.

Declining Number of Public School Districts

Despite continuing increases in the general population, as well as a 13% increase in public school enrollments between 1984 and 1994 (National Center for Educational Statistics, 1995a), the number of school districts in America has continued to decline. Before World War II, there were approximately 119,000 districts; today the number is estimated to be approximately 15,000. Even so, only about 10% of the school districts enroll more than 5,000 pupils (Ornstein, 1993). The decline is attributable almost entirely to school district consolidation, a process that continues in states such as Illinois and Nebraska (Ramirez, 1992).

The merger of school districts, especially when the result of coercion by state government, usually produces resentment. Ornstein (1993) offered the following comments on this issue:

> [C]onsolidating districts usually means closing some schools, and this has proved to be a serious and emotional matter, especially in small and rural school districts, where the local school may be a focal point of the community's identity. (p. 169)

Opposition to consolidation also may be associated with economic motives. In very small districts, the public generally has greater control over tax rates and school budgets. That is to say, citizens are more likely to have access to school board members and thus be able to influence decisions in areas such as employee salaries, transportation policies, capital outlay, and instructional budgets. Yet school district consolidation continues to be encouraged in many states. Why? Arguments favoring consolidation usually pertain to economic efficiency, the adequacy and equity of educational programming, and the expansion of student services. Table 2–1 outlines the more persuasive reasons.

History has not made school district consolidation a less controversial topic. While the destruction of small community identity and a loss of liberty continue to be reasons for opposing consolidation, more recent arguments against it have focused on economic and educational outcomes. Most notably, these include failures of consolidation to produce economic efficiency and failures to enhance student learning. The former is based on the belief that as districts become larger, they simply become more bureaucratic, and rather than saving money, they result in new tiers of administration and new employee categories. The latter stems from the judgment that large school districts spawn large-enrollment schools, and large-enrollment schools are often seen as cold, uncaring institutions where some students simply get lost. With less than convincing evidence that larger districts have a positive effect on student learning (Ramirez, 1992), critics frequently point to the potential social and personal problems thought to be more prevalent in larger schools (e.g., alienation, value conflicts).

Arguments in favor of maintaining very small districts—and many of these districts still exist—have been aided by cooperative services agreements (e.g., joint services contracts among school districts for special education and vocational education), intermediate districts (discussed in the previous chapter), and technology (which allows long-distance learning and access to worldwide webs of information). Also, they have been helped by the current popularity of decentralization concepts (such as site-based management) and the renewed emphasis on the political pursuit of liberty in American life.

Conditions regarding the size, number of school districts, number of pupils served, and per-pupil expenditures still differ significantly across the states. Consider the following facts:

Table 2–1
Common reasons for school consolidation

Category	Specific Reason	Rationale
Economic efficiency	Greater fiscal equity	As school districts become larger, inequities in fiscal capacity (i.e., assessed valuation per pupil) are diminished.
	Increased tax base	Greater total wealth often enhances a district's ability to enter into capital projects because many states continue to place much of the burden for facility costs on local taxpayers.
	Economies of scale	By purchasing goods and services in larger volumes, school districts operate more efficiently and reduce per-pupil costs.
Educational programs	Expanded curriculum	Larger schools, especially at the secondary level, are able to offer students a broader curriculum (e.g., more choices in foreign language, advanced science classes, vocational programs).
	Individual student needs	In larger schools, instruction can be geared to specific student needs, especially the needs of nonaverage students (e.g., special education classes for low-incidence disabilities, different sections of a high school course predicated on ability and achievement).
	Increased staff quality	Larger school districts are able to provide individuals with more specialized talents (e.g., teachers for the gifted and talented, curriculum directors in the central office).
Student services	Expanded opportunities	Larger schools offer students more choices in extra and cocurricular programs.
	Scope of special services	Larger school districts are more likely to employ social workers, attendance officers, counselors, and psychologists.
	Support services quality	Larger school districts are more apt to have modern transportation programs, diverse food services programs, and modern facilities.

- One state, Hawaii, has a single system of education; several other states essentially have only one school district in each county (e.g., Florida, Kentucky, Louisiana); hence, the average enrollment per district in these states is quite large.
- Some predominately rural states have many small districts. For example, Oklahoma, Maine, South Dakota, Vermont, Nebraska, and Montana have average school district sizes of below 1,000 pupils.

- Larger school districts are most often located in or near large cities; smaller districts tend to be in the outer rings of suburbs or in rural areas (Ornstein, 1992).

- The number of students enrolled in elementary and secondary education within a given state varies considerably. In the fall of 1993, California had just over 5.3 million students enrolled, while North Dakota had just over 119,000 enrolled (National Center for Education Statistics, 1995a).

- Expenditures for public elementary and secondary education vary considerably among the states. In 1992–93, New Jersey had a per pupil average expenditure of $8,770, while in Utah this figure was only $2,967 (National Center for Education Statistics, 1995b).

Because of these considerable differences, generalizations about local school districts cannot be very meaningful.

Arguments for school district consolidation based on the principles of adequacy, efficiency, and equity persist. However, the current popularity of decentralization and socially driven concerns for local community autonomy counterbalances such arguments. As a result, the issue of how school districts will be organized in the future remains uncertain. Further consolidation is likely in states where counties still have many small districts. Mergers are also possible in urban areas where problems plaguing big-city districts could result in state government legislating such organizations out of existence (the districts would essentially be divided into pieces that are then annexed by their contiguous suburban districts) (Kowalski, 1995).

Social and Economic Contexts

Schools have never totally controlled the lives of children. Students also are influenced by their families and communities, and unfortunately, many students enter kindergarten already at risk of becoming educational casualties. The inescapable link between schools and the wider environment is a critical consideration in school reform. If administrators and policymakers do not understand changing social and economic conditions, or if they determine such conditions to be irrelevant to schools, are they likely to provide students with relevant learning experiences? Without a real understanding of student needs and community wants, neither visioning nor strategic planning is likely to be productive. As such, the changing face of American society has become a central issue for school district leadership.

Changing Demographics

Robert Huelskamp (1993) wrote, "Perhaps more than any other factor, the changing demographic makeup of the student body will have a profound effect on future educational requirements" (p. 720). Three demographic trends appear to be especially significant in this regard:

1. Changes in the geographic distribution in the country's population
2. Increasing ethnic and racial diversity
3. Age transitions in the country's population

Increases and declines in population almost always create problems for public schools. This is true because patterns among and within states are dissimilar. The population is continuing to shift away from the east and north to the west and south; some eastern states have had substantial declines in school-age population (Riddle, 1992). The most significant growth is occurring along two corridors: in the southwest, from Texas to California, and in the southeast, from Virginia to Florida. And although the total population of the country increased by just over 22 million from 1980 to 1990, several states actually lost population during this period; for example, Iowa, North Dakota, and Wyoming (United States Bureau of the Census, 1991). Thus, superintendents in some states are still struggling with school closings, while superintendents in other states are addressing problems of opening new schools.

The country is rapidly becoming more ethnically and racially diverse. Two factors are responsible: increased levels of immigration and an imbalance in fertility rates among women of different racial groups and educational groups. While most Americans readily recognize that the nation is becoming a more heterogeneous society, Americans tend to underestimate the rate at which this is occurring. In the mid-1990s, about one fourth of the population was classified as minorities (Ward, 1994). Comparisons between the 1980 and 1990 official census data provide clear evidence of an accelerating rate of diversity. Table 2–2 contains data showing the rate of population growth within the racial and ethnic categories as identified in the official United States census.

During the 1980s, minority categories had substantially larger increases in percentage than did the majority white population. Population projections, however, generally indicate that current growth rates (but not actual populations) for most minority groups will decline, especially if immigration laws and quotas become more restrictive. In 1990, there were approximately 248,710,000 residents in the

Table 2–2

Changes in population by racial and ethnic groups between 1980 and 1990

Category	1980	1990	Percent Increase
White (non-Hispanic)	176,544,000	187,137,000	6.0%
African American	26,489,000	29,986,000	13.2%
Native American, Eskimo or Aleut	1,421,000	1,959,000	37.9%
Asian or Pacific Islander	3,500,000	7,274,000	107.8%
Hispanic	14,610,000	22,354,000	53.0%

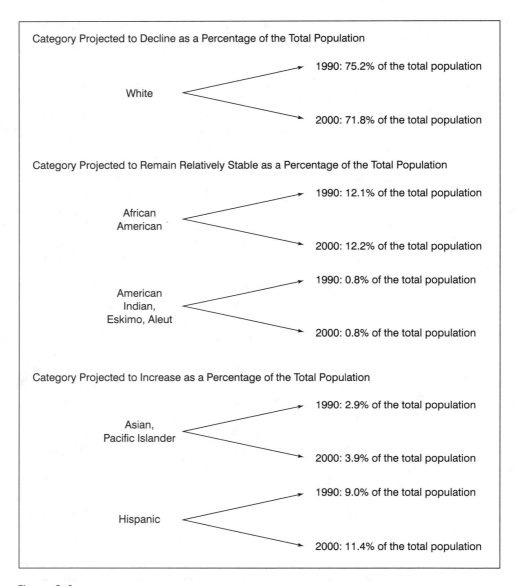

Figure 2–1
Racial composition of the population of the United States: 1990 and 2000

United States; this figure is projected to increase to 274,633,000 in the year 2000. Figure 2–1 shows actual and projected figures for race categories as percentages of the total population. The distribution of 1993 public school enrollments by race is shown in Figure 2–2. From comparisons of 1990 population figures with 1993 public school enrollments, it is obvious that minorities are represented to a higher degree in public schools than they are in the general population.

Figure 2–2
1993 public school enrollment: percentages by race

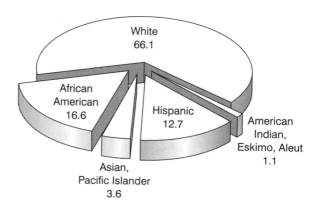

In addition to immigration, growth in minority populations stems from birthrates. Hispanic females have fertility rates higher than African American women, and African American women have fertility rates higher than white women. Perhaps even more relevant, women with the lowest level of formal education generally have the highest fertility rates. Since there are definite connections between a lack of education and poverty, this fact helps explain the growing number of children being born into poverty.

As expected, states with the fastest growth rates "tend to be states with a high percentage of minorities, especially minority youth" (Hodgkinson, 1992, p. 3). Large districts in Florida, such as Dade County and Broward County, are gaining as many as 10,000 students per year, and a significant portion of these students are immigrants from economically poor Caribbean countries.

Immigration rates in the United States are higher than ever. However, unlike the past when immigrants came predominately from Europe, most now come from Asian and Hispanic countries (America's Changing Face, 1990). In Texas, New Mexico, Arizona, and California, the Hispanic population is growing rapidly; between 1973 and 1993, the percentage of elementary and secondary students in the United States who were Hispanic doubled (from less than 6% to 12%) (National Center for Educational Statistics, 1995b). Demographers estimate that as many as 5 million immigrant children will enter K–12 schools in America during the 1990s. The white student population is projected to decline from 68.6% in 1990 to 49.4% by 2030 (U.S. Bureau of the Census, 1993). Already 150 different languages are spoken by children in our schools (Huelskamp, 1993). Immigrant children often enter schools with a number of special problems. In addition to language difficulties, they often must overcome personal health problems and poverty. More important, many enter schools unprepared to deal with the cultural diversity that they find.

The changing population with new and different needs presents challenges to public education. Minority children and those living in poverty already constitute a significant portion of the public school enrollment in the United States, and the immigration and birthrate trends suggest a more diverse population in the future. Consider these statistics:

- In 1993, there were over 11 million African American children under the age of 18 in the United States (Bennett, 1995). In 1996, only 66% of the children in this country were classified as nonminority; this is a decrease from 74% in 1980 (Federal Interagency Forum, 1997).

- Minority students are far more likely to be enrolled below the modal grade for their age; approximately 40% of Hispanics, 37% of African Americans, and 25% of whites are below the modal grade for their age (Orum, 1986). In 1996, 14% of Hispanic youth were neither in school nor working; this compares with only 8% of the white youth (Federal Interagency Forum, 1997).

- In 1989, 43% of all 16– to 24–year-old Hispanics who were born outside the United States had not completed high school or earned a GED (National Center for Educational Statistics, 1995b).

- From 1979 to 1995, the number of school-age children who spoke a language other than English at home virtually doubled; in 1995, there were nearly 2.5 million children in this category (Federal Interagency Forum, 1997).

- Growth in minority populations has occurred at a time when the national economy and youth job markets have undergone substantial change (Rury & Cassell, 1993). Youth who do not succeed in the educational system create problems for themselves and society.

- On the Scholastic Aptitude Test (SAT), African American students "still average nearly 200 points lower than whites. Similarly, the scores of Hispanics and Native American students trail the scores of whites by more than 100 points" (Huelskamp, 1993, p. 719).

- Status dropout rates (that is, dropout rates representing a proportion of all dropouts rather than dropouts for just a single year) for 16– to 24-year-olds in 1992 showed that whites had a rate of 7.7%, African Americans had a rate of 13.7%, and Hispanics had a rate of 29.4% (McMillen, Kaufman, Hausken, & Bradby, 1993).

- In 1970, nearly 90% of white children under the age of 18 lived in families where both parents were present, but by 1992, that figure dropped to 77%. In 1970, just under 60% of African American children lived in two-parent families; by 1992, that figure dropped to 36%. In 1970, 78% of Hispanic children lived in two-parent families; by 1992, that figure dropped to 65% (Educational Research Service, 1995).

- In married couple families, 8.8% of white children, 16.1% of African American children, and 26.3% of Hispanic children ages of 6 to 17 live in poverty. In female, one-parent families, those figures increase to 38.2% of whites, 63.5% of African Americans, and 62.2% of Hispanics (Educational Research Service, 1995).

- While just over 40% of the students living in poverty are white, Hispanic and African American students are more likely to be raised in poverty. Hispanic students constitute about 13% of the total school enrollment, but over 21% of the children living in poverty; African Americans constitute about 15% of the total school enrollment, but about 33% of the children living in poverty (U.S. General Accounting Office, 1993).

Some large-city school districts already have predominately minority student populations (e.g., Washington, D.C.); however, many nonmetropolitan school districts across America also are becoming more heterogeneous (Hobbs, 1994). The rising enrollment of minority students in public schools has brought up some significant educational issues. For example, issues relating to bilingual education and multicultural education often divide communities and spark heated debates among educators.

The third noteworthy demographic trend relates to the population's age distribution. Compared to 1980, the average citizen is older, and the over-35 cohort is expected to continue increasing more rapidly than younger cohorts (Kennedy, 1993). However, age-related trends are uneven across states. Consider the situation in Florida. Long a haven for retirees, the state also has grown in younger population because of immigration. In other states, however, a longer life span and declining birthrates result in a smaller percentage of the population being in the 18-and-under cohort. Several critical issues are associated with an increasing average age in America. Among them are the following:

- Senior citizens often oppose efforts to raise taxes for education because they have fixed incomes, are negatively affected by property taxes, and no longer have children in the public schools.

- In many states, only about 1 in 4 taxpayers perceives a direct personal benefit from public education (that is, they still have children in school). Often they are reluctant to support school improvement initiatives.

- Transitions to an information-based society and global economy have stirred public opinion about the importance of education. Demands for lifelong learning, for example, reflect a pragmatic judgment about the value of information. Frequently, local school districts face demands for more adult programming.

- Within numerous communities, school districts operate the largest food service and transportation programs, and school buildings constitute the largest investment in public property. Demographic changes often lead to proposals calling for school resources to be used for emerging needs (e.g., using school facilities for preparing meals for the elderly, allowing public access to school libraries and computers).

In summarizing the effects of an escalating average age, Paul Bauman (1996) wrote the following:

The 'graying' of America translates to increased political power among those who do not have children in school and a concomitant lessening of the proportion of voters with school-age children. The trend has direct implications for efforts to achieve excellence in the public schools that rely on broad public support. (p. 92)

Symbiotic relationships between public schools and communities are more difficult because of the demographic changes identified here. For example, social and ethnic diversity can magnify philosophical differences over public education; a perceived lack of benefits can erode political and economic support among older taxpayers. Fifty years ago, when superintendents were guided by principles of efficiency, they were comfortable making critical decisions in isolation. Now, enlightened superintendents openly seek community involvement and partnerships with businesses and other public agencies as a means of maintaining support for schools.

Deterioration of the Family

In the 1950s, the typical child was reared in a family consisting of a working father, a stay-at-home mother, and two or more siblings. In addition, the child was likely to spend a considerable amount of time with grandparents and other relatives, some of whom resided in the same community. Now many school-age children are raised in single-parent households, their home life is dysfunctional (describing situations in which the development of children is either not supported or is actually impaired), and they rarely see relatives outside of their immediate family. Consider the following facts about family structure:

- The divorce rate in the United States doubled between 1950 and 1989, and the rate at which divorced fathers abandoned their children doubled between 1970 and 1990 (Reitzug, 1996).
- In 1990, over 74% of the mothers whose youngest child was between the ages of 6 and 13 were either working or seeking work (Natale, 1992); 82% of all children under age 18 now have working mothers (Hodgkinson, 1992).
- Half of the single women with children in America live in poverty (Kirst & McLaughlin, 1990).
- In 1990, one fourth of all children were born to unmarried parents, and about 350,000 babies were born to drug-addicted mothers (Hodgkinson, 1992).
- Compared with white children, African American children are four times as likely, and Hispanic children twice as likely, to be reared in single-parent families (Reitzug, 1996).

In both single- and two-parent families, more and more children are facing what Sylvia Hewlett (1991) coined a "time deficit"—decreased time parents spend with children compared with previous generations. According to the Family Research Council, today's parents spend just 17 waking hours per week with their children compared to an average of 30 hours in 1965 (Stratton, 1995).

Clearly, family instability has encouraged calls for schools to provide more services. Preschool programs, social work services, and expanded psychological services serve as examples. Less obvious issues relating to these changes are a host of legal and quasi-legal questions, such as guardianship, access to private records by noncustodial parents, and other policies regarding parental rights and responsibilities (Duncan, 1992).

Destructive and Antisocial Behaviors

Changes in family and societal values obviously alter student behaviors and the problems that educators perceive about their students. Consider a comparison of teacher concerns in the 1940s and 1980s from surveys conducted by the California Department of Education:

- During the 1940s, teachers' major concerns about students were (1) talking in class, (2) chewing gum, (3) making noise, (4) running in the halls, (5) getting out of turn when in line, (6) wearing improper clothes, and (7) not putting refuse in the wastebaskets.
- During the 1980s, teachers' major concerns about students were (1) drug abuse, (2) alcohol abuse, (3) pregnancies, (4) suicide, (5) rape, (6) robbery, (7) assault, (8) burglary, (9) arson, (10) bombings, (11) murder, (12) excessive absenteeism, (13) vandalism, (14) extortion, (15) gang warfare, (16) abortion, and (17) venereal disease (Fernandez & Underwood, 1993)

Many children no longer receive moral and ethical codes from their families, communities, and churches. Instead their behavioral standards are determined by "pop" culture and peer influence. Research on the effects of television, for example, shows that quantity and quality of exposure to this medium influence the incidence of violence among children and their performance on standardized tests (Stratton, 1995). The following statistics exhibit the extent of destructive behavior among school-age children:

- Overwhelmingly, the general public believes that violence in schools has increased across the nation in recent years; 68% believe it has increased a great deal, and 21% believe it has increased some (Elam & Rose, 1995).
- One out of every 4 deaths among teenagers is due to gunshot wounds (Hull, 1993).
- In 1994, children under the age of 18 were 244% more likely to be killed by guns than they were just 7 or 8 years earlier (Adler, 1994).
- In inner-city schools, 45% of male students say they either have been threatened with a gun or someone actually shot at them while they were coming to or going from school (Portner, 1994).

Violence is not the only manifestation of moral and ethical problems. In 1990, over a half million girls under age 20 gave birth—the fourth consecutive year that the number had increased (Caldas, 1994).

Changing Roles for Schools

Discussing differing conceptions of the purposes of public education, Philip Schlechty (1990) described three conflicting goals shaping curriculum, instruction, and educator behavior. These were (1) preserving values and beliefs of a dominant culture, (2) preparing individuals for the work force, and (3) compensating for injustice and inequity. Each has its own associated image of schools, teachers, and administrators. Through much of the 20th century, the purposes of education were dictated by external forces (that is, forces outside of schools and school districts). And since economic, social, and political transitions were often extreme, schools were expected to change course quickly.

One of the best examples of this pattern is found in the period from roughly 1957 to 1970. About the beginning of this era, William Van Til (1971) wrote the following:

> With the launching of the Russian *Sputnik* in 1957, American social hysteria increased, and the schools proved to be a handy scapegoat. Magazines called for the closing of the 'carnival' in the schools; intellectual leaders who had not been in an elementary or secondary school since their own graduations loftily condemned the schools for a lack of academic rigor. (p. 3)

Dissatisfaction with the social order spawned a number of efforts to increase rigor in the disciplines (especially in subjects such as science and mathematics); the passage of the National Defense Education Act of 1958, in particular, was intended to push schools toward academic excellence. A few years later, however, American society turned its attention inward as the government struggled with issues relating to civil rights, poverty, mounting racial tensions, and an unpopular war in Vietnam. Again the social order was disrupted, but this time, alienation, disillusionment, and distrust of government took center stage (Van Til, 1971). And again, schools were blamed for society's imperfections. Almost immediately, the agenda of excellence was displaced by an agenda of equity.

Current reform efforts have been primarily directed toward achieving excellence. They include goals such as raising graduation rates, raising standardized test scores, and making students computer literate. Ironically, these efforts have also served to rekindle concern for inescapable questions about the responsibility of public education to provide children with reasonably equal opportunities. Table 2–3 provides examples of reform initiatives related to both equity and excellence.

For school superintendents, responding to educational needs arising from social and economic problems is only part of the total picture. More fundamental are philosophical questions guiding institutional vision and planning—and ultimately, policy. The long-standing balance between state and local control of public education is being seriously challenged by dissimilar interests and needs among those who can influence education policy. Demands for excellence often translate into demands for liberty, that is, higher levels of local control. Concerns for equity often translate into demands for more centralized governmental control, that is,

Table 2–3
Examples of critical issues for public education in a more diverse society

Issue	Educational Perspectives	Potential Political Conflict
Alternative schools	A growing number of students are not coping in regular schools; these students require a different instructional format, curriculum, or institutional setting.	Alternative schools are viewed as unnecessary by some taxpayers; critics charge that these schools convey the message that all types of behavior will be tolerated.
Bilingual education	A growing number of non-English-speaking students are entering public school; their learning is delayed by language barriers.	Many Americans view bilingual education negatively because they see it as contributing to divisions in society; some point to continuing problems in French-speaking Quebec, Canada, as proof.
Discipline	As more and more students live in poverty or come from dysfunctional families, discipline problems in schools increase.	Many Americans demand "get tough" policies for discipline without considering the potential effects on society if large numbers of students fail in school.
Full-service schools	A growing number of students bring social, physical, and emotional problems to school; these problems require more special personnel (e.g., counselors, social workers) and programs.	Many Americans continue to insist that schools have a limited mission to teach academic skills; there is a reluctance to fund additional operations, which are seen as outside the scope of this responsibility.
Measuring and testing	There is compelling evidence that failing students increases the likelihood of their never finishing high school; many tests are culturally biased.	Many Americans continue to demand that schools sort students; scores on standardized tests and grade retention rates are seen as measures of quality.
Multicultural education	Potential success for ethnic and racial minorities in public education is often affected by racism and other forms of discrimination—conditions sustained by not understanding/appreciating other cultures.	Multicultural education is opposed by some who believe that it presents multiple perspectives of history and perpetuates the separation of cultures in American society.
Tracking	Student placements in tracks are often done using questionable criteria; once placed in low tracks, students are rarely able to move to higher-level groups.	Many Americans believe that separating students on the basis of ability and achievement facilitates good education.

state intervention designed to equalize educational opportunities among school districts. Thus, the present arrangement for school governance might be most effective when there is a simultaneous pursuit of excellence and equity. Unfortunately, there are no clear lines describing a sufficient level of equity (for example, as exhibited in school finance litigation). If local school boards fail to keep principles in balance, they invite state governments to establish basic educational goals and the means by which they will be achieved (Bauman, 1996).

Beyond the seemingly endless list of problems associated with changing social and economic conditions, educational leaders are also challenged by an ageless question, What knowledge is of most worth? In a shrinking world constantly reshaped by technology, and in an information-based society, schools are expected to develop students as thinkers, problem solvers, and creators (Schlechty, 1990). In addition, as the national goals for education stipulate, schools are expected to graduate at least 90% of their eligible students.

Unfortunately, statistics suggest that schools are not meeting these expectations. The separation between rich and poor is becoming wider, and poverty is a major factor placing students at risk of becoming educational casualties. Rapidly, America is also becoming a country divided between the "information rich" and the "information poor," categories defined by economic status and education (Hodgkinson, 1992).

Even in school districts with decentralized governance plans, the superintendent is expected to be the primary catalyst for change. As the leading administrator, the superintendent bears the responsibility of educating others so they understand and accept the need to build a new generation of American schools. This process begins with educating principals and teachers, but it ultimately extends to educating the community at large. "The superintendent, in fact, becomes the chief educator of the community, for the superintendent's role is to educate the community about education" (Schlechty, 1990, p. 44). Perhaps more than ever before, the superintendency is drifting toward the role of educator-scholar. Superintendents are expected to enlighten the community; they are expected to nurture a sensitivity to the evolving educational needs; they are expected to fashion democratic procedures for reaching critical decisions; and they are expected to create cultures and climates enabling schools to redefine their purposes. These are tasks requiring professional knowledge and political skills.

PUBLIC DISSATISFACTION

Writing about the politics of education in the 1980s, Frank Lutz and Laurence Iannaccone (1986) described the value of understanding *dissatisfaction theory*. They called public dissatisfaction a disease that could be predicted by monitoring changes in the socioeconomic and political indicators of a community. As the illness progresses, special-interest groups and others intensify efforts to influence policy; there is an increase in voter turnout for school board elections; and incumbent school board members get defeated or choose not to seek another term. Ultimately, the disease causes a change in the superintendency and a disruption to the school system. The theory suggests that this disease is not as sudden as it often appears to the casual observer, but rather it is a long-term illness, usually exhibiting a variety of symptoms in the early stages.

If superintendents are to lead schools into the future successfully, they must recognize the symptoms of discontent, accurately measure its levels of intensity, and understand its underlying causes. Dissatisfaction theory is especially helpful in the first task—recognizing the symptoms of discontent. Unfortunately, measuring levels of dissatisfaction is usually more difficult. Superintendents often get mixed signals, especially from their own profession.

Many educators, for example, argue that the level of public dissatisfaction with education has been exaggerated (e.g., Clark & Astuto, 1990). The Phi Delta Kappa/Gallup polls, probably the most widely used barometer for opinions about public education, have generally found that parents are satisfied with their schools (Elam, 1995). The 1997 poll, for example, found that people continue to rate schools in their own communities much higher than they rate schools across the country— and the closer they get to schools, the higher the ratings (Rose, Gallup, & Elam, 1997). Others, however, have concluded that public support for education is tenuous. They caution that neither those who seek radical reform nor those who oppose it should feel confident that the American public is on their side (e.g., Bradley, 1995).

That the public has mixed opinions about school effectiveness is not surprising. Sources of displeasure frequently have deep philosophical roots, especially differences about values and beliefs regarding the purposes of public education and who should pay for it. Many taxpayers remain dubious about educational innovations and the will of educators to return schools to the basics and stern discipline. So while people often appear to be enthusiastic about change at the national and state levels, their support for specific reform ideas quickly wanes when costs are disclosed (Coombs & Wycoff, 1994).

Purposes and Dissatisfaction

In a perfect world, public opinion about education would be based on a set of commonly accepted goals, and success would be determined by an objective assessment of progress toward these goals. Unfortunately, not even the first element, consensus of purpose, has been achieved. Consequently, public perceptions of schools are often shaped by self-interest and secondhand information supplied by the media or special-interest groups. For example, 52% of the respondents to the 1988 Phi Delta Kappa/Gallup Poll on education said they relied on newspapers for their information about schools (Elam, 1995). At best, we know that most of us accept two broad goals for public education, to serve the individual and to serve society. These are often described as the private and social missions for schools (Bauman, 1996).

Many Americans overlook the fact that more students today are staying in school and graduating. And while some contend students are not learning what they should learn, compared with past decades, "schools are surely doing no less" (Schlechty, 1990, p. 30). In truth, the "good old days" often are exaggerated; describing periods when less than half of those between the ages of 25 and 29 had graduated from high school (a common condition until 1950), many critics of current schools proclaim unqualifiedly that the public schools then were highly effective. Unlike today when the focus is placed on those who do not succeed, judgments about the past are usually based on the achievers. Then families, churches, neighborhoods, and other social units addressed many of the needs of youth—especially those not deemed to be the responsibility of schools. For the children in the past, the development of morals, ethics, and civic responsibility occurred more naturally (Finn, 1991). In addition, good-paying jobs awaited those who did not graduate from high school.

In large part, current dissatisfaction flows from changes about the purposes of public schools. The previously mentioned shift from the post-*Sputnik* quest for excellence to the mid-1960s pursuit of equity was just one of many abrupt policy transformations. They were provoked by what Larry Cuban (1988) described as the menacing dilemma of choosing between two basic values in American life. A variety of destabilizing consequences for schools have been the result:

> Courses change, laws change, and even teacher and administrator behaviors change—but only temporarily. The basic structure of schools remains intact, waiting for the next swing of the imaginary pendulum of public concern. (Kowalski & Reitzug, 1993, p. 280)

Skepticism about the need for change among educators is also fueled by realizations that the road to reform is paved with myths. For instance, many critics of public education suggest that meaningful school renewal will not require additional resources, and they argue that what is required is revolutionary action. Those who truly understand the process of education and the history of public schools realize that such assumptions are unfounded. True reform requires highly specific, systemic, and structured methodologies, new technologies, and adequate materials. Furthermore, the most important changes in public education have tended to be incremental (Pogrow, 1996).

Movement away from the equity agenda of the 1960s toward a focus on excellence provides a good example of the American public's tendency to embrace new purposes for elementary and secondary schools. Although often attributed to the report, *A Nation at Risk* (National Commission on Excellence in Education, 1983), a transition toward excellence actually had started in the 1970s. The famous report merely legitimatized the public concern about low test scores and student performance in basic subjects (Finn, 1991). In 1982 (a year before publication of the report), there was ample evidence that many taxpayers were already concerned about the quality of public education—only about 20% of the population rated the performance and quality of the nation's public schools as above average (Gallup, 1982).

Many of the initiatives emerging in the 1980s were imposed by state governments and were "intensifications" of previous mandates. Ideas such as longer school years, longer school days, more homework, and increased graduation requirements were often enacted in the absence of (1) a clear societal consensus regarding expectations for schools, (2) support from the education profession, and

CURRENT CONDITIONS OF PRACTICE

(3) evidence that individuals desired change for "their" local schools. Hence, most recent reform initiatives did not start at the grassroots level as a result of wide-spread public dissatisfaction; rather they were initiated by governmental officials and powerful interest groups (Coombs & Wycoff, 1994). The general public dissatis-faction with education simply reduced opposition to their ideas.

As previously mentioned, people often rate their local public schools higher than they rate the nation's public schools (Rose et al., 1997). This fact is probably due to people's reliance on secondhand information—that is, many citizens depend on the news media or pressure groups to describe the processes and outcomes of public education. Nevertheless, negative perceptions also appear to stem from lack of confidence about the future. While social reformers and economic conservatives often reach different conclusions about purposes of public education, they collec-tively worry that the next generation of adults will be unable to maintain the nation's status in the world. And beneath their expressions of concern and discon-tent, many Americans still believe that better schools make a better society (Tyack & Cuban, 1995). Repeatedly seeing schools portrayed as unproductive and dangerous institutions is undoubtedly disheartening. A significant portion of society has con-cluded that "too many public schools are not providing the minimum prerequisites for education—a safe, orderly environment and effective teaching of 'the basics'" (Johnson & Immerwahr, 1994–95, p. 4). Approximately 85% of those who partici-pated in the 1995 Phi Delta Kappa/Gallup Poll on Education said they favor higher standards for both promotion and graduation (Elam & Rose, 1995).

Given the manifold expectations society has for public education, a certain amount of dissatisfaction is unavoidable. Even in small, rather homogeneous com-munities, different—and sometimes contradictory—purposes for schools are evi-dent. Captains of industry, for instance, want high schools to produce graduates who are computer literate, loyal, honest, and dependable; others desire schools to prepare responsible citizens; others expect schools to set very high expectations and to challenge students academically; and still others count on schools to com-pensate for the difficulties faced by disadvantaged students. These perspectives essentially can be reduced to the principles of excellence and equity, with one side believing intelligence and ability are inherited and the other side believing human abilities are universal. For the former, schools should serve the purpose of nourish-ing the assets of intelligence and ability; for the latter, schools should provide equalizing opportunities (Parker & Parker, 1995).

Doing More or Doing Less?

Divisions over equity and excellence have resulted in two distinct reform agendas. First, those emphasizing equity as a prerequisite to excellence believe that public education has a responsibility to provide all students with a reasonable opportu-nity for success. This requires educators to be sensitive to diversity and to compen-sate for the negative effects of poverty, abuse, and dysfunctional homes. Jo Anna Natale (1992) wrote:

> One of the best hopes for improving children's lot in America, experts say, can be found in programs that link health, social, and instructional services under one roof—the schoolhouse roof. Inaccessibility of services—whether real or perceived—can keep children and their families from getting the help they need when they need it. (p. 26)

Social reformers argue that meaningful reform should include reconceptualizations of educational equity, additional programs for the disadvantaged, and coordinated efforts with other community agencies (e.g., Garcia & Gonzalez, 1995; Kirst, 1994; Negroni, 1994).

Those who argue that social issues and equity should be infused into school reform policies are generally guided by these beliefs:

- There is a dual system of education in America—one for the poor and one for everyone else. To date, school reform has not addressed the problems associated with having separate and unequal schools. Schools will remain ineffective as long as racism and poverty are ignored (Kozol, 1992).

- Business leaders have unfairly blamed schools for the nation's economic problems, and it is unjust for them to expect schools to be reconstructed solely on the basis of economic goals (Schnieder, 1992).

- Business leaders want to increase accountability and efficiency without increasing financial responsibility or equity. By imposing private-sector values on public schools, they undermine responsibility of citizens for collective action to improve schools for all (Moffett, 1994).

- Many low-income and minority children do not adjust well to traditional schools, which have little continuity with their personal lives. Reform should focus on increased services and relevant experiences for disadvantaged students (Banks, 1993).

In essence, these reformers contend that excellence and equity should be pursued simultaneously.

The nearly opposite reform position grows out of the beliefs that schools already waste too much money and pay too little attention to nonacademic matters. For these critics, the application of economic and business strategies can result in greater productivity without an increase in fiscal resources (or even in some instances, with a reduction in fiscal resources). In recent years, advocates for this position have dominated the political arena. Their calls for excellence often portray students as lazy, educators as incompetent, and schools as inefficient bureaucracies; more important, their suggested solutions—ideas such as vouchers, choice, and charter schools—focus on a redistribution of financial resources. Because their initiatives often require little or no sacrifice from taxpayers, and because their agenda emphasizes liberty for taxpayers and hard work for teachers and educators, their ideas have appealed to large segments of society. Adherents of this position include a significant number of business leaders, elected government officials, ultra-conservative political and religious organizations, and disgruntled taxpayers.

Many in this group measure educational success with an economic yardstick, but others use a combination of economic, social, political, and moral criteria. Among the problems they see in public education are a lack of discipline, waste and inefficiency, a "dumbing down" of standards, a preoccupation with political correctness, an overdependency on government to care for individuals, and a lack of accountability. Conservative critiques of public education have not been peculiar to the United States; similar criticisms have been voiced in Canada and Great Britain over the past decade (Elliott & MacLennan, 1994).

Many who rely entirely on economic perspectives to identify academic short-comings feel that the sole purpose of schools is to prepare dutiful workers. They charge that corporate America is paying dearly for insufficiently educated workers (e.g., Groennings, 1992). Being preoccupied with economic matters, these critics are usually indifferent to moral and political issues that extend beyond the acquisition of knowledge (Soder, 1995). They believe national economic problems constitute a sufficient reason for school reform, and they are especially enamored with ideas calling for new governance structures (e.g., decentralization), revisions in professional preparation and licensure (e.g., reducing emphasis on pedagogy and increasing emphasis on disciplines), and competition among schools (e.g., vouchers, choice) (Ehrlich, 1988). They often see evolutionary change as ineffective and demand radical reforms similar to those carried out by major corporations such as General Motors during the 1970s and 1980s (e.g., Shreve & Lidell, 1992). These critics express pessimism about the ability and willingness of school administrators to lead a significant reform movement, and as a result, they view imposing change as an appropriate tactic.

By contrast, those who combine economics, politics, and religion come at the problem somewhat differently. The Christian Right, for instance, has refocused its efforts from issues such as secular humanism to issues having wider appeal—ones such as questioning multiculturalism, sex education, and outcomes-based education (Jones, 1993). Ralph Reed, Jr. (1993), the former leader of the Christian Coalition, one of the most prominent organizations among the Christian Right, blamed the radical left for perpetuating images of his organization as being solely interested in causes such as censorship and school prayer. He viewed his organization's agenda as being mainstream in that it seeks parental rights, drug-free schools, an emphasis on basic skills, and competition. Similarly, Robert Simonds (1993), leader of Citizens for Excellence in Education, put forth a three-pronged agenda for improving schools: (1) a return to academic excellence in education, (2) a return to moral sanity and family values, and (3) the election of parents to community and statewide school boards "who will hire parent-sensitive superintendents when these boards don't listen" (p. 20). He also noted that his group's goals were quite similar to those stated by the National Commission on Excellence in Education—the group that authored the report *A Nation at Risk*. Observing the growing influence of the Religious Right, George Kaplan (1994) concluded: (1) their work has been energized by a pervasive belief that schools are failing and (2) they have become more powerful by skillfully targeting problems that concern most Americans.

There are several plausible explanations as to why lasting change in education has been so evasive. Consider the following:

- Educators tend to frame educational problems and develop policy largely from the perspective of social theories, while many policymakers and legislators frame problems from the perspective of economic theories (Boyd, 1992). Thus, changes imposed on schools through statewide policies and laws do not necessarily affect the minds and hearts of educators.
- The American public has always had difficulty reaching consensus on the primary purposes of schooling (Wagner, 1993). Compromises reached in past reform eras have often papered over the basic conflicts over equity and excellence (Tyack & Cuban, 1995).
- Both public discontent and claims about the nature and severity of educational deficits have been common throughout the history of the United States (Harris, Hunt, & Lalik, 1986). Often policymakers and legislators have mistakenly interpreted this recurring attitude as a mandate for radical change.
- The persistence of bureaucratic-like structures in many school districts reflects the fact that schools were designed to be agencies of control rather than agencies of change (Kowalski & Reitzug, 1993). Neither academic preparation nor incentives in the workplace have encouraged administrators to be change agents.
- Rather than being expressions of citizen trusteeship, reform debates have typically been dominated by power elites who "have tried to persuade the public that their definition of problems and proposed solutions were authoritative" (Tyack & Cuban, 1995, p. 59). Hence, change initiatives often lack a broad base of support.

A more basic perspective on the public's attitude toward educational reform was offered by Martin Haberman (1994):

> The basic condition preventing significant school change is that the public doesn't want it. Using demography as a scare tactic to make the public more amenable to change doesn't work either, because there are no explicit connections made between the reforms proposed and the statistical horrors used to state the problem. (p. 692)

For the superintendent on the firing line, public discontent and demands for change have created a hydra-headed monster. Administrators are pushed by business and government leaders to make schools more effective and efficient while they are pulled by their profession, fellow educators, and their consciences to make schools an equalizing force in a changing society. What is the consequence for school superintendents? Insightful practitioners realize that their primary task is to improve schools for children in a democratic fashion that incorporates the entire community's concerns. To accomplish this, they must create environments that encourage an informed and thoughtful exchange of ideas about the purposes of public education and how those purposes can be achieved (Wagner, 1993). The moral tone for governance, that is the climate in which goal setting and planning occurs, is set by superintendents and school boards. In this respect, these local officials help determine if reform will focus on excellence or a combination of excellence and equity. After all, school district employees, students, and other members of the community "know what is expected by seeing what is inspected and respected" (Schlechty, 1992, p. 28).

A number of years ago noted education critic, Seymour Sarason, wrote a thought-provoking book, *The Culture of School and the Problem of Change* (1971). In it, he argued that all public schools—regardless of location and clientele—exhibited regularities associated with an imposed culture. Thus, the structure and instructional activities in a classroom in rural Idaho were not too dissimilar from those found in an urban school. He concluded that externally imposed mandates often failed because they ignored the deeply held values and beliefs that were responsible for such regularities. Revisiting his thesis 25 years later, Sarason (1996) remains pessimistic about school reform. He found classroom structures and activities as still lacking "almost all the hallmarks of productive learning" (p. 333). In large measure, he blames this condition on the passivity of educators. He criticizes them for not engaging in the professional responsibility of reading journals and books. Most noteworthy here, he sees internally driven change as unlikely because administrators and teachers do not adequately understand organizational culture and change. One of the consequences, he observes, is that educators do not engage in meaningful dialogue about their work in schools:

> What I find discouraging and even frightening is that school personnel rarely (if ever) raise and seriously discuss two questions. What is the overarching purpose of schooling, a purpose which if not realized makes the attainment of other purposes unlikely, if not impossible? What are the characteristics of contexts for productive learning? (p. 379)

While many educators believe that Professor Sarason's analysis is overly pessimistic, few take issue with his judgment that the American public is now extremely impatient. That is, they are becoming less and less willing to wait for educators to transform schools.

THE INFLUENCE OF TECHNOLOGY

The current nature of the role of school superintendent is also being shaped by technology. Both the process of education and the execution of administrative duties have changed markedly in the past few decades because of innovations such as the microcomputer, fax machines, and distance learning (a process of delivering instruction to remote sites via television). As far back as the late 1970s, several forward-thinking scholars were predicting that technology would improve access to information and increase the importance of information to organizational survival

(Lipinski, 1978). While this prophetic conclusion has had universal relevance to a society moving away from a manufacturing base, it is particularly significant for leaders in public institutions for at least two important reasons:

1. Schools are often perceived as inefficient institutions and computers present opportunities for increasing productivity (Kearsley, 1990).
2. Public institutions in a democratic society are expected to be open to their community environments. More precisely, they are expected to exchange information openly and continuously—a goal made more attainable because of modern technologies.

Many observers have described technology as a revolutionary development for education; in truth, its impact has been and will continue to be evolutionary. Its influence on educators and students is really an ongoing series of developmental phases, and the future promises of technology can be summed up by five key trends:

1. Increased processing speed
2. Greater memory capacity
3. Miniaturization
4. Decreased cost
5. Increased ease of use (Dyrli & Kinnaman, 1994, p. 92)

These trends in technology will make it increasingly possible for superintendents to achieve greater productivity and to make the climate of their schools more open.
   In this vein, consider the following potential effects that technology offers:

- Communication can be reconceptualized from a one-way process (distributing information) to a two-way process (distributing and receiving information).
- Access to information allows decisions to be made in a more informed and more timely manner.
- Internal communication (within the school system) and external communication (with outside agencies or individuals) can occur more frequently and at a lesser expense.
- Efficiency can be increased in a number of managerial tasks such as budgeting, accounting, inventories, personnel records, student records, bus routing, building maintenance, and food services.
- Higher levels of efficiency are possible in a number of leadership ventures such as curriculum development, strategic planning, and staff development.

There is mounting evidence that administrators are recognizing the promises of technology and integrating it into their practice, e.g., approximately 10% of all computers purchased by public school systems are used for administrative work (Wall, 1994).

As professionals, today's leaders ought to be expected to rethink how they conceptualize and implement organizational communication (Toth & Trujillo, 1987). Robert Woodroof (1996) noted that advancements in technology are compelling professionals to do just that. Table 2–4 presents examples of modifications in professional behavior he has identified as common expectations. In addition to enhancing personal practice, technology also can provide advantages to administrative teams. Telecommunication and computer technologies, for instance, enhance leadership functions by (1) aligning and connecting education's psychological and physical workplaces, (2) generating and moving information through voice, video, and data connections available to educators, and (3) breaking through the real and assumed barriers that often isolate decision makers (Rhodes, 1988).

Technology is not just about information, it is also about communication. Accordingly, it is changing long-standing ideas about schools and practices within them. The following illustrate this point:

Table 2–4
Effects of technology on professional behavior

New Demand	Interpretation
Seeking the highest level of communication skills	While increasing a superintendent's ability to reach targeted audiences, technology forces him or her to become very effective in the process. Because most people enjoy increased access to information, they become selective in sending and receiving information.
Learning to communicate continuously	Fax machines, electronic mail, and other forms of technology have changed the way superintendents can engage in the communication process. For many, communication occurs around the clock and even when the superintendent is out of town.
Engaging in lifelong learning	Superintendents have instantaneous access to information that can inform practice. Administrators are able to remain current in their profession. Perhaps most important, using technology for learning allows the superintendent to lead by example.
Using critical thinking and analytical skills	Activities such as visioning and strategic planning are dependent on accurate information. Technology permits superintendents to use databases and to complete both trend analyses and impact analyses.
Accepting accountability for system performance	Access to information provided by technology allows superintendents to be better informed about operations throughout the school system. Consequently, they can be more accountable for organizational operations.

Source: Based on "Public Relations and Technology" (pp. 75–82) by R. H. Woodroof, in T. Kowalski (Ed.), *Public Relations in Educational Organizations: Practice in an Age of Information and Reform,* 1996, Upper Saddle River, NJ: Merrill/Prentice Hall.

- Schools are no longer seen as the sole depository for teaching and learning resources.
- The act of teaching is no longer seen as the mere transfer of information from teacher to student; accessing and using information independently have become more relevant in the curriculum.

Research examining the use of technology in schools is beginning to reveal some positive outcomes. Several studies (e.g., Sheingold & Hadley, 1990; Stuhlmann, 1994) have found that classrooms using computers shifted from teacher-centered to student-centered instructional approaches and that in them, perceptions of student performance changed.

Partly because of technology's potential to increase learning, its availability raises a number of possible concerns for superintendents. Consider the following questions, which are commonly posed to school administrators:

- Compared with other school districts, are the students in your district provided reasonable access to technology?
- Are technology resources equitably distributed in your school district?
- Are teachers and administrators adequately prepared to use technology resources, and are they encouraged to do so?
- Will your school district be able to protect its investments in technology? That is, will your district have the fiscal resources necessary to maintain and upgrade the technology you have purchased?

Questions such as these reveal the many hidden costs associated with technology. The most relevant include staff development and maintenance of up-to-date hardware and software.

Technology also can create personal problems for superintendents. Because computers are such powerful tools in accessing and analyzing information, they can give administrators a false sense of security (Brody, 1988). Computers, for instance, may be seen as objective machines capable of sifting through complex data to produce rational decisions. However, the decisions facing school superintendents are almost always too complex to be reduced to the mere level of data analysis. No computer can appropriately integrate values, ethics, politics, and craft knowledge into critical decisions affecting the lives of people. While a computer can facilitate management tasks, it can never become a substitute for professional and political judgment. The improper use of technology can also create problems by dehumanizing the administrative process. A superintendent, for example, may avoid face-to-face meetings with others, opting instead to communicate continuously via electronic mail and faxes.

Even though the possibility for misusing technology exists, this concern is significantly outweighed by its likely positive contributions. For example, ventures such as distance learning are giving new life to small schools. Through intermediate districts and other cooperative ventures, secondary schools with low enrollments are increasingly able to offer students a broader curriculum. In this respect, technology may prevent further consolidation of rural districts and of small-enrollment schools within districts. E. Robert Stephens (1994) wrote, "The potential that technology holds for enriching the curricular offerings of rural schools in particular seems irrefutable" (p. 175).

Technology is also reshaping the instructional process, making teaching a more individualized and relevant experience. Table 2–5 provides examples of functions that can be positively affected by the use of computers and other technologies.

One of the greatest promises of technology relates to its capacity to facilitate normative, reeducative change strategies—that is, strategies directed toward attitudes, values, skills, and opinions (Chin & Benne, 1969). Redesigning at an organizational level is becoming more evident as states move toward the broader policy initiative of deregulation and as school districts move toward decentralization. Cultural change strategies are highly dependent on communication and, hence, are dependent on accessing, storing, and using information.

One reason technology is such a central issue arises from its potential to be either beneficial or detrimental. Another reason has to do with public expectations. Because technology has had such a major impact on American society, parents and other taxpayers are becoming intolerant of educators who are unable to integrate technology into their work. This intolerance has been more evident in the area of teaching, but it is rapidly becoming the case with administrators, too (Tyack & Cuban, 1995). Shortly, students who were educated in computer-rich environments will assume the roles of policymakers and taxpayers—and as they do, expectations for superintendents to use technology will be even greater.

 ## FOR FURTHER REFLECTION

The conditions of practice for most school superintendents have changed markedly over the past 50 years. Today there are fewer school districts, districts have more heterogeneous populations, and schools are having to respond to a growing number of social, economic, and political problems. Poverty may well be the most debilitating circumstance affecting young children in the United States and their education. In the eyes of many Americans, schools have become unsafe places where expectations for learning are declining.

Not surprisingly, such perceptions spawn concern about the welfare of the nation. Are our public schools preparing students sufficiently? Will our country's economic and political stature in the world suffer in the future? There is growing evidence that many Americans are not satisfied with public education; their discontent prompts many of them to accept radical reform proposals. Pressures to restructure public education, or at least to place the schools in a competitive environment, come at a time when many taxpayers no longer have family members attending elementary and secondary schools. Under these circumstances, it has

Table 2–5
Examples of applications of technology in school districts

General Area	Function	Examples of Specific Tasks
Administration	Business management	Accounting procedures Budgeting/budget management Employee contract information Employee insurance programs Inventories Payroll Personnel records Purchasing
	Facility management	Energy management Equipment inventories Insurance management Maintenance schedules Security systems Work assignments
	Leadership	Communication Data analysis Decision support systems Information exchanges Planning Policy development/analysis
	Transportation services	Fleet insurance Fleet and parts inventories Fleet maintenance schedules Parts inventories Routing
Instruction	Instructional planning	Faculty/administration communication Lesson planning Needs assessments
	Program delivery	Computer networking Distance learning Individualized instruction Scheduling
	Student services	Attendance records Counseling and occupational information Food services Grade reporting Student record files Test scoring Transcripts

not been uncommon for communities to support reform but to oppose tax increases that may be necessary for implementing reform initiatives.

Likewise, technology has changed the conditions of practice for superintendents. Computers and telecommunications are especially meaningful in two critical areas: increasing productivity in administrative tasks and creating open organizational climates. The opportunities afforded by technology are pertinent to the critical task of rebuilding bridges to the community. By moving to two-way communication, by using information to revamp the instructional strategies used in schools, and by employing technology to make schools more accessible to all citizens, superintendents can make great strides toward this goal.

As you consider what you read in this chapter, answer the following questions:

1. Why is the United States becoming a more diverse society? Is this a trend that is driven by national policies? by local and state conditions?

2. In what ways has school consolidation improved the quality of public education? Is there a negative side to consolidation?

3. Why is school consolidation such a controversial topic?

4. In some urban schools, school health clinics have been established to deal with problems such as pregnancies and venereal disease. Are such clinics controversial? Why or why not? Are they more likely to be controversial in large cities than they are in suburban or rural areas?

5. In your own community, has there been a demand for schools to do more? If so, what additional services are being sought?

6. Why is poverty an especially debilitating circumstance for students? What can schools do to compensate for poverty?

7. Are most teachers and administrators adequately prepared to work with diverse cultures? To what extent does your local school system deal with issues relating to multicultural education?

8. When computers became available to schools in the early 1980s, were educators prepared to use them? How were computers integrated into your local school system?

9. In what ways can technology increase the productivity of educational administration?

10. Are most people in your community dissatisfied with schools? What information leads you to answer this question?

CASE STUDY

Following World War II, Tylerville became one of the fastest-growing suburbs in the United States. Located just 30 minutes from downtown Chicago, the community attracted primarily middle-class families. By 1970, most available land in the suburb had been developed into housing subdivisions. Apartment complexes and strip malls consumed the remaining land in the early 1970s. During the period of 1950 to 1970, the school district witnessed the construction of 7 new schools, a 175% increase in enrollment, and a 160% increase in the number of employees. Most of the new employees were young teachers who had just graduated from college.

The district experienced its first enrollment decline in 1973. Over the next 13 years, the district's enrollment dropped from 11,500 to 6,400, and several school buildings were closed. In 1986, the pattern of decline was reversed. Slight increases, about 2% per year, have occurred ever since. The upturn in enrollments was attributable to the changing population in the community. Families who had moved to Tylerville in previous decades were now moving out of Tylerville to more affluent suburban communities. A comparison of 1975 and 1995 is presented below:

Factor	1975	1995
Percentage of district enrollment classified as minority	5%	60%
Percentage of children living with only one parent	9%	43%
Percentage of students receiving free or reduced-price lunches	6%	39%
Percentage of students not completing high school before age 19	12%	32%

Substantial changes also occurred among the employees of the school district.

Factor	1975	1995
Average age of administrators	41	54
Average age of teachers	29	51
Percentage of minority administrators	5%	20%
Percentage of minority teachers	4%	18%
Percentage of professional employees living in the community	76%	41%

Dr. Robert Stephan became superintendent of the Tylerville Community School District just about 1 year ago. He had served as superintendent of a 1,500-student school district in a small southern Illinois farming community. At the age of 43, he had 9 years of classroom experience, 6 years of building-level administrative experience, and 4 years of central office experience—all in smaller, more rural communities. Having lived in small communities his entire life, Dr. Stephan, his wife, and their two children (ages 14 and 17) had mixed feelings about moving to an urban area. However, a $30,000 increase in salary, an attractive benefit package, and permission from the school board to reside outside the school district made the job sufficiently appealing. He was also favorably impressed with the fact that the school board had been very stable. Two of the members had served more than 20 years, 4 had served more than 12 years, and the remaining board member had served 4 years.

Although there were many challenges for Dr. Stephan in Tylerville, he considered the escalating dropout rate to be the most critical. After several months in the community, he appointed a special task force consisting of three administrators and seven teachers to study the problem. Their charge was to determine what was causing the escalation in the dropout rate. Among their findings were the following:

- The curriculum in the district's high school still focused heavily on college preparation. In fact, the courses had changed very little in the last 25 years. There was no school-to-work transition program.
- Pregnancies and expulsions accounted for much of the increase in dropouts. Although pregnant students could continue in school, most elected not to do so. More than half of the students who were expelled for one semester never returned to school. Most expulsions were for fighting, illegal drugs or alcohol, and excessive unexcused absences.
- Students in the district could attend classes at an area vocational school, but very few did so. Students received information about vocational courses, but there was no concerted effort to recruit students for these programs.
- The number of high school graduates enrolling in 4-year colleges had dropped from a high of 73% in 1970 to a low of 38% in the previous school year. A lack of interest in higher education may have contributed to dropout rates.
- There was no alternative school program in the district.
- While the number of white students in the district was declining, the number of Hispanic and African American students was increasing.
- Gangs and racial tension were becoming greater concerns.
- The school district had little contact with other community agencies; most of the school employees were not involved in community activities.

Using the findings from the task force report, Dr. Stephan presented three goals to the school board:

1. The district should establish an alternative high school to serve students unable to function in a normal school setting. Students expelled for disciplinary reasons would be eligible to attend.
2. The district should increase the number of minority employees; both Hispanic and African American educators should receive preferential consideration for employment.
3. The high school should revamp its entire curriculum; greater emphasis should be placed on school-to-work programs for students not planning to attend college.

Issues for Discussion

1. Is the demographic pattern of Tylerville typical for older suburban communities?

2. Many of the teachers in Tylerville were employed when demographics were different; they accepted employment immediately after graduating from college. Are these facts important? Why or why not?

3. Do you agree with Dr. Stephan that the dropout problem is critical?

4. What are the advantages and disadvantages of alternative schools? How might the addition of an alternative school affect Tylerville?

5. The school district has not had much contact with other community agencies. Is this fact important? Why or why not?

6. Do you agree with the superintendent's recommendation to revamp the high school curriculum? Does he have sufficient information to establish this as a goal?

7. If you were the superintendent, what steps would you take to ensure that the school system would be more responsive to community needs?

8. In what ways might technology be useful in addressing the task of revamping the high school curriculum?

9. Do you agree with Dr. Stephan's recommendation that Hispanics and African Americans should be given preferential consideration for employment as teachers and administrators? Are there legal problems associated with his recommendation?

10. Is the stability of the school board in this case a positive factor? In general, is board stability a positive factor? Why or why not?

11. Do you agree that the declining number of students enrolling in 4-year colleges represents a declining interest in education? Why or why not?

12. Why do you think the curriculum at the high school had changed very little during the past 25 years?

13. Assuming that resources are scarce, should priority be given first to revamping the curriculum or developing an alternative school?

14. Do you think it is an important issue that the superintendent has chosen to live outside the district?

15. If you had been selected as the new superintendent of schools, what approach would you have taken to determine the direction of the district?

16. After reading the case, would you accept the superintendency in this district? Explain your answer.

17. What additional information should be collected to help guide the future of the school district in Tylerville?

REFERENCES

Adler, J. (1994, January 10). Kids growing up scared. *Newsweek,* pp. 43–49.

America's changing face. (1990, September 10). *Newsweek*, pp. 44–50.

Banks, C. A. (1993). Restructuring schools for equity: What we have learned in two decades. *Phi Delta Kappan, 75*(1), 42–44, 46–48.

Bauman, P. C. (1996). *Governing education: Public sector reform or privatization.* Boston: Allyn and Bacon.

Bennett, C. E. (1995). *The Black population of the United States: March 1993 and 1994.* (ERIC Document Reproduction Service No. ED 381 600)

Boyd, W. L. (1992). The power of paradigms: Reconceptualizing educational policy and management. *Educational Administration Quarterly, 28*(4), 504–528.

Bradley, A. (October 18, 1995). Public backing for schools is called tenuous. *Education Week*, *30*(7), 1, 13.

Brody, E. W. (1988). *Public relations programming and production.* New York: Praeger.

Burroughs, W. A. (1974). *Cities and schools in the gilded age.* Port Washington, NY: Kennikat.

Caldas, S. J. (1994). Teen pregnancy: Why it remains a serious social, economic, and educational problem in the U.S. *Phi Delta Kappan, 75*(5), 402–406.

Chin, R., & Benne, K. D. (1969). *General strategies for effecting changes in human systems.* In W. Bennis, K. Benne, & R. Chin (Eds.), The planning of change (2nd ed.) (pp. 32–59). New York: Holt, Rinehart, & Winston.

Clark, D. L., & Astuto, T. A. (1990). The disjunction of federal education policy and educational needs in the 1990s. In D. Mitchell & M. Goertz (Eds.), *Education politics for the new century* (pp. 11–26). London: Falmer Press.

Coombs, F. S., & Wycoff, C. E. (1994). *The public's role in school reform.* Paper presented at the Annual Meeting of the American Educational Research Association, New Orleans.

Cuban, L. (1988). Why do some reforms persist? *Educational Administration Quarterly, 24*(3), 329–335.

Dewey, J. (1899). *The school and society.* Chicago: University of Chicago Press.

Duncan, C. P. (1992). Parental support in schools and the changing family structure. *NASSP Bulletin, 76*(543), 10–14.

Dyrli, O. E., & Kinnaman, D. E. (1994). Preparing for the integration of emerging technologies. *Technology and Learning, 14*(9), 92, 94, 96, 98, 100.

Educational Research Service (1995). *Demographic factors in American education.* (ERIC Document Reproduction Service No. ED 379 773)

Ehrlich, E. (1988, September 19). America's schools still aren't making the grade. *Business Week* (3070), pp. 129, 132, 134–136.

Elam, S. M. (1995). *How America views its schools: The PDK/Gallup Polls, 1969–1994.* Bloomington, IN: Phi Delta Kappa Foundation.

Elam, S. M., & Rose, L. C. (1995). The 27th annual Phi Delta Kappa/Gallup Poll of the public's attitudes toward the public schools. *Phi Delta Kappan, 77*(1), 41–56.

Elliott, B., & MacLennan, D. (1994). Education, modernity and neo-conservative school reform in Canada, Britain, and the U.S. *British Journal of Sociology of Education, 15*(2), 165–185.

Federal Interagency Forum on Child and Family Statistics (1997). *America's children.* Washington, DC: Author.

Fernandez, J. A., & Underwood, J. (1993). *Tales out of school: Joseph Fernandez's crusade to rescue American education.* Boston: Little, Brown.

Finn, C. E. (1991). *We must take charge*. New York: The Free Press.

Gallup, G. H. (1982). The 15th annual Gallup poll of the public's attitudes toward the public schools. *Phi Delta Kappan, 64*(1), 37–50.

Garcia, E. E., & Gonzalez, R. (1995). Issues in systemic reform for culturally and linguistically diverse students. *Teachers College Record, 96*(3), 418–431.

Groennings, S. (1992). The politics of education. In T. Brothers (Ed.), *School reform: Business, education and government as partners* (pp. 15–16). New York: The Conference Board.

Haberman, M. (1994). The top 10 fantasies of school reformers. *Phi Delta Kappan, 75*(9), 689–692.

Harris, L., Hunt, T., & Lalik, R. (1986). Are public schools failing? Assessing the validity of current criticisms. *Clearing House, 59*(6), 280–283.

Hewlett, S. A. (1991). *When the bough breaks: The cost of neglecting our children*. New York: Basic Books.

Hobbs, D. (1994). Demographic trends in nonmetropolitan America. *Journal of Research in Rural Education, 10*(3), 149–160.

Hodgkinson, H. L. (1991). Reform versus reality. *Phi Delta Kappan, 73*(1), 8–16.

Hodgkinson, H. L. (1992). *A demographic look at tomorrow*. Washington, DC: Institute for Educational Leadership.

Huelskamp, R. M. (1993). Perspectives on education in America. *Phi Delta Kappan, 74*(4), 718–721.

Hull, J. D. (1993, August 2). A kid and his gun. *Time,* pp. 21–27.

Johnson, J., & Immerwahr, J. (1994–95). First things first: What Americans expect from the public schools. *American Educator, 18* (4), 4–6, 8, 11–13, 44–45.

Jones, J. L. (1993). Targets of the Right. *American School Board Journal, 180*(4), 22–29.

Kaplan, G. R. (1994). Shotgun wedding: Notes on public education's encounter with the new Christian Right. *Phi Delta Kappan, 75*(9), K1–K12.

Kearsley, G. (1990). *Computers for educational administration.*. Norwood, NJ: Ablex.

Kennedy, P. (1993). *Preparing for the twenty-first century*. New York: Random House.

Kirst, M. W. (1994). Equity for children: Linking education and children's services. *Educational Policy, 8*(4), 583–590.

Kirst, M. W., & McLaughlin, M. (1990). *Rethinking children's policy: Implications for educational administration*. Bloomington, IN: Consortium on Educational Policy Studies.

Kowalski, T. J. (1995). *Keepers of the flame: Contemporary urban superintendents*. Thousand Oaks, CA: Corwin.

Kowalski, T. J., & Reitzug, U. C. (1993). *Contemporary school administration: An introduction*. White Plains, NY: Longman.

Kozol, J. (1992). Inequality and the will to change. *Equity and Choice, 8*(3), 45–47.

Lipinski, A. J. (1978). Communicating the future. *Futures, 10*(2), 126–127.

Lutz, F. W., & Iannaccone, L. (1986). *The dissatisfaction theory of American democracy: A guide for politics in local school districts*. (ERIC Document Reproduction Service No. ED 274 041)

McMillen, M. M., Kaufman, P., Hausken, E. G., & Bradby, D. (1993). *Dropout rates in the United States: 1992*. Washington, DC: National Center for Education Statistics.

Moffett, J. (1994). On to the past: Wrong-headed school reform. *Phi Delta Kappan, 75*(8), 584–590.

Natale, J. (1992). Growing up the hard way. *American School Board Journal, 179*(10), 20–27.

National Center for Educational Statistics (1995a). *Digest of education statistics 1995*. Washington, DC: Author.

National Center for Educational Statistics (1995b). *The condition of education 1995.* Washington, DC: Author.

National Commission on Excellence in Education. (1983, April). *A Nation at risk: The imperative of school reform.* Washington, DC: U.S. Government Printing Office.

Negroni, P. J. (1994). The transformation of America's public schools. *Equity and Excellence in Education, 27*(1), 20–27.

Ornstein, A. C. (1993). School consolidation vs. decentralization: Trends, issues, and questions. *Urban Review, 25*(2), 167–174.

Orum, L. S. (1986). *The education of Hispanics: Status and implications.* (ERIC Document Reproduction Service No. ED 274 753)

Parker, F., & Parker, B. J. (1995). A historical perspective on school reform. *Educational Forum, 59*(3), 278–287.

Pogrow, S. (1996). Reforming the wannabe reformers. *Phi Delta Kappan, 77*(10), 656–663.

Portner, J. (1994, January 12). School violence up over past 5 years, 82% in survey say. *Education Week,* 9.

Ramirez, A. (1992). *Size, cost, and quality of schools and school districts: A question of context.* (ERIC Document Reproduction Service No. ED 361 162)

Reed, R. E.(1993). The agency of the Religious Right: The Christian Coalition. *School Administrator, 50*(9), 16–18.

Rhodes, L. A. (1988). *Technology as a leadership tool.* (ERIC Document Reproduction Service No. ED 305 193)

Riddle, W. C. (1992). *The distribution among the states of school-age children in poor families, 1990 versus 1980: Implications for Chapter I.* (ERIC Document Reproduction Service No. ED 355 319)

Reitzug, U. C. (1996). Changing social and institutional conditions. In T. Kowalski (Ed.), *Public relations in educational organizations: Practice in an age of information and reform* (pp. 23–40). Upper Saddle River, NJ: Merrill/Prentice Hall.

Rose, L. C., Gallup, A. M., & Elam, S. M. (1997). The 29th annual Phi Delta Kappa/Gallup poll of the public's attitudes toward the public schools. *Phi Delta Kappan, 79*(1), 41–56.

Rury, J. L., & Cassall, F. A. (1993). *Seeds of crisis: Public schooling in Milwaukee since 1920.* Madison, WI: University of Wisconsin Press.

Sarason, S. B. (1971). *The culture of the school and the problem of change.* Boston: Allyn and Bacon.

Sarason, S. B. (1996). *Revisiting "the culture of the school and the problem of change."* New York: Teachers College Press.

Schlechty, P. (1990). *Schools for the twenty-first century: Leadership imperatives for educational reform.* San Francisco: Jossey-Bass.

Schlechty, P. (1992). Deciding the fate of local control. *American School Board Journal, 178*(11), 27–29.

Schneider, E. J. (1992). Beyond politics and symbolism: America's schools in the years ahead. *Equity and Excellence, 25*(2–4), 156–191.

Sheingold, K., & Hadley, M. (1990). *Accomplished teachers: Integrating computers into classroom practice.* (ERIC Document Reproduction Service No. ED 322 900)

Shreve, D. L., & Lidell, S. A. (1992). The GM school of reform. *State Legislatures, 18*(5), 39–41.

Simonds, R. L. (1993). Citizens for Excellence in Education. *School Administrator, 50*(9), 19–20, 22.

Soder, R. (1995). American education: Facing up to unspoken assumptions. *Daedalus, 124*(4), 163–167.

Spring, J. (1990). *The American school: 1642–1990* (2nd ed.). New York: Longman.

Stephens, E. R. (1994). Recent education trends and their hypothesized impact on rural districts. *Journal of Research in Rural Education, 10*(3), 167–178.

Stratton, J. (1995). *How students have changed*. Arlington, VA: American Association of School Administrators.

Stuhlmann, J. M. (1994). Telecommunications and teaching practices: What leads to change? *Journal of Information Technology for Teacher Education, 3*(3), 199–211.

Toth, E. L., & Trujillo. N. (1987). Reinventing corporate communications. *Public Relations Review, 13*(4), 42–53.

Tyack, D., & Cuban, L. (1995). *Tinkering toward utopia: A century of public school reform*. Cambridge, MA: Harvard University Press.

U.S. Bureau of the Census. (1991). *Statistical abstract of the United States, 1991*. Washington, DC: U.S. Government Printing Office.

U.S. Bureau of the Census. (1993). *Population projections of the United States, by age, sex, race, and Hispanic origin: 1993 to 2050*. Washington, DC: Author.

U.S. General Accounting Office. (1993). *School-age demographics: Recent trends pose new educational challenges*. Washington, DC: Author.

Van Til, W. (1971). Contemporary criticisms of the curriculum. In W. Van Til (Ed.), *Curriculum: Quest for relevance* (pp. 1–8). Boston: Houghton Mifflin.

Wagner, T. (1993). Systemic change: Rethinking the purpose of school. *Educational Leadership, 51*(1), 24–28.

Wall, T. J. (1994). Working smarter. *Executive Educator, 16*(4), 48–51.

Ward, J. G. (1994). Demographic politics and American schools: Struggles for power and justice. In C. Marshall (Ed.), *The new politics of race and gender: The 1992 yearbook of the Politics of Education Association* (pp. 7–18). Washington, DC: Falmer Press.

Woodroof, R. H. (1996). Public relations and technology. In T. Kowalski (Ed.), *Public relations in educational organizations: Practice in an age of information and reform* (pp. 73–91). Upper Saddle River, NJ: Merrill/Prentice Hall.

Chapter 3

Expectations for Dynamic Leadership

Key Concepts

- ✧ Defining leadership, management, and administration
- ✧ Transactional and transformational leadership
- ✧ Growing emphasis on leadership in the superintendency
- ✧ New professional perspectives of practice
- ✧ Understanding the concept of directed autonomy
- ✧ Ethical and moral practice
- ✧ Implications of technology for leadership

The statement that superintendents need to be leaders would appear to be axiomatic. However, this actually is not the case. Historically, Americans have viewed public education largely as a community-driven experience, and they have perceived administrators as being the guardians and managers of the community's mission of education. In the context of the recent intense efforts to restructure schools, these beliefs are changing. Distinctions are now being drawn between management and leadership. While a superintendent's management role remains important, the leadership role in areas such as policy and planning is increasingly stressed. This chapter explores the meanings of leadership, reasons for the growing demand for leadership in the superintendency, and changing professional perspectives associated with leadership in the superintendency. Later in the book (chapter 8), the specific responsibility of instructional leadership is addressed.

UNDERSTANDING LEADERSHIP

The concept of organizational leadership has evolved over time in the form of distinct movements. Each movement in organizational studies over the last hundred years has had its impact on views of the superintendency.

The first, commonly known as scientific management, was based largely on the work of Max Weber (1947), a noted German sociologist who lived from 1864–1920, and Frederick Taylor (1911), an American engineer. The principles of scientific management dominated American industry in the early 1900s. In the formative years of public education, many school board members and large-city superintendents accepted the tenets of scientific management as being highly applicable to school administration (Callahan, 1962). Consequently, the principles of efficiency, control, and legitimate power (that is, the power vested in a position) became dominant themes both in the academic preparation of school administrators and in their day-to-day practice.

However, even in the early years, insightful scholars realized that schools were not factories. This perception was reinforced by the second stage in the development of studies of organizations: namely, the human relations approach. This theory, which became prominent in the 1930s, focused on analysis of human behavior and the importance of the human factor in organizations. For schools, this meant that the attitudes, feelings, beliefs, and ideas of employees, students, and parents played a significant role in shaping individual and group behavior. Leading scholars associated with the human relations approach (e.g., Lewin, 1939, 1951) emphasized that activities such as participation and democratic decision making required leaders to have an understanding of organizational culture and the dispositions of individuals in that culture, in addition to understanding organizational design and work distribution.

The third stage of organizational studies focused on the behavioral sciences. Especially during the 1950s and 1960s, research based on the behavioral sciences approach improved and expanded theory in school administration. However, while this stage of organizational studies expanded the professional knowledge base and captured the attention of many professors and doctoral students, its impact on practitioners was minimal. By the late 1970s, the behavioral sciences approach was being criticized for attempting to simplify human interaction and behavior to a state of predictability—an approach that could be considered unrealistic and even irrational (Foster, 1980).

Concepts of leadership evolved through each of these three stages of organizational theory. Students in the area of educational administration were enlightened by advances in thought that provided richer, more comprehensive descriptions of behavior in organizations. However, much of the research that supported the evolving theories was done in nonschool environments. Persons studying principals and superintendents eventually concluded that leadership in schools was idiosyncratic; many of the observations made in industrial and business settings were not completely valid when applied to schools. As public institutions, schools provide a service, not a product. The primary activities of educators require professional knowledge about education (e.g., pedagogy, child development) and not just management. As public entities, schools function within a political context in which there are constant interventions from the community, the courts, and governmental agencies. The inescapable conclusion is that while there are aspects of leadership in the superintendency that are common to leadership in all types of organizations, there are also aspects of leadership in the superintendency that are truly unique.

Defining Leadership

Although the words *management*, *leadership*, and *administration* are often used interchangeably, they possess different meanings. In simple terms, *management* is a process of implementing strategies and controlling resources in an effort to achieve organizational objectives. *Leadership* focuses on determining organizational objectives and strategies, building consensus for meeting those objectives, and influencing others to work toward the objectives. *Administration* has a broader meaning, one encompassing both management and leadership (Kowalski & Reitzug, 1993).

Leadership as a component of school administration has been addressed in literally thousands of articles and hundreds of books. Research studies on this topic have targeted a number of variables, including personal traits, on-the-job behaviors, motives, and power. Unfortunately, the findings have been inconclusive, and at times even contradictory (Yukl, 1989). Describing difficulties surrounding understandings of leadership in modern practice, E. Mark Hanson (1996) wrote the following:

> The concept is a many-facetted one, surrounded by a mass of myth, conventional wisdom, idealism, and illusion. Part of the reason for this confusion is that as a social science concept, as well as in popular usage, the idea of leadership evolves from the particular perspective one holds. (p. 153)

In large measure, interpretations of leadership vary because researchers have approached their work with less than uniform perspectives, foci, and methods. Their observations and conclusions were influenced by the people they studied, the contexts in which they did their research (e.g., the school climates and cultures from which data are collected), the particular tasks and responsibilities they studied, and their own biases and errors.

Because leadership entails both deciding what should be done and influencing others to work toward those goals, leadership has both symbolic and political dimensions (Bolman & Deal, 1994). Management, which entails directing people and resources toward accepted outcomes, has focused on the use of legitimate and punishment-centered power. By contrast, leadership has focused on noncoercive approaches that are cultural in orientation and rely more heavily on expert or referent power (that is, influence based on being seen as an ideal leader). Leaders devote a good bit of their energy to determining whether climate and culture "aid or hinder the fulfillment of the organization's mission" (Schein, 1985, p. 320), and they use their skills to reshape values and beliefs as a means for renewing their organizations. Typically, they rely on practices grounded in their professional knowledge base and the principles of democracy. They are more likely than managers to see organizational change as an evolutionary process.

Because there are so many different definitions of leadership, several authors have attempted to categorize them. Gary Yukl (1989) described four broad approaches to research in this area: (1) power-influence approach, (2) trait approach, (3) behavior approach, and (4) situational approach. These approaches are explained in Table 3–1. For purposes of basic understanding, the essence of leadership can be further reduced to three elements:

> . . . (1) the presence of unique psychological traits or behavior characteristics (*people*); (2) the art of compelling compliance or inducing compliance (*processes*); (3) the presence of formal structure, informal structure, differential problem situations (e.g., task complexity, personnel competence), or the external organizational environment (*systems*). (Hanson, 1996, p. 156)

In isolation or collectively, these elements help explain differences in concepts of leadership.

The leadership function assumed by superintendents is distinctively different from the more commonly understood managerial and political roles of the position. Collectively, these roles encompass a number of different functions such as organizing, facilitating, planning, and allocating. While all superintendents probably spend some time in each role and with each function, differences in actual work behaviors are likely to be in emphasis rather than in kind (Sergiovanni, Burlingame, Coombs, & Thurston, 1992). Arthur Blumberg (1985) observed that management and leadership present opposing demands on most superintendents. This is exemplified by dispositions toward conflict. On the one hand, a superintendent is expected to assume a maintenance role that is largely reactive, e.g., keeping the school district running smoothly. In this role, conflict needs to be man-

Table 3–1
Research approaches to leadership

Approach	Examples of Foci
Power-influence	Sources of administrative power; the acquisition and/or loss of power; reciprocal influence processes; influence tactics used by administrators
Trait	Personal attributes of leaders such as personality type, creativity, intelligence; specific skills (e.g., technical, analytical); administrator motivation
Behavior	
Nature of work	Pace of work and general time allocation; content of administrative work; roles, functions, and practices; job description studies; activity patterns
Behavior patterns	Performance and job satisfaction; administrative influence on subordinate satisfaction; task versus people orientations; participative versus isolated administration
Situational	
Behavior determinants	Similarities in administrative behavior across organizations; similarities in administrative behavior at different levels of an organization; role conflict resolution
Contingency models	The effectiveness of behavior patterns or traits in different situations; variables contributing to situational effectiveness; flexibility in administrative approaches

The categories in this table are based on those in G. A. Yukl, 1989, *Leadership in Organizations* (2nd ed.), Upper Saddle River, NJ: Prentice Hall.

aged. On the other hand, superintendents are expected to influence the culture and character of school districts. This responsibility for organizational renewal can lead the superintendent to view conflict as a vehicle for change. Here, the discussion of leadership in the superintendency focuses on differentiating between style and strategy and transactional and transformational concepts.

Style and Strategy

Two words commonly used in conjunction with leadership are *style* and *strategy*. *Style* usually describes the way an administrator handles specific aspects of his or her job (Bassett, 1970). This could include activities such as personal relationships, setting expectations for others, and delegating authority. Variation in style is usually described along a continuum from autocratic to democratic. Style is an intricate mix of personal philosophy, professional knowledge, experience, and situational variables. Thus, theories and models focusing on leadership style concentrate on one or more of these factors.

Among the most widely recognized and used models for leadership style is Douglas McGregor's Theory X and Theory Y. In Theory X, the administrator has a dim view of workers because he or she accepts three pessimistic assumptions: (1)

people generally dislike work and try to avoid it; (2) because of a negative disposition toward work, employees must be pushed and controlled if they are to attain organizational goals; (3) because they lack personal responsibility, employees seek managerial control (McGregor, 1990a). In Theory Y, the administrator is more optimistic and emphasizes the potential contributions of employees. His or her disposition is based on three assumptions, very different from those associated with Theory X: (1) conditions in the workplace affect employee commitment, responsibility, and productivity; (2) in positive environments, employees often become committed to organizational goals and work diligently toward their attainment; (3) employees possess the ability to solve problems they encounter, but this potential is either not recognized or not utilized in many organizations (McGregor, 1990b). In general, leadership style relates to questions such as these: Is a superintendent orientated toward tasks or toward people? Is a superintendent autocratic or democratic?

Strategy, by contrast, describes broader, longer-term, and more comprehensive patterns of leadership behavior (Bassett, 1970). Whereas style is largely connected to an individual administrator, strategy often has more of an organizational connection. Consider, for instance, a large school district in which a new superintendent, not previously employed in the system, has implemented a decentralization governance plan. The strategy has both educational and political objectives. Success depends heavily on the commitment and behavior of principals and central office support staff. These administrators, however, have been socialized to a culture in which rewards have been linked to avoiding problems; thus, their personal leadership styles are incompatible with the new strategy. For them, risk taking (e.g., allowing school-based councils to make critical decisions) is not justified in terms of potential rewards and punishments. Caught in this web, they must make the critical decision between either adjusting their personal leadership style to the new situation or resisting personal change in anticipation that the implementation of the new school reform program will not continue.

Differentiations between style and strategy are especially significant in the current era of school reform. Because schools have historically been agencies of stability (Spring, 1990), the dominant strategy to which most administrators have been socialized is failure avoidance. That is, they have been rewarded for dodging conflict and preventing problems from reaching higher levels of the organization. Even when the failure avoidance is in conflict with personal convictions, many practitioners

> . . . accept their "symbolic" world whole cloth and conceive of their role entirely in symbolic terms. In doing so they become dependent upon the organization for their very character, with the result that they put themselves at its mercy. (Bassett, 1970, p. 223)

Each time an administrator is rewarded (or protected) for avoiding conflict and resisting change, his or her leadership style becomes more ingrained. Contemporary critics blame local school boards for tolerating and contributing to this inertia. They charge that boards have failed to provide "far-reaching or politically risky leadership for reform" (Danzberger, 1994, p. 369). In order to appreciate the difficulty of changing administrative practice, it is necessary to distinguish between leadership style and leadership strategy. While leadership strategy may be organizationally imposed, the leadership style remains largely a matter of personal conviction.

Transactional and Transformational Leadership

The literature on educational leadership often includes distinctions between transactional and transformational leadership. James Burns (1978) is credited with elucidating these concepts, which describe the nature of interactions between a person holding legitimate authority and those over whom he holds authority.

Transactional leadership is defined as an exchange between an administrator and subordinate for purposes of achieving one or more goals they deem important. Here is an example of transactional leadership. Consider a situation in which a superintendent creates a special committee to study discipline policies. The committee will meet outside the school day, and it will include parents, students, and community leaders. Because the potential for conflict exists and because this assignment will add more hours to the principals' workweek, no principal has volunteered to serve on the committee. The superintendent decides to offer a deal to a principal who has submitted a request to attend a national meeting. In exchange for serving on the committee, the superintendent will approve the principal's travel request. The exchange satisfies a personal interest of each party.

Much of the work in organizations has been predicated on politically driven behaviors identified as transactional leadership (Bennis & Nanus, 1985). That is to say, administrators have commonly attempted to motivate employees by appealing to the employees' self-interests (Yukl, 1989). Underlying this approach are the beliefs that individuals are focused inwardly and that they have little or no commitment to the organization.

Whereas transactional leadership appeals to baser emotions such as fear, greed, and jealousy, *transformational leadership* seeks to influence behavior by appealing to "higher ideals and moral values such as liberty, justice, equality, peace, and humanitarianism" (Yukl, 1989, p. 210). It entails the pursuit by both the leader and followers of commonly held higher-level goals. Components of transformational leadership are the following:

- *A commitment to a common goal.* Both the leader and followers desire the same goal.

- *The pursuit of higher levels of morality.* The emphasis is on moral values to govern behavior.

- *A reliance on higher-order needs.* The leader focuses on more advanced human needs when considering motivations. (Burns, 1978).

Warren Bennis (1984) described four essential competencies of leadership through transformational behaviors:

- *Attention.* A commitment to a vision.
- *Meaning.* Communication of a vision.
- *Trust.* Believing in people and remaining focused.
- *Self.* Knowing your skills and deploying them.

These competencies nurture empowerment, a state in which people feel significant and capable of improving their work. They also symbolically emphasize the value that learning and competence are truly important in settings in which people can control their own destiny. Finally, they promote a sense of community, an environment in which people base their behaviors on commitments. The topic of community building is explored in the next chapter.

Transformational leadership occurs at both the personal level (e.g., exchanges between two individuals) and organizational level (e.g., cultural change) (Yukl, 1989). It can be exemplified by an administrator who seeks to build community within a school or school district. Rather than encouraging or accepting pragmatic accommodations to achieve cooperation for the sake of mutual advantage, he or she values "the ideal of group solidarity and a commitment to norms of care and responsibility" (Power, 1993, p. 159). The goal is the achievement of "collective norms of caring, trust, and shared responsibility, norms that go beyond the strict requirements of justice" (Power, 1993, p. 159).

The relevance of distinctions between transactional and transformational leadership is "nested in a larger debate regarding whether the purpose of schooling should be the transmission and reproduction of existing culture, or the empowerment of individuals to transform existing unjust and inequitable components of society" (Kowalski & Reitzug, 1993, p. 234). It is also embedded in fundamental questions about life in a democratic society. Since political power is rarely distributed evenly in society and organizations, public institutions allowing self-interests to drive policy almost always are unjust to those with little or no power.

While the American public may not agree on the effectiveness of public education or its future goals, virtually all citizens agree that improvement is necessary (Odden, 1995). After more than 100 years of failed attempts to politically mandate change in a top-down fashion, enlightened reformers have reached two critical conclusions:

- School renewal is more likely if it occurs at the micro level, that is, at the school or school district level, rather than at the national or state level.
- Meaningful improvement is more likely if criteria such as professionalism, shared authority, shared responsibility, morality, and ethics guide the change process.

This reconceptualization of the reform process is forging a new context for administrative practice and is prompting practitioners to reconsider leadership style and strategies. Michael Fullan and Andy Hargreaves (1991) offered the following advice to administrators regarding their role as change agents:

- *Understand the culture.* You can't change what you don't understand.
- *Value your teachers: Promote their professional growth.* Learn to value something in every teacher; treat teachers as total persons, not just a bundle of competencies.
- *Express what you value.* Your behavior and the example you provide are what really matter.
- *Promote cooperation, not cooptation.* Proprietary claims and attitudes, e.g., *my vision*, suggest personal rather than collective ownership and responsibility.
- *Make menus, not mandates.* Collaboration can take many forms; commit to the principle, but democratically decide on a strategy.

In many states, local school districts are now being given an opportunity to experiment and self-determine change targets. This increased liberty is accompanied by greater demands for accountability. That is to say, state officials are becoming more active in establishing broad expectations for public schools, but they are simultaneously moving toward deregulating, allowing local officials greater flexibility in meeting these expectations. In this political context, new expectations for the superintendency are evolving. For example, greater emphasis is being placed on conceptual skills; school boards are becoming more tolerant of risk taking; and a greater premium is being placed on democratic, transformational leadership.

EMERGING NEED FOR LEADERSHIP

For a period of approximately 25 years following World War II, school superintendents exercised considerable influence over both local district decisions and state regulations and policies. School board members and state officials often relied exclusively on superintendents for advice and counsel on key policy decisions. However, this power began to erode in the 1970s and 1980s

> . . . as the inward-focused operational style of the superintendent as dominant decision maker atop the hierarchical pyramid of the school district organization clashed with collective bargaining, demands for involvement of more diverse constituencies in the education policy process, new roles for women administrators, increased decision making by state and federal political leaders, and, by the end of the 1980s, single issue citizens, and the religious right. (Odden, 1995, pp. 213–214)

Transitions affecting the superintendent's role became even more apparent as the school reform movement gained momentum in the mid-1980s.

As noted earlier, through much of the 20th century, superintendents were expected to be the guardians and managers of the concept of public schools as agencies of social stability (that is, institutions that socialized children, especially from immigrant families, to the norms of American society). Evaluation of job performance was often based exclusively on tasks such as fiscal control, facility development, and compliance with state regulations and laws. Even local policy making often was nothing more than the establishment of enforcement criteria for state mandates. Superintendents frequently devoted much of their work day to interactions with top assistants (e.g., associate and assistant superintendents), school board members, governmental officials, and other politically influential citizens. Especially in large-enrollment districts, direct communication between the superintendent and teachers or principals was rare; this task was usually relegated to administrative aides.

Because superintendents were both managers and guardians and because critical policy was almost always imposed on schools by either state government or lay school boards, superintendents adopted a bureaucratic disposition toward conflict—that is, they perceived conflict as being inefficient and threatening to the traditional role of the public school. Hence, superintendents typically acted instinctively and swiftly to eradicate any tensions, whether generated externally or internally. These arose from parties such as the courts, special-interest groups, disgruntled employees, and student groups. A superintendent who was truly skilled in avoiding conflict often was able to "gain the reputation of being a manager who is able to keep things under control and who can keep the system out of trouble, or at least keep aggravating problems at a low level" (Blumberg, 1985, p. 209).

Changing behaviors that have always appeared sensible is truly a difficult task (Sergiovanni, 1992). Most practitioners in educational administration have been taught to see school districts as organizations tied together by political compromises among individuals and groups. They have also been socialized to bureaucratic structures in which essential policies have been promulgated by powerful governmental officials. As long as these concepts remain, superintendents will be inclined to replicate past practices (that is, they emulate behaviors that they have seen rewarded). Almost always this pattern of conflict avoidance results in the perpetuation of transactional styles of leadership. To break this cycle, issues embedded in the minds and hearts of superintendents and other educators need to brought to the surface (Fullan & Hargreaves, 1991).

Shifts in expectations for administrative behavior are also associated with conditions in the external environments of schools. One method for describing these conditions is a continuum ranging from placid to turbulent. These two positions describe the opposite ends of the possible ecosystem of an organization. In the case of public schools, the ecosystem may be the local community, state, and/or nation. Gradations on this continuum are generated by technology changes, shifts in market demand, governmental action, increased competition, value shifts, economic conditions, and demographic transitions (Hanson, 1996). In virtually all organizations, the condition of the environment has a direct effect on role expectations of the administrator. Consider these two examples:

- Role expectations for officers in the armed services often change when the country faces a military crisis. Whereas emphasis on rank, status, and failure avoidance dominates in periods of peace, threats to national security escalate the importance of, and tolerance for, creativity, boldness, and risk taking.

- A university with a series of losing seasons in football hires a coach with a record of recruiting violations or other problems at another institution. The decision to employ him is prompted by the demands of disgruntled alumni, faculty, and students who want to be associated with a winning team.

For the most part, schools are now functioning in conditions of high turmoil. There is uncertainty about the future; many people are anxious about the transition from an industrial-based economy, which provided the tax base for schools in many communities; and many taxpayers perceive schools to be ineffective and unsafe. Those entrusted with the power to select superintendents are increasingly inclined to pick a risk taker; they are increasingly more likely to focus on potential gains than potential losses.

Today there are growing expectations that superintendents can provide leadership that will allow schools and districts to reinvent themselves (Odden, 1995). This task requires the integration of three attributes, as shown in Figure 3–1. The first is professional knowledge. A superintendent needs sufficient theoretical and practical information about schools, institutional behavior, decision making, planning, and the like to permit leadership to occur. Second, the individual must possess a leadership style that facilitates change. This includes a proclivity toward risk taking and an orientation toward experimentation and new ideas. Third, the individual must possess a personal disposition (attitudes) congruent with the dominant themes of contemporary restructuring efforts. That is, the superintendent should philosophically support concepts such as democracy, professionalism, shared decision making, empowerment, and shared responsibility.

Figure 3–1
Attributes for contemporary superintendents

CHANGING PROFESSIONAL PERSPECTIVES

Human behavior is complex, and it is especially so in institutional settings. Years ago Jacob Getzels and Egon Guba (1957) provided a model for understanding behavior in a social system. Predicated on two dimensions (a normative dimension defining organizational expectations and a personal dimension defining self), the model viewed behavior as the interface of institution with individual, role with personality, and role expectation with need dispositions. This paradigm was later refined to include cultural dimensions (at both the normative and personal levels) (Getzels, Lipham, & Campbell, 1968) and a communities dimension (Getzels, 1978). By providing a deeper view of socialization—that is, the ways in which values, norms, rules, and operating procedures are communicated and learned in work environments (Miklos, 1988)—these refinements help bring into focus the complexity of administrative behavior. Superintendents are socialized to the school administration profession in graduate school and the workplace; both environments contribute to their enculturation to the profession (Goodlad, 1990).

A disjunction between theory and practice has been a long-standing problem in educational administration. In part, this disharmony represents a time gap between theoretical realignments (e.g., adjustments to the knowledge base and the application of new technologies) and role expectations transmitted in professional preparation and practice. For instance, students in educational administration are taught that performance evaluation has two dimensions, formative (helping the employee to improve) and summative (deciding if performance is acceptable). However, when they enter practice, existing policies and established norms often pressure them to concentrate solely on making summative judgments regarding reemployment, merit salary increases, and the like. Among the many realignments occurring in educational administration, four are especially relevant to the superintendency: (1) a focus on attitudes, values, and beliefs (rather than a preoccupation with organizational structure); (2) a focus on directed autonomy (rather than a preoccupation with total centralization or decentralization); (3) a focus on ethical and moral practice (rather than a preoccupation with political considerations); and (4) a focus on the incorporation of technology into administrative work.

Focusing on Attitudes, Values, and Beliefs

One lesson learned from failed initiatives over the past few decades is that schools cannot be made sufficiently effective by tinkering with perceived weaknesses. This "fix the broken parts" strategy is grounded in the assumption that significant improvement can be realized by addressing selected elements of the schools. At the very heart of this reform approach are attitudes and beliefs that label programs and people as being at fault. More specifically, critics who promote this strategy believe that students are lazy, educators are incompetent, and programs are ineffective. Even in the face of clear evidence that problems in school are far more complex than this, these critics cling to their beliefs and attitudes.

They see the educational community's emphasis on addressing issues such as poverty, child abuse, economic transitions, and dysfunctional families as a diversionary tactic.

In a similar fashion, exposing an administrator to new knowledge, especially knowledge that contradicts personal attitudes, beliefs, and values, does not ensure a behavioral change. Just requiring administrators to take more college courses or providing them with staff development does not guarantee a change in behavior. Rather, behavior is linked to attitudes, beliefs, and values, and although knowledge can reshape these variables, there is no guarantee any modification will occur (Hersey & Blanchard, 1993). The thinking and behavior of administrators are influenced greatly by the culture of a district and of individual schools in it. Often this cultural influence outweighs official policies, programs, rules, and regulations (Hopkins, Ainscow, & West, 1994). If knowledge alone were sufficient to change behavior, warning labels on packages, units of instruction in health classes, and public service announcements on television should have virtually eradicated smoking in America. Attitudes determine how individuals treat knowledge; they can cause a person to mistrust facts and to see new knowledge as threatening (Waterman, 1987). Unfortunately there is little research examining how superintendents use their professional knowledge, but available evidence usually shows that information and new knowledge are filtered by existing personal attitudes when critical judgments are made (e.g., Kowalski, 1995; Lasher, 1990).

Today there are many calls for new leadership in public education, but they come from a variety of directions. Consequently, leadership continues to have different meanings. Government officials and captains of industry who still view administration largely as a managerial function, see leadership as a solution to problems "that lie in the spheres of management and economics rather than in the realms of values and politics" (Giroux, 1992, p. 7). For them, leadership is a more forceful iteration of management. This perception is at odds with the definition of leadership provided earlier in the chapter—which included determining organizational objectives and building consensus for meeting those objectives. Those who enter the superintendency are almost always caught between divergent perceptions of ideal practice. As practitioners attempt to deal with the resulting tension, they rely heavily on their own beliefs and attitudes.

The critical nature of attitudes is illustrated in Figure 3–2, which presents a range of potential superintendent behaviors in school reform. Because of role conflict (different expectations placed on superintendents), differences between what administrators say and what they really believe are not uncommon. Philosophy, attitudes, and beliefs of administrators are just as important as skills and capabilities, especially in knowledge-based organizations such as schools (Senge & McLagan, 1993).

Decentralization offers an excellent example of the importance of attitudes. Studies of administrators frequently show high levels of support for concepts such as shared decision making and site-based management (probably because they are widely accepted reform initiatives). However, the reasons for support often

Figure 3–2
Range of potential behaviors regarding current reform strategies

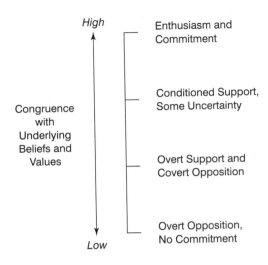

vary (Weiss & Cambone, 1994). Deeper probing often reveals serious apprehensions about key facets of these concepts (Kowalski, 1994). Often attitudinal change is associated with introspection. A person tries to reconcile self-interests and role expectations with new knowledge. Frequently, there is conflict between the interests of the school (and people who constitute the school) and the personal interests of the administrator (e.g., safety, security, recognition). For instance, principals might resist decentralization because they are (1) insecure and weak (they fear the responsibility of decentralization); (2) politically powerful (they have a political advantage in the current system); or (3) autocratic (they philosophically reject shared decision making) (Brown, 1991).

Describing attempts to implement shared decision making and site-based management in his school district, one superintendent noted, "We have opened the door of the cage but some of the canaries are refusing to fly. It was as if a cat was sitting outside the cage door" (Mitchell, 1990, p. 23). In his enlightening book, *Teaching the Elephant to Dance: Empowering Change in Your Organization*, James Belasco (1990) used the training techniques for elephants to illustrate how we are all conditioned by our institutional experiences:

> Trainers shackle young elephants with heavy chains to deeply embedded stakes. In that way the elephant learns to stay in its place. Older elephants never try to leave even though they have the strength to pull the stake and move beyond. Their conditioning limits their movements with only a small metal bracelet around their foot—attached to nothing. (p. 2)

This example illustrates the power that attitudes, beliefs, and values have on behavior. If the role of the superintendency is to be truly transformed, the profession must find ways of overcoming those obstacles that continue to socialize practitioners to essentially managerial and political roles.

Moving Toward Decentralization

Earlier in the book, the current practice of melding centralization and decentralization as a reform strategy was discussed. While this strategy may appear contradictory, it has been used since the earliest days of public education in this country to reduce tensions between state government and local authorities over the control of schools—tensions stemming from the principles of liberty, equity, and adequacy. Emphasis among these three principles, however, shifts continually. Currently, the following pattern is prevalent in many states:

- Adequacy has become a driving force for setting higher standards and expectations. Rather than dictating programs, however, states are setting broad policies and making local officials accountable for outcomes.
- Liberty has become more important in a political climate denouncing over-regulation and too much government. Some states have even passed legislation requiring local school councils (a rather intriguing approach to democracy).
- Equity has been deemphasized, but state officials keep a nervous eye on how increased local decision making could draw them into another round of legal disputes (e.g., litigation over school finance equity, imbalances in programs offered by local districts).

The result is a combination of centralization-decentralization policy that is more skewed toward decentralization than it was just a decade ago.

Movement toward decentralization is also associated with continuing perceptions of school districts as ineffective bureaucracies, a perception that has permeated the literature for almost a century. In his seminal work on the development of public schools during and immediately following the Industrial Revolution—that is, covering the period from approximately 1900 to 1920—Raymond Callahan (1962) described how superintendents and school boards embraced the cultures and climates of burgeoning industries to satisfy the most powerful in the community. But while schools adopted aspects of bureaucracy, especially the principles of centralization and a reliance on rules and regulations, superintendents rarely were able to amass levels of power possessed by their business counterparts. School administrators were constrained by the need to delegate certain functions to others and by the reality that subordinate units could affect decisions and procedures officially deemed to be administrative domains (Corwin & Borman, 1988). Further, school boards often relegated superintendents to management functions, symbolically affirming to employees and taxpayers that administrators were not true leaders.

An ideal bureaucracy and a totally decentralized organization represent polar positions on a continuum. Rather than reaching either extreme, public school districts fall somewhere between the two. Thus, school districts and superintendents always experience some degree of autonomy and some degree of control from above. For the superintendent, the level of autonomy is determined by three factors: (1) the amount of freedom state government gives to school districts, (2) the amount of freedom a school district gives to individual schools, and (3) the amount of freedom a school board gives to a superintendent. These zones are illustrated in Figure 3–3. Placement on the three continua helps provide a way to view the amount of autonomy given to a superintendent. A state, for example, may pass reform legislation giving local districts greater freedom to set curriculum; the school boards may respond by giving individual schools more freedom to determine instructional materials. But neither of these changes may affect the degree of freedom the school board gives a superintendent.

Because the balance between control and autonomy shifts and because it never gets skewed completely to either extreme on the continuum, preparing superintendents as if they had either complete authority or absolutely no control would be unrealistic and counterproductive. Politically and legally, state governments are required to maintain a degree of control over public education. Likewise, school districts, as legal entities, maintain a degree of responsibility for what occurs in individual schools. Even in the worst case situations, in which school board members micromanage on a daily basis, superintendents have some legitimate power granted by statutes. These realities prompt several change theorists to conclude that school improvement requires a balanced approach. They argue that selecting either total centralization or total decentralization is a mis-

Figure 3–3
Zones of autonomy for school
superintendents

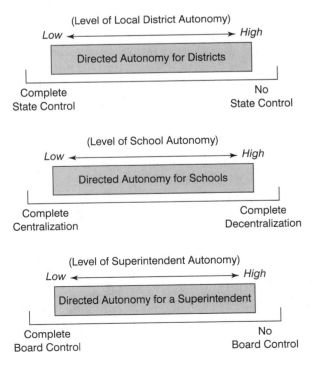

take because the former errs in the direction of overcontrol, while the latter errs in the direction of chaos (Fullan & Stiegelbauer, 1991).

Despite all the rhetoric about decentralization, current change in public schools does not constitute a radical shift away from centralization. Rather districts engaged in reform are experiencing incremental movements toward autonomy. What results is a reapportioning of the mixture—more autonomy and less control. The product is a concept called *directed autonomy*. Describing this concept in business enterprises, Robert Waterman (1987) wrote the following:

> . . . people in every nook and cranny of the company are empowered—encouraged, in fact—to do things their way. Suggestions are actively sought. But this all takes place within a context of direction. People know what the boundaries are; they know where they should act on their own and where not. The boss knows that his or her job is to establish those boundaries, then truly get out of the way. (p. 75)

For superintendents, directed autonomy means that they empower others to have greater discretion over their work and greater freedom to determine how they meet broad policies and goals. Hence, directed autonomy provides a new recipe for enhancing autonomy of individuals in the school organization.

The use of directed autonomy in education takes on added significance because teachers and administrators view themselves as professionals. As such, they often expect some level of empowerment when making determinations of how to apply their professional knowledge. Even in the most rigid and controlled school districts, teachers and principals cannot be supervised intensively; they have always had at least a modicum of autonomy in their classrooms and offices.

Efforts to move school districts toward higher levels of autonomy concentrate on empowering teachers and principals to enact policies that extend beyond their traditional domains of power—their individual classrooms and offices (Kaczmarek, 1994). These efforts arise out of defensible conclusions about teaching and learning. For example, a local school is likely to be more successful if programming can be structured to meet the needs of individual students, rather than the needs of an imaginary average student. In short, a teacher is more likely to increase student learning if he or she is able to individualize instruction.

Interestingly, decentralization is embraced by both political leaders and leaders in the educational profession, albeit for different reasons. While greater autonomy appeals to citizen demands for liberty, it also is congruous with decentralization theory (the closer the process of governance is to those affected the more responsive it is to real needs and wants).

Ethical and Moral Practice

Over the years, there have been numerous distinctions made between the work of school administrators and private sector managers. One of the more recent is the recognition of the moral character of schools. Colleen Capper (1993) wrote the following:

> [T]he American public school is fundamentally a moral institution by virtue of its goal of preparing children to assume the roles and responsibilities of citizenship in a democratic society. While there are other goals that schools seek to accomplish, none is so central as this, and it is this moral socialization function of public schools that distinguishes the work of the school administrator from that of administrative counterparts in other organizational contexts. (p. 268)

Similarly, William Greenfield (1995) noted, "The dual conditions of involuntary membership and being subjected to socialization processes and purposes not of the children's choosing make the administration of schools a highly moral enterprise" (p. 64). Perhaps the most important element regarding school effectiveness is not the curriculum or the daily class schedule, but rather the educational experiences the school generates (Etzioni, 1983). These experiences play a very important role in the lives of individual students; they help determine students' character, civility, civic responsibility, and other desirable goals. Because of their power to affect lives and help society attain its goals, among all administrators, those who work in schools should be guided by high ethical and moral standards.

Until recently, preparation programs for superintendents have not paid much attention to the ethical and moral dimensions of leadership (Kirby, Paradise, & Protti, 1992). Criticizing the lacks in leadership preparation, Thomas Sergiovanni (1992) noted that leadership has been viewed as "behavior rather than action, as something psychological rather than spiritual, and as having to do with persons rather than ideas" (p. 3). He also observed that a superintendent's bureaucratic, psychological, and technical-rational authority has been overemphasized, while professional and moral authority has been neglected. "In the first instance, we have separated the hand of leadership from its head and its heart. In the second, we have separated the process of leadership from its substance" (p. 3). Increasingly, those who prepare superintendents agree with his observations.

Ethical constructs are commonly perceived in legal contexts, but the meaning of administrative ethics is broader than this. Referring to administrators in all types of organizations, Kenneth Blanchard and Norman Vincent Peale (1988) proposed a simple, three-part "ethics check" for leaders: (1) Is it legal?, (2) Is it balanced?, (3) How will it make me feel about myself? (p. 27). In the specific context of school administration, ethics extend beyond legalities to such issues as bias, discrimination, nepotism, violating confidentiality, commitment to work responsibilities, and playing politics for purposes of self-interest (Howlett, 1991; Kimbrough & Nunnery, 1988). Table 3–2 provides a categorization of administrative ethics. Perhaps the least recognized area of ethical practice is in the category of routine professional issues—those issues that relate most directly to personal leadership style.

Robert Starratt (1991) formulated three foundational themes for ethical practice. They include the ethic of critique, the ethic of justice, and the ethic of caring. The first theme addresses issues such as hierarchy, privilege, and power (e.g., Who controls public schools? Who defines the future of public education?). The second addresses issues such as democratic participation and equal access to programs and resources (e.g., How are scarce resources allocated? How are critical decisions

Table 3–2
Categorization of administrative ethics

Category	Description	Examples
Nonroutine issues of morality and personal practice	Ethical choices that occur on an irregular basis that are guided by laws and social expectations	A conflict of interest causing the administrator to make a decision for personal benefit; misuse of petty cash funds
Nonroutine issues of professional practice	Ethical choices that occur on an irregular basis that pertain to professional responsibilities	Terminating a teacher who has not been properly supervised or given an opportunity to improve; giving a relative preferential treatment in employment/promotion (nepotism)
Routine issues of professional practice	Constant and pervasive issues that have a long-term effect on schools	Abusing one's power; not allowing others to participate in a democratic manner; unfairly manipulating individuals

Based on *Contemporary School Administration: An Introduction* (pp. 368–369) by T. J. Kowalski and U. C. Reitzug, 1993, New York: Longman.

made?). The third addresses issues focusing on human relationships such as cooperation, shared commitment, and friendship (What do personal relationships demand from superintendents, other administrators, and teachers?). While the first two themes have received some attention in school administration literature, the third has been largely ignored.

For many observers, leadership in the superintendency has become "less a matter of aggressive action than a way of thinking and feeling—about ourselves, about our jobs, and about the nature of the educational process" (Mitchell & Tucker, 1992, p. 31). More precisely, moral leadership requires attention to what schools are all about and what they do. Successful schools typically benefit from both leadership vision and high levels of consensus; the former sets direction and the latter provides a basis for action. Both are critical to school effectiveness, and they constitute a process of leadership called purposing—a process for enhancing performance and productivity of people and the organization (Sergiovanni, 1992). Now that school districts are being given more latitude to make programming decisions, moral leadership has become central to determining how decisions are made, as well as the nature of those decisions. Purposing allows members of the school community to identify goals and strategies that can be supported by all.

Technology and Leadership Expectations

Just as changes in societies and market conditions force businesses to reconsider purposes, strategies, and operations, evolving educational and social needs force schools to be adaptive and responsive to emerging needs and wants. Dynamic conditions require leaders who are willing and able to act without waiting for revelation or request (Heifetz & Laurie, 1997). Technology, discussed in the previous chapter, enables superintendents to adjust to this emerging role expectation in two critical ways. First, computers can reduce the time requirements and complexity of many managerial responsibilities. For example, budgeting, payroll, and inventory maintenance become far less cumbersome when they are computerized. Second, increased access to information permits administrators to be more effective in policy-related functions, such as planning, goal setting, facilitation, and evaluation. In essence, technology permits educators to overcome barriers, such as isolation in the workplace and a lack of time, that previously prevented them from discussing philosophy and collaborating on the development of purposes and goals. Networked computers, for example, allow superintendents to communicate with all employees and with a broader spectrum of the community; such information exchanges facilitate leadership activities associated with decentralized governance and shared decision making (Brandt, 1993). In some schools, cable television also is being used to enhance communication (e.g., televising school board meetings or public forums on controversial topics) (West, 1996).

Leadership functions require information sharing. The superintendent's responsibility to keep the school board informed can be aided by a range of emerging technologies. For example, several districts provide computers to board members to connect them with the school district network. This access not only allows school board members to communicate with the superintendent through e-mail but also provides them with databases available to school employees. There is a gain in efficiency, and the school board members can also experience firsthand some of the potentialities and benefits of technology (Vail, 1996).

Interest in technology as a leadership tool has increased because the public simply expects its institutions to be more responsive in an age of information. However, the use of technology has also grown because superintendents recognize that it can provide a significant tool to help them meet expanding role expectations. Most superintendents already work more than 60 or 70 hours a week; realistically, meeting new demands have to be accommodated within that already demanding time frame. By accessing and using information more efficiently, superintendents can increase their productivity. In essence, technology offers a means of empowering administrators. Put in the context of school reform, technology is a vehicle for accessing, disseminating, and using knowledge (Woodruff, 1996)—a prerequisite in any attempt to change attitudes and beliefs.

Given the widely recognized power of technology to affect administrative practice and given the explosion of technology in public school districts, it is truly disappointing that its potential for superintendents has received so little attention. Some departments of educational leadership have created technology application courses, and others are using technology for simulations in which students gain opportunities to try out knowledge and management skills (Bozeman & Wright, 1994–95). However, there is still a long way to go. At a time when school administration is increasingly focusing on transformational strategies and community building—issues dependent on human relations—technology ought not to be applied thoughtlessly and haphazardly. Communication via computers and cable television can be a cold and insensitive experience—but it does not have to be. Some practitioners have used technology to bring more people into the decision-making process; some have set up databases to facilitate planning and evaluation; some have moved to two-way communication processes with employees and the community. These achievements need to be documented and become part of the professional knowledge base in educational administration.

FOR FURTHER REFLECTION

The focus of this chapter was on definitions of leadership, the growing need for leadership in the superintendency, and changing professional perspectives of leadership in the superintendency. Leadership was differentiated from management and described as a process of deciding what should be done and influencing others to work toward those goals. Leadership style was contrasted with leadership strategy, and the concepts of transactional and transformational leadership were reviewed.

The growing need for leadership in the superintendency was explained in the context of current reform strategies that simultaneously call for centralization and decentralization. New perspectives are being driven by (1) recognition of the importance of attitudes, beliefs, and values in institutional change; (2) the concept of directed autonomy; (3) a deeper concern for ethical and moral practice; and (4) the potential of technology.

As you consider what you read in this chapter, answer the following questions:

1. How is management differentiated from leadership? How does each concept relate to administration?

2. Is it possible or likely that the superintendency will evolve to a state in which management will be relatively unimportant?

3. What is the difference between leadership style and leadership strategy? What are the determinants of each?

4. What is the difference between transactional and transformational leadership? In which category would you place superintendents you have known?

5. The need for leadership in the superintendency is associated with new perspectives on school reform. What strategies of reform were dominant for much of the 1980s? What strategies are dominant today? Why do current strategies demand high levels of leadership from the superintendent?

6. Given the example of warning consumers about the danger of smoking cigarettes, why is knowledge often insufficient to change a person's behavior? How does this issue relate to school reform?

7. What forces support a transition toward decentralized governance in school districts?

8. Many argue that decentralization concepts, such as site-based management, will make the burdens of the superintendency lighter. Do you agree? Why or why not?

9. What is the concept of *directed autonomy?* Why has it become an issue for many superintendents?

10. Why are schools "moral institutions"?

11. Do superintendents have a greater responsibility for ethical and moral leadership than do corporate executives? Why or why not?

12. Are superintendents more inclined to be guided by political considerations or ethical and moral considerations? What evidence do you have for your response?

13. To what extent is technology being used by administrators in school districts in your area? To what extent have the superintendents made use of technology?

14. What forces may prevent a superintendent from being a moral and ethical leader?

CASE STUDY

Dr. James Summers became superintendent of the Fort Davis Community School District approximately 15 months ago. With 22 schools enrolling about 17,000 students, it is one of the larger school systems in this southwestern state.

In seeking a new superintendent, the school board in Fort Davis emphasized its commitment to change. All 7 board members agreed that the district had not moved forward sufficiently to address community needs and wants. Hence, they sought a leader with a proven track record in the area of reform; they wanted a person of vision, someone who would lead the district into the next century. Dr. Summers appeared to meet all of their expectations. At the age of 53, he had been superintendent in two other districts where he spearheaded substantial change. In his previous position, Superintendent Summers received a national award for implementing technology in his school district.

Shortly after becoming superintendent in Fort Davis, Dr. Summers revealed a plan he labeled, "Fort Davis Schools in the 21st Century." It emphasized three broad goals:

- A massive investment in information technology in the schools. It included a minimum of 4 computers in each classroom and 2 computer laboratories in each school, distance learning capabilities (e.g., a satellite dish or cable access), and information systems integrating voice, video, and data in each classroom. Additionally, the entire district was to be networked.

- A transition to site-based management, which required each school to create a governance council consisting of teachers and parents
- A major investment in staff development to prepare employees to use technology and to master the new teaching strategies they would select for their schools

The school board cheered the plan publicly and encouraged its implementation as soon as possible. However, the administrators and teachers were apprehensive. Many of the employees in the district were not accustomed to change. Nor were many inclined to accept the need for change. They judged they were already doing a pretty good job, albeit in a rather traditional format. Even though principals in the district recognized this attitude on the part of employees, they elected not to voice any concern with the plan. They still were uncertain about Dr. Summers' leadership style, and they knew the board had quickly given the superintendent its stamp of approval.

Having lived through change processes in other districts, Dr. Summers expected most principals and teachers to be apprehensive. He decided to move forward because he considered that there was a window of opportunity during his first year in the district. To help alleviate staff fears, he established a coordinating council, consisting of the principal and one teacher from every school in the district. This group was given the task of guiding the implementation of his plan. Additionally, he visited each school and spoke to the employees about the plan and its goals. His message was the following:

"This plan for change will benefit you in many ways. For those of you who have never used computers or integrated information systems, you are going to learn a great deal. For those of you who always wanted to be true professionals, your school councils will provide a vehicle for greater autonomy. Put simply, you will become better teachers. And while we will all grow as professionals, our schools will become more responsive to the real needs of our students. After all, that's the reason we are here."

Neither the establishment of a district-wide council nor Dr. Summers's visits to the schools, however, reduced opposition to his plan. For 6 months following the announcement of the plan, little progress was made in developing the school councils. Principals made dozens of excuses why they were behind schedule. The technology portion moved forward because a consulting firm was employed to make decisions about equipment and software, and several inservice sessions were held for teachers and administrators on technology use. But the core element of the plan, the implementation of school-based councils, was stalled.

Dr. Summers reported his disappointment to the school board. Uniformly, they encouraged him to move forward and restated their complete support for his efforts. One board member, who was vice-president of a local manufacturing company, responded more specifically. "Dr. Summers, sometimes you have to push real hard to get people to change. Our schools are too important to let a few stubborn teachers and principals block progress."

Issues for Discussion

1. How would you describe the leadership strategy being employed by Dr. Summers?

2. How would you describe his leadership style? To what extent is his style compatible with his strategy?

3. To what extent was the board's behavior in this case typical? Do school boards usually believe they can achieve radical change by employing a new superintendent?

4. Dr. Summers had many issues to weigh in determining what he would do. Differentiate political considerations from ethical and moral considerations.

5. Evaluate the superintendent's behavior. The superintendent was prompted to announce a plan so soon after assuming the superintendency because he thought support would be greatest during his first year. Is this a reasonable assumption? What evidence do you have to support your response? Could the school board election cycle influence a new superintendent's decisions?

6. The case suggests that Dr. Summers had led two other districts through a change process. What, if any, inferences can you make from this information?

7. Change efforts and the leadership behaviors that drive them always have a symbolic dimension. How would you describe the symbolism associated with the leadership of Dr. Summers?

8. What other leadership tactics could have been employed by Dr. Summers? What roles might teachers and parents play in the change process?

9. Are there occasions when superintendents must impose their will on others for the good of the school district? If so, what are they?

10. To what extent is the resistance to change among the teachers and administrators in Fort Davis typical?

REFERENCES

Bassett, G. A. (1970). Leadership style and strategy. In L. Netzer, G. Eye, A. Graef, R. Drey, & J. Overman (Eds.), *Interdisciplinary foundations of supervision* (pp. 221–231). Boston: Allyn and Bacon.

Belasco, J. A. (1990). *Teaching the elephant to dance: Empowering change in your organization*. New York: Crown Publisher.

Bennis, W. G. (1984). The four competencies of leadership. *Training and Development Journal, 38*(8), 14–19.

Bennis, W. G., & Nanus, B. (1985). *Leaders: The strategies for taking charge*. New York: Harper & Row.

Blanchard, K., & Peale, N. V. (1988). *The power of ethical management*. New York: William Morrow and Company.

Blumberg, A. (1985). *The school superintendent: Living with conflict.* New York: Teachers College Press.

Bolman, L. G., & Deal, T. E. (1994). Looking for leadership: Another search party's report. *Educational Administration Quarterly, 30*(1), 77–96.

Bozeman, W., & Wright, R. H. (1994–95). Simulation applications in educational leadership. *Journal of Educational Technology Systems, 23*(3), 219–231.

Brandt, R. (1993). On restructuring roles and relationships: A conversation with Phil Schlechty. *Educational Leadership, 51*(2), 8–11.

Brown, D. J. (1991). *Decentralization: The administrator's guide to school district change.* Newbury Park, CA: Corwin.

Burns, J. M. (1978). *Leadership.* New York: Harper and Row.

Callahan, R. E. (1962). *Education and cult of efficiency.* Chicago: University of Chicago Press.

Capper, C. A. (1993). *Educational administration in a pluralistic society.* Albany, NY: SUNY Press.

Corwin, R. G., & Borman, K. M. (1988). School as workplace: Structural constraints on administration. In N. Boyan (Ed.), *Handbook of research on educational administration* (pp. 209–238). New York: Longman.

Danzberger, J. P. (1994). Governing the nation's schools: The case for restructuring local school boards. *Phi Delta Kappan, 75*(5), 367–373.

Etzioni, A. (1983). Restructuring the schools: A set of solutions. *Learning, 11*(8), 86–93.

Foster, W. (1980). A demonstration and the crises of legitimacy: A review of Habermasian thought. *Harvard Education Review, 50*(6), 496–505.

Fullan, M. G., & Hargreaves, A. (1991). *What's worth fighting for? Working together for your schools.* Andover, MA: Regional Laboratory for Educational Improvement.

Fullan, M. G., & Stiegelbauer, S. (1991). *The new meaning of educational change* (2nd ed.). New York: Teachers College Press.

Getzels, J. W. (1978). The communities of education. *Teachers College Record, 79*, 659–682.

Getzels, J. W., & Guba, E. G. (1957). Social behavior and the administrative process. *School Review, 65*, 423–441.

Getzels, J. W., Lipham, J., & Campbell, R. (1968). *Educational administration as a social process.* New York: Harper & Row.

Giroux, H. A. (1992). Educational leadership and the crisis in democratic government. *Educational Researcher, 21*(4), 4–11.

Goodlad, J. I. (1990). *Teachers for our nation's schools.* San Francisco: Jossey-Bass.

Greenfield, W. D. (1995). Toward a theory of school administration: The centrality of leadership. *Educational Administration Quarterly, 31*(1), 61–85.

Hanson, E. M. (1996). *Educational administration and organizational behavior* (4th ed.). Boston: Allyn and Bacon.

Heifetz, R. A., & Laurie, D. L. (1997). The work of leadership. *Harvard Business Review, 75*(1), 124–134.

Hersey, P., & Blanchard, K. H. (1993). *Management of organizational behavior: Utilizing human resources* (6th ed.). Upper Saddle River, NJ: Prentice Hall.

Hopkins, D., Ainscow, M., & West, M. (1994). *School improvement in an era of change.* New York: Teachers College Press.

Howlett, P. (1991). How you can stay on the straight and narrow. *Executive Educator, 13*(2), 19–21, 35.

Kaczmarek, P. (1994). Empowerment philosophies and practices in business and educational settings. *Performance and Instruction, 33*(8), 26–29.

Kimbrough, R. B., & Nunnery, M. Y. (1988). *Educational administration: An introduction.* New York: Macmillan.

Kirby, P. G., Paradise, L. V., & Protti, R. (1992). The ethical reasoning of school administrators. *Journal of School Leadership, 2*(2), 178–186.

Kowalski, T. J. (1994). Site-based management, teacher empowerment, and unionism: Beliefs of suburban school principals. *Contemporary Education, 65*(4), 200–206.

Kowalski, T. J. (1995). *Keepers of the flame: Contemporary urban superintendents.* Thousand Oaks, CA: Corwin.

Kowalski, T. J., & Reitzug, U. C. (1993). *Contemporary school administration: An introduction.* New York: Longman.

Lasher, G. C. (1990). Judgment analysis of school superintendent decision making. *Journal of Experimental Education, 59*(1), 87–96.

Lewin, K. (1939). Field theory and experiment in social psychology: Concepts and methods. *American Journal of Sociology, 44*(6), 868–896.

Lewin, K. (1951). *Field theory in social science.* New York: Harper.

McGregor, D. (1990a). Theory X: The integration of individual and organizational goals. In J. Hall (Ed.), *Models of management: The structure of competence* (2nd ed.) (pp. 11–18). Woodlands, TX: Woodstead Press.

McGregor, D. (1990b). Theory Y: The integration of individual and organizational goals. In J. Hall (Ed.), *Models of management: The structure of competence* (2nd ed.) (pp. 19–27). Woodlands, TX: Woodstead Press.

Miklos, E. (1988). Administrator selection, career patterns, succession, and socialization. In N. Boyan (Ed.), *Handbook of research on educational administration* (pp. 53–76). New York: Longman.

Mitchell, D. E., & Tucker, S. (1992). Leadership as a way of thinking. *Educational Leadership, 49*(5), 30–35.

Mitchell, J. E. (1990). Coaxing staff from cages for site-based decisions to fly. *School Administrator, 47*(2), 23–24, 26.

Odden, A. R. (1995). *Educational leadership for America's schools.* New York: McGraw-Hill.

Power, F. C. (1993). Just schools and moral atmosphere. In K. Strike and P. Ternasky (Eds.), *Ethics for professionals in education* (pp. 148–161). New York: Teachers College Press.

Schein, E. (1985). *Organizational culture and leadership.* San Francisco: Jossey-Bass.

Senge, P. M., & McLagan, P. A. (1993). Transforming the practice of management. *Human Resource Development Quarterly, 4*(1), 5–32.

Sergiovanni, T. J. (1992). *Moral leadership: Getting to the heart of school improvement.* San Francisco: Jossey-Bass.

Sergiovanni, T. J., Burlingame, M., Coombs, F. S., & Thurston, P. W. (1992). *Educational governance and administration* (3rd ed.). Boston: Allyn and Bacon.

Spring, J. (1985). *American education: An introduction to social and political aspects* (3rd ed.). New York: Longman.

Spring, J. (1990). *The American school 1642–1990: Varieties of historical interpretation of the foundations and development of American education* (2nd ed.). New York: Longman.

Starratt, R. J. (1991). Building an ethical school: A theory for practice in educational leadership. *Educational Administration Quarterly, 27*(2), 185–202.

Taylor, F. W. (1911). *The principles of scientific management.* New York: Harper and Brothers.

Vail, K. (1996). It's time your board got wired. *Executive Educator, 18*(3), A16–17.

Waterman, R. H. (1987). *The renewal factor: How the best get and keep the competitive edge*. New York: Bantam Books.

Weber, M. (1947). *The theory of social and economic organization*. New York: The Free Press.

Weiss, C. H., & Cambone, J. (1994). Principals, shared decision making, and school reform. *Educational Evaluation and Policy Analysis, 16*(3), 287–301.

West, P. T. (1996). Effective programming at the unit level. In T. Kowalski (Ed.), *Public relations in educational organizations: Practice in an age of information and reform* (pp. 133–156). Upper Saddle River, NJ: Merrill/Prentice Hall.

Woodroof, R. H. (1996). Public relations and technology. In T. Kowalski (Ed.), *Public relations in educational organizations: Practice in an age of information and reform* (pp. 73–91). Upper Saddle River, NJ: Merrill/Prentice Hall.

Yukl, G. A. (1989). *Leadership in organizations* (2nd ed.). Upper Saddle River, NJ: Prentice Hall.

Chapter 4

School Districts: Purpose, Conceptualizations, and Design

Key Concepts

✧ Legal status and purpose of school districts

✧ Differences among school districts

✧ School districts from an organizational perspective

✧ Importance of climate and culture

✧ School district organization (centralized and decentralized governance)

✧ Directed autonomy as an element of school district organization

Reflecting on school reform efforts in recent decades, Luvern Cunningham (1991) advised policymakers to shift their focus "away from hobby-horse, special-interest driven, often trivial ideas about educational improvements, toward investment in democratically anchored efforts to concentrate on the everyday needs of all Americans" (p. 246). In essence, such recommendations are shaped by the belief that centralized governance inevitably becomes consumed with attempting to create "one size fits all" schools by tinkering with aspects of structure rather than reconsidering fundamental philosophical issues and changing societal conditions. Correspondingly, reform efforts started in the early 1980s have attempted to broaden the base of lay involvement in school governance, "with more and more influence being exercised by those outside the established educational community" (Danzberger, Kirst, & Usdan, 1992).

As calls for more decentralized governance capture the public's attention, significant questions about the structure and purpose of local districts inevitably surface. This chapter explores the nature of school districts, the organizational aspects of these districts, and emerging ideas for reconfiguring this traditional institution.

NATURE OF SCHOOL DISTRICTS

The local school district is the basic unit of government in the organizational structure of public education. Created by the state, this entity provides a mechanism designed to satisfy citizen demands for liberty and local self-determination. In this respect, school districts are political agencies of state government that ensure a degree of balance between state and local control. They come in many different sizes and configurations, a situation resulting more from political preferences than documentation of effectiveness (Ramirez, 1992). However, while there is little evidence showing a connection between school district size or design and student learning, it is quite clear that this unit of government does much more than simply distribute resources to individual schools. Yet somewhat surprisingly, the school district has been basically ignored by those who seek to reform public education (Hannaway, 1992). Nevertheless, organizational concepts such as site-based management, charter schools, and choice are circuitously revealing the important role played by these governmental units.

Legal Status

The legal status of local school districts differs among the states. In some states, they are identified as municipal corporations (a public entity that functions at the local level and provides governmental services); more commonly, they are classified as quasi-corporations (an entity that acts as if it were a municipal corporation) (Guthrie & Reed, 1991). As "quasi-corporations," districts are a special type of municipal corporation in which "local interest and advantage rather than execution of state policy are its determining characteristics" (Edwards, 1955, p. 54). While acting as though they were municipal corporations, quasi-corporations have more limited authority. For this reason, school districts are often referred to as limited municipal corporations (Knezevich, 1984). In Indiana, for example, school districts are legally titled school corporations.

Several states have had litigation seeking to clarify the status of school districts. Often these disputes center on the right of one unit of local government to impose its regulations on another unit of local government operating within its boundaries. For instance, can a city impose its building codes on a local school district that exists within that city? Decisions on such questions have not been consistent across states. In some cases, the courts have ruled that municipalities have such power; in other instances, they ruled that school districts, as extensions of state government, are immune from municipal dictums (Campbell, Cunningham, Nystrand, & Usdan, 1990). Thus, a precise, universal definition of the status of a local school district as a quasi-corporation is not possible.

As a subdivision of the state, the local district is subject to the plenary powers of the legislature. Such powers must be exercised within the constitutional provisions for that state. This means that the legislature can alter a district's jurisdiction, boundaries, and powers; the legislature can even eliminate a local district (Lunenburg & Ornstein, 1991). Because the powers granted by the state are limited to the specific purposes of public education, school districts often have less power and authority than city or county governmental units. Typically, the power granted to local districts includes (1) those expressly granted by statute, (2) those fairly and necessarily implied from powers expressly granted by statute, and (3) those that are discretionary and essential to operations (Knezevich, 1984). Because state constitutions and statutes are not uniform, the level of autonomy enjoyed by local districts differs among the states and not uncommonly among classifications of districts within a state (Campbell et al., 1990).

From 1940 to 1992, slightly fewer than 102,000 school districts were eliminated in the United States (National Center for Educational Statistics, 1993); between 1940 and 1980, the mean number of districts in a state declined from 2,437 to 318 (Strang, 1987). The reason for these massive reductions, as noted earlier in this book, was school district consolidation. This movement, which produced fewer and larger school districts, transformed administrative structures and behaviors. Districts became more bureaucratic-like and authority in them became more centralized. Centralization occurred as a result of placing more schools under a single school board and superintendent, thus increasing the likelihood that "consolidated districts would be more susceptible to central initiatives across a range of policy issues" (Strang, 1987, p. 364).

Today many reform efforts represent a form of devolution. That is, they are attempting to reverse some of the effects of school consolidation. Most notably, ideas such as school councils represent a conscious effort to put some degree of policy making back into individual schools—a setting in which decision making should prove to be more sensitive to real student and community needs.

Types of School Districts

Many adjectives are used to describe school systems in legal terms, and these terms are not always well understood. Classifications may be based on (1) statutory provisions for creating districts, (2) fiscal independence, (3) levels of educational opportunity provided, (4) scope of territory served, and (5) geographic description. Table 4–1 provides a summary of classification systems for school districts.

Statutory Base

In some states, school districts are described by the law under which they are organized. Largely because of a desire after World War II to reduce the number of local units within a state, state governments often provided incentives and encouragements to centralize. The incentives were for citizens to merge school districts or to move away from the old township trustee system—a situation in which a single trustee rather than a school board had legal responsibility for the schools. Since conditions varied across a given state, legislators in some states provided local communities options for reorganization by passing several different laws. This strategy allowed local citizens to reorganize their district under a law most favorable to their needs and philosophy. In states like Indiana and Iowa, for instance, the official name of a school district is usually indicative of the law

Table 4–1
Descriptors used in conjunction with school districts

Category	Explanation	Common Descriptors
Statutory basis	Formal classification is based on the state statute under which the school district is organized and functions.	Community school districts Metropolitan school districts School city districts
Fiscal independence	Formal classification is based on a school district's independence in determining budgets and tax rates.	Independent districts Dependent districts
Levels of education provided	Formal classification is based on grade levels included in the school district.	Unit or unified districts Elementary school districts High school districts
Scope of territory served	Largely informal classification is based on a school district's relationship with townships, towns, cities, and counties.	County school districts City school districts Township school districts
Geographic description	Informal classification is based on a geographic portrait of the school district.	Urban districts Suburban districts Smaller city or town districts Rural districts

under which the district was formed and operates, and not necessarily indicative of the geographic setting of the district. For example, a rural district in Indiana may be called a metropolitan school district, and a rural district in Iowa may be called a community school district.

Fiscal Classification

Either officially or unofficially, school districts may be referred to as *dependent* or *independent*. These words describe a local district's power (as granted by the state) to levy property taxes for the support of its operations. Basically, independent districts can set their own budgets and tax rates; dependent districts cannot. Approximately 90% of all districts in the United States are classified as independent. Twenty-three states have only independent districts, four states have only dependent districts, and the remainder have both (Campbell et al., 1990).

Dependent districts must have their budgets and tax rates approved by another agency of government (e.g., a county council, a city council). Proponents of dependence argue that tax rates for government services should be coordinated to protect the public from uncontrolled, unnecessary, or excessive increases. They believe that needs for public education should be weighed against all other needs for local government. Proponents for independence contend that educational needs are too important to be subjected to political battles centering on the distribution of scarce resources. In truth, few districts have plenary powers to set taxes. In most states, budgets and tax-related decisions of local school boards are subjected to reviews by state agencies or restricted by statutes. More accurately, "independence" refers to the initial fiscal decisions at the local level.

Level of Educational Opportunity

The vast majority of school districts are *unit* or *unified districts*, connoting the provision of educational programs for grades pre-kindergarten through 12. Several states (e.g., California and Illinois) have both unit districts and *dual districts*. Dual districts refer to separate *elementary* and *secondary school districts* (the latter often called *high school districts*). Elementary districts include grades pre–K to 6 or pre–K to 8; secondary districts include grades 7 to 12 or 9 to 12.

Potentially, dual districts can enhance the principles of liberty and adequacy. Residents in them pay taxes to support two school systems, and as such, they have access to two school boards. The tax codes may allow dual districts to actually raise more in local funds (that is, more collectively) than a unit district. Where this occurs, dual districts may be able to generate more operating funds than unit districts of comparable wealth (that is, districts with similar assessed valuations per pupil). In several states, community colleges, junior colleges, or technical schools serving students beyond grade 12 may also be part of a public school district.

Scope of Territory

School districts can also be classified according to descriptions of the territory served, e.g., township district, county district. This classification is largely informal, reflecting the relationship of the school district to townships, towns, cities, and counties. Some districts may be quite small and serve only part of a township; some may include an entire county. In the case of Hawaii, there is only one district in the state. In most parts of the United States, multiple-school districts within a county are the norm. In southern states, however, a single school district in each county is common (several southern states have only all-county school districts). The reasons can be traced to colonial times, when the Church of England was predominant in the southern colonies. Rather than following the pattern of community-based school districts like the one developed in New England, the South opted for centralized governance. This decision was influenced by the close relationship that existed between church affairs and public affairs in the southern colonies. Several states outside of the South (e.g., Utah and Nevada) also have chosen to use all-county school systems (Campbell et al., 1990).

Geographic Description

Another informal classification is based on the geographic setting of school districts. Here, labels such as *urban*, *smaller city or town*, *suburban*, and *rural* are used as descriptors. These geographic designations may be meaningful in discussions about demographic variables and educational needs in school districts. For example, the designation of "urban" often spawns perceptions of diverse populations, large-enrollment schools, high rates of poverty, and so on. Indirectly, geographic labels also produce mental images of quality, which may or may not be accurate. In several states, school districts are officially categorized according to their geographic setting.

ORGANIZATIONAL CONTEXT OF SCHOOL DISTRICTS

The study of schools and school districts has been conducted largely in an organizational context. This does not mean, however, that educational institutions are identical to other organizations. In fact, public schools are rather different from most private, profit-seeking enterprises, and the degree of diversity among districts, even within a given state, is often substantial (Hannaway, 1992). Yet each of these units of government possesses certain attributes that constitute a common thread running through all organizations. These elements are fundamental to understanding the structure, purpose, behavior, and resistance to change of school districts.

School Districts as Organizations

In very simple terms, organizations are "social inventions accomplishing goals through group effort" (Johns, 1988, p. 10). In virtually all definitions of organizations, two recurring themes are evident: (1) an organization is a *social unit* and (2) an organization has identifiable *goals* (Kowalski & Reitzug, 1993).

1. *Organization as a social unit.* This refers to the fact that organizations are composed of individuals and groups that establish some level of interdepen-

dency and that inevitably have some level of interaction. People in an organization can be likened to the various cells and molecules in our bodies. A problem in one area often has a systemic effect on our total health.

2. *Identifiable goals*. The element of identifiable goals indicates organizational purpose. Purpose could range from producing profits to providing recreation to ensuring health care. Organizations are pervasive; we are born into them and we live our lives in them. They vary in goals, size, environmental conditions, incentive systems, and leadership and authority (Knoke & Prensky, 1984).

One of the most serious problems facing school districts is a condition called *organizational uncertainty*. It arises from ambiguity in one or more of the following components: philosophy, mission, structure, purposes. In the case of public education, a lack of clarity with regard to purpose continues to be problematic. Throughout the history of public education in America, "debate over purpose in public education has been a continuous process of creating and reshaping a democratic institution that, in turn, helped create a democratic society" (Tyack & Cuban, 1995, p. 142). This fact is of the utmost significance since purpose has implications for school organization, curriculum, and instructional strategies.

While current societal transitions have made us aware of the need for change, they have not provided a clear direction for the process. This is because perceptions of purpose are a complex mix of personal philosophies and societal needs, which vary across communities and states. In the absence of agreed-upon purposes, people arrive at different conclusions about the need for, and content of, school reform. This lack of consensus contributes to organizational uncertainty in school districts, a situation that intensifies the risks of leadership, particularly in the realm of decision making (March & Simon, 1958).

Varying theories have been used to describe and study organizational behavior. Three of the most dominant are *classical theory*, *social systems theory*, and *open systems theory*. While each of these theories is represented in contemporary management thinking, "they entered the mainstream of thought at different historical periods" (Hanson, 1996, pp. 4–5).

As pointed out in the previous chapter, classical theory, or bureaucratic theory, emerged during the Industrial Revolution, at the end of the 19th century. It emphasizes five mechanisms for controlling and coordinating people and groups: (1) maintaining firm hierarchical control of authority and providing close supervision of workers, (2) establishing and maintaining adequate vertical communication (top-down, one-way communication), (3) developing a myriad of rules and regulations to guide actions, (4) having clear plans and schedules for workers to follow, and (5) adding supervisory positions to the hierarchy if changing conditions or problems require additional supervision and control (Owens, 1998). Applications in school districts concentrate on predicting and controlling the behavior of teachers, students, and other employees.

Social systems theory, also called sociopolitical group theory, emerged in the 1930s and was an outgrowth of the human relations approach to studying behavior in organizations. Unlike classical theory—which concentrates on organizational goals—social systems theory recognizes the existence of both organizational needs and individual or group needs. Thus, workers may be motivated not only by money and job security, but also by a need to be socially accepted within groups. Additionally, social systems theory explores the relationships between formal and informal power within an organization (Hanson, 1996). In school districts, for instance, unions represent a formal group that often is able to direct teacher behaviors; in many schools, power is also possessed by those who have no legitimate claim to it (e.g., an informal but influential group of teachers who are able to control the principal).

Open systems theory became popular in the 1960s. Unlike classical theory and social systems theory—which concentrate on the inner workings of the organization—open systems focuses on interactions between the organization and its wider environment (e.g., community, state). The development of open systems theory was associated with the behavioral sciences approach to studying organizational behavior. Behavior is seen in the context of cycles of events, consisting of outputs the organization gives to the environment and the inputs it receives from the environment (Hanson, 1996). For schools, open systems perspectives are especially significant, given the expectation that public institutions are highly sensitive to community needs and wants. In this frame of reference, organizational survival is more dependent on adaptability to changing social needs than the predictability of employee behaviors (Snyder & Anderson, 1986).

Metaphors also have been used to describe organizations. This approach takes into account the complexity of behavior and provides another framework for planned change. Gareth Morgan (1986), for example, developed eight separate metaphors:

- *Organizations as machines* (seeing organizations as a set of interlocking parts with defined roles; the essence of bureaucratic theory)
- *Organizations as organisms* (seeing organizations as unique social systems; examining how organizations are created, develop, are able to adapt, and so on)
- *Organizations as brains* (seeing how information is processed, how learning occurs, how knowledge is accumulated and used)
- *Organizations as cultures* (seeing how values, norms, and basic assumptions determine and sustain behavior)
- *Organizations as political systems* (seeing how interest, conflict, and power shape behavior)
- *Organizations as psychic prisons* (seeing how people and groups become trapped by their own thoughts, ideas, or unconscious goals)
- *Organizations as flux and transformation* (seeing how organizations change or recreate themselves)
- *Organizations as instruments of domination* (seeing how organizations use employees, the community, or the state to achieve self-determined ends)

Metaphors, like theories, provide insights into organizational behavior, and they encourage critical thinking among leaders.

Unfortunately many school administrators dismiss theories and metaphors as impractical. For instance, they view theory as being synonymous with speculation, supposition, or idealistic conceptions. In truth, theory is related to practice in three ways: "First, theory forms a frame of reference for the practitioner. Second, the process of theorizing provides a general mode of analysis of practical events. And third, theory guides decision making" (Hoy & Miskell, 1996, p. 7). Because of this potential to inform practice, superintendents should possess a thorough understanding of schools as organizations; they should be familiar with major organizational theories and their applications to school districts. However, rather than utilizing theory as an appropriate tool, administrators often become wed to a single view of organizational life. Consequently, it is virtually impossible for them to gain a full understanding of the motivations and dynamics of individual and group behavior (Bolman & Deal, 1989).

Critical Elements of Climate and Culture

When we walk into a school, we immediately form impressions based on what we see and how we are treated. If the environment is warm and colorful or if people are friendly and helpful, our perceptions are more likely to be positive. Later, we may even refer to the school as having had a friendly climate. The total environment of an organization constitutes its climate. A critical component of the total environment is the element of culture. Both individual schools and school districts have climates and cultures that contribute to their uniqueness. Factors such as community politics, revenues, local resources, enrollment, community characteristics, and student demographic and performance characteristics produce substantial diversity among school districts (Hannaway, 1992). School districts also possess symbolic idiosyncrasies predicated on tradition, values, and norms.

School District Climate

The concepts of organizational climate and culture are often confused, and some theorists identify them as overlapping concepts. However, culture is commonly defined as a symbolic element of climate. Climate represents the atmosphere in a school district that generates perceptions of expectations for work-related behavior (Miskel & Ogawa, 1988). Climate has been used as a descriptive metaphor and an explanation as to why schools and school districts are often different (Miskel & Ogawa, 1988); it conveys to administrators, teachers, other employees, and students what is expected of them (Owens, 1998). Frequently, climate in schools is described by using a continuum ranging from closed to open. These terms may refer to the degree to which a school district interacts with its environment: closed districts have little interaction, while open districts have a great deal of interaction. More commonly, however, these polar positions describe characteristics of employee behavior predicated on factors such as morale, disengagement, and leadership behavior; closed climates are characterized by apathy and inertia, while

Table 4–2
Elements of school district climate

Element	Description	Examples
Ecology	Physical and material features of the school district	School buildings, equipment, technology
Milieu	People who compose the school district	Administrators, teachers, students, and other employees; their needs, wants, motivations, and dispositions
Social system	The organizational nature of the school district	Line and staff relationships, grade organization, how conflict is addressed, calendars and schedules
Culture	The symbolic nature of the school district	Values, beliefs, and norms that are characteristic of the people who compose the school district; beliefs and values held in common by employees

Based on "The Concept of Organizational Climate" (pp. 11–32), by R. Tagiuri, in R. Tagiuri & G. Litwin (Eds.), *Organizational Climate: Explorations of a Concept,* 1968, Boston: Harvard University, Graduate School of Business, Division of Research.

open climates are characterized by energetic and lively behaviors that move the organization toward its goals (Lunenburg & Ornstein, 1991).

The most commonly used description of climate was developed by Renato Tagiuri (1968). His conceptualization divides elements of climate into four groups: (1) ecology, (2) milieu, (3) social system, and (4) culture (Owens, 1998). These elements are described in Table 4–2.

The social system dimension has clearly received the most attention from researchers over the years. That is, research frequently has focused on organizational designs, formal roles, and instructional designs. By contrast, the physical and material aspects of schools have often been overlooked in studying climate. This is particularly true with respect to understanding how physical spaces and instructional materials and equipment affect (1) teaching and learning, (2) individual behavior, and (3) group behavior (Pfeffer, 1982). Even though people and groups within schools have received considerable attention in the literature over the past 50 years, research in this area also has been limited.

In the current context of school reform, culture has received special attention. This is because meaningful improvement requires a strategy that addresses fundamental elements of culture—values and beliefs of educators (Fullan & Stiegelbauer, 1991).

School District Culture

Organizational culture is rooted in sociology and anthropology; rather than focusing on what a school district possesses, culture deals with what a school district is (Hanson, 1996). Edgar Schein (1992) formally defines a group's culture as the following:

A pattern of basic assumptions that the group learned as it solved its problems of external adaptation and internal integration, that has worked well enough to be considered valid and, therefore, to be taught to new members as the correct way to perceive, think, and feel in relation to those problems. (p. 12)

More succinctly, it is the shared beliefs, expectations, values, and norms of conduct for individuals and groups who make up the school district; it is a normative structure defining "both 'what is'—knowledge, beliefs, and technology—and 'what ought to be'—values and norms—for successive generations (Firestone & Corbett, 1988, p. 335). The culture of a school district is composed of an educational environment (community needs and wants, competition, prevailing practices), values (shared basic concepts and beliefs), heroes (individuals who personify the shared values), rites and rituals (systematic and programmed routines), and a network (mechanisms for disseminating shared values) (Deal & Kennedy, 1982). While part of a school's culture is factual, other aspects are likely to be mythical. This is because individuals and groups establish meaning for themselves by interpreting the conditions around them (Bates, 1984).

Each school district, while embracing some values and beliefs commonly found in all school districts, is a unique entity with its own culture and subcultures. Organizational cultures are described on the basis of strength, that is, along a continuum ranging from weak to strong. Weak cultures are fragmented and difficult to discern; teachers and administrators, for example, hold varying views about professional responsibility, student discipline, and the like. In strong cultures, by contrast, there is widespread acceptance of the basic values and their related elements. In school districts, especially larger school districts, individual schools may have distinctively different cultures (which in effect are subcultures of the district). Hence, it is possible to have a relatively weak district culture composed of schools that have relatively strong cultures. In most organizations, including school districts, "there are often different and competing value systems that create a mosaic of organizational realities rather than a uniform corporate culture" (Morgan, 1986, p. 127). In part, this explains why lasting change in large institutions is so difficult to achieve.

Often the true culture of a district is not readily apparent; superintendents usually must engage in purposeful assessment to determine what truly exists. Taher Razik and Austin Swanson (1995) noted the following about assessing school cultures:

The integration, fragmentation, and differentiation perspectives are all available to the researcher/observer. This approach offers us a crucial illustration of the organization's "ethos," its historical purpose, power shaping, motivations, beliefs, informal settings, symbolic expression, visual data, and more. Culture is a part of the organization, and it is the organization. (p. 211)

The task of assessing school culture, however, is intricate. In large measure, this is because the real identity of a culture is found in varying levels of the school district that range from tangible overt manifestations (those that you can see and feel) to deeply embedded, unconscious assumptions (Schein, 1992). Accordingly, the administrator who only assesses what is apparent on the surface is not likely to gain a true picture of the school district. Edgar Schein (1992) described three layers of culture:

1. *Artifacts.* These are visible structures and processes such as school buildings, the overt behavior of teacher groups, and the applications of technology.

2. *Espoused values.* These are visible in the school district's philosophy statements, planning goals, and leadership strategies. These values may or may not accurately depict what actually occurs in a school district. For example, a school district may stress student self-discipline in its philosophy statements, but day-to-day practices may reveal a very different set of values.

3. *Basic assumptions.* These are explicit assumptions that guide behavior. They are typically not confronted or debated. For instance, all administrators and teachers in a school district may share the basic assumption that corporal punishment is an ineffective discipline measure; in this district, paddling children would be an inconceivable behavior.

When culture is defined in this way, the difficulty of cultural change is made more understandable. True change requires addressing that which is typically nonnegotiable—the basic assumptions guiding the behavior of administrators and teachers on a day-to-day basis. Over the past several decades, there have been many examples of superintendents who have tried to reconstruct school districts imposing new values, heroes, rituals, and networks. Almost always such efforts have proven to be futile. These would-be change agents, and the board members who encourage their efforts, fail to understand the power of an organization to protect itself. This capacity is manifested in varying ways. Writing about the power of organizations to enculturate new members, Ann Weaver Hart (1991) noted, "Organizations, however, protect against the intrusion of new members, values, and beliefs by routinization and through formal and informal social mechanisms, one of which is socialization" (p. 469). The basic assumptions that exist at the deepest level of culture are passed to new teachers and administrators; and in strong cultures, those who resist are not likely to survive.

The futility of imposed change has been most evident in troubled urban school districts. School boards in many of these districts have purposely sought out individuals who overtly embraced espoused values that clashed with the real behaviors occurring in the schools. Almost always the existing culture proves to be stronger than the new superintendent. And even though the pattern repeats itself, such boards continue to search for the ultimate change agent. Most likely, their behavior reflects both a lack of understanding and politics. With regard to the latter, they feel compelled to respond to public pressures for change. However, rather than really pursuing change, they merely provide the community with an illusion of change; they lead the public to believe that one individual can miraculously re-create a school district (Kowalski, 1995a).

Importance of Climate and Culture

Because meaningful and lasting change is dependent on attitudes as well as knowledge, the values and beliefs of administrators and teachers are critical to school renewal. Support for this statement is clearly visible in the different conditions that already exist among school districts. For example, why are some districts highly decentralized, while others are highly centralized? In large measure, it is because educational philosophy and organizational design are endogenous to local districts (Hannaway, 1992). Studying the effects of local political pressures on school district design, Jane Hannaway (1993) found that even in districts with similar institutional environments and technologies, differences could be observed in organizational design and procedures for decision making. In summarizing her research, she offered the following conclusion:

> The results suggest that the assumption implicitly made by many educational reformers that schools are free to choose their organizational structure is, at least to some significant degree, overdrawn. External political pressure at the local level appears to constrain managerial arrangements. (p. 160)

Such findings suggest that climate and culture are not manufactured entirely by school boards and administrators. Rather they evolve over time through a myriad of internal and external interactions. Consequently, what we see as the visible manifestations of climate and culture are the products of an intricate mix of school district and community characteristics—attributes such as the political environment of the community, available resources, demographics, tradition, values, and norms. Given this situation, there is little reason to believe that mandates will appreciably change school districts, especially if the variables producing the dominant basic assumptions remain unaltered.

The importance of understanding the complexity of organizational change, especially as it relates to school districts, lies in the fact that meaningful change is more probable if it is evolutionary and inclusive. Climate and culture provide frameworks for beginning the process of change. Reform should commence with an accurate assessment of strengths and weaknesses followed by a diagnosis of barriers that prevent meaningful improvement. Each major element of climate should be examined. For example, improved instructional approaches may be hindered by a physical environment that is inflexible or lacks technology (elements of ecology); more democratic procedures for decision making and planning may be obstructed by existing disposition toward conflict (an element of the social system).

Almost always a superintendent finds that culture is the most immutable aspect of climate. This is especially true in districts with relatively strong cultures. Widely embraced values and assumptions constitute the glue for an organization (Firestone & Corbett, 1988), and it is these beliefs that determine real roles (that is, what administrators and teachers accept as their responsibility and the behaviors that are appropriate in carrying out those responsibilities) (Prestine & Bowen, 1993). Behavior in a school district is not random; rather, there are fundamental consistencies influenced by a complex network of interactions among individuals and formal and informal groups within a cultural context (Robbins, 1986). This is why cultural transitions are rarely achieved by simply replacing personnel or juggling organizational charts.

Put simply, understanding culture and climate has become more essential to effective practice because these factors are integral to organizational renewal. Not only do superintendents need to understand the essence of these concepts, they must also be able to accurately assess these attributes in their given situation and transform their knowledge into effective strategies. Additionally, they must be able to educate others who become participants in a more democratic and more decentralized governance structure; they must facilitate consensus while providing appropriate professional guidance.

Because superintendents continuously interact with others, they transmit symbolic messages that reveal personal values; not all, however, step back occasionally to relate these messages to the core values of the prevailing culture. All too often, superintendents enter new positions announcing an agenda for change even before they accumulate sufficient information about prevailing, deeply rooted assumptions. Often they feel compelled to do so because their time frame for achieving change is unrealistically short. For many of them, especially for those who were hired from outside the school district, diagnosing the prevailing culture may take as long as 1 or 2 years. In the absence of this critical information, a superintendent cannot make an informed decision as to whether the current culture should be maintained (Dumaine, 1990). Despite this fact, some school boards continue to believe that a new superintendent with a predetermined agenda can transform a district in 1 or 2 years.

ORGANIZATIONAL PARADIGMS IN SCHOOL DISTRICTS

Basically, the distribution of authority in public education revolves around three control-related tensions:

- The tension between states and local districts
- The tension between school districts and schools
- The tension between legitimate control and professionalism (that is, administrators and teachers) (Kowalski, 1995b)

Each relationship plays some part in determining how authority is distributed. Not all states give local districts the same level of legitimate power; not all school districts give schools the same degree of autonomy; not all principals give teachers the same degree of independence to make professional judgments. As previously noted, reasons for these differences are an intricate mix of external (e.g., laws) and internal variables (e.g., politics, tradition, and philosophy).

Configurations of power distribution between school districts and schools are largely a matter of local policy (although some states have recently passed legislation requiring some aspects of decentralized governance, such as school councils). As such, superintendents and school boards have significant influence on the size of administrative staff, the distribution of administrative authority and responsibility, and the formal relationships among administrators in the district. Decisions for these matters are often based on personal and institutional dispositions toward centralized or decentralized authority.

The Centralized School District

The centralized school district is characterized by a concentration of power and authority in the upper echelons of the organization. There is an inverse relationship between the number of employees at a given level and their power, creating a pyramidal configuration of authority in the organization. This concept is illustrated in Figure 4–1. The greatest concentration of legitimate power and authority is in the superintendency, an employment category of one; the lowest concentrations are in the largest employee groups such as teachers, secretaries, and custodians. Centralized authority is also discernible in line and staff charts illustrating a chain of command in the school district. Figure 4–2 shows the organizational relationships for administrators in a school district with 14,000 students. Note that only one person, the deputy superintendent, reports to the superintendent, but supervisory responsibilities become more extensive for lower-level administrators. If the chain of command were strictly enforced, a directive from the superintendent to an elementary principal would be processed through three other positions (the director of elementary education, the associate superintendent for instruction, and the deputy superintendent).

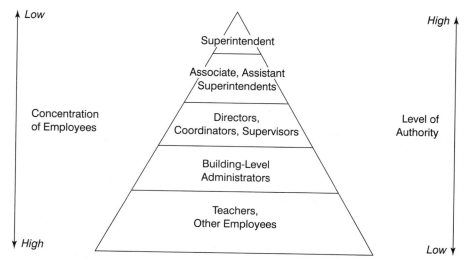

Figure 4–1
Hierarchy of authority in a school district

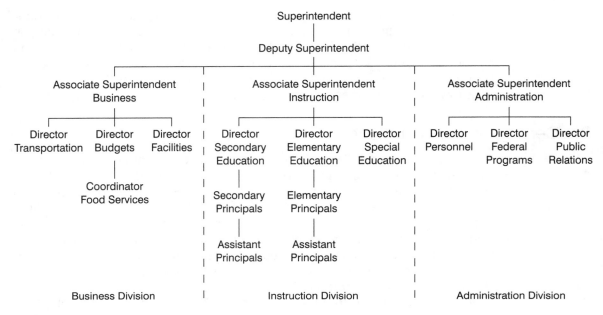

Figure 4–2
Divisions of authority in a district with an enrollment of 14,000 students

The concept of centralized authority is rooted in classical theory of organizational structure. At its core are beliefs such as these:

- Efficiency is the sole measure of productivity.
- Human behavior is rational.
- Work should be separated into units and closely supervised.
- Uniform policies, rules, and regulations are necessary to ensure proper control.
- Individuals are not inclined to work hard.
- A hierarchy of authority is necessary to establish organizational goals and to coordinate efforts toward their achievement (Hanson, 1996).

As described earlier, classical theory had a significant impact on the formation of early urban school districts, and in turn, these districts became the models for other school systems.

Over time, however, the bureaucratic structure of school districts has been criticized for many of its erroneous assumptions and negative by-products. Critiquing the failures of educational reform, Frank Smith (1995) aptly observed:

> We delude ourselves when we think of education (or the economy) as something coherent, logical, and rational that human beings have reflected upon and designed with a clear purpose in mind, like the internal combustion engine, a jet aircraft, or even the common teakettle. (p. 587)

Schools are complex social institutions, not factories. Behavior in them is not always rational, and efficiency is not an appropriate measure of effectiveness—at least not in a democratic society.

Many critics myopically judge that the perpetuation of centralized authority in schools is the result of administrator self-interests (that is, protection of their own power) and teacher resistance (or the resistance of their unions) to reconfigurations that may create greater levels of conflict and accountability. While these two factors may have a limited effect on local policy decisions in some school districts, they have far less effect on organizational design than do more global social and political variables. Consider the following three examples:

1. School districts during the 1960s and 1970s moved toward greater centralization because of a growing orientation toward compliance, which made school board members and administrators wary of litigation and state-imposed sanctions (Tyack, 1990). A series of federal and state laws in areas such as civil rights, the rights of those with disabilities, and employment discrimination indirectly led superintendents and school boards to adopt more policies, rules, and regulations and to insist on closer supervision with regard to their enforcement.

2. State constitutions and statutes permit, and often require, legislatures and state departments of education to exercise control over local schools. The intensity of that control is periodically elevated by political pressures resulting from dissatisfaction (Kowalski, 1995b). Many state interventions contribute to centralized governance structures in local districts. In the case of school consolidation laws, for example, having fewer, but larger, school districts with a centralized administration made relationships between state departments of education and local districts more manageable (Strang, 1987). Complex accreditation procedures, fiscal controls, and curriculum mandates also encourage the creation of central administration and the employment of specialists who can manage these functions.

3. Tensions between equity and excellence constitute another reason why superintendents and school boards may be apprehensive about relinquishing too much control. Current demands for decentralization are fueled by expectations of greater quality and excellence. Advocates believe, for instance, that educational productivity suffers because bureaucratic administrators are too detached from the teaching process. However, previous educational policy shifts toward quality and excellence inevitably have recreated concerns about equity and redistribution (Weiler, 1990). School finance litigation provides an excellent example.

These examples illustrate that the retention of centralized authority in school districts is really the product of numerous intertwined variables reflecting social, economic, political, and legal considerations.

As commonly used in school administration, centralization does not describe a specific level of authority distribution, but rather a range of distributions skewed in the direction of centralized authority. Line and staff charts are insufficient to determine the degree of centralization in a school system; this is more accurately identified by assessment procedures such as climate audits. In many school districts, for instance, the degree of centralization shifts depending on the types of decisions that need to be made (Abbott & Caracheo, 1988). Generally speaking, however, there are specific problems commonly attributed to centralized authority. The more prevalent are presented in Table 4–3. Largely because of the failures to change schools in the 1980s through top-down mandates, general problems such as those listed in the table are frequently employed to argue the case for school restructuring away from centralization.

Table 4–3
Examples of commonly criticized attributes of school district centralization

Attribute	Perceived Problem(s)
Concentration of power and authority	Because decisions are affected by divisions of labor and tiers of authority, change is improbable; an administrator at each level of authority could veto an initiative (Hanson, 1996).
One-way communication	Communication occurs in a top-down fashion; administrators may screen and filter information as it moves through the tiers of the district; teachers may withhold information from principals because they are excluded from critical decisions (Lunenburg & Ornstein, 1991).
Excessive control over instructional decisions	Teachers are unable to render professional decisions based on individual student needs; good teachers often leave the profession because they have little freedom to practice as true professionals.
Standardization of curriculum	Instructional programs are targeted to an imaginary "average" student; even within a school district, needs may vary depending on community and student demographics.
Assumed relationship between professional knowledge and legitimate authority	Those in the highest positions of authority are presumed to possess the greatest level of professional knowledge; often critical instructional decisions are not based on real needs nor are they formulated using the best resources available.
Divisions of responsibility	Functions and responsibility are often divided into administrative divisions, resulting in either political battles over resources or jurisdiction disputes; fiscal considerations may take precedence over educational needs.
Reliance on rules and regulations	Rather than being guided by professional commitment and responsibilities, the work of principals and teachers is shaped by rules and regulations; such conditions either attract employees who seek high levels of control or they result in most rules and regulations being ignored.

The Decentralized School District

Decentralization, just as centralization, does not occur as an absolute in public education. Rather, *decentralization* is properly defined as the delegation of prescribed levels of authority to individual schools by the superintendent and school board. Districts self-identified as decentralized may differ significantly in the amount and types of authority granted to individual units. For instance, one district may have decentralized only those decisions involving textbook selection and acquisitions of instructional materials; another district may have decentralized all basic decisions in the areas of instruction, budget management, and employment. Clearly, the level of decentralization differs in these two districts, yet both may overtly claim to be decentralized.

Decentralization is not a recently developed concept. Urban growth in the 1950s and 1960s resulted in many big-city districts serving an increasingly diverse student population. The concept of decentralization was used to mollify ethnic and racial demands for greater representation (Lunenburg & Ornstein, 1991). More recently, the concept has been promoted for both political and professional reasons. Politically, decentralization has been tied to liberty, and as such, it has wide support among citizens. The notion that taxpayers ought to have greater influence over their social institutions has become a theme of many elected officials in recent decades. Professionally, decentralization is linked to research into effective schools, which suggests that instructional effectiveness is diminished by placing educators in a quagmire of bureaucratic rules and regulations. Although decentralization as applied to the education profession more accurately relates to tensions between administrators and teachers, many policymakers have argued that it is not likely to be achieved unless schools are given greater degrees of freedom from centralized authority in their districts.

Arguments for organizational decentralization are often predicated on the anticipation of achieving the following goals:

1. *Increasing flexibility.* Schools are able to respond more quickly and directly to new needs.
2. *Using human resources more effectively.* Teachers can contribute to the decision making process.
3. *Decision making.* The structure ensures that decisions are made at the level closest to the problems (Certo, 1989).

Writing specifically about schools, Daniel Brown (1991) identified three key beliefs underlying decentralization:

1. Some variability is good.
2. Schools often know best.
3. Schools are usually trustworthy (pp. 12–15).

Interestingly, the words *some, often,* and *usually* reveal the conceptual challenges faced by administrators. How much decentralization? Which schools should be more autonomous? How does a superintendent determine if a school is not trust-worthy? Ambivalence is also caused by other perplexing questions: What evidence exists to verify that decentralization increases student learning? Does a superinten-dent remain personally responsible for violations of law or state policy that may occur in individual schools? Is decentralization truly the new standard for gover-nance, or is it just another in a long line of passing fancies in public education?

There are a myriad of potential problems associated with reconfiguring authority relationships in a school district. Some of the most commonly cited are summarized in Table 4–4. Perhaps the most intriguing question centers on the potential for conflict between the teaching profession and the community. If school councils are given substantial authority, will decisions reflect the political interests of taxpayers, the personal interests of school employees, or the common good of the community and students? Can schools move toward professionalism (giving teachers greater power to control their own practice) and democracy (increased liberty, shared decision making) at the same time?

Because there are so many unanswered questions and because school dis-tricts are such unique entities, decisions about decentralization are best made on a district-by-district basis. The choice ought not be perceived as one of choosing centralization or decentralization; rather, it should be one of determining the appropriate balance given the needs of a specific community.

Further, decentralization entails much more than a school board policy deci-sion regarding school authority; power and authority are also dispersed between the state and local districts and between administrators and teachers (see Figure 4–3). Imbalances among these dimensions become yet another source of conflict. Highly centralized state systems of education provide local districts with fewer opportunities to decentralize; the benefits of giving greater authority to individual schools can be negated by principals who refuse to share power and legitimate authority with teachers and others in the school community.

Despite its potential pitfalls, decentralization is more likely than top-down mandates to produce meaningful renewal in public education. Success, however, must be determined on two fronts. First, it must be measured by the degree to which progress is being made toward predetermined collective visions (that is, visions established by individuals and groups composing the school). Second, it must be measured by the extent to which outcomes satisfy state-imposed expec-tations in the areas of excellence and equity .

PURSUING CHANGE IN THE CONTEXT OF DIRECTED AUTONOMY

The concept of directed autonomy was discussed in the previous chapter, and it was noted that the nature of public schools and their relationship to state govern-ment make complete decentralization most improbable. However, there is sub-stantial evidence that the structure of schools will not change unless administra-

Table 4-4

Examples of commonly criticized attributes of school district decentralization

Attribute	Perceived Problem(s)
Adequate representation for the entire community	Often school site councils are composed of school employees and parents; if a centralized school board does not maintain a certain degree of authority, a high percentage of taxpayers (those who are not parents) may be disenfranchised (Danzberger, Kirst, & Usdan, 1992).
Potentiality of chaos	Districts that become too decentralized run the risk of erring on the side of chaos (Fullan & Stiegelbauer, 1991).
Tensions between liberty and professionalism	Liberty reflects political demands for greater, not less, lay control of schools; professionalism reflects greater teacher autonomy and control over their practice; decentralization generates consequential questions about conflict between these interests (Strike, 1993; Zeichner, 1991).
Creation of inequities	By giving schools greater freedom to be different, inequities may become more pronounced among school districts in a state and among schools within a district; schools most needing improvement may have fewest human and material resources in such an educational market.
Lack of evidence regarding success	While decentralization may appeal to the political interests of taxpayers and to personal interests of teachers and principals, there is little evidence showing that the concept has been successful (Weiler, 1990).
New power struggles are created	Rather than resolving conflict over power, decentralization may create new turf battles within the school; this is especially likely if decentralization does not move beyond governance to address issues of knowledge, information, and finances (Odden, Wohlstetter, & Odden, 1995).
Lack of support within the school	Despite the fact that decentralization is being promoted for both political and professional reasons, some teachers and principals may not want additional responsibility and accountability; some people opted to work in education because it has been a highly regulated, quasi-profession (Kowalski, 1995b).

tive control and teacher empowerment are reconsidered. Can teachers be sufficiently empowered so that they can be more responsive to the real needs of their students without creating political and legal problems? This is the essential question that leads administrators to consider directed autonomy as a feasible option. In basic terms, directed autonomy is an arrangement in which employees are empowered, and even encouraged, to do things their own way. But this empowerment is not without boundaries (Waterman, 1987). Along a continuum from total

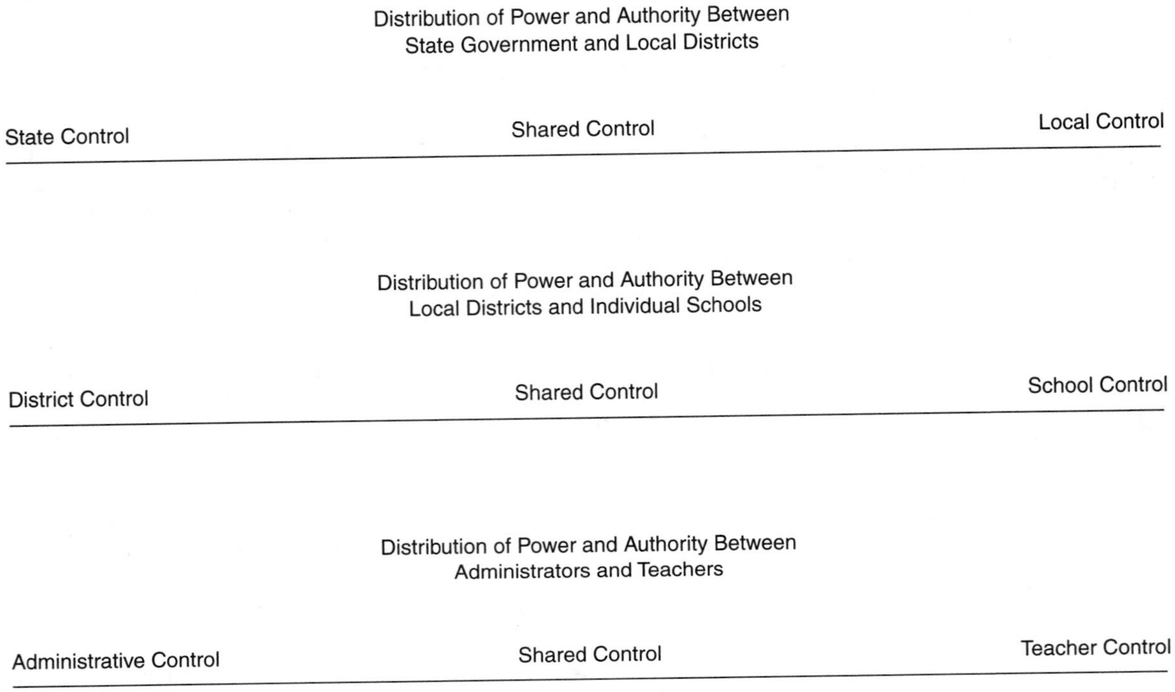

Distribution of Power and Authority Between
State Government and Local Districts

State Control   Shared Control   Local Control
_____

Distribution of Power and Authority Between
Local Districts and Individual Schools

District Control   Shared Control   School Control
_____

Distribution of Power and Authority Between
Administrators and Teachers

Administrative Control   Shared Control   Teacher Control
_____

Figure 4–3
Three levels of potential tension involving decentralization of authority

centralization to total decentralization, directed autonomy is found in zones that are skewed toward decentralization. This is illustrated in Figure 4–4.

Those who understand social systems theory may argue that shared power already exists in schools because these institutions are not true bureaucracies, but instead *loosely coupled systems*, that is, the units that compose the school system are only partially linked to each other (Weick, 1976). From a sociological perspective, a loosely coupled system is one in which "goals are ambiguous, hierarchies of authority are not closely integrated, technologies are unclear, participation is fluid, and organizational units are partially autonomous from their social organization (Corwin & Borman, 1988). For instance, teachers, even in very rigid schools (that is, those with many rules and regulations), have always had considerable

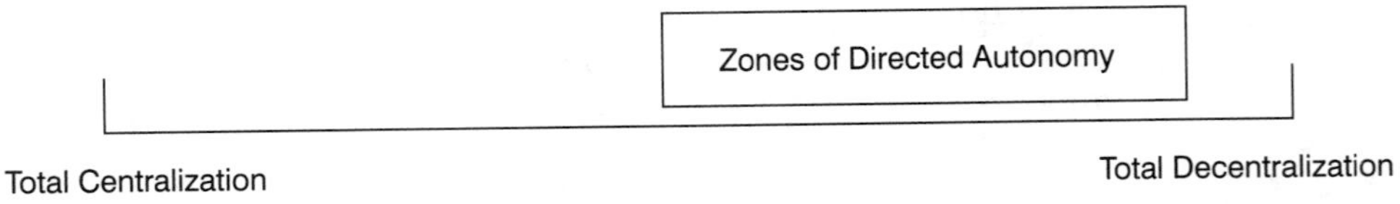

	Zones of Directed Autonomy

Total Centralization   Total Decentralization

Figure 4–4
Zones of directed autonomy

leeway to determine classroom activities for most of the school day. Although the curriculum and instructional periods may be precisely defined and although instructional expectations (e.g., required lesson plans) are detailed for teachers, administrators do not continuously supervise teachers to ensure compliance. This form of autonomy, however, exists for teachers within the informal organization. This means the exercise of power is the product of processes and behaviors that are unplanned, spontaneous, and reflective of teacher needs (Hanson, 1996).

Directed autonomy by comparison entails a distribution of authority sanctioned, and even encouraged, by school district policy. Largely because administrators and teachers are members of the same profession, empowerment involves three distinct domains for decision making: (1) responsibilities controlled by administrators, (2) responsibilities controlled by teachers, and (3) responsibilities controlled by both administrators and teachers. For example, decisions about adopting mathematics textbooks could be divided into the following domains:

1. The central administration determines which texts are eligible, assumes responsibility for obtaining review copies, and establishes guidelines and time frames for the review process.
2. Teachers determine the criteria for review, outline specific goals, and bring their professional knowledge on teaching mathematics.
3. Collectively, the administrators and teachers reach consensus on the selection of texts.

Figure 4–5 illustrates an example of directed autonomy in a school and Figure 4–6 illustrates an example of directed autonomy in a school district. The most criti-

Domain of Administrative Authority		
Record Keeping		Performance Evaluation
Annual Calendar	General Policy Enforcement	
Facility Management	Food Services	Budget Management
Domain of Shared Authority		
Staff Development		Visioning and Planning
Curriculum Design	Pupil Conduct	Daily Schedule
Program Evaluation	Community Relations	Budget Development
Domain of Teacher Authority		
Instructional Methods		Instructional Priorities
Grading Practices		
Learning Goals	Use of Technology	Student Assessment	Instructional Materials

Figure 4–5

Domains of directed autonomy in a school, with examples of areas of authority

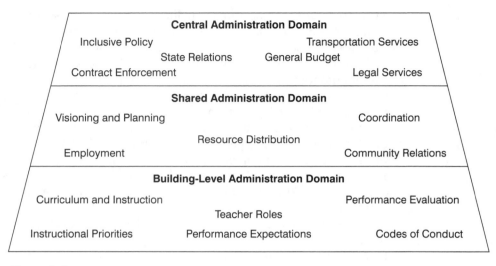

Figure 4–6
Domains of directed autonomy in a school district, with examples of areas of authority

cal institutional decisions, those involving purpose, curriculum, staff development, and the like are most apt to fall in the shared domain. This is why leading and facilitating have become so essential to the contemporary role of a superintendent.

Clearly, school reform is more likely if the proposed initiatives and structural transitions are congruent with the values of American society. Spencer Maxcy (1995) identified three beliefs deeply ingrained in democracy:

- A dedicated belief in the worth of the individual and the importance of the individual in participation and discussion regarding school life
- A belief in freedom, intelligence, and inquiry
- A conviction that projected designs, plans, and solutions be results of individuals pooling their intelligent efforts within communities (p. 73)

Thomas Sergiovanni (1994) argues that resistance to change is often associated with mental images of schools as organizations and behavior in them as organizational behavior. He advocates reconceptualizing the school as a community. He has made the following observation:

> Life in organizations and life in communities are different in both quality and kind. In communities we create our social lives with others who have intentions similar to ours. In organizations relationships are constructed for us by others and become codified into a system of hierarchies, roles, and role control. (p. 4)

Rather than relying on imposed policy, rules, and regulations, communities create a culture in which behavior is dependent on "norms, purposes, values, professional socialization, collegiality, and natural interdependence" (Sergiovanni, 1994, p. 4).

Recasting schools as communities, however, will be an extremely difficult task for at least two reasons. First, most people who work in schools have only known the culture that currently exists in their workplace. Most teachers, for example, have been socialized to accept many of the basic assumptions driving behaviors in the traditional school. Even for those who prefer nontraditional values and beliefs, the process of change produces anxiety. Second, the relationship of states to local school districts—a relationship historically rooted in the quest to build a common school experience—serves to restrict excessive autonomy for school districts and schools. Concerns are already being raised about the potential effects of fragmentation, pluralization, decentralization, and radical individualism on public education (e.g., Maxcy, 1995). Hans Weiler (1990) argues that there is a basic tension between decentralization and "the tendency of the modern state to assert or reassert centralized control over the educational system" (p. 433). The modern state, he concludes, increasingly faces serious challenges regarding its need and value. At the same time local districts are being given greater leeway to determine how they will meet statewide goals, states are demanding higher levels of accountability. More precisely, states are imposing evaluation procedures that unavoidably restrict the degrees of freedom that can be exercised by schools. Thus, some form of state control appears inevitable, particularly in light of the fact that the dismantling of centralized authority eventually results in centrifugal tendencies undermining accountability (Moloney, 1989).

The very same tensions that create a control dilemma for state government are relevant to school districts. Decentralization rhetoric and policy are at the same time politically advantageous and vexatious. If schools are able to become communities having the authority to determine their own purpose, direction, and goals, are school districts necessary? Both state governments and school districts are likely to fight to preserve some control over public education—in essence they predictably fight to legitimize their continued existence. In this context, neither total centralization nor total decentralization appears to be a reasonable choice for school renewal. Rather than experiencing total devolution, school districts are moving gradually from more centralized governance to more decentralized governance as power is being formally dispersed into the three distinct domains of authority cited previously—central administration, building-level administration, and shared administration.

FOR FURTHER REFLECTION

This chapter reviewed the nature of school districts as legal, political, and social units of government. Differences with regard to their legal setup as statutory base, fiscal classification, levels of educational opportunity, scope of territory, or geographic location were examined. In addition, school districts were viewed as organizations, with special attention given to the importance of their organizational climate and culture. Both the centralized and decentralized school districts were described in the context of school reform initiatives, and potential tensions associated with decentralization were identified at three levels: the state, the school district, and the school. Finally, directed autonomy was suggested as an alternative to the misguided notion that superintendents had to choose between a highly centralized or highly decentralized governance format.

As you consider what you read in this chapter, answer the following questions:

1. Some individuals believe that public education is a responsibility of local government. Are they correct? What are the reasons for your opinion?

2. In what ways are school districts legal entities, political entities, and social entities?

3. What is the fundamental difference between a dependent and an independent school district?

4. Several scholars in school administration argue that schools and school districts should be conceptualized as communities rather than organizations. Do you agree? Is this reconceptualization possible?

5. Why are metaphors valuable to understanding organizational behavior? Are the metaphors identified in this chapter relevant to school districts? Discuss the reasons for your opinions.

6. The climate of a school district was discussed in this chapter. What potential barriers to change exist within a district's climate?

7. Cultures are often described along a continuum from "weak" to "strong"; climates are often described along a continuum from "closed" to "open." How do you define the polar positions of these two continua?

8. What factors are most likely to contribute to a highly centralized governance system in a school district? Does enrollment or the number of attendance centers (schools) typically have an influence on centralization?

9. What forces are responsible for the increased popularity of decentralized governance in education? How has decentralization been perceived in other types of organizations, such as giant business corporations?

10. Both state government and local school districts have a legitimate role in public education. What does this mean? To what extent does decentralization threaten the legitimate roles of these agencies?

11. In what ways does centralization serve to ensure equality of educational opportunity in school districts?

CASE STUDY

The Haddington School District is located in the heart of America's "rustbelt." In 1970, the school system enrolled just over 42,000 students; today, there are fewer than 23,000. Since 1970, the district has closed 12 schools, and 7 different individuals have occupied the superintendency. The district also has suffered through two teacher strikes in the last 15 years, primarily over disagreements about policies in reducing the number of teachers. But the fortunes for Haddington appear to be changing. The enrollment is becoming stable, and several new businesses have recently opened in the community.

The current superintendent, Walter Mayhew, is an experienced administrator who has held two previous superintendencies in smaller school systems. Although he had not previously worked in the Haddington school system, he was well aware of its past problems when he accepted the job. Virtually all of his professional experience has been in the same state in which Haddington is located, and the rapid turnover in that district's superintendency was a popular topic at administrative meetings across the state.

Two factors influenced Dr. Mayhew's decision to move to Haddington. First, after many years of decline, the demographic situation of the district appeared to be turning around. Additionally, the school board had expressed deep concerns about turnover in the superintendency. Thus, Dr. Mayhew judged that a prolonged tenure was very possible. Second, the new superintendent was given the authority to make changes he desired with regard to his central office staff. The school board members recognized that change was necessary if the schools were going to improve. Dr. Mayhew exercised this authority to employ a long-time associate, Dr. Helen Carey, as his deputy (a position that had become vacant because of a retirement).

When the two administrators arrived in Haddington, they were amazed to find that the rigid, centralized governance system that existed in 1970 was still in place. Although several central office positions had been eliminated, four layers of administration continued to separate the superintendent from principals. Although the previous superintendent had attempted to force change by requiring schools to establish advisory councils, he did nothing to alter the district's basic governance structure. From what Dr. Mayhew and Dr. Carey could determine, the school advisory councils were created simply to mollify critics who were demanding decentralization. After they became operational, there was little evidence that the councils actually did anything important. All the signs pointed to "business as usual."

After 4 months in the district, the superintendent and the deputy superintendent arrived at different conclusions about a course of action for changing the Haddington school system. Dr. Carey wanted to move rather quickly to redesign the governance structure, making individual schools more autonomous and accountable. She told Dr. Mayhew, "You know we have only a limited window of opportunity to make a difference in this district. Despite what the board members may say about wanting to have a long-term superintendent, they are not going to be tolerant if things remain the same. It would take us 3 to 5 years to weed out the weak administrators and change attitudes. I don't think the board will be that patient. The previous superintendent may have been both right and wrong. I think he was correct to start moving quickly; his approach was wrong. We shouldn't start with school councils, but rather with the basic administrative structure of the district. Let's get rid of some of administrative positions and use the money to bolster individual school budgets. These people are not going to learn to swim unless we push them into the water."

Dr. Mayhew's perspective was quite different. He told his deputy superintendent, "You may be right about the time frame, but I don't believe that we can change things rapidly. Previous superintendents have attempted to impose change, and look where they got. My strategy is to develop a long-range plan calling for evolutionary change. We have to get the school board members to buy into it; they have to realize this is going to take more than 3 years. And, there is a lot more about this district we need to learn. Certainly there are some strengths we can use as building blocks. We are not likely to change the minds and hearts of the teachers and administrators if we simply destroy their culture. My plan is to start with a staff development program for administrators. We have to expose them to emerging knowledge about school reform. Then we may be ready to do the same with teachers. And only after we have made these efforts can we reasonably expect everyone to participate in fashioning a new vision and new goals. Sure, it's a gamble. But what do we accomplish if we impose change?"

Issues for Discussion

1. Do you think it is common for a school district to experience considerable enrollment changes without altering administrative structure? Why or why not?

2. Why do some superintendents place four or five layers of administration between themselves and school principals?

3. Is it reasonable for the school board members to simultaneously expect stability in the superintendency but change in the school district? Discuss the reasons for your opinion.

4. How do you respond to Dr. Carey's contention that there is only a 3- or 4-year window of opportunity to change the school district? What evidence do you have, from the case and from the professional literature, to support your position?

5. Assess the positions taken by Dr. Mayhew and Dr. Carey. Which do you favor? What elements of the professional knowledge base influence your decision on this matter?

6. Can you make any judgments about the strength of the culture in this district? Why or why not?

7. Beyond the suggested actions presented by the superintendent and his deputy, are there courses of action that you would prefer if you were superintendent?

8. Can you make any judgments about the turnover in the superintendency and the invariability of the school district's administrative structure?

9. How long should it take a superintendent in a district of this size to identify the system's strengths and weaknesses?

10. In private business, and especially in electoral politics, a change in leadership is often accompanied by significant changes in support staff. Would school districts be better served if new superintendents could bring their own administrative teams with them? Why or why not?

REFERENCES

Abbott, M. G., & Caracheo, F. (1988). Power, authority, and bureaucracy. In N. Boyan (Ed.), *Handbook of research on educational administration* (pp. 239–257). New York: Longman.

Bates, R. J. (1984). Toward a critical practice of educational administration. In T. J. Sergiovanni & J. Corbally (Eds.), *Leadership and organizational culture* (pp. 64–71). Urbana, IL: University of Illinois Press.

Bolman, L., & Deal, T. E. (1989). *Modern approaches to understanding and managing organizations*. San Francisco: Jossey-Bass.

Brown, D. J. (1991). *Decentralization: The administrator's guidebook to school district change*. Newbury Park, CA: Corwin.

Campbell, R. F., Cunningham, L. L., Nystrand, R. O., & Usdan, M. D. (1990). *The organization and control of American schools* (6th ed.). Upper Saddle River, NJ: Merrill/Prentice Hall.

Certo, S. C. (1989). *Principles of modern management: Functions and systems* (4th ed.). Boston: Allyn and Bacon.

Corwin, R. G., & Borman, K. M. (1988). School as workplace: Structural constraints on administration. In N. Boyan (Ed.), *Handbook of research on educational administration* (pp. 209–238). New York: Longman.

Cunningham, L. L. (1991). Putting the pieces together: Toward a comprehensive program of social reform (reformulating our approaches to school governance). *Planning and Changing, 22*(3), 240–247.

Danzberger, J. P., Kirst, M. W., & Usdan, M. D. (1992). *Governing public schools: New times new requirements*. Washington, DC: The Institute for Educational Leadership.

Deal, T. E., & Kennedy, A. A. (1982). *Corporate cultures: The rites and rituals of corporate life*. Reading, MA: Addison-Wesley.

Dumaine, B. (1990). Creating a new company culture. *Fortune, 121*(2), 127–131.

Edwards, N. (1955). *The courts and the public schools*. Chicago: University of Chicago Press.

Firestone, W. A., & Corbett, H. D. (1988). Planned organizational change. In N. Boyan (Ed.), *Handbook of research on educational administration* (pp. 321–340). New York: Longman.

Fullan, M., & Stiegelbauer, S. (1991). *The new meaning of educational change* (2nd ed.) New York: Teachers College Press.

Guthrie, J. W., & Reed, R. J. (1991). *Educational administration and policy: Effective leadership for American education.* Boston: Allyn and Bacon.

Hannaway, J. (1992). *School districts: The missing link in education reform.* (ERIC Document Reproduction Service No. ED 359 644)

Hannaway, J. (1993). Political pressure and decentralization in institutional organizations: The case of school districts. *Sociology of Education, 66*(3), 147–163.

Hanson, E. M. (1996). *Educational administration and organizational behavior* (4th ed.). Boston: Allyn and Bacon.

Hart, A. W. (1991). Leader succession and socialization: A synthesis. *Review of Educational Research, 61*(4), 451–474.

Hoy, W. K., & Miskel, C. G. (1996). *Educational administration: Theory, research, and practice* (5th ed.). New York: McGraw-Hill.

Johns, G. (1988). *Organizational behavior: Understanding life at work* (2nd ed.). Glenview, IL: Scott, Foresman and Company.

Knezevich, S. J. (1984). *Administration of public education: A sourcebook for the leadership and management of educational institutions* (4th ed.). New York: Harper & Row.

Knoke, D., & Prensky, D. (1984). What relevance do organizational theories have for voluntary associations? *Social Science Quarterly, 65*(1), 3–20.

Kowalski, T. J. (1995a). *Keepers of the flame: Contemporary urban superintendents.* Thousand Oaks, CA: Corwin.

Kowalski, T. J. (1995b). Preparing teachers to be leaders: Barriers in the workplace. In M. O'Hair & S. Odell (Eds.), *Educating teachers for leadership and change: Teacher education yearbook III* (pp. 243–256). Thousand Oaks, CA: Corwin.

Kowalski, T. J., & Reitzug, U. C. (1993). *Contemporary school administration: An introduction.* New York: Longman.

Lunenburg, F. C., & Ornstein, A. C. (1991). *Educational administration: Concepts and practices.* Belmont, CA: Wadsworth.

March, J. G., & Simon, H. A. (1958). *Organizations.* New York: John Wiley.

Maxcy, S. J. (1995). *Democracy, chaos, and the new school order.* Thousand Oaks, CA: Corwin.

Miskel, C., & Ogawa, R. (1988). Work motivation, job satisfaction, and climate. In N. Boyan (Ed.), *Handbook of research on educational administration* (pp. 279–304). New York: Longman.

Moloney, W. J. (1989). Restructuring's fatal flaw. *Executive Educator, 11*(10), 21–23.

Morgan, G. (1986). *Images of organization.* Beverly Hills, CA: Sage.

National Center for Educational Statistics (1993). *Digest of educational statistics: 1993.* Washington, DC: U.S. Government Printing Office.

Odden, A., Wohlstetter, P., & Odden, E. (1995). Key issues in effective site-based management. *School Business Affairs, 61*(5), 4–16.

Owens, R. G. (1998). *Organizational behavior in education* (6th ed.). Boston: Allyn and Bacon.

Pfeffer, J. (1982). *Organizations and organization theory.* Marshfield, MA: Pitman.

Prestine, N. A., & Bowen, C. (1993). Benchmarks of change: Assessing essential school restructuring efforts. *Educational Evaluation and Policy Analysis, 15*(3), 298–319.

Ramirez, A. (1992). *Size, cost, and quality of schools and school districts: A question of context.* (ERIC Document Reproduction Service No. ED 361 162)

Razik, T. A., & Swanson, A. D. (1995). *Fundamental concepts of educational leadership and management.* Upper Saddle River, NJ: Merrill/Prentice Hall.

Robbins, S. P. (1986). *Organizational behavior: Concepts, controversies, and applications* (3rd ed.). Upper Saddle River, NJ: Prentice Hall.

Schein, E. H. (1992). *Organizational culture and leadership* (2nd ed.). San Francisco: Jossey-Bass.

Sergiovanni, T. J. (1994). *Building community in schools.* San Francisco: Jossey-Bass.

Smith, F. (1995). Let's declare education a disaster and get on with our lives. *Phi Delta Kappan, 76*(8), 584–590.

Snyder, K. J., & Anderson, R. H. (1986). *Managing productive schools: Toward an ecology.* Orlando, FL: Academic Press.

Strang, D. (1987). The administrative transformation of American education: School district consolidation, 1938–1980. *Administrative Science Quarterly, 32*(3), 352–366.

Strike, K. A. (1993). Professionalism, democracy, and discursive communities: Normative reflections on restructuring. *American Educational Research Journal, 30*(2), 255–275.

Tagiuri, R. (1968). The concept of organizational climate. In R. Tagiuri & G. Litwin (Eds.), *Organizational climate: Explorations of a concept* (pp. 11–32). Boston: Harvard University, Graduate School of Business, Division of Research.

Tyack, D. (1990). Restructuring in historical perspective: Tinkering toward utopia. *Teachers College Record, 92*(2), 170–191.

Tyack, D., & Cuban, L. (1995). *Tinkering toward utopia: A century of public school reform.* Cambridge, MA: Harvard University Press.

Waterman, R. H. (1987). *The renewal factor: How the best get and keep the competitive edge.* New York: Bantam Books.

Weick, K. E. (1976). Educational organizations as loosely coupled systems. *Administrative Science Quarterly, 21*(1), 1–19.

Weiler, H. N. (1990). Comparative perspectives on educational decentralization: An exercise in contradiction? *Educational Evaluation and Policy Analysis, 12*(4), 433–448.

Zeichner, K. M. (1991). Contradictions and tensions in the professionalization of teaching and the democratization of schools. *Teachers College Record, 92*(3), 363–379.

Chapter 5

School Boards

Key Concepts

✧ Role and responsibilities of school boards

✧ Profiles of school boards

✧ Relationships between boards and superintendents

✧ Board member perceptions of the superintendent

✧ Common causes of conflict between boards and superintendents

✧ Practices for positive relationships with boards

✧ Sources of conflict between superintendents and boards

✧ Future directions for school boards

In recent years, school reformers have turned their attention to governance issues in public education. As such, school boards have increasingly been scrutinized in an effort to determine whether they are an asset or liability in the quest for educational renewal (Todras, 1993). While there are serious questions regarding the suitability of this 18th century institution to govern effectively in a rapidly changing society, the idea of local control is "deeply embedded in grass-roots American political values" (Danzberger, Kirst, & Usdan, 1992, p. 1). Consequently, many citizens are not eager to see the demise of local school boards, even if their eradication promises to expedite school restructuring.

The history of school districts, including the creation of school boards, was addressed in previous chapters. The purpose here is to examine the role and responsibilities of school boards more closely and to provide a profile of them as they function today. Much of this chapter is devoted to discussing the critical issue of relationships between school boards and superintendents; common causes of conflict and positive practices are reviewed. The chapter concludes with a vision of the future: Will school boards exist in the next century? And if they survive, should their role be changed?

LOCAL SCHOOL BOARDS TODAY

Statutes pertaining to the regulation of public education by local boards vary from state to state; even so, "all states dictate such matters as the corporate nature and size of local boards as well as the powers delegated to them" (Russo, 1994, p. 7). While the context of public education has changed markedly over the past 100 years, many statutes regulating school boards have remained unchanged. Despite massive alterations in the social, economic, and political structure of American society, despite substantial population increases and despite movement toward fewer but larger school districts, the present arrangement for local control in public education—a system through which states delegate authority to elected or appointed school boards—remains very much as it was in the early 20th century (Danzberger & Usdan, 1994). However, there are growing signs that legislators are becoming more willing to revamp long-standing education statutes. Recent legislative actions in Illinois, Kentucky, and Massachusetts provide evidence of this. In 1990, the legislature in Kentucky enacted a massive reform package that essentially required all public education laws, policies, and regulations in that state to be rewritten. More often, however, state legislatures have expressed concerns about public schools by acting against single districts. In the late 1980s, for instance, the Illinois legislature passed a law requiring the troubled Chicago school system to implement aspects of decentralized governance (e.g., school councils); in 1996, concerned by a lack of progress, the legislature passed another law—this time giving the Chicago mayor unprecedented authority over the public schools. Similarly, state officials in Massachusetts abolished the nation's first elected school board (in Boston) and gave the mayor the authority to appoint new members (Todras, 1993). In some instances, the state simply acts under its existing powers and assumes the responsibility of operating a local district. Such action occurred in 1989 when the state of New Jersey took control of the Jersey City schools.

Nine states (Arkansas, Georgia, Kentucky, New Jersey, New Mexico, Ohio, South Carolina, Texas, and West Virginia) already have "takeover statutes," which permit state government to assume administrative responsibility for troubled local districts (Pancrazio, 1994). Other states have provisions for exercising fiscal control over school districts that are operating at a deficit. In Indiana, for example, a school district can be declared a "controlled corporation" and placed under the fiscal jurisdiction of the state's Property Tax Control Board. The local board is not removed; however, every major financial transaction—including the development of the annual budget, tax rates, salary increases, and capital outlay—must be approved by the controlling state agency.

Now that governance has become a reform issue, a myriad of questions are being raised about the functions of school boards and the statutes that grant them power. More states are likely to pass "takeover" laws (Pancrazio, 1994), and state officials are continuously seeking ways to make local policymakers more accountable for their actions. Within this context, several additional issues emerge. Should board members be elected or appointed? Are schools boards really necessary, or do they just provide another layer of bureaucracy? While the answers remain uncertain, there are clear signs that momentum is building for overhauling the governance system for public elementary and secondary education (Harrington-Lueker, 1993).

Ideal and Real Roles

Historically, the literature on public school boards has concentrated on two issues. First, the policy-making role of school boards has been constantly examined, and second, considerable attention has been given to inappropriate behaviors on the part of school boards—especially those behaviors that involve intrusions into administration. Far less attention has been given to what school boards ought to do in fulfilling their broad policy mission. It is not surprising, therefore, that a degree of confusion and controversy continues to exist with regard to the ideal role of school board members (Campbell & Greene, 1994).

As an agency of state government, the school board assumes a control function that is implemented through policy decisions. This responsibility has both external and internal dimensions. Externally, the school board's decisions should represent the will of the district's citizens. This requires the board members to maintain communication with the community so that they are able to accurately represent citizen interests. Internally, the responsibilities of the school board include ensuring proper administrative control through the office of the superintendent, making primary fiscal decisions about budgets and taxes, and examining the district's outcomes with respect to student learning (Campbell, Cunningham, Nystrand, & Usdan, 1990).

Recently, the National School Boards Association attempted to define the school board's role in concise terms. They identified more than two dozen specific responsibilities, which fall into four broad categories:

1. The establishment of a long-term vision for the school system
2. The establishment and maintenance of a basic organizational structure for the school system, including employment of a superintendent, adoption of

an annual budget, adoption of governance policies, and creation of a climate that promotes excellence

3. The establishment of systems and processes to ensure accountability to the community, including fiscal accountability, accountability for programs and student outcomes, staff accountability, and collective bargaining

4. Advocacy on behalf of children and public education at the community, state, and national levels (Campbell & Greene, 1994, p. 392)

Figure 5–1 provides an outline of role expectations.

For both external and internal role expectations, there is a fine line separating what superintendents usually interpret as appropriate and inappropriate school board member behavior. For example, board members are expected to maintain two–way communication with the public. Through this process, they frequently receive positive feedback about programs and employees, but occasionally they also uncover perceived problems or negative attitudes. Clearly, the acquisition of such information falls within the scope of a board member's role. However, when board members choose to act on such information rather than relaying it to the superintendent, conflict typically ensues.

School board members often have to choose between two distinctively differ-ent concepts of their role: being a trustee and being a delegate. The former relates to representing broad public interests; the latter is more representative of individual interests or special–interest groups. Trustees tend to make their own

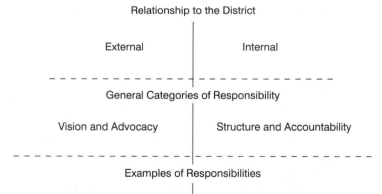

Figure 5–1
Role expectations for school boards

judgments on policy matters; delegates tend to be highly sensitive to the political interests of their constituents (McCurdy, 1992). Board members may also have to choose between aligning themselves with professional leadership and aligning themselves with political factions. Because problems exist with both choices of being a trustee or being a delegate, many board members seek a middle ground that allows them to move in and out of the two roles depending on the particular issue in question.

From the earliest decades of the 20th century, ideal school board behavior (the role of trustee) was outlined as follows:

1. Boards should act in the public interest rather than the selective interests of individuals or groups.
2. Boards should govern rationally rather than politically.
3. Policy is the domain of the school board and implementation is the domain of expert administrators (Zeigler, Jennings, & Peak, 1974).

These ideals, however, were never fully understood or accepted by many citizens. Since the 1960s, "local boards have evolved back into politicized boards, increasingly involved in the operations and administration of their school districts" (Danzberger & Usdan, 1994, p. 366). Some citizens believe that they should have open access to school board members; they commonly expect board members to be personal advocates who listen, respond, and intervene. Studying the responsiveness of New Jersey school board members to parent and community groups, Kenneth Greene (1990) found that the amount of responsiveness among these individuals varied considerably and that their behavioral differences were affected by "[t]he level of electoral competition in the district, the complexity of the district, and whether or not they [board members] plan to run for reelection" (p. 374). Summarizing the determinants of board member behavior, he concluded that neither the entreaties of professional associations nor the aura of expertise surrounding educational administration was sufficiently convincing to overcome pragmatic, political considerations.

More recently, reformers have focused on content-centered role conflict. That is to say, they have become increasingly interested in topics that are either ignored or insufficiently addressed by board members. This scrutiny has produced a list of common criticisms of school boards, which include (1) not spending sufficient time on educational matters, (2) not working effectively with other community agencies, (3) not providing adequate policy oversight, (4) not effectively communicating educational outcomes to the community, and (5) failing to provide a long-term vision for the school system (Danzberger, 1994). To some degree, these oversights are caused by community expectations that school board members devote themselves to the issues of the day rather than becoming preoccupied with abstract, long-term objectives. Such expectations usually result in school boards spending virtually all of their time attempting to handle day-to-day issues that have little consequence for the teaching and learning process.

Role expectations for school board members are important because the boards set standards for superintendents. Board members who become mired in the politics of community conflict are likely to set role expectations for their superintendents that are primarily political and managerial. Board members also face the public's reluctance to relinquish control to an individual administrator (Blumberg, 1985). Those elected to the school board are constantly reminded by their constituents that no single person, no matter the level of education and experience, should dominate the school system. So what has evolved over time is a delicate compromise between the professional role of the superintendent in running the school system and the desire of taxpayers to influence critical decisions through school board members. At the same time that communities overtly accept and support the ideal roles for school board members, there is a less discernible demand for political involvement on the part of school boards. Recognizing this condition, many school board members refuse to accept a clear line of demarcation separating policy from administration (Trotter & Downey, 1989), and their behavior is influenced by their own political instincts, and not codes of values.

Profile of the Contemporary School Board Member

During much of the first half of the 20th century, school board members were white males who were often politically powerful in their communities. This was especially true in the large-city system (Kowalski, 1995). Today it is more difficult to describe a typical board member. Between 1989 and 1994, for example, the following demographic transitions were occurring:

- More women were being elected or appointed to school boards. (In 1989, approximately 32% of the board members were female; in 1994, that percentage increased to just over 40%.)
- School boards were becoming slightly more diverse with respect to race and ethnicity. (In 1989, just under 94% of all board members were white; in 1994, that percentage dropped to just over 90%.)
- The percentage of board members over age 40 was increasing. (In 1989, just under 23% of all board members were under the age of 40; in 1994, that percentage dropped to about 18% [Education Vital Signs, 1994, p. A20]).

Statistics for specific demographic groupings of school boards often provide a somewhat different picture. An early 1990s study of large school systems (those with enrollments over 33,500) found that 58% of the board members were males and 28% were nonwhite (Ornstein, 1992).

A national study of school board presidents just prior to the 1990 census revealed the following:

- Approximately 3 out of 10 (29%) were women.
- 97% were white (of the remaining 3%, 2% were African American and 1% were Hispanic).

- About 4 out of 10 (41%) had less than a bachelor's degree.
- These individuals held varying forms of employment, with a third indicating that the nature of their work was managerial or administrative.
- 94% reported being married.
- Incomes were very diverse, with about 13% reporting annual incomes greater than $75,000 and 20% reporting annual earnings of less than $25,000 (Feistritzer, 1994).

In 1994, just about 41% of all board members did not have children in public schools (Education Vital Signs, 1994). While this figure may seem high, one should keep in mind that in many communities, 75% to 80% of all adult residents do not have children enrolled in the public schools. Also noteworthy is the political philosophy of board members. Just under two out of three (64%) identify themselves as conservatives (Education Vital Signs, 1994).

Many, but not all, school board members are entitled to receive compensation for their service (this is in addition to reimbursements for expenses). Statutes vary among the states, and laws concerning compensation for school board members can be placed into three broad groups: (1) states permitting all board members to be compensated, (2) states permitting some board members to be compensated, and (3) states not permitting compensation for board members. An early 1990s study of school districts located in larger cities (populations between 50,000 and 100,000) found that just over half of the school boards (50.8%) provided members compensation; the average compensation per board member was just under $5,000 per year (Needham, 1992). A national study (with 43 states reporting) found that 31 states permitted board members to receive salaries, 6 states permitted limited salaries, 2 states were pursuing legislation to permit salaries, and only 4 states did not allow board members to receive salaries (Krumm & Grady, 1997). In some very large districts, school board members may be paid over $20,000 per year, receive an office, and have access to secretarial services. To date, there is no conclusive evidence indicating that compensation influences decisions to seek board election or appointment; nor is there conclusive evidence showing that compensation affects board members' behavior. This is not to say that compensation has no influence; rather, there is a lack of research on this topic.

Methods of Selection

Basically, school board members are either appointed or elected to office. Each option can occur in several ways as detailed in Table 5–1. State statutes either detail selection methods or provide a range of options for local districts. In rare instances, school boards may have several members who are elected and several members who are appointed. Regionally, appointed boards are more common in the South than in other areas of the country; according to district enrollment, appointed boards are more likely in larger school systems (Campbell et al., 1990).

Appointive systems for selecting board members are becoming slightly less popular, possibly because some voters believe appointed board members are less

Table 5–1
Methods for selecting school board members

Category	Options	Explanation
Appointment	By an external official or group	Appointments to the school board are made by a mayor, city council, county council, judge, or some other person or official agency (depending on relevant laws and policies).
	By the school board	In a number of states, school boards are given the authority to replace a school board member who leaves office prior to the expiration of his or her term of office; if board members are not elected to office initially, then appointments for unexpired terms are often made by the person or group making the initial appointment.
Elected	Partisan or nonpartisan	The vast majority of school board elections are conducted on a nonpartisan basis; in some districts, however, individuals are the official candidates of political parties.
	At-large or districted candidacy	In some school districts, some or all seats on the school board are legally associated with specified areas or districts; that is, candidates can only seek the seat(s) on the school board that is designated for his or her specific area of residence; the concept of districted candidates is the same as the one used to elect representatives to the U. S. House of Representatives; elections involving districted candidates may be based on at-large or districted voting (depending on relevant laws and policies).
	At-large or districted voting	At-large voting allows all voters in a school district to vote for all contested seats, even if the seats themselves are districted.

responsive to constituent needs and wants. In 1992, Virginia, the only state that did not allow school board elections, changed its statutes (Underwood, 1992). Movement away from appointed school boards has been very gradual. Over the past two decades, the percentage of appointed boards has declined by 1% or less; in the early 1990s, just over 94% of all boards were elected (Glass, 1992). In that group, the overwhelming majority (approximately 86%) was selected through nonpartisan elections (Campbell et al., 1990). A more recent study of state laws (43 states reporting) found that only 6 states permitted board members to be either elected or appointed (Krumm & Grady, 1997).

Both appointed and elected boards have their proponents; common arguments for each option are outlined in Table 5–2. Support for appointed school boards is often dependent on the specifications of the law, especially that part of the law identifying the person and group who is to make the appointment. In large cities, for example, superintendents may be wary of mayoral appointments, which could give city hall added political leverage over the public schools.

Change in board member selection almost always moves from appointed boards to elected boards. Although this switch has occurred in a number of school districts over the past 4 or 5 decades, there is little information detailing the political consequences. Certainly, the potential exists for instability during the transition period, especially if members who previously had been appointed to the school board either do not seek election or are defeated if they do so. In addition, adoption of the election process often results in new political alliances within the community and new political arrangements for policy making (Godfrey, 1987).

School board elections, like all other elections, may be influenced substantially by the activities of political action committees or similar pressure groups. In recent years, however, some of these coalitions have changed their tactics. In an effort to gain control of a local school board, they have selected and financed "stealth" candidates—individuals who do not disclose their affiliation or true agenda until elected (Ledell, 1993). Describing the efforts of one pressure group, Christian fundamentalists, Zita Arocha (1993) wrote the following:

> [R]eligious fundamentalists are using the democratic process effectively, sometimes joining forces with taxpayers, senior citizens, and other conservative religious groups that share their agenda. They are winning seats on local and state school boards and they are using hard-won power to reshape educational policy. (p. 9)

Such efforts expose the continuing philosophical differences that exist in American society. Members of the most zealous groups believe that the country is engaged in a cultural war, and clearly, they have decided to make the public schools a battleground. The result has been intense emotional struggles, tensions, and even hostility.

However, despite concerns about stealth candidates and pressure groups, public preference for elected boards remains strong. Perhaps the major reason is that elected boards are more likely to be responsive to parents and community groups seeking to influence policy or administrative decisions (Greene, 1990).

RELATIONSHIPS BETWEEN BOARDS AND SUPERINTENDENTS

Rapid turnover in the superintendency is often attributed to poor relationships between a superintendent and his or her school board members (Weller, Brown, &

Table 5–2
Perceived advantages and supporting arguments for appointed and elected school boards

Category	Perceived Advantage	Supporting Argument
Appointment	Greater emphasis on credentials	The person making the appointment may be more inclined than the voting public to examine issues such as academic credentials, relevant experiences, philosophy, and intentions.
	Greater likelihood of accepting the role of trustee	Since appointees are less indebted to political groups, they may be more inclined to support the broad interests of the public rather than the narrow interests of individuals or groups.
	Improved pool of candidates	Some who are well prepared to serve on school boards do not want to subject themselves to the elective process; the appointment system may be more appealing to influential citizens.
	Greater likelihood of collaboration	Because appointments are often made by key governmental officials or groups, appointees may be less inclined to be territorial; they may exhibit a greater willingness to collaborate with other community agencies.
	Less likelihood of intrusion into administration	Appointees are not politically obligated to individuals who may urge them to get involved in administrative matters; their reappointment is more likely to be based on an assessment of total service rather than their vote on a single incident.
Election	Congruence with democracy	In a democratic society, election is the preferred mechanism for selecting public representatives.
	Accountability	The schools belong to the people and those governing should be answerable to the people.
	Representative boards	Elections are more likely to produce a school board that is representative of the total community.
	Public awareness	The election process makes citizens aware of issues and needs in education.
	Public participation	The school board election is one avenue of citizen involvement in schools; with approximately 75% of the voters not having children enrolled in the public schools, this is an important issue.
	Making the public aware of philosophies and issues	The election process often spawns public debates over values, beliefs, and critical issues.

Flynn, 1991). For this reason, relationships with school boards are obviously of interest to those seeking superintendent posts. But this topic also has captured the attention of a growing number of scholars who recognize that a poor relationship between a superintendent and his or her school board also deters school improvement (e.g., Danzberger et al., 1992). Critical reform efforts, such as collaborative visioning and long-range planning, are made less likely by political battles and frequent changes in top-level administration in a school district. In essence, poor relationships diminish the effectiveness of both superintendents and school boards.

Several studies have shown that superintendents have a proclivity to characterize relationships with a school board in terms of individual associations rather than associations with the board as a unit (Blumberg, 1985; Kowalski, 1995). This is to be expected for at least two reasons:

1. School boards commonly are composed of political factions that place the superintendent in a difficult position. He or she must decide whether to align with one of the factions or try to remain neutral. In either instance, personal relationships become the focal point for power relationships (Kowalski, 1995).

2. The superintendent's reputation and job survival are largely dependent on his or her ability to influence critical policy decisions. Most often, efforts to sway votes occur on a one-to-one basis between the superintendent and an individual board member (Blumberg, 1985).

A multitude of ethical, moral, professional, and social issues provide the context for the relationship between a superintendent and school board members. For instance, superintendents have the professional and ethical obligation to make recommendations to the board on policy matters. While board members are ethically bound to listen, they certainly are not obligated to follow the superintendent's recommended course of action. Hence, communication, both formal and informal, becomes an essential part of policy making, and effective communication certainly depends on positive relationships.

Building a Positive Relationship

How do superintendents build and maintain positive relationships with school board members? The foundation for such associations is laid during the hiring process. Written application materials, job interviews, and subsequent communication with a candidate provide board members with information about an applicant's values, beliefs, qualifications, experiences, and aspirations. Board members have two critical expectations in candidates for such an important position: (1) they expect candidates to be aware of their personal philosophies and leadership style and (2) they expect candidates to candidly share this information. If a candidate misrepresents his or her positions, this fact almost always becomes obvious to the school board as the superintendent begins to work with others in the school district and community. When initial expectations are not met, the integrity of the superintendent is placed in doubt. For this reason, self-awareness and honesty are foundational to good relationships.

Providing knowledge and assistance to school board members about their role is an essential responsibility for superintendents for several reasons. Many board members begin their service without any formal training for their complex duties. Approximately 90% of the states do not even have laws specifying minimum educational qualifications for school board members (Krumm & Grady, 1997). While board members may have access to workshops conducted by school board associations, not all will be able or inclined to enroll in them. In a national study of school superintendents, Thomas Glass (1992) found that nearly half of the superintendents indicated that they provided board members with their primary orientation to their role as school board members. Additionally, changes in statutes and state-level policies often require superintendents to make interpretations for even the most experienced board members. Community groups often expect board members to be knowledgeable about emerging educational issues, and superintendents are usually in the most convenient position to provide orientation activities and continuing education experiences for board members. Research conducted by Marilyn Tallerico (1991), however, indicated that superintendents probably overestimate their influence with respect to the orientation of new board members. Her outcomes revealed that board members employ a broad framework of resources to adjust to their new role. It is likely that board member socialization varies across districts. The prevailing culture, past practice, the individual board member, and the individual superintendent are influential variables determining how the process occurs.

One of the primary responsibilities of the superintendent is to keep board members informed about all issues that affect policy development, policy implementation, and community relations. This requires a process of open, two-way communication—a process that entails both distributing and collecting information on a regular basis. One of the major causes of conflict between board members and superintendents, for instance, is failure to discuss the role expectations they have of each other (McCurdy, 1992). In essence, these role expectations provide a code of conduct for both parties.

Lasting and solid relationships require commitment from the parties involved. This means that they willingly and cooperatively reach agreement about the nature of their relationship. In some school districts, the school board may be comfortable giving the superintendent an unusually high level of authority; in other situations, the school board may demand much greater involvement for themselves. The bonding element for good relationships between board members and superintendents is not dominance, but rather mutual respect. That is to say, the parties in the relationship honor one another's roles and views. Mutual respect extends beyond simply liking or even tolerating another person; it entails honoring divergent views, especially those views that are rooted in personal philosophy and culture.

Respect is another building block for positive relationships. Thomas Shannon (1996), executive director of the National School Boards Association, noted that superintendents should have high regard for the local school board as an American institution of representative governance. This means both respect for the board as a policy-making entity and respect for individual board members as public officials.

Although the role responsibilities of superintendents and school boards are commonly separated by the categories of administration and policy making, the line of demarcation between the two areas is not clear-cut, and there are broad areas of overlap. In reality, both parties rely on each other for successful outcomes. This is why divisive behaviors are so damaging. In situations where factions exist on the school board, the superintendent's responsibility to work with all board members is made even more difficult. Positive associations require *cooperation*, and this means a willingness to help one another; it also means sharing commitment and responsibility.

The ultimate attribute of a positive relationship between a superintendent and school board is *trust*. In its absence, suspicions, misinterpretations, accusations, insecurity, and political behavior flourish. Not surprisingly, studies of positive relationships often reveal that trust is ranked as the important factor (McCurdy, 1992). The critical elements of a good relationship between a superintendent and board members are shown in Figure 5–2.

Philosophical and Style Compatibility

One of the most important, yet complex, elements of relationships between superintendents and school board members involves personal disposition. It is not unusual for discussions of values and beliefs about governance to first surface

Figure 5–2
How superintendents build and maintain positive relationships with school board members

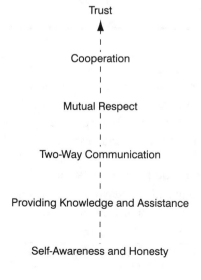

Trust

↑

Cooperation

Mutual Respect

Two-Way Communication

Providing Knowledge and Assistance

Self-Awareness and Honesty

months after a superintendent has been employed. Typically a conflict situation or major problem sparks discussions of values. If board members totally accepted the codes of ethics provided by their state associations and if all superintendents behaved ethnically, there would be less need for such discussions. Consider three common points found in codes of ethics for board members: (1) board members should not engage in administration, (2) board members should refer complaints to the superintendent, and (3) board members should act on policy matters only after receiving and considering the superintendent's recommendation. Clearly, not all board members abide by these standards, and core values and beliefs about public institutions are at least part of the reason that they do not.

However, studies often reveal that superintendents and board members hold similar views about their roles. An early 1990s study of these two groups (Freeman, Underwood, & Fortune, 1991), for example, examined perceptions of the characteristics of effective board members. The ranks of importance for the top 8 characteristics are presented in Table 5–3. As this study reveals, superintendents and school board members appear to hold quite common perceptions about the ideal role of effective board members. Responses to such surveys, though, may reflect respondents' ideas about what is politically correct rather than serve as a candid assessment of real behaviors and beliefs.

Studying the interactions of superintendents and board members in 6 school districts, Marilyn Tallerico (1989) found differences in the ways both school board members and superintendents collected and used information related to decision making. As a result of her observations, she placed school board members into three groups: (1) those who refused to engage in administration and relied substantially on the superintendent's leadership, (2) those who cultivated a wide

Table 5–3
Characteristics of effective board members as perceived by superintendents and board members

Characteristic	Rank Order of Importance	
	Board Members	**Superintendents**
Maintaining focus, even amid criticism and controversy	1	3
Abiding by the board-established code of ethics	2	2
Clearly differentiating between policy making and administration	3	1
Encouraging citizen involvement and promoting school-community cooperation	4	6
Using established procedures to evaluate the superintendent	5	4
Communicating clearly and regularly with constituencies	6	8
Following policy regarding contact with the media	7	7
Having the trust of school district employees	8	5

From "What Boards Value" by J. L. Freeman, K. E. Underwood, & J. C. Fortune, 1991, *American School Board Journal, 178*(1), p. 33. Adapted by permission.

range of information sources and engaged in oversight and management activities, and (3) those who cultivated a wide range of information sources but deferred to the superintendent's authority. She placed superintendents into two groups: (1) those who were more control oriented and inclined to persuade board members to their position and (2) those who were less control oriented and inclined to have board members seek a wide range of information and present divergent views.

Malcolm Katz (1993) formulated similar characterizations. He described the behavior of school boards as falling along a continuum from "corporate board style" and "familial board style." The former was characterized by reliance on the superintendent for data and recommendations, formality, and commitment to standards; the latter was characterized by informality, informal communication, and extreme loyalty to the community. He categorized superintendent behavior along a continuum from task orientation to relationship orientation (a distinction he adopted from leadership theory). He concluded that productive relationships occurred when task-oriented superintendents were matched with corporate-type board members or when relationship-oriented superintendents were matched with familial-type board members.

Groupings such as these help us understand the importance of achieving philosophical and stylistic compatibility between a school board and its superintendent. Communication and working relationships are likely to be more effective when the superintendent understands board member perceptions relative to conflict, decision making, and governance (Newman & Brown, 1992). Unfortunately, convictions about governance are either not discussed or not given ample consideration during the employment process. As a result, superintendents and board members discover their true identities only after they are bound by an employment contract.

IDENTIFYING AND MANAGING CONFLICT WITH SCHOOL BOARDS

Aspiring superintendents often ask, How do I avoid falling into the traps that may cause severe conflict between the school board and me? Unfortunately, there is no foolproof answer to this question. Negative relationships may be caused by any number of variables, and often when things go sour, both parties share some of the blame. Because school districts are unique by virtue of their cultures, community settings, and people (the individuals and groups making up the school district), generalizations about conflict are difficult to make. Nevertheless, when asked to identify factors that detract from positive relationships, board members and superintendents tend to voice recurring concerns about each other.

Common Problems Attributed to School Board Members

In the eyes of most school administrators, the vision of an ideal school board member is shaped by several basic assumptions. They include the following:

- The primary, if not exclusive, role of board members is policy making.
- Decisions by board members should be directed by the broad needs of the community, and not the special interests of individuals and pressure groups.
- Board members should be supportive of the superintendent and respect his or her professional knowledge.
- Board members ought to act ethically and morally and not use their office for personal gain.

These notions on the part of those in educational administration are strengthened in graduate study and during the socialization process that occurs in schools. They are also reinforced in the codes of ethics provided by state and national associations for school board members and administrator organizations. For most superintendents, these tenets constitute the framework through which they judge appropriate behaviors for board members.

Although school boards are legal entities, and although their official authority is limited to matters within their jurisdiction, superintendents are likely to discuss school boards from a sociopolitical rather than legal perspective (Blumberg, 1985). Expectations superintendents establish for school board members are usually based on an intricate mix of ethical, moral, social, and political standards. Perceptions of negative behavior on the part of school board members are based on these standards. Among the more prevalent are the following:

1. *Pursuing single issues*. This problem is characterized by a board member who has little interest in the general needs of the community; he or she is focused on a particular problem or objective. Often, the board member is affiliated with a pressure group and is elected to advance the agenda of that group. Or this board member may simply have an ax to grind, such as seeking revenge against one or more school officials.

2. *Pursuing personal gain*. This problem is characterized by a board member who seeks election or appointment to the school board because it may be a stepping-stone to a higher political office. Or the problem may be caused by more basic self-interests such as being able to get jobs for relatives or friends.

3. *Rejecting the professional status of the superintendent*. This problem is characterized by a board member who sees and treats the superintendent as just another political appointee. The professional knowledge of the superintendent either is not respected or is just ignored. Even for policy decisions involving critical educational issues, this board member relies on personal instinct and "gut feelings" rather than on the professional leadership of the superintendent.

4. *Pursuing personal power*. This problem is characterized by a board member who has a need to dominate and control. This person shows little respect for other viewpoints, and frequently he or she engages in conflict with both fellow board members and the superintendent.

5. *Failing to maintain confidentiality.* This problem is characterized by a board member who discloses confidential information about personnel, legal matters, or delicate problems. This behavior often surfaces in matters related to employee dismissal or collective bargaining.

6. *Causing factionalism.* This problem is characterized by a board member who continuously exhibits divisive behaviors that result in splitting the school board into competing factions. This person may be prompted by an inability to achieve a desired level of power and status within the context of the entire board. Personal rivalries among board members (e.g., two board members who simply do not like each other) may also be a contributing factor.

7. *Intruding into administration.* This problem, clearly the most commonly cited in the literature, is characterized by a board member who consistently and egregiously crosses the fine line separating policy and administration. This person typically spends an inordinate amount of time becoming involved in school matters; he or she maintains regular communication with school employees, visit schools regularly, and often contacts parents and other interested parties when problems occur.

Additionally, superintendents may voice concerns about board members who they feel are simply unprepared for their responsibilities. That is, the board members are perceived as lacking basic necessary skills to deal with the complexity of policy making. The issue of educational requirements for school board service is not new, and some state legislatures have been urged to review their statutes on this matter.

Common Problems Attributed to Superintendents

Because most board members neither complete a course of study in school administration nor share the socialization experiences of administrators, their perceptions of superintendent behavior are likely to be formed by personal convictions. That is to say, they have some mental image of what superintendents should do, but that image is not necessarily consistent with the ideal role described in textbooks. Among the problems commonly attributed to superintendents are the following:

1. *Lacking integrity.* This problem is characterized by a superintendent who simply is not trustworthy in the eyes of the school board. Board members have doubts about the accuracy of information they receive from administration.

2. *Lacking respect for board members.* This problem is characterized by a superintendent who exhibits little respect for the board's ability to understand and deal with complex issues. This type of superintendent is seen by board members as aloof and condescending.

3. *Failing to maintain confidentiality.* This problem is characterized by a superintendent who discloses confidential information to employees, the media,

or others. This often occurs when the board in engaged in deliberations involving sensitive matters such as employee dismissal, potential budget cuts, or collective bargaining.

4. *Subordinating rather than cooperating.* This problem is characterized by a superintendent who must constantly assert legitimate authority over the school board. This person does not see the board as a legislative body, but rather as a subordinate group.

5. *Failing to lead.* This problem is characterized by a superintendent who either does not understand leadership or is reluctant to lead. This person neither plays a major role in visioning and planning nor facilitates others who are attempting to identify and achieve institutional goals. Most commonly, this person is reluctant to make recommendations to the school board.

6. *Failing to manage.* This problem is characterized by a superintendent who either does not understand management or is reluctant to assume responsibility for managing. Critical decisions relating to resources are either ignored or the responsibility for them is relegated to others.

7. *Failing to be accessible.* This problem is characterized by a superintendent who is unavailable to school board members and the community (and possibly school board employees). This person rarely accepts telephone calls, usually does not see anyone without an appointment, and shows little interest in community involvement.

8. *Failing to communicate.* This problem is characterized by a superintendent who is unable or unwilling to maintain open, two-way communication with the school board. This person's shortcomings often result in surprises for the school board.

9. *Failing to comply with ethical and moral standards.* This problem is characterized by a superintendent who engages in either illegal, immoral, or unethical behaviors.

Studying the dismissal of superintendents in rural districts, Edward Chance and James Capps (1992) identified the most common reasons for dismissal as being financial mismanagement, financial malfeasance, communication issues, and marital infidelity. In urban school systems, superintendent dismissal is more often caused by complex political issues such as unrealistic expectations for radical institutional change and political changes relative to the composition of the school board (Kowalski, 1995).

The Issue of Social Contact

Should superintendents establish personal friendships and socialize with school board members? Does familiarity breed contempt in relationships between board members and superintendents? The traditional view expressed by many seasoned practitioners is that such associations should be avoided or kept to a minimum.

The reasons for this stance have to do with potential conflict and politics. That is, friendships may lead to a loss of objectivity or expectations that special favors should be granted. Or, social contacts could lead to unnecessary tensions such as disagreements about religion or partisan politics.

In truth, there is no hard and fast rule about social contacts with school board members. Superintendents do not lose their jobs because of personal contacts with board members; they may experience difficulties, however, because of tensions generated by those contacts. When a superintendent and board members meet socially, a different, more informal atmosphere surrounds their personal contacts—and this can be both good and bad. If mutual respect is present, both the board member and superintendent should be able to honor the ethical and legal boundaries of their associations in a professional context.

Monitoring Relationships

Relationships between board members and superintendents also may deteriorate because they are not properly monitored. To avoid this problem, superintendents ought to periodically engage the board in discussions designed to provide at least an informal evaluation of their relationship. Not only does this allow the superintendent to detect early warning signs of relationship problems, it also creates a forum for resolving conflict that already exists (Castallo, Greco, & McGowan, 1992). Periodic retreats with the school board constitute one mechanism for engaging in such evaluation activities.

Often it is helpful to begin discussions about relationships by collecting perceptions from individuals. For example, board members can assess the degree to which they believe the superintendent is meeting critical role expectations. Likewise, the superintendent can assess the degree to which he or she believes the board is meeting role expectations. To accomplish this, everyone can fill out an assessment sheet either before the meeting or as the first activity in the meeting. These data then become a starting point for discussions. This process does not replace the formal annual evaluation of a superintendent, but it should enhance the meaning and accuracy of that process. Examining the status of board-superintendent relationships only once a year may be insufficient; checkups every three or four months are more advisable (Castallo et al., 1992).

The monitoring of relationships is accomplished in some districts by formal evaluations for both the superintendent and the school board. For school boards, this may entail a formal self-evaluation. This process, focusing on the group and not individual members, may serve multiple purposes such as these:

* Identifying and clarifying the purpose of the board as a policy-making body
* Identifying operational strengths and weaknesses
* Assessing past successes and failures
* Exhibiting accountability to the public
* Providing a mechanism for avoiding abuses of power

- Providing a framework for goal setting
- Examining the working relationship with the superintendent
- Enhancing an understanding of and appreciation for the process of performance evaluation (Kowalski, 1981).

In addition, board self-evaluation helps to build credibility and aids board members to distinguish properly between administration and policy making (Robinson & Bickers, 1990).

While many observers may assume that school boards consistently evaluate superintendents within the normal course of performing their duties, this is not necessarily true. A national study in 1984, for instance, revealed that only 32% of the school districts examined provided their superintendents with formal evaluations (Sonedecker, 1984). Two more recent studies conducted within individual states (Koryl, 1996; Simpson, 1994), however, reveal that while the frequency of formal evaluations appears to have increased, approximately one fourth of the superintendents still do not receive formal evaluations.

In school districts without self-evaluation by boards and formal evaluation of the superintendent, communication about relationships between the board and superintendent is unlikely. The same reasons that make the parties reluctant to engage in performance assessment and evaluation probably make them reluctant to discuss operational relationships.

THE FUTURE OF SCHOOL BOARDS

By the late 1980s, most educational reformers had become convinced that intensification mandates could only produce slight improvement in student performance. Consequently, their attention shifted toward more radical reform proposals such as school restructuring. When this transition in strategy occurred, the issue of school and district governance was, de facto, drawn into the school reform debate. In 1992, two national reports, *Facing the Challenge* (funded by the Twentieth Century Fund and Danforth Foundation) and *Governing Public Schools* (produced by the Institute for Educational Leadership), found the current system of school governance to be inadequate; both reports recommended "sweeping changes in the ways school boards are organized and operate" (Harrington-Lueker, 1993, p. 31). Since these reports have been published, the attention being given to boards has been steadily increasing.

Given that the local school board remains a bastion of liberty in American society, why is this honored institution now under such intense scrutiny? There are at least three reasons.

1. The first involves concerns about the declining length of tenure for school superintendents. Most observers have reached an a priori conclusion that organizational change is more likely if it occurs in an evolutionary manner.

The probability of meaningful and lasting renewal is diminished, therefore, when there is a revolving door on the superintendent's office. While the declining tenure of superintendents is not solely attributable to dismissals or forced resignations (Glass, 1992; Kowalski, 1995), the escalating friction between the superintendent and school board members in many districts is seen as a primary cause of leadership instability. This is even more trouble-some in light of the fact that tensions between superintendents and board members often have little to do with the most essential functions of public education; more commonly the tensions are related to personal and political conflict.

2. The second reason why the future of school boards is being questioned has to do with the types of reforms being advanced. Ideas such as charter schools, choice, and decentralization inevitably provoke questions about the need for district school boards and the role they should assume. Site-based management, for example, forces boards and superintendents to redefine boundaries between centralized and individual school authority. As greater power and autonomy are given to school councils and principals, there is less need for central administration to manage. At the same time, though, the need for facilitation, coordination, and program evaluation becomes greater. Under this new configuration, board members will be expected to spend more of their time dealing with curricular frameworks, bridging reform initia-tives with district policy, ensuring adequate and equitable experiences across the school district, and developing systems to review the success levels of individual schools (Danzberger, 1994).

3. Uncertainty about the future of school boards is also related to a general dis-satisfaction with the current system. School board members, themselves, often admit that they are concerned about their lack of effectiveness. An early 1990s study conducted by the Institute for Educational Leadership, for exam-ple, found that "boards, by their own admission, are not functioning well as strategic planning and goal-setting policy bodies" (Danzberger et al., 1992, p. 58). Moreover, there are growing concerns about the degree to which school boards are truly representative of their communities and about the low level of communication that often occurs between boards and the general public. Such problems are exacerbated by what the public often perceives to be high levels of conflict, not only between board members and the superintendent, but also among board members themselves (Danzberger et al., 1992).

Despite these imperfections, most policy analysts argue that the institution of the local school board should be sustained—but they do so with the proviso that the central role of the board be reconfigured. Given the need to transform the organizational structure of schools, it is difficult to argue that true school reform can occur unless there is a corresponding restructuring of school boards (Danzberger, 1994). This does not mean that there are no effective boards or that no current practice is worth sustaining. Rather, much can be learned by focusing on best practice. Describing the most effective school boards, Phillip Schlechty (1992) noted the following behaviors exhibited by board members:

They do:
- Create a consensus vision
- Develop and implement a plan for engaging the community in discussion about the vision
- Empower leaders to achieve the vision and evaluate the extent of implementation
- Ensure that policies and regulations contribute to achieving the vision

They don't:
- Engage in micromanagement
- Act as advocates for narrow parochial interests
- Separate themselves from teachers and administrators for political protection from public criticism

The last point is especially noteworthy, since some school board members act as if they have no responsibility for problems or deficiencies. By separating themselves from other elements in the school district, they are able to deflect criticism rather than respond to it.

Because school boards are an extension of state government, changes in their role expectations and duties most probably will be initiated by statutes. The 1992 report issued by the Institute for Educational Leadership (Danzberger et al., 1992) recommended that state legislatures repeal all current laws regarding school boards; they urged that school boards should officially be renamed "Local Education Policy Boards" (p. 87). The role of such boards would revolve around responsibilities for visioning, planning, curriculum development, community interactions, and budget and contract approvals. Under this plan, school boards would no longer do the following:

- Serve a quasi-judicial function (e.g., presiding over appeals or other hearings)
- Have a fiduciary responsibility (e.g., approving claims, purchase orders)
- Engage in budget management
- Manage details of construction projects
- Be involved in personnel matters other than those pertaining to the superintendent
- Approve routine travel requests such as field trips (Danzberger et al., 1992)

If implemented, these recommendations would radically change the role now assumed by many school boards.

There are also other calls for change that more directly challenge the traditional relationship between a superintendent and board members. This movement is exemplified by disgruntled board members who claim that a lack of progress in school reform is attributable to existing school cultures and superintendents who place board members in a subordinate role. One such board member recently published an article in which she too advocated that school boards become policy boards, but her perception of this new role was clearly different from the one recommended by the Institute for Educational Leadership. She wrote the following:

> Traditionally few boards ever have meetings without the superintendent physically present: they are much like children relying on a parent—or students relying on a teacher. Just as we see kids in a classroom, when excellence is not demanded, when thoughtfulness is not valued, and when self-directed meaningful work is not required, then apathy and mediocrity result. Is it any wonder trustees have abdicated their responsibilities over the years? (Zlotkin, 1993, p. 24)

This board member also advocated that the superintendent occasionally take a back seat, that board members attend seminars and conferences, and that board members be helped to build relationships with staff members other than the superintendent.

An important point that needs to be made is that there are different perceptions of what policy boards should do, and those who call for school boards to move in this direction may have very different motives. The roots of the dissimilarities appear to be philosophical. At one end of the spectrum, there are those who seek to make board members catalysts for democratic discussions about the most critical elements of public education (vision, mission, purpose). These reformers acknowledge the value of professional knowledge, and thus, see the superintendent as a vital source of information in policy making. With regard to administration, they believe that the implementation of policy and routine management can be carried out without board member involvement. At the other end of the spectrum are those who see transitions to the status of policy board largely as a reconfiguration of power between board members and administrators. These reformers are more likely to question the need for superintendents to make policy recommendations. They are more likely to either (1) reject the assertion that superintendents possess a professional knowledge base essential to school improvement or (2) believe that board members can act independently if they acquire basic educational knowledge by attending periodic workshops and conferences. Even though leaders in school administration have sought recognition for their profession for nearly 100 years, such a tendency to disregard the value of professional knowledge shows that the goal has not been fully achieved. Unfortunately, social and political factors have influenced professional study and practice more than research and theory (Goldhammer, 1983). So even to this day, many influential reformers remain unconvinced that superintendents are the best-prepared individuals to lead the process of school restructuring.

Any significant statutory change involving school boards ought to be grounded on consensus about the role these governmental units are expected to assume. The primary purpose of school boards should be to transform the real needs of the community into a vision that reflects the best interests of the entire community and society. The school board "must represent the best and finest thinking in the community regarding the purposes of education in a democracy" (Schlechty, 1992, p. 28). This is more likely to be accomplished if school boards devote their time and energy to building community consensus for the fundamental issues that frame policy.

FOR FURTHER REFLECTION

This chapter reviewed the duties and responsibilities of school boards and school board members, and it gave a profile of the contemporary school board member. Of special note is the distinction between the concept of *trustee* and the concept of *delegate*. Focused attention was given to the critical issue of the relationship between board and superintendent. With the tenure of superintendents declining across all types of districts and with boards becoming increasingly divided politically, greater attention is being given to those practices that enhance or destroy a positive working relationship between a superintendent and board members. Finally, the future of school boards was discussed; a growing number of reformers are calling for laws defining this legislative body to be rescinded and replaced with statutes establishing local education policy boards. If accomplished, this statutory revision would significantly redefine the ideal role of school board members.

As you consider what you read in this chapter, answer the following questions:

1. What are the fundamental differences between the concepts "control board" and "policy board"?
2. What are the fundamental differences between the concepts "trustee" and "delegate"?
3. In your own community, what are the primary functions of the school board? Do the school board members become highly involved in day-to-day school activities?
4. Some board members rely heavily on the superintendent for leadership and information; others prefer to involve themselves and to collect their own information. What factors contribute to these different perspectives of a board member's role?
5. If you were going to interview for a superintendency in a community with which you were not familiar, how might you learn the dispositions of individual board members toward the role of superintendent?
6. Develop a list of superintendent behaviors you have observed that you believe enhance personal relationships with others. To what extent are these behaviors common among all superintendents?
7. Why do school boards often elect to spend most of their time dealing with management issues such as discipline, finances, and purchasing?
8. Should superintendents socialize with board members? Why or why not?

9. If school boards are reconfigured as policy boards, would you favor requiring a college degree for service on a school board? Why or why not?

10. If school boards are reconfigured as policy boards, which of the following options would you support for member selection?

   a. Appointment by the mayor or city (county) council

   b. Board seats designated to specific areas, but all members elected on an at-large basis

   c. All members run and are elected on an at-large basis

   Defend the option you select.

11. Do most school board members accept the assertion that superintendents possess a specialized body of knowledge that is critical to policy making and school improvement? Why or why not?

12. In what ways do ideas such as charter schools, choice, and decentralization force a reconsideration of the role of school boards?

CASE STUDY

George Collins has been an educator for 20 years. His experiences have included 7 years as a classroom teacher, 8 years as an elementary principal, and just over 5 years as a director of curriculum. Over the past 2 years, he has developed the desire to become a school superintendent. Judging that the superintendency would not likely become vacant in the district in which he was employed, he began applying for positions in school districts within a 100-mile radius of his current place of residence. He was invited to interview for two positions.

George's first interview was with the Hampton Unified District #1, a predominately rural district with an enrollment of just over 1,000 students. During the interview, George was asked to characterize his leadership style and personal strengths. He responded in the following manner:

"When I was a teacher and principal, I respected administrators who involved me in important matters. This is how I will treat others. Next, I believe the community should be highly involved in what occurs in the schools; collectively, the board and administration have the responsibility of creating opportunities for such involvement. I believe that the superintendent and school board should act as partners, not as adversaries. The board's job is to approve policy; the superintendent's job is to recommend policy to the board and to assume responsibility for its implementation. My leadership style is to treat others as professionals; teachers and principals should be given responsibility and autonomy. If they don't perform up to my standards and your standards, then we need to intervene. Finally, I support decentralization of authority. Schools should have greater freedom to pursue specific needs."

The school board members reacted positively to George's message, and the board president commented, "Mr. Collins, I think we agree with your philosophy. It is a pleasure to hear someone be so candid about values and beliefs." George left the interview thinking that he would be offered the position.

Less than a week after his interview in Hampton, George had a second interview with the board in the Rogers City Unified Schools, a district with about 1,800 students. While the two districts were not that different in enrollment, they were quite dissimilar with regard to other demographic characteristics. Whereas Hampton was predominately rural and agriculturally based, Rogers City was an industrial-based town in which most residents worked in the mining industry.

During the interview in Rogers City, George was not asked to describe his leadership style and philosophy—but he volunteered to do so. He told the board, "Ladies and gentlemen, I think you need to know what I am about and what I believe about education." He then went on to state the beliefs and values he had articulated a few days earlier in Hampton. But the reaction in Rogers City was different. One board member commented, "There are a lot of fancy ideas and dreams about the way things should be, but the fact is that superintendents don't survive unless they are good managers and stay on top of things. We have had more than our share of union problems in this district, and the taxpayers are fed up with it. Our last superintendent had a lot of trouble dealing with the teachers' union, and eventually, he became totally frustrated."

Another board member offered her views, "We expect the superintendent to be fair, but tough. If you don't demand that people work hard, they probably won't. Our biggest problems here are money and facilities. We don't have enough money, and our buildings desperately need attention. Quite frankly, I don't think we have time or resources to be experimenting with decentralization."

The board president was the next to speak. "As you can see, Mr. Collins, we are not shy about saying what we believe. Now, we don't always agree. Personally, I think that a superintendent and school board have to learn to work together. So, I'm not that concerned about philosophy. We all have our dreams, but the reality is that we have to sit down together and decide what we need to do. I do agree with my colleagues on the board that this probably isn't the best time to be trying a lot of new ideas in Rogers City."

George left the interview in Rogers City certain he was not going to get the job. He was not discouraged, however, because he remained confident he would be offered the job in Hampton—clearly his preference. Four days following his interview in Rogers City, he received a telephone call from the board president in Hampton informing him that although the board thought he was an outstanding candidate, they had decided to offer the job to an administrator already working in the school district. That very same day George received another call, this time from the board president in Rogers City.

"Mr. Collins, this is Fred Drover, president of the school board in Rogers City. We had a special meeting this morning and decided to offer the superintendency to you. Now before you give me an answer, I want you to know that we are aware you are a finalist for the job in Hampton. Personally, I think our job is a better opportunity for you, and to convince you of that, I am going to offer an $85,000 salary for the first year, a 3-year contract, and a very nice fringe benefit package that includes a leased automobile."

George was surprised, "I really did not expect to hear from you again, Mr. Drover. The discussion during the interview left me with the impression that at least several board members were not exactly thrilled by what I had to say."

The board president responded, "Well, that's real perceptive of you. There are two board members who would like to offer the job to someone else, but the other four members and I think that you are the best candidate. As I told you in the interview, my opinion is that people worry too much about their disagreements and not enough about what they might have in common. We are prepared to do what it takes to get you to come to Rogers City."

George asked for 48 hours to consider the offer, and Mr. Drover agreed. During that time, George identified his options and discussed them with his wife. While he was concerned about having 2 board members not supporting his employment, he felt that he might not have many more opportunities to become a superintendent. He was currently making $25,000 less than the salary offered by Mr. Drover. His wife told him that it was his decision to make. George felt he had some leverage with the school board in Rogers City and decided to counter Mr. Drover's offer. At least this way, he would find out if they truly wanted him as their next superintendent.

"Mr. Drover, this George Collins calling," he told the board president. "My wife and I have talked this over, and I want you to know that I am truly flattered by your offer. I will take the job provided that you meet two requests that I have. First, can you increase the salary for the first year of the contract to $88,000? Second, can the school district pay my moving expenses?"

Without hesitation, Mr. Drover answered both questions affirmatively. Six weeks later, George Collins was the new superintendent in Rogers City.

Within one month after starting his new job, George discovered that the school board was politically divided into two factions; the 5 members who voted for his employment constituted one and the other 2 members constituted the other. The two factions disagreed on virtually everything. The dominant faction led by Mr. Drover expected total loyalty from George; the other faction urged him to remain neutral.

The first regularly scheduled school board election occurred approximately 1 year after George became superintendent. Two of the 7 members were running for reelection—both were part of Mr. Drover's faction. They were opposed by two candidates hand-picked by the other faction. Everyone in Rogers City realized that this election could change the balance of power between the two factions. With the election drawing near, the local newspaper endorsed the two challengers in an editorial. Mr. Drover was furious. He went to George's office to discuss the matter.

"As I see it, George, we both have a lot at stake here. You realize that if these challengers get elected, I won't be president. More important for you, you will have a new majority controlled by 2 board members who did not support your employment. Further, these are people who want to run the show—to get more involved in managing the schools. You have impressed a lot of people in the short time you have been here. The teachers' union president likes you, and they are not backing the challengers. I think it would be good for you to do an interview with the paper and indicate that you think the two incumbents are doing an excellent job. Your feelings could sway some votes. Our backs are against the wall. We can help each other. Will you do it?"

Issues for Discussion

1. George Collins had only one interview with two different districts. Was it unusual for each district to have only one interview? What information do you have about how many interviews are typically given to applicants for the position of superintendent?

2. What could George have done to learn more about the school boards in these two communities?

3. Is it typical for administrators to accept jobs knowing that their personal philosophy and leadership style are not compatible with the expectations of some board members?

4. If you were George, what conclusions would you have drawn from the statements made by the 3 board members during his interview?

5. If you were George, what would you have done differently (if anything) before giving Mr. Drover an answer about accepting the superintendency?

6. What causes school board members to form factions?

7. Identify the advantages and disadvantages of George agreeing to do the interview with the newspaper.

8. Are there ever circumstances when a superintendent should get involved in a school board election? Why or why not?

9. This chapter presented several factors commonly found in positive relationships between school boards and superintendents. Which, if any, are relevant to this case?

REFERENCES

Arocha, Z. (1993). The Religious Right's march into public school governance. *School Administrator, 50*(9), 31–34.

Blumberg, A. (1985). *The school superintendent: Living with conflict.* New York: Teachers College Press.

Campbell, D. W., & Greene, D. (1994). Defining the leadership role of school boards in the 21st century. *Phi Delta Kappan, 75*(5), 391–395.

Campbell, R. F., Cunningham, L. L., Nystrand, R. O., & Usdan, M. D. (1990). *The organization and control of American schools* (6th ed.). Upper Saddle River, NJ: Merrill/Prentice Hall.

Castallo, R. T., Greco, J., & McGowan, T. (1992). Clear signals: Reviewing working relationships keeps board and superintendent on course. *American School Board Journal, 179*(2), 32–34.

Chance, E. W., & Capps, J. L. (1992). *Superintendent instability in small/rural schools: The school board perspective.* (ERIC Document Reproduction Service No. ED 350 121)

Danzberger, J. P. (1994). Governing the nation's schools: The case for restructuring local school boards. *Phi Delta Kappan, 75*(5), 367–373.

Danzberger, J. P., Kirst, M. W., & Usdan, M. D. (1992). *Governing public schools: New times new requirements.* Washington, DC: The Institute for Educational Leadership.

Danzberger, J. P., & Usdan, M. D. (1994). Local education governance: Perspectives on problems and strategies for change. *Phi Delta Kappan, 75*(5), 366.

Education Vital Signs. (1994). A supplement to the *American School Board Journal, 181*(12), A1–A31.

Feistritzer, C. E. (1994). A profile of school board presidents. In P. First & H. Walberg (Eds.), *School boards: Changing local control* (pp. 125–150). Berkeley, CA: McCutchan.

Freeman, J. L., Underwood, K. E., & Fortune, J. C. (1991). What boards value. *American School Board Journal, 178*(1), 32–36, 39.

Glass, T. E. (1992). *The 1992 study of the American school superintendency.* Arlington, VA: American Association of School Administrators.

Godfrey, M. (1987). *Case study in change: Appointed to elected school board.* (ERIC Document Reproduction Service No. ED 300 926)

Goldhammer, K. (1983). Evolution in the profession. *Educational Administration Quarterly, 19*(3), 249–272.

Greene, K. R. (1990). School board members' responsiveness to constituents. *Urban Education, 24*(4), 363–375.

Harrington-Lueker, D. (1993). Reconsidering school boards. *American School Board Journal, 180*(2), 30–36.

Katz, M. (1993). Matching school board and superintendent styles. *School Administrator, 50*(2), 16–17, 19–20, 22–23.

Koryl, M. (1996). *Formal evaluation of Indiana school superintendents: Practices and superintendent perceptions.* Unpublished doctoral dissertation, Ball State University, Muncie, Indiana.

Kowalski, T. J. (1981). Why your board needs self-evaluation. *American School Board Journal, 168*(7), 21–22.

Kowalski, T. J. (1995). *Keepers of the flame: Contemporary urban superintendents.* Thousand Oaks, CA: Corwin.

Krumm, B. L., & Grady, M. L. (1997). *A national study of school boards.* Paper presented at the Midwest Educational Research Association, Chicago.

Ledell, M. A. (1993). Taking the steam off pressure groups. *School Administrator, 50*(9), 31–34.

McCurdy, J. (1992). *Building better board-administrator relations.* Alexandria, VA: American Association of School Administrators.

Needham, J. D. (1992). To pay or not to pay? *American School Board Journal, 179*(3), 40–41.

Newman, D. L., & Brown, R. D. (1992). Patterns of school board decision making: Variations in behavior and perceptions. *Journal of Research and Development in Education, 26*(1), 1–6.

Ornstein, A. C. (1992). School superintendents and school board members: Who are they? *Contemporary Education, 63*(2), 157–159.

Pancrazio, S. B. (1994). State takeovers and other last resorts. In P. First & H. Walberg (Eds.), *School boards: Changing local control* (pp. 71–90). Berkeley, CA: McCutchan.

Robinson, G. E., & Bickers, P. M. (1990). *Evaluation of superintendents and school boards.* (ERIC Document Reproduction Service No. ED 320 273)

Russo, C. J. (1994). The legal status of school boards in the intergovernmental system. In P. First & H. Walberg (Eds.), *School boards: Changing local control* (pp. 3–20). Berkeley, CA: McCutchan.

Schlechty, P. C. (1992). Deciding the fate of local control. *American School Board Journal, 178*(11), 27–29.

Simpson, E. H. (1994). *Practices and procedures used in the evaluation of public school superintendents in South Carolina as perceived by superintendents and school board chairpersons.* Unpublished doctoral dissertation, University of South Carolina, Columbia.

Shannon, T. A. (1996). Lessons for leaders. *American School Board Journal, 183*(6), 19–22.

Sonedecker, J. W. (1984). *Evaluation of the American public school superintendent.* Unpublished doctoral dissertation, Ohio State University, Columbus.

Tallerico, M. (1989). The dynamics of superintendent-school board relationships: A continuing challenge. *Urban Education, 24*(2), 215–232.

Tallerico, M. (1991). School board members development: Implications for policy and practice. *Planning and Changing, 22*(2), 94–107.

Todras, E. (1993). *The changing role of school boards.* (ERIC Document Reproduction Service No. ED 357 434)

Trotter, A., & Downey, G. W. (1989). Many superintendents privately contend school board "meddling" is more like it. *American School Board Journal, 176*(6), 21–25.

Underwood, K. (1992). Power to the people. *American School Board Journal, 179*(6), 42–43.

Weller, L. D., Brown, C. L., & Flynn, K. J. (1991). Superintendent turnover and school board member defeat: A new perspective and interpretation. *Journal of Educational Administration, 29*(2), 61–71.

Zeigler, L. H., Jennings, M. K., & Peak, W. G. (1974). *Governing American schools: Political interaction in local school districts.* North Scituate, MA: Duxbury.

Zlotkin, J. (1993). Rethinking the school board's role. *Educational Leadership, 51*(3), 22–25.

Chapter 6

Policy Statements: Purpose, Analysis, and Implementation

Key Concepts

✧ Nature of school district policy

✧ Purposes of policy in public education

✧ Development of policy statements

✧ Political environment of policy development

✧ Role of values in school district policy

✧ Professional input in developing policy statements

✧ Superintendent responsibilities for policy

✧ Policy implementation

✧ Policy statements and regulations

The literature in educational administration has commonly distinguished between the role of the school board and the role of the superintendent by focusing on policy. Ideally, local school boards are expected to set policies in areas not covered by state laws and regulations; administrators, under the direction of the superintendent, are supposed to ensure that the board's policies are followed. This demarcation of authority is made less than clear, however, by two main factors. First, policy has many different meanings, and hence, the public, board members, and even administrators often attach their own meanings to the word. Second, the tasks of establishing, implementing, and enforcing policy are difficult to separate precisely; superintendents frequently play an influential role in setting policy and board members often play an influential role in implementing policy.

As noted in the previous chapter, the critical role of school boards was largely ignored in reform initiatives produced in the 1980s. Now that school improvement is focusing more sharply on restructuring of school systems and on a new distribution of power, governance for school districts is receiving much more attention (Bauman, 1996). As such, local policy making has been more intensely scrutinized. This chapter explores the meaning of policy and how it is developed, analyzed, and evaluated. Particular attention is given to the school board's responsibilities and leadership expectations from superintendents. Distinctions are made between policy statements and administrative regulations. The primary purposes of the chapter are to place school district policy making in the context of school reform and to show that superintendents do have a critical role in policy development.

ESSENCE OF POLICY

Educational policy is developed at the national, state, and local levels. Collectively, policy development is commonly associated with five broad areas:

1. Setting goals and objectives for the educational enterprise
2. Determining for whom educational services are provided
3. Determining the level of investment in population quality (for example, education) to promote economic growth and the general welfare
4. Allocating resources to and among educational services
5. Determining the means by which educational services are provided (Swanson & King, 1997, pp. 19–20)

As policy moves from the national to the local level, it logically becomes more targeted and specific. School district policy is often most evident in areas such as student discipline, transportation programs, extracurricular programs, and the use of school facilities during evenings and on weekends. One of the more conspicuous ways that school district policy touches the general population is via tax decisions. However, despite its importance, the essence of policy is often misconstrued.

Defining Policy

In most general terms, *policy* "designates the behavior of some actor or set of actors, such as an official, a governmental agency, or a legislature, in a given area of activity" (Anderson, 1990, p. 4). To varying extents, all organizations rely on policies to provide broad guidelines that direct individuals and groups toward goal attainment. The term *public policy* "refers to the action of government and the intentions that determine those actions" (Cochran, Mayer, Carr, & Cayer, 1986, p. 2). Accordingly, policy established by a local school board falls under the general category of public policy. A school board may establish policy within the powers granted to it by the state legislature, and all such decisions must conform to the limitations of relevant constitutional provisions, statutes, federal and state regulations, and common law (Imber & Van Geel, 1993). Specific policy decisions made by school boards are commonly referred to as *policy statements*. Such a statement is supposed to be "a guide for discretionary action, a statement of purpose rather than a prescription for action" (Clemmer, 1991, p. 20).

Four factors help explain why definitions of public policy are varied. First, the word *policy* can be used very broadly to describe a general course of action or very narrowly to describe a specific decision. From the former perspective, for example, a person might refer to general school board policies on pupil conduct and discipline—"The board's policy on discipline is really strict." From the latter perspective, a person might refer to a specific discipline policy—"The board has instituted a new, very rigid policy on truancy." When policy is discussed broadly, it is seen as a series of more or less related activities (Anderson, 1990). For larger governmental units, e.g., state government, policy more commonly has broad connotations; for school districts, the term is more frequently used to describe discrete decisions.

Second, ambiguity is caused by ill-defined distinctions between what is intended and what actually occurs (Anderson, 1990). Assume that a school board establishes a policy that mandates an automatic expulsion of a student for any second offense involving possession of an illegal drug. Further, assume that the board occasionally has granted exceptions to this policy because of extenuating circumstances; that is, some students were not expelled even though they were caught a second time. When asked about the school board's policy on the possession of illegal drugs, some in the school community might respond, "A second offense results in an automatic expulsion." They describe the policy in its official form (that is, the way in which it appears in the policy manual). Others, however, may respond, "The board's policy is to usually expel students for a second offense." These individuals describe the policy from the basis of experience.

Third, confusion typically surrounds differences between policy and regulations (or rules). Assume that a school board promulgates a policy that states, "Principals shall be responsible for evaluating the performance of all employees assigned to his or her school annually." Citing this policy, a principal indicates to teachers that each of them "shall be observed in the classroom by the principal at least twice each semester." Is the number of observations a policy or a regulation? Even though most administrators would describe this as a regulation (because it is a matter established by an administrator within the scope of granted authority), teachers may commonly refer to it as policy. Distinctions between policy and regulations are discussed more fully later in this chapter.

Fourth, ambiguity is associated with formality. That is, must all policies be formally enacted at school board meetings and placed in the school district's policy manual? Both practically and legally, the answer is no. Assume that a school district has no formal policy regarding participation in extracurricular activities and academic performance. Over time, however, the board has consistently approved recommendations submitted by the superintendent to bar students who have received one or more failing grades from participating in athletics. Even though there is no written policy on this matter, the courts are likely to determine that consistent rulings, recorded in the official minutes of the school board, constitute a de facto policy. Because policies can exist informally, employees and the general public become less certain about the nature of policy.

The literature also contains distinctions between the concepts of *policy as stated* and *policy in use*. The latter has been defined as follows:

> Policy in use refers to policy that is created as guidelines to be interpreted, mandated characteristics are weighed, differential priorities are assigned, action theories are applied, and ideas come to life in the form of implementing decisions and professional practice. Policy in use is the policy that is felt by students and teachers as schooling takes place. (Sergiovanni, Burlingame, Coombs & Thurston, 1992, p. 59)

Such distinctions remind us that overt statements do not provide a sufficient basis for accurately evaluating policy. Both intent and application are important. This is especially true when such statements are highly nonprescriptive.

DEVELOPING POLICY STATEMENTS

As noted in the early portions of this book, local school boards have been granted the authority to set policies in areas that do not conflict with established statutes and state regulations. In most states, certain matters pertaining to employees, pupils, and fiscal operations fall into this category. This would include areas such as performance evaluation, grade reporting, and compensation programs. The primary purposes of policy are to provide *direction* to decision makers and *information* to those who may be affected by the decisions of school district officials. While the legal dimensions of policy are commonly recognized, the symbolic attributes are often overlooked. Collectively, the decisions of the school board convey messages about objectives, values, beliefs, and priorities. Policy statements also serve an important orientation function by informing persons who are new to the school community—this includes new board members and new employees (Rebore, 1984).

Elwin Clemmer (1991) noted that effective policy can "save time, clarify objectives, promote consistency, and assign responsibility" (p. 12). Conversely, poorly developed policy can be unduly restrictive and prevent education professionals from exercising appropriate judgments. The current interest in giving teachers greater latitude in making decisions in their own classrooms represents a response to state policies that often prescribe curriculum, textbooks, and even the precise number of minutes for instruction in various subjects. The degree to which policy achieves its potential depends on a proper mix of control and freedom. This is why policy has become a focal issue in efforts to decentralize the governance of school districts. It determines the division of responsibilities between central administration and individual school administrators; it provides guidance for dealing with issues that have been decentralized; it promotes consistency and fairness across all subdivisions of the organization. Even in highly decentralized districts, uniformity of action remains critical in certain areas of administration that are bound by legal parameters, e.g., employment procedures. One of the indirect benefits of policy is that it serves to inform board members and the larger community about the school district's intentions.

Generally, school boards are allowed to set policies in areas of expressed and implied power, provided that such policies are not unconstitutional, in discord with existing laws, or contrary to state regulations. Policy decisions made by school boards may be shaped by four critical considerations: (1) laws, (2) politics and political behavior, (3) values, and (4) organizational and professional influences. These factors are illustrated in Figure 6–1, and they are covered in detail in this section.

Figure 6–1
Critical considerations shaping
school district policy

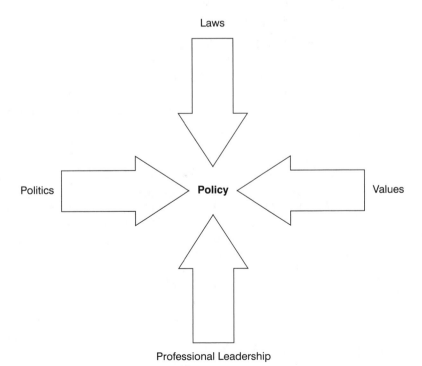

Laws

Politics

Policy

Values

Professional Leadership

Laws

While it is unnecessary for school districts to have policies that restate existing laws and while school boards cannot legally rewrite laws via policy, laws can be an essential consideration in policy formation. This is especially true with regard to new statutes that affect students or school employees. Relevant examples include civil rights statutes, legislation for those with disabilities, and equal opportunity employment laws. Even though these laws are relatively explicit, there may be a need for school districts to develop new policy statements to ensure compliance. Broader legal matters, such as court rulings, also serve to set parameters for policies. James Anderson (1990) noted, "public policy, at least in its positive form, is based on law and is authoritative" (p. 8). For example, taxation is a binding matter. Unlike policies developed for private companies, policy in education has an authoritative and legally binding quality.

Aspects of school reform are likely to make the legal dimension of policy making even more evident in coming years. Since the early 1980s, most of the activity in the arena of reform has occurred in state legislatures. There are growing signs, however, that this center of activity will shift to the courts in the near future (Heise, 1995). As reform-related laws in areas such as equity financing are tested, the decisions may result in additions and revisions to school district policies.

Politics and Political Behavior

Political behavior is a recurring element affecting public policy development. Competition for fiscal resources, power, participation, and prestige exemplify considerations that influence the decisions of school board members. Each board member determines the criteria he or she uses to make decisions. Political behavior may be pursued through public opinion, pressure groups, group affiliations, and deference (deferring to the judgment of others). Political influence is exemplified by a situation in which a school board, faced with a critical policy issue, establishes a blue ribbon committee to recommend a decision. While such actions are arguably democratic, they also provide the school board with a mechanism for relegating a high-conflict task to another group.

Ideally, board members are viewed as trustees who act independently in the best interests of the community; they are also expected to avoid conflicts stemming from self-interests. As trustees, they should give due consideration to the less powerful and to minority opinions. This disposition, known as *public spirit*, is a political form of altruism that comes in two distinguishable forms: (1) an emotional attachment to others and community (love) and (2) a rational commitment to a set of principles (duty) (Mansbridge, 1994). As communities become more diverse, and consequently as political pressures placed on school board members intensify, it becomes increasingly difficult to formulate policy that is in the interest of the whole community. Board members become both trustees and delegates (that is, representatives of specific constituencies). In the most demographically diverse school districts, for example, board members often represent specific pressure groups with whom they identify, both physically (neighborhoods, race, ethnicity) and philosophically (values and beliefs).

One of the greatest difficulties for superintendents and school boards is to objectively and accurately determine the public's best interests. James Anderson (1990) summarized three possible approaches:

- look at policy areas where there is intense conflict to understand constituent positions,
- search for widely and continuously shared interests,
- look at the need for organization and procedure to represent and balance interests, to resolve issues, to effect compromise in policy formation, and to carry public policy into effect. (pp. 124–125)

Schools commonly rely on forms of information gathering to determine public interest. One is the development of data banks providing information about students, their needs, and their performance (e.g., formal needs assessments). Another is two-way communication as part of a comprehensive program of school and community relations. By creating opportunities for citizen involvement and participation in governance matters, administrators and board members gain a greater awareness of real needs and wants in the larger community.

Ideological, Institutional, and Personal Values

The political aspects of policy making are related to deeply held values that have influenced public education in America from its very origin (Stout, Tallerico, & Scribner, 1994). More precisely, education policy has been the result of constant interplay among the values of *equality*, *efficiency*, and *liberty* (Guthrie & Reed, 1991). In recent decades, two other values, *adequacy* (or *excellence*) and *fraternity*, have played prominent roles in national and state education decisions. Adequacy relates to the quantity and quality of education provided; fraternity refers to notions of community life in a democratic setting. These five primary values are shown in Figure 6–2.

Figure 6–2
Ideological values in a democratic society

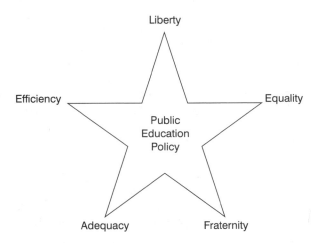

The pursuit of social metavalues inevitably creates tension. For example, a state that gives local districts tremendous latitude to determine both tax rates and levels of educational spending is certain to face challenges with regard to equity (that is, wealthy districts are likely to spend substantially more than poor districts and/or poor districts will have much higher tax rates than wealthy districts). Additionally, none of the values has been sufficiently powerful to stand alone as a reform agenda (Sergiovanni et al., 1992). Consequently, policy shifts often reflect a combination of these values. Consider the following two examples:

- In the mid-1960s, federal programs aimed at education emphasized equity and efficiency—a form of bureaucratic liberalism.
- In the mid-1980s, reform efforts were characterized by the pursuit of excellence and efficiency—a form of bureaucratic elitism (Sergiovanni et al., 1992).

While the tensions associated with pursuit of social values has been most evident at the national and state levels, they also are relevant to local policy making. Today, for example, many districts are contemplating issues such as in-district choice and decentralized budgets—matters that will result in emphasizing some social values over others.

Institutional values also influence policy. Often these values are viewed as inherently defensive of professional and bureaucratic interests by policymakers (Kogan, 1975). For example, teachers may object to a proposed policy statement that they perceive as being counter to their role as decision makers in the classroom (e.g., a policy that prescribes penalties for not doing homework). The potency of institutional values depends on the distribution of power among individuals and groups within the system. Teachers' unions, for instance, often are able to sway policy decisions because of their access to the school board and administration via collective bargaining.

In addition to these ideological and institutional values, school district policies also may be shaped by personal values (Anderson, 1990). For example, a school board president may decide that he or she does not want to be the first president to preside over a deficit budget. Hence, that person's decisions on budgetary matters are influenced by a degree of self-interest associated with protecting a reputation. Unfortunately, the tendency has been to judge the behavior of board members as either being altruistic or being self-serving rather than a mix of the two. Because policy positions are an intricate mix of ideological values, personal values, and other considerations, observers often underestimate the effects of altruism, even in situations in which self-interests may be rather obvious (Mansbridge, 1994). Most major reforms in public education during the 20th century reflect ideological values and altruistic behavior on the part of policymakers (e.g., eliminating segregated schools, school finance reform designed to increase equity in wealth and spending) (Guthrie & Reed, 1991).

Links between national, state, and local district policies are becoming more obvious in an environment in which state government sets broad goals and establishes parameters for accountability while granting local school boards greater discretion in instructional and operational matters (Shannon, 1994). As such, ideological values shaping policy at the macro level are not insignificant to policy decisions in local school districts. The influence of national leaders is often overlooked in this respect. National goals for education, for instance, are influential in a political sense because they provide ideological values that shape state laws and regulations. In turn, state laws and regulations set parameters for policy making at the district level.

Professional Direction

There are two primary sources of professional input that may influence policy decisions.

1. One is the superintendent, who commonly makes recommendations to the board based on organizational and professional considerations.
2. The other is legal input, which usually is provided by the school district attorney, but in some instances may be provided by special legal consultants (e.g., in matters related to enforcement of federal laws prohibiting discrimination).

In the absence of such professional input, board members are left to rely on ideological values, personal values, and political influences.

A number of writers (e.g., Sergiovanni et al., 1992) have made distinctions between policy statements and the actual use of policies. That is to say, the words contained in a policy statement may not be truly reflective of how the policy is actually implemented. There is a fine and often indistinguishable line between policy and administrative practice (Sergiovanni, et al., 1992). To a significant degree, the real effect of policy is determined by the context in which it is applied. This includes a mix of the decision makers, problems, and environmental conditions. Thus, factors such as leadership style, the prevailing school climate, and the school's culture are essential elements that determine whether policy will accomplish its intended goals. However, board members commonly set policy without understanding how administrators' professional knowledge base can guide them (Holdaway, 1983) or without knowing the prevailing conditions within the district. Partly for this reason, the responsibility of incorporating these considerations into policy deliberations almost always rests with the superintendent. A potential policy statement regarding teacher conduct, for example, ought to consider the history of, and prevailing attitudes toward, personal responsibility for professional conduct; it should consider the actual roles of principals and their dispositions toward enforcing policy in this area. Such information serves to inform policymakers about potential impact of the specific policies they are making.

The superintendent has a responsibility to provide professional leadership by translating his or her knowledge base related to education into policy recommendations. Many board members may recognize the need for such professional direction when contemplating instructional policies (e.g., grading policies), but they often are less inclined to seek the superintendent's input for other matters. When establishing pupil discipline policies, for example, board members may feel that community values, public opinion, and common sense provide sufficient guidance for their decisions. Accordingly, they may not be made aware of current research on topics such as corporal punishment, child development, social behavior, and relationships between discipline actions and learning—information that should be supplied by superintendents. Virtually all decisions in a complex institution have a systemic effect, and thus all policy decisions in a school district potentially influence student learning and personal growth. However, experiences with school reform efforts since the early 1980s have shown that policymakers are often influential community members who are not experts in education (Katz, 1993). These individuals often rely entirely on personal ideology, personal values, and prevailing political circumstances.

Legal guidance is advisable for policy matters that have clear legal implications. The legal advice may relate to the board's authority to set policy in a given area, or it may relate to interpretations of law that affect a policy statement that is being developed. This input can take two forms. One option is to have the legal consultant give advice directly to the school board members either in a written document or verbally. The other option is to have the legal adviser provide input to the superintendent, who then integrates this information into his or her ultimate recommendation and supporting rationale. Past practice, leadership style, and board member preferences often determine which path is followed.

There is growing concern among many administrators that educational policy is increasingly being controlled by the courts and by legal interpretations of court decisions. This situation creates tension between the superintendent's role to inform policy from an educational and leadership perspective and the school attorney's role to inform policy from a legal perspective.

Not all board members support the notion that superintendents should render recommendations for policy decisions (McCurdy, 1992). In addition to declaring that policy is their domain, these individuals often argue that their objectivity is reduced by having to consider a superintendent's recommendation. That is, they feel that support for the superintendent often becomes a consideration outweighing the policy matter itself. If they do not support the recommendation, their relationship with the superintendent may deteriorate; or the public may interpret their negative votes on a policy matter as being indicative of a more general dissatisfaction with the superintendent. Some board members also may contend that they cannot meet the public's expectation that they be effective leaders if superintendents control policy making. These concerns certainly have merit, but can they be addressed while maintaining the benefits of bringing a superintendent's organizational and professional values into the decision-making process?

In the healthiest situations, superintendents and board members develop trust and mutual respect regarding roles and responsibilities (McCurdy, 1992). Policy development is not seen as a "win-lose" situation. Rather, board members appreciate the need for professional leadership and realize that political issues and values should not be their only decision-making compass. Superintendents appreciate the fact that board members have a duty to represent the community; they are not devastated by negative votes. While textbooks continue to suggest that boards set policy and administrators execute it, effective practice is most likely when the two parties accept their mutual dependency.

THE PROCESS OF POLICY DEVELOPMENT

Policy development does not occur in a uniform manner across all school districts. While some systems utilize an elaborate process that ranges from needs assessment to impact forecasts, other systems rely on necessity; that is, they build policy extemporaneously as it becomes necessary to do so. Reporting the findings of a survey conducted by the National School Boards Association, Patricia First (1992) summarized a number of reasons why some boards fail to develop policy statements:

- Lack of time
- A lack of staff
- Poor administrative leadership
- Negative attitudes about written policies
- Lack of knowledge and skill in the policy-making process
- Lack of continuity (frequent turnover of board members and superintendents)
- Lack of fiscal resources for consultant services
- Lack of resource information

The important task of developing policy statements can be categorized broadly as encompassing making (1) decisions related to the development of new policy statements, (2) decisions related to revisions of existing policy statements, (3) decisions related to deletions of existing policy statements, and (4) decisions related to interpreting and enforcing policy statements. Examples for each of these are provided in Table 6–1. Recurring problems in the fourth category usually indicate that a policy needs to be revised.

There are multiple stages to creating and implementing school district policy. The process typically consists of five distinct stages: (1) problem formation/identification, (2) policy formulation, (3) policy adoption, (4) policy implementation, and (5) policy evaluation (Portney, 1986). The first two stages can be split into more definitive tasks as illustrated in Figure 6–3.

Table 6–1
Examples of policy initiatives

Type of Action	Example
Development of new policy statements	A school district is experiencing problems with requests to place students in accelerated classes; previous decisions have been left to principals and teachers. The potential for litigation leads the superintendent to recommend a consistent policy statement in this area.
Modification of existing policy statements	A school district has a policy allowing community groups to rent school buses; an insurance audit raises questions about the district's liability in such matters. The current policy is revised to accommodate these concerns.
Deletions of policy statements	A school district decides to rescind a policy concerning student conduct because a court ruling brings into question the legal status of the policy.
Interpretation and enforcement of policy statements	A school district has a policy concerning student clubs, which is interpreted differently by a new superintendent. Because principals disagree with the new interpretation, they request that the school board review the policy and how it is currently being enforced.

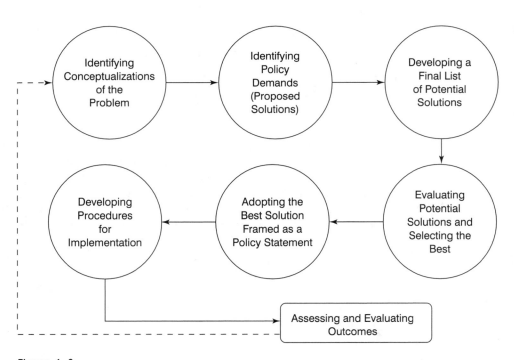

Figure 6–3
Stages for creating and implementing school district policy statements

Preadoption Tasks

The development of school district policy almost always begins with the identification of a problem. Problem identification can occur through planned, purposeful activities (e.g., needs assessment), or it can be the product of natural circumstances (e.g., an emergency or crisis). This fundamental first step to policy development is one of the most difficult and complex in the overall policy process. This is true because problems are not framed in a totally objective manner; rather, problem definitions represent the conceptions of the people who formulated them. For example, if a school district has a very high rate of teen pregnancies, not all individuals and groups are likely to see and define the situation in the same way. Some might view the problem from a social perspective, while others see it as an educational issue. The existence of multiple conceptualizations is critical because if the problem is improperly defined, then the proposed solution may be inherently flawed (Dery, 1984). Policymakers are more likely to define the problem correctly if they identify and analyze the various perspectives from which a problem can be viewed.

Conflicting perceptions not only facilitate the accurate framing of a problem, they also serve to inform the superintendent of alternative solutions that may be preferred by various constituencies. In the case of teen pregnancies, some may want the schools to establish health clinics; others may seek a greater emphasis on sex education; and still others may want firm disciplinary action designed to punish the students. Multiple problem definitions, together with the suggested solutions they generate, permit the superintendent to develop a final list of alternative proposals for dealing with the issue (Cochran et al., 1986).

Because these developmental stages are so interrelated, policymakers should have detailed information about each. For the superintendent, this means providing school board members with various formulations of the problem and various proposals for solutions. The superintendent can gather the needed information for this task by communicating with various individuals and groups who are affected by the issue being studied. While all board members may not be involved in preadoption deliberations, each should receive detailed information about this stage. Most often, this background information is conveyed in the rationale that accompanies the superintendent's policy recommendation.

Adoption and Implementation

Approval by the school board at one of its public meetings is the final stage of adoption of a policy. It is preceded by the process of analyzing alternative solutions and selecting the preferred course of action. Historically, school districts have not done this; rather, trial and error was the common path to establishing policy. Today superintendents are unlikely to have the luxury of trying alternative policies until they find the one that works best. Instead, they are turning to analytical procedures that attempt to predict the impact of proposed policies. The goal is to select the one option most likely to address the identified problem. After the preferred course of action is determined, a policy statement is developed and recommended to the school board for adoption. Individual board members may or may not be involved in analyzing the alternative solutions. Often the nature of the problem (and its potential political ramifications) determines whether board members actually participate in the formulation of the policy statement. The supporting rationale for a statement should include a clearly stated goal or set of goals, that is, the objectives that are anticipated as a result of implementing the policy.

Drafting the policy statement is a task requiring thought and care. One consideration pertains to the relationship between the proposed policy and existing policies. A certain number of policies are needed to direct administrative decisions, but problems emerge when a school district has too many policies or has policies that are too prescriptive. Thus, new policies should be evaluated with regard to necessity, fit (that is, the compatibility of the statement with existing policy), and effectiveness. If a proposed policy is redundant with regard to laws and state regulations or if it is a new interpretation of an existing policy, it is unnecessary. Effectiveness is an attribute that is associated with the following characteristics:

- *Completeness.* The statement is sufficiently instructive to communicate purpose and rationale.
- *Flexibility.* The statement has provisions for review and amendments; it can modified rather easily (Clemmer, 1991).
- *Clarity.* The statement is sufficiently clear to guide the decision maker and to inform those who may be affected; the statement will have high reliability in interpretation and implementation (Conran, 1989).
- *Brevity.* The statement includes essential information but is not unduly prescriptive or descriptive.
- *Stability.* The statement does not become less effective because of personnel changes (Rebore, 1984).

Between adoption and implementation decisions, the superintendent should consider how affected members of the public will be informed of the policy statement. Because school board meetings are usually covered by reporters, general dissemination of information typically occurs through the news media. In addition, it is advisable to provide all employees with some internal communication detailing the new policy and the reasons for its adoption. In many districts, each employee has a policy manual, and the adoption, revision, or rescinding of any policy statement requires the superintendent to distribute updated material.

Putting a policy statement into practice may entail several different functions. These tasks are associated with the following types of questions: Will additional funds be required? How will the policy be communicated? Does implementation require a plan of action? What measures will be required for enforcement? Implementation of decisions, a responsibility that clearly belongs to the superintendent and other administrators, plays a critical role in determining whether policy statements will achieve their intended objectives (Cochran et al., 1986). The common approach to ensuring proper implementation is the development of administrative rules and regulations. In addition, superintendents may hold briefing sessions for their administrative staffs after a policy statement has been approved.

Evaluation

As with all programmatic elements in education such as the curriculum, evaluation is often the most neglected process in policy making. Often policy statements are adopted, placed in the school district's policy manual, and literally forgotten until conflict emerges. Evaluation involves studying the impact of policy and determining whether the statement achieved its objective. To accomplish these tasks, the superintendent should decide how outcomes will be assessed and how the resulting information will be evaluated. If goals are not attained, revisions of the policy statement or a totally new policy statement may be in order.

In addition to determining whether a policy statement has served its intended purposes, the evaluation process may include a more general judgment regarding its impact on the school district. For instance, a policy on teacher absenteeism may have achieved the intended goal of reducing the district's expenditures for substitute teachers, but it also may have encouraged teachers and administrators to come to work when they were ill. Policy statements may have unanticipated consequences that are overlooked unless a global perspective is used in the evaluation process.

ADMINISTERING POLICY

The superintendent's role with regard to policy is most often described in the context of ensuring compliance. In this regard, the superintendent (or designees) has two essential responsibilities. The first involves the development and maintenance of a school district policy manual; the second relates to establishing rules and regulations that facilitate compliance.

The Policy Manual

Board policies should be maintained and codified in a notebook commonly called a policy manual. The Educational Policies Service of the National School Board Association is one agency that provides a classification system that may be used by school districts for their policy manuals. "The coding of policies and regulations is simply the process by which they are assembled, numbered, and indexed for ready access by all users" (Clemmer, 1991, p. 185). Thomas Glass (1992) wrote that a policy manual should be "a living document that serves as the chief guide for district management and, therefore, is a signpost for administrators, board members, teachers, and other staff who are responsible for carrying out their duties" (p. 237).

Since board policy serves to inform decision making, each employee in the school district ought to be provided with a policy manual or given reasonable access to one. Parents, students, and the general public also should have access to the manual. Access is accomplished by placing manuals in (1) public and school libraries, (2) administrative offices, (3) employee workrooms, and (4) community centers. To ensure accuracy, a system of disseminating updates (that is, additions, deletions, or revisions) needs to be established. Additionally, an annual check of manuals is advised to determine if the document remains complete and accurate (Conran, 1989).

Administrative Regulations

The term *regulation* has several meanings. From a legal perspective, the word is often used to describe nonconstitutional and nonstatutory rules promulgated by public departments, agencies, or bureaus (Imber & Van Geel, 1993). Within school districts, however, regulations commonly refer to administrative directives developed in conjunction with policy statements. Unlike policy statements, regulations are not formally adopted by the school board; typically they are approved by the superintendent. Because board policy and administrative regulations are intermingled in many districts, employees and others are often unable to determine who is responsible for having approved particular statements. This is especially likely if regulations are indiscriminately placed in the board's policy manual without being specifically designated as regulations.

Regulations can be written so as to give decision makers various degrees of freedom for enforcing policy. The following categories of regulations demonstrate this flexibility:

- *Mandatory.* These regulations are designed to accomplish absolute consistency in implementation; the emphasis is on prescribing action, not on encouraging administrative thinking.
- *Directory.* These regulations may suggest certain actions, but they typically allow some administrative discretion in application (e.g., to account for the idiosyncrasies of individual schools).
- *Discretionary.* These regulations permit wide discretion on the part of the administrator.
- *Proscriptive.* These regulations merely inform the administrator of prohibited actions or specify which selected personnel may take action (Clemmer, 1991).

As school improvement becomes more dependent on local policy and regulations, the superintendent's role is becoming more critical (Rubin, 1984). The trend of states giving local districts more latitude to determine instructional decisions heightens both the need for comprehensive planning and the need to interconnect policy and regulations with planning initiatives (Kowalski & Reitzug, 1993).

Occasionally a proposed regulation may have legal implications, and in these instances, the superintendent may prefer to have formal approval from the school board. For such regulations, it is important to determine if the regulation is consistent with policy and whether its approval changes the meaning or intent of policy. Once put into effect, regulations become an extension of policy. As such, they should be reviewed in the process of evaluating policy. In some instances, a policy may not achieve its intended goal just because the corresponding regulations are inappropriate or ineffective. Regulations may not be necessary for all board policy statements.

POLICY IN THE FUTURE

In recent years, the role of local school boards has been called into question. Critics have charged that these legislative bodies spend far too much time with political and noneducational matters, while largely ignoring critical policy issues that relate more directly to education (e.g., Danzberger, Kirst, & Usdan, 1992). Reformers fear that in school districts where this is true, efforts such as decentralization and shared decision making will be hindered by a centralized authority preoccupied with management and power struggles. Rather than promulgating policy that permits individual schools to address specific needs, and rather than permitting teachers and principals to perform as professionals, school boards may perpetuate institutional cultures that stress control and uniformity.

One alternative is to change the focus of local school boards by making them educational policy boards. This would require some deregulation at the state level permitting local districts to exercise greater discretion concerning what is taught and how it is taught. It would mean discontinuing expectations that school boards have quasi-judicial and fiduciary responsibilities. It would imply that boards concentrate on providing broad goals and directions for educational programs (Danzberger et al., 1992). While this proposed change may appear to be sweeping, it really is not too different from what is already advocated by the National School Boards Association. A 1992 statement issued by that organization recognizes four major school board functions: (1) envisioning a community's future educational program, (2) establishing organizational structures and community environments that facilitate the education program, (3) ensuring performance assessment systems to enhance accountability, and (4) serving as primary advocates for children (Fisher & Shannon, 1992).

A reconfiguration of local school boards into educational policy boards certainly has many consequences for superintendents. Professional leadership on the part of the superintendent in policy making is likely to become both more necessary and more visible (although board members would be expected to increase their knowledge in these areas). As school improvement becomes less of a state responsibility, superintendents are expected to issue recommendations that improve, not merely maintain, their school systems. Not only does this require them to take a more active role in policy formulation, but it also pushes them toward a risk orientation. However, politically, assertive leadership in policy formation on the part of the superintendent may not be interpreted positively by the public, and it is likely to increase political tensions between superintendents and school boards (Burlingame, 1988).

FOR FURTHER REFLECTION

This chapter examined the meaning of policy and how it can be developed, implemented, and evaluated at the school district level. These tasks are being redefined as a result of recent school improvement initiatives that are spurring reconsideration of the traditional policy-making roles assumed by school boards and superintendents. A shift in authority from the state to school districts, for instance, increases the importance of local policy statements. It also places greater responsibility on the superintendent to lead rather than manage.

As you consider what you read in this chapter, answer the following questions:

1. What restrictions are placed on a local school board with regard to setting policy?
2. What rationale can be provided for having the superintendent make recommendations on policy statements?
3. How do ideological values, institutional values, and personal values influence policy decisions that are adopted by school boards?
4. What are the primary differences between school board policy statements and administrative regulations?
5. Should regulations be placed in the school board's policy manual? Why or why not?
6. Who should receive a school board policy manual?
7. What is the purpose of policy statements?
8. From a legal perspective, must policies be in writing? Explain your answer.
9. To what extent do personal philosophy and experience influence the way individuals define problems and potential solutions?
10. What is the difference, if any, between regulations developed by a state department of education and regulations developed by a school district superintendent? How does each affect the scope of policy that may be developed by school boards?
11. Why is it advantageous to evaluate policy statements periodically?
12. As communities become more diverse, and as school governance becomes more decentralized, will the superintendent's role in policy formation become less political? Why or why not?

CASE STUDY

Bill Davis obtained his first superintendency in Buffalo Falls School District last July. After having been a middle school principal in another school district for 12 years, he accepted the top position in this predominately rural district of 1,350 students knowing that the previous superintendent had been dismissed. At the age of 47, he thought he would have to take some risks to acquire a superintendent's position. Although the district has had three superintendents in the last 9 years, Bill was impressed with the board members and the administrators he had met during his two interviews.

One of the areas that was never discussed during the interviews was school board policy. Bill assumed that the board had a policy manual similar to the one he was accustomed to using in his former job. However, when he started his new position, he discovered that this was not the case. Discussions with the board president, Bart Williams, indicated that the board never felt the need for a manual. The board had relied on official minutes to provide a record of policy statements. Bill convinced Mr. Williams that such a manual was beneficial for several reasons. First, it would provide a reference for administrators when making decisions; second, it would serve to inform employees and others in the school community of existing policy; third, it would provide a codified document that could be used periodically to evaluate policy.

Mr. Williams agreed that the development of a manual should be pursued. Both the superintendent and board president urged this action at the subsequent school board meeting. The 4 other board members supported the idea, and Bill was directed to move forward to develop the document.

After reviewing board minutes for the past 12 years, Bill was convinced that the board did not have policies in a number of areas. For example, there was no policy concerning the use of school buildings by community groups; there was no policy regarding school bus rental by outside agencies; there was no policy concerning an annual evaluation of the superintendent. Bill developed a list containing approximately 15 areas in which he believed the board needed to consider policy statements.

When Bill presented the list to Mr. Williams, the board president appeared surprised. He asked the superintendent, "Are you sure we need to make policy in all these areas? This seems like it will be a lot of work. We seem to have gotten along without policy statements all these years." Bill explained that these were areas in which problems were likely to arise. He said he would feel better if policy statements existed for these functions so that administrators could be guided uniformly in their decisions. Mr. Williams indicated that he wanted the board attorney, Madeline Iber, to look at the list.

The school attorney took the position that policy was not necessary in all of these areas since the board could be guided by state statutes and regulations. She told the 5 board members, "I think you can develop policy for everything on this list. However, I don't think it is necessary. Take the use of school buildings by community groups. You have always made a decision on this matter on a case-by-case basis."

Sensing that the board might reject the idea of developing these policies, Bill said, "Why don't I develop recommendations for policy statements in each of these areas? After you read them, then you can decide if you want to move forward."

Mr. Williams appeared puzzled. "What do you mean develop recommendations? Policy is the board's responsibility. The last two superintendents who were here complained about board members becoming involved in the day-to-day functions of administration. The state school boards' association indicates that the board should set policy and the superintendent should enforce it. If you start making recommendations on policy, won't we be creating the same problem but in a different direction?"

Bill responded, "I believe it is the superintendent's responsibility to make recommendations on every action that is pending before the school board except his own employment—and that includes policy matters. You don't have to follow my recommendations, but I think it is my duty to tell you what I believe is in the best interests of the school district."

Mr. Williams looked at the other 4 board members as if he was seeking someone else to speak. No one did. So he responded to the superintendent, "It's easy to say that we don't have to follow your recommendations, but if we don't, you may get mad. If we follow your recommendations, some in the community will charge that we're nothing but a 'rubber stamp' for the superintendent. Seems to me that we have problems almost any way we go. So, maybe we should continue as we always have."

"How is that?" Bill inquired.

"I mean, we probably don't need all these new policies, and we certainly do not need a recommendation from the superintendent every time we take a vote. Sure, there are educational matters that require your input—for example, adopting a mathematics textbook. But if we're deciding whether to let the local little league baseball team rent one of our buses, it seems that we can do that ourselves. Besides, I would think you would feel more comfortable not having to stick your neck out all the time. We have been through a lot of superintendents lately, and we would like to see you succeed. We would like to have you be our superintendent for a number of years."

The other board members acknowledged that they agreed with the board president. They also uniformly indicated that they would work hard not to interfere in the administration of the school system. One of them put it this way, "Some of our patrons are not going to be happy if they ask us to look into a matter and we tell them, 'Sorry, you have to talk to the superintendent.' Now if we have the superintendent directing us on every decision we make, how is the public going to look at us? We accepted some of the blame for the problems with the last two superintendents; we have agreed to correct our mistakes. I just think agreeing to have you make recommendations on virtually everything is a step in the wrong direction. It would restrict our ability to be objective."

Issues for Discussion

1. What would have been the advantages for Bill and the school board of discussing the issue of policy during the employment interviews?

2. Is Bill correct in his assertion about the role of the superintendent in policy making?

3. Could Bill have accomplished the goal of providing guidelines to his administrative staff by simply developing administrative regulations in all of these areas? Why or why not?

4. Given the board's commitment to stop interference in administrative functions, should Bill push the matter of policy at this time? Why or why not?

5. What are the advantages and disadvantages if a school board relies almost entirely on state statutes and regulations to provide guidelines for administrative decisions?

6. What would be the advantages of having a widely disseminated policy manual?

7. The board is willing to create a manual but reluctant to establish new policy statements. Should Bill move forward to establish the manual or insist that the project be delayed until the board approves new policies?

8. One avenue that Bill could pursue is to have an official from the state school boards' association and an official from the state superintendents' association talk to the board members about policy development. Would you advise him to do so?

9. Do you know whether the school district in which you reside (or work) has a policy manual? If so, is the document available to the general public?

10. Among the issues raised in this case are the superintendent's responsibility to make recommendations on policy matters and the board's promulgating policy statements in areas identified by the superintendent. How crucial is it for a superintendent to always make a recommendation?

11. If a school board promulgates policy without a superintendent's recommendation, what factors are likely to influence the outcome?

REFERENCES

Anderson, J. E. (1990). *Public policymaking: An introduction.* Boston: Houghton Mifflin.

Bauman, P. C. (1996). *Governing education: Public sector reform or privatization.* Boston: Allyn and Bacon.

Burlingame, M. (1988). The politics of education and educational policy: The local level. In N. Boyan (Ed.), *Handbook of research on educational administration* (pp. 439–452). New York: Longman.

Clemmer, E. F. (1991). *The school policy handbook.* Boston: Allyn and Bacon.

Cochran, C. E., Mayer, L. C., Carr, T. R., & Cayer, N. J. (1986). *American public policy* (2nd ed.). New York: St. Martin's Press.

Conran, P. C. (1989). *School superintendent's complete handbook.* Upper Saddle River, NJ: Prentice Hall.

Danzberger, J. P., Kirst, M. W., & Usdan, M. D. (1992). *Governing public schools: New times new requirements.* Washington, DC: Institute for Educational Leadership.

Dery, D. (1984). *Problem definition in policy analysis.* Lawrence, KS: University of Kansas Press.

First, P. F. (1992). *Educational policy for school administrators.* Boston: Allyn and Bacon.

Fisher, E. H., & Shannon, T. A. (1992). Some good ideas despite pernicious and unsubstantiated negativism. *Phi Delta Kappan, 74*(3), 230–231.

Glass, T. E. (1992). The district policy manual. In P. First (Ed.), *Educational policy for school administrators* (pp. 234–238). Boston: Allyn and Bacon.

Guthrie, J. W., & Reed, J. R. (1991). *Educational administration and policy: Effective leadership for American education* (2nd ed.). Boston: Allyn and Bacon.

Heise, M. (1995). The courts vs. educational standards. *Public Interest, 120,* 55–63.

Holdaway, E. A. (1983). Educational policy and educational research. *Education Canada, 23*(4), 10–14.

Imber, M., & Van Geel, T. (1993). *Education law.* New York: McGraw-Hill.

Katz, L. G. (1993). *Trends and issues in the dissemination of child development and early education knowledge.* (ERIC Document Reproduction Service No. ED 360 102)

Kogan, M. (1975). *Educational policy-making.* Hamden, CT: Linnet Books.

Kowalski, T. J., & Reitzug, U. C. (1993). *Contemporary school administration: An introduction.* New York: Longman.

Mansbridge, J. (1994). Public spirit in political systems. In H. Aaron, T. Mann, & T. Taylor (Eds.), *Values and public policy* (pp. 146–172). Washington, DC: Brookings Institute.

McCurdy, J. (1992). *Building better board-administrator relations.* Alexandria, VA: American Association of School Administrators.

Portney, K. E. (1986). *Approaching public policy analysis.* Upper Saddle River, NJ: Prentice Hall.

Rebore, R. W. (1984). *A handbook for school board members.* Upper Saddle River, NJ: Prentice Hall.

Rubin, L. (1984). Formulating education policy in the aftermath of the reports. *Educational Leadership, 42*(2), 7–10.

Sergiovanni, T., Burlingame, M., Coombs, F., & Thurston, P. (1992). *Educational governance and administration* (3rd ed.). Boston: Allyn and Bacon.

Shannon, T. A. (1994). The changing local community school board: America's best hope for the future of our public schools. *Phi Delta Kappan, 75*(5), 387–390.

Stout, R. T., Tallerico, M., & Scribner, K. P. (1994). Values: The "what?" of the politics of education. *Journal of Education Policy, 9*(5–6), 5–20.

Swanson, A. D., & King, R. A. (1997). *School finance: Its economics and politics* (2nd ed.). New York: Longman.

Chapter 7

Four Conceptions of the Superintendency

Key Concepts

✧ Role expectations for superintendents

✧ Superintendents as professional educators

✧ Superintendents as chief executive officers

✧ Superintendents as democratic leaders

✧ Superintendents as social scientists

✧ Professional knowledge and skills

✧ Role conflict

✧ Adjusting to changing needs

I deal characterizations of the superintendency found in textbooks rarely are found in practice. This is true not because the ideal is rejected, but rather because the actual work performed by superintendents is formed by a myriad of contextual and personal variables. These are conditions over which the superintendent has little or no control. The culture of a school district, the climate of a community, prevailing problems, and access to resources are examples of critical issues that influence leadership strategies, priorities, and other aspects of the superintendent's actual role.

The first chapter of this book presented four conceptions of the superintendency that have been prevalent since the Civil War:

1. The superintendent as scholarly leader
2. The superintendent as business manager
3. The superintendent as educational statesman in democratic schools (that is, democratic leader)
4. The superintendent as applied social scientist (Callahan, 1966)

The primary purpose of this chapter is to explore the meaning of these distinctively different, but interrelated, roles. In particular, attention is given to the roots of each conception and the degree to which each conception remains part of contemporary practice.

THE TEACHER OF TEACHERS

From the mid-1800s to approximately 1910, superintendents devoted much of their energy to issues such as maintaining orderly schoolhouses, supervising teachers, and implementing uniform curricula. As such, the role of instructional leader became the primary conception of the superintendency during that era. It was forged by prevailing conditions in society and within the teaching profession. Now in the context of school reform, this role is again receiving considerable attention. The forces responsible for its resurgence, however, are quite different from those that originally promoted the concept.

Formative Years

The school district superintendency rose out of the quest to make public education a uniform experience in America. Noted reformers, such as Horace Mann and Henry Barnard, envisioned the public schools providing a common education to the entire population—a goal that required centralized control, the elimination of local idiosyncrasies, and the standardization of curriculum. This philosophy was the foundation that molded public schools into incipient bureaucracies (Spring, 1990). In the formative years, during the early 1800s, powerful policymakers sought to institutionalize educational experiences as a means of assimilating students into American life, and this purpose had a profound effect on the role of the earliest school district superintendents.

As the position of superintendent evolved following the Civil War, instructional leadership became its primary and most visible responsibility. Near the turn of the century, for example, big-city superintendents often devoted much of their time to visiting schools and observing the work of teachers; rather than being consumed with management issues, they wrote frequently about philosophy, history, and pedagogy (Cuban, 1988). Clearly, those who ascended to the superintendency during this era perceived themselves to be teachers who had assumed supervisory responsibilities. This self-image was to be expected for several reasons. Schools during the late 1800s were often small structures (many being one-room schoolhouses) in which a teacher or several teachers performed a wide range of duties including building maintenance, resource management, and delivery of instruction. Distinctions between administration and teaching were not as pronounced as they are today. In addition, universities had not yet developed courses for the study of school administration. Thus, neither socialization in graduate school nor the culture of schools separated educators into specialized categories. For example, administrators and teachers belonged to the same professional organization (National Education Association).

However, superintendents were often among the most influential at defining codes of ethics and effective practice for the educational profession. Most significant in defining the role of the superintendent was perhaps the common school philosophy. Since the primary objective of this educational model was to standardize students' educational experiences through a common curriculum, administrators were expected to have a comprehensive understanding of pedagogy and to be able to determine whether teachers were properly following the state-prescribed courses for instruction.

The essence of the conception of superintendent as teacher-scholar was summarized in an 1890 report on urban superintendents that defined the responsibility of the emerging position:

> It must be made his recognized duty to train teachers and inspire them with high ideals; to revise the course of study when new light shows that improvement is possible; to see that pupils and teachers are supplied with needed appliances for the best possible work; to devise rational methods of promoting pupils. (Cuban, 1976a, p. 16)

However, even in these early years, there appeared to be tensions regarding the ideal role of superintendents. Many big-city superintendents in the late 19th century attempted to use professionalism as a shield against the intrusions of powerful business executives and city politicians into the schools. When confronted with a problem regarding management, these superintendents "resolved it by having the business aspects of administration handled either by the Board or by a subordinate official" (Callahan, 1966, p. 193).

Current Practice

Widespread efforts to reform public education have rekindled emphasis on the instructional leadership role of the school superintendent. Initiatives such as school-based management, deregulation, and competition with private schools raise expectations that superintendents can provide leadership to redesign curriculum and forge new instructional strategies relevant in an age of information (see Table 7–1). This responsibility requires collaboration and risk taking, but it also necessitates a mastery of the professional knowledge base. In this regard, the superintendent's role in school renewal has been likened to the symphony conductor who cannot provide essential leadership unless he or she has a mastery of the knowledge base in music (Kowalski & Oates, 1993).

Central to the revitalized interest in the superintendent's role as a teacher of teachers is professionalization. One by-product of the common school movement has been the creation of centralized systems of education that have restricted administrators and teachers to the task of implementing highly standardized cur-

Table 7–1
Reform-related initiatives contributing to a renewed interest in instructional leadership

Initiative	Example	Implications for Instructional Leadership
Higher expectations for student performance	Periodic testing, exit exams	Mandated programs for assessing student progress raise expectations that superintendents can adjust curricula and provide appropriate remediation programs; superintendents are expected to interpret and communicate issues of student progress to the community.
Higher expectations for teacher performance	Performance evaluation, inservice	Both performance evaluation and staff development become more essential; the superintendent is expected to provide growth and remedial opportunities for professional employees.
Decentralization	School-based management	Superintendents are expected to encourage, facilitate, and evaluate instructional innovations; as schools become less standardized in curricula, coordination and instructional supervision become more essential.
Controversial paradigms	Outcome-based education	New concepts for teaching and evaluation already have proven to be problematic for superintendents. As schools experiment with new programs, superintendents are expected to protect community values and provide direction for instructional decisions.
Competition for public schools	Vouchers, charter schools, choice	Many policy elites have accepted the argument that competition will force improvements in public schools; superintendents are expected to make public schools more competitive by improving instructional programs.

ricula. As a consequence, teachers have not been expected to act as true professionals (that is, practitioners who make individualized decisions related to the needs of their clients), and they have been socialized to roles that are guided by failure avoidance rather than by risk taking (Kowalski, 1995b).

Linda Darling-Hammond (1988) astutely noted that there have been two very different streams of reform policy based on dissimilar ideas of teaching and learning. One led policymakers to conclude that schools needed improved regulations, and the other led them to conclude that schools needed better teaching. Reliance on intensification mandates through much of the 1980s exemplified the belief that educational outputs, especially as measured by standardized tests, would increase if students and educators were simply required to do more of what they were already doing. This strategy was distinctly visible in new state laws increasing school years, school days, and graduation requirements; it was also obvious in legislation that made it more difficult for educators to become licensed (e.g., competency examinations for teachers and administrators, the elimination of life licenses). Largely because these efforts have failed to produce the intended improvements, critics now are pursuing an alternative strategy: they are calling for the removal of regulatory bonds that restrict the instructional decisions of educators (Hanushek, 1995).

Thus, the current impetus for superintendents to be scholars in the education profession is driven by motives substantially different from those that existed in the late 19th century. Today's superintendents are expected to increase their contact with teachers and individual schools not so much to ensure compliance with state-mandated curricula, but rather to determine if effective decisions are being made by teachers and principals functioning in quasi-deregulated environments.

Within this contemporary context, weighty questions emerge regarding the extent to which a superintendent should assume the role of a teacher of teachers. For instance, should the professionalization of educational administration draw administrators back into the teaching profession, or should it create even more distinct lines separating administration and teaching? Thomas Sergiovanni (1991) has argued that recent efforts to redefine the core technologies of administration and teaching present an opportunity to reinstitute a single profession. Taking the position that administration should once again become an integral part of the teaching profession rather than a distinct and supposedly superior function, he wrote the following:

> I propose that we build a more limited and hierarchically flatter profession of educational administration, one based on shared educational expertise with teachers, limited specialized knowledge in management and organization, and blurred role distinctions that open rather than restrict access to the profession. (p. 526)

While there are differing opinions regarding the extent to which superintendents should devote their time to working in the domains of teachers, there is little disagreement that issues such as decentralization and teacher professionalization have served to resurrect the role expectation of superintendent as teacher-scholar.

THE SUPERINTENDENT AS BUSINESS MANAGER

The second conception of the superintendency focused on the management of human and material resources. This role expectation was an outgrowth of industrial and demographic changes that occurred in the United States at the end of the 19th century and the beginning of the 20th century. People were moving from farms to cities, immigration was making the country more heterogeneous, and a new field of study—industrial management—was capturing the attention of academics, civic leaders, and policymakers. These developments and the continued emphasis on the concept of the common school experience contributed to expectations that superintendents be more than teachers of teachers.

The Era of Efficiency

The development of the conception of the superintendent as business manager began to emerge at the end of the 19th century as urban school districts came into being. Writing about this period, Larry Cuban (1976a) noted the following:

> By 1890 disagreement over the nature of the superintendency was expressed in speeches, articles and heated discussions (conducted, however, with genteel courtesy). The lines of argument crystallized over whether the functions of a big-city superintendent should be separated into two distinct jobs, i.e., business manager and superintendent of instruction. (p. 17)

The operation of multischool systems created responsibilities that increasingly compelled superintendents to reduce the amount of time they devoted to instructional functions.

Although there were many issues that came together to set the stage for the role expectation that superintendents become efficient business managers, four were especially significant. First, the population in the United States was moving toward urban areas. This transition necessitated large school districts in the cities—a unique challenge for American public education. In these institutions, the management of human and material resources was a far more demanding responsibility than it was in small, rural schools. Second, approximately 14 million immigrants, mostly from the poorest socioeconomic groups in eastern and southern Europe, had come to the United States between 1865 and 1900. The vast majority of them moved in big cities where they could obtain jobs as laborers, and their presence necessitated thousands of additional classrooms. Third, critics began to charge that public education was an inefficient enterprise. Particularly noteworthy in this regard was the report *Laggard in Our Schools*, authored by Leonard Ayres in 1909. This study used age- and grade-level distributions to support an argument that fiscal resources were being wasted. Although ignoring critical data, such as social and economic problems and the age at which children started school, Ayres succeeded in convincing many policymakers that public education was rife with inefficiency (Callahan, 1962). And fourth, superintendents did not possess much political power; hence, they were institutionally weak and unable to resist the demands placed on them (Callahan, 1966).

The conception of superintendent as business manager blossomed during the early 1900s. Perceived successes using scientific management to transform American industry, the presence of business leaders on big-city school boards, and the creation of management courses by education professors were especially influential in the development. More affluent members of society, in particular, became enamored with scientific management. And since more than half of all school board members in cities during that era were either from the business or professional classes (Butts & Cremin, 1953), urban superintendents were pushed in the direction of efficiency. As a result, the image of ideal superintendent changed from teacher-scholar to executive, and this conception reached its zenith toward the end of the 1920s (Griffiths, 1966).

Typical of the successful superintendents during that era was Ernest Hartwell, who eventually became superintendent of St. Paul, Minnesota, and Buffalo, New York. He embraced a business model of operation that emphasized efficiency and standardization, and he promised his patrons that his management would "assure greater returns in their tax investments in education" (Thomas & Moran, 1992, p. 28). Superintendents who accepted the role of business manager were often able to convince the public that administration had become a profession separate from teaching; more important, they were able to establish themselves as essential managers who acted in the public's interest by preventing teachers and students from being inefficient (Callahan, 1962; Thomas & Moran, 1992). The emergence of the management conception created role conflict for many superintendents in office during that era, especially those who believed that instructional leadership was their primary responsibility.

Current Practice

A simple distinction between leadership and management is that leaders are concerned with *what* should be done and managers are concerned with *how* things should be done (Kowalski & Reitzug, 1993). Clearly, school renewal efforts have increased demands for leadership on the part of superintendents, but have they correspondingly reduced expectations for management? There is no evidence that the public expects less from superintendents today with regard to efficiently controlling resources. If anything, the mounting cost of public education has intensified beliefs that administrators have a responsibility to avoid excessive spending and to eradicate waste.

Some of the most compelling evidence of persisting demands for the management role of the superintendent is found in the criteria for professional membership, both with regard to professional preparation and subsequent licensure. The criteria continue to stress management knowledge and skills (e.g., business management, personnel management, school facility management)—and for rather good reasons. School districts are multimillion dollar enterprises.

Experiences with attempted school reform reveal that the leaders of American industry continue to play a pivotal role in determining educational policy. The economic power of these individuals provides them access to public policymakers, who in turn set the parameters for school districts, and indirectly, the expectations for superintendents (see Figure 7–1). Unfortunately, these influential citizens often have exhibited a lack of understanding of public institutions and the process of education. Discussing common tensions between American government policy and American business, Laurence Iannaccone (1990) wrote:

> Ideologically, the two systems are profoundly different. The business system is philosophically and operationally exclusive; in its competitions it tends toward secrecy; it is highly differentiated in its statutes and fosters a concentration of power. The political system rests upon numbers of votes, is broadly equalitarian, and avidly seeks publicity in its competitions. (p. 162)

Justifications for the management role of the superintendent become muddled largely because of the differences between business and education. While efficiency is a reasonable expectation with regard to material resources, providing efficiency is less important as a standard for a superintendent than providing adequacy and equality with regard to educating the nation's youth. Policymakers, and those who influence their decisions, frequently have failed to consider these differences.

Today superintendents are less inclined to believe that emphasizing their role as business manager is sufficient for successful practice. Studies of practitioners conducted after 1950 often showed that superintendents in districts with larger enrollments were able to make adaptations in their behavior and time commitments when organizational or community conditions suggested that such changes would be advantageous (e.g., Burroughs, 1974; Cuban, 1976b; Tyack, 1972). That is to say, they were able to shift among their various roles to accommodate the most pressing needs of the day. Noting that contemporary practice

Figure 7–1
Pattern of influence of business and professional elites on the role of superintendent

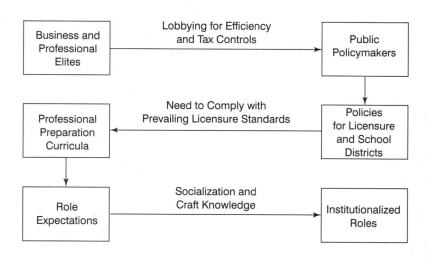

requires an intricate blend of management and leadership, Joseph Murphy (1991) observed the following:

> The image of the steely-eyed, top-down manager who has all the vision and all the answers must be coupled with a gentler, less heroic image . . . The effective superintendent, then, must be both a tough manager with solutions and a caring educator who listens—who is an active learner, an enabler, a catalyst who make good things happen for children. (p. 512)

Unquestionably, the conception of superintendent as business manager remains relevant, but in a contemporary context, this role is neither exclusive nor dominant.

THE SUPERINTENDENT AS DEMOCRATIC LEADER

There have been a myriad of attacks against the conception of superintendent as business manager. They occurred not because the business function was regarded as unimportant, but rather because of a belief that autocratic administration in schools was inappropriate. Like the business executives they emulated, many big-city superintendents successfully centralized power and authority in their organizations by claiming that their acts were necessary to achieve efficiency. However, by 1930, critics were attacking what they believed to be an obsession with efficiency; more specifically, they argued that public schools should practice and model democracy and develop symbiotic relationships with the communities in which they functioned.

The Rise of the Democratic Leader

The third conception of the superintendence, as democratic leader, emerged because of a combination of gnawing philosophical questions and pragmatic concerns about resources. Several scholars, such as John Dewey and George Sylvester Counts, were deeply troubled by the fact that critical education decisions were being made by relatively few individuals whose legitimate power was ensured by climates and cultures that they had created. In the highly bureaucratic school districts that had developed, both teachers and taxpayers were disenfranchised. Rather than modeling the democratic society they served, these school systems indirectly transmitted the message that efficiency was more important than either liberty or community. Commenting on school administrators' obsession with efficiency, George Counts (1952) wrote the following:

> The drive for mechanical efficiency has been unfortunate, not because efficiency is not desirable. The contrary is clearly the case. But efficiency is secondary to the ends that are to be served. It seems probable that the transference to education of a principle of operation developed in relation to the production of material things is a fundamental mistake. Unfortunately, moreover, many of the best minds of the profession have been engaged in the study of the mechanics of education at a time when the consideration of its substance has been imperative. Primary concentration on school

efficiency during a period of cultural crisis and transformation is both a form of escape and a way of compounding the troubles of the age. (pp. 30–31)

Such criticisms did not argue against the need for management; rather, they attempted to put management in its proper perspective.

The emergence of the conception of superintendent as democratic leader occurred at a time when resources were especially scarce. Common sense suggested that even the most efficient school districts would have less than they desired or needed; thus, school districts were increasingly forced to compete with other governmental agencies for limited resources. Prior to 1930, however, political involvement by superintendents was discouraged, largely because of the fear that the corruption that permeated the governmental structures in many large cities would seep into public education. Many leaders within the profession feared that playing politics would result in the city bosses taking control of the schools, a condition that would then allow mayors and city councils to exert considerable control over district employment decisions, taxes, and budgets. To a large extent, the change in disposition toward engaging in politics was a pragmatic decision; that is, aversions to political involvement began to lessen as school superintendents realized that they had to take part in the political arena to secure additional fiscal resources.

Gradually after 1920, leading figures in school administration developed the new conception of superintendent as statesman in professional journal articles and speeches. In 1925, for example, Jesse Newlon, who had served as superintendent of schools in Denver and as professor of education at Teachers College, Columbia, presented his vision of this new role at a national administrators' conference. He argued that being relegated to the role of bookkeeper was not in the best interest of the superintendency, and he called for democratic leadership that would permit teachers to participate more fully in addressing the needs of public education (Callahan, 1966). Inherent in this new conception was increased sensitivity to the importance of community and to the diversity of groups from which school superintendents needed both financial and moral support (Cuban, 1976b).

Transition to the conception of democratic leader intensified after World War II because of renewed interest in the meaning of community life in America. During this period the concept of community education was formalized in the writings of Ernest Melby, a prominent scholar who had served as dean of the College of Education at Northwestern University. Melby (1955) emphasized the centrality of community in strengthening the democratic process; he argued that the entire community was an educational resource. Perhaps most important, he believed that one purpose of public education was to address the needs and wants of all citizens. As such, public schools became the hub of action for a learning community.

Current Practice

In an article first published in *Saturday Review* in 1962, noted educator, William Van Til (1971) asked the profound question, Is progressive education obsolete? This article was written during a period when educators were absorbed by issues of technology, national defense (in the aftermath of Russian satellite *Sputnik*), and higher academic standards for the basic disciplines (e.g., mathematics, science). Responding to this fundamental question, Van Til argued that issues raised by educational progressives such as John Dewey, William Heard Kilpatrick, and Boyd Bode would never really die because they were fundamental to life and education in a democratic society:

> The central questions posed and the relevant contributions toward workable answers for our times made by such interpreters of the progressive movement in education are not obsolete. They must and will persist. In time, they will be embodied in the form of new proposals for modern education, new syntheses which build upon our predecessors, as is common in the world of ideas. The overanxious gravediggers, and those who currently give them comfort, will discover as this twentieth century moves along that what they have mistaken for a corpse is indeed very much alive. (Van Til, 1971, p. 17)

In the context of current reform, Van Til's insights have proven to be extremely prophetic.

The concept of democratic leader has two dimensions. Seeking to broaden participation in essential educational decisions is one; the other relates to managing a political environment created by that participation. The emergence of teacher unionism in the 1960s occurred at a time when interest in the conception of a democratic leader was waning. Collective bargaining challenged traditional power relationships in school districts, thus it became the source of considerable conflict (Kerchner, 1979). In large measure, teachers turned to unions because they felt powerless to influence local policies, even those policies that directly related to them (e.g., those pertaining to working conditions and compensation). Superintendents who continued to see themselves primarily as managers reacted angrily to collective bargaining laws and condemned teachers who joined the union. Others, however, were more diplomatic. They treated the conflict generated by collective bargaining as an opportunity to make their districts more democratic.

Most practitioners and scholars in school administration agree that the political aspects of practice have become greater in the past few decades. This fact is visible in both traditional and new frames of political activity for superintendents. In the former, superintendents continue to compete with other governmental agencies for scarce resources. The public simply expects school officials to be aware of and responsive to community demands (Tucker & Ziegler, 1980), and because of demographic changes in American society, these demands are often beyond the scope of traditional services provided to children in grades K–12 (e.g., adult education, recreation programs, and expansions of food and transportation services). Superintendents need to address community desires and weigh competing demands for services. In the emerging frame, superintendents face realities associated with diminishing control and altered power structures (Spring, 1985); state and federal governments, for example, have appropriated increasingly greater portions of decision-making policy from local boards of education (Iannaccone & Lutz, 1994). Consequently, contemporary superintendents, either individually or collectively, are prone to engage in lobbying activities designed to influence policy development beyond the scope of their school districts.

The role of democratic leader is also sustained by the desire to make schools truly democratic institutions. A society committed to democracy ought to have institutions and institutional leaders who symbolize the values and beliefs of this philosophy (Slater, 1994). Democracy is anchored in a faith in human intelligence and in the power of pooled and cooperative experience (Dewey, 1993). As such, schools cannot be truly democratic unless teachers, students, and parents are given legitimate opportunities to participate in determining their purpose and future programming. Spencer Maxcy (1995) summarized three critical values that shape the school as a democratic institution:

> . . . (a) a dedicated belief in the worth of the individual and importance of the individual in participation and discussion regarding school life; (b) a belief in freedom, intelligence, and inquiry; (c) a conviction that projected designs, plans, and solutions be results of individuals pooling their intelligence efforts within communities. (p. 73)

Research often shows that effective schools and districts are led by individuals who believe that schools should be inclusive (that is, schools that invite community participation) (Lezotte, 1994). Successful change is more likely if professionals within a school are bonded by a sense of community, making them more capable of developing a joint vision and working collectively to achieve it (Glickman, 1992).

THE SUPERINTENDENT AS APPLIED SOCIAL SCIENTIST

In the mid-1950s, the idealistic view of the superintendent as democratic leader was replaced by a new conception that viewed the superintendent as a combination educational realist and applied social scientist (Callahan, 1966). This image suggested that administrators needed to be well prepared academically in the behavioral sciences, so that they would be able to analyze and direct the behavior of individuals and groups. Disciplines such as psychology, anthropology, and sociology became important in the preparation of administrators; concepts such as systems analysis became an integral part of administrative courses.

Forces Shaping the Social Scientist Perspective

The integration of the behavioral sciences into the study and practice of school administration occurred in two ways. First, new courses were introduced into the curricula for degree and certification programs in educational administration; some of these were interdisciplinary in nature. Second, social science units, concepts, and research were incorporated into existing administration courses. A study of doctoral programs in school administration conducted in the mid-1960s found that all had included course work in the behavioral sciences either as separate courses or as part of existing courses. The disciplines most commonly included were sociology, economics, political science, psychology, and anthropology (Delacy, 1966).

Raymond Callahan (1966) cited four factors responsible for the replacement of the conception of the superintendent as statesman (democratic leader) by a new image as social scientist:

1. There was growing dissatisfaction with the idealistic notion of democratic administration; by 1962, the concept had apparently run its course.
2. The social sciences developed rapidly after World War II; there was widespread interest in applying this knowledge to the practice of school administration.
3. The Kellogg Foundation provided a considerable amount of fiscal resources to major universities to enhance teaching and research in school administration; some of this money was used to bring noted social scientists into educational administration programs.
4. A new round of criticism against public education emerged in the 1950s; school administrators responded by encouraging superintendents to become prepared in the social sciences.

Interest in the social sciences was predicated on the belief that superintendents could become more effective in practice by using theory to predict the consequences of their administrative actions. Such theories "attempt to determine what effective leaders do by identifying both the behavior of leaders and the effects leader behavior has on subordinate productivity and work satisfaction" (Razik & Swanson, 1995, p. 41). Interest in the social sciences was fueled by the belief that schools, like much of the world, were defined by underlying patterns of logic and order. In this vein, scholars pursued improved practice in school administration by presenting students with rational models that could be applied to problematic situations (Owens, 1998). Administration textbooks published in the 1950s and 1960s exhibited a growing interest in theory as a primary guide to practice (Glass, 1986).

Especially relevant for the superintendency was the development of planning models based on the assumption that school districts were integrated systems. Perhaps the best-known integrated paradigm is systems analysis. During the 1970s, systems analysis models were used rather widely to study problems and chart institutional change in schools. Interest in such paradigms heightened interest in the behavioral sciences as a component of school administration (Milstein & Belasco, 1973).

Current Practice

The role of superintendent as social scientist remains essential, but it has been revised since 1980. Prior to that time, the infatuation with the behavioral sciences was associated with the belief that theory could both explain organizational behavior and predict the consequences of administrative decisions. Much of the research used for theory building in the period of 1940 to 1980 was based on traditional laboratory-type methods designed to ensure unbiased outcomes. Largely ignored were the insightful caveats of several scholars (e.g., Rudner, 1954) who had pointed out that such efforts necessarily entailed value judgments that almost always affected objectivity. Describing this period of organizational studies (commonly called the Modern era), Robert Owens (1998) wrote the following:

> . . . at least until the mid-twentieth century, the pervasive assumption in Western cultures was that the world we live in must be characterized by some underlying patterns of logic, system, and order. From that assumption arose the belief that these patterns could be discovered only by using systematic methods of study, generally called the scientific method, that were controlled and circumscribed by strict rules of procedure and evidence. . . . Claims to knowing based on other rules of procedures and evidence could be dismissed as intuitive, anecdotal, or otherwise unscientific and therefore not to be taken terribly seriously. (p. xix)

Commenting on the consequences of the behavioral science era, Joseph Murphy (1995) noted the following: "Knowledge was something that was created at the university and applied in the field. It was a nonrecursive relationship" (p. 69).

Attacks upon social science commonly stemmed from a rejection of the assumption of rationality. That is to say, critics were unwilling to accept that schools were rational organizations and that administrators always acted rationally. Technical rationality is an epistemology of practice that evolved from positivist philosophy (Schon, 1987). In the real world of practice, superintendent's actions are usually affected by biases related to the acquisition of information, the processing of information, and selection of responses to problems (Wagner, 1993).

The social science approach also has been criticized as having an androcentric bias (Hoy & Miskel, 1996; Owens, 1998). That is, research and the development of theory have been influenced by male perspectives of the world, management, power, and so on. "Androcentric bias occurs when male experience is treated as the norm, whereas female realities are not considered or are relegated to the abnormal" (Epp, Sackney, & Kustaski, 1994, p. 451). Studies of popular theories and articles published in respected journals have lent support to the contention that such a bias has existed (e.g., Epp et al., 1994; Shakeshaft, 1989; Shakeshaft & Hanson, 1986).

Still others practitioners have rejected the social science approach because they view the perspective as being too theoretical and essentially detached from the day-to-day problems they encounter.

Donald Schon (1987), a scholar who has written extensively on professions and professionals, has attacked the notion that technical knowledge is sufficient for effective practice. In developing the concept of reflective practice—a process of integrating experiences into one's professional knowledge base—he noted that outstanding practitioners in all professions eventually confront problems that defy scientific theory. Accordingly, the most outstanding practitioners are not commonly described as having more professional knowledge than their colleagues, but rather their higher level of performance is associated with factors such as "wisdom," "talent," "intuition," or "artistry" (Schon, 1987, p. 13). These attributes fall within the craft domain of school administration; they are acquired by personal experience and working with masters in the craft. They are honed through reflection as the practitioner integrates experiences into his or her knowledge base.

Today superintendents are expected to possess a sufficient knowledge base to enter practice. Arguably, they need to understand society, communities, organizational behavior, and their own performance. However, practice has been redefined as an intricate balance between science and craft. If the superintendency were still conceived as a technician's job, then scientific knowledge accumulated in graduate school would still be deemed as sufficient for effective practice. Even the common sense of many school board members, however, leads them to conclude that experience and professional growth attained through practice make a critical difference in superintendent performance.

SYNTHESIS

Since the end of the 19th century, each of the four conceptions of the role of superintendent discussed in this chapter has enjoyed a period of dominance. However, even in the earliest years, aspects of each conception of the role could be discerned. This remains true in contemporary practice, although which conception is dominant varies from district to district. Contextual variables, such as the size of a school district, prevailing climate and culture, the extent of state deregulation, and the extent of decentralization, blend to shape specific role expectations for each superintendent. Actual roles are also significantly influenced by personal leadership styles and philosophies.

In the early decades of the 20th century, outstanding superintendents were often characterized by their personal power and by that conferred on them by their position. They were able to exert considerable influence over other school district employees simply because they were the top bosses. Today the ability of one individual to exert so much control is less likely. Schools and society are more complex, and philosophically, fewer Americans are willing to allow any one individual to have absolute power. However, this does not mean the superintendents are inconsequential to school reform and improvement. As Susan Moore Johnson (1996) noted, "the fact that positional power is limited does not mean that it is unimportant or useless, for while people may be ambivalent about formal leaders, they do not ignore them" (p. 11). The challenge for the superintendent is to integrate the various roles so that professionalism, management, politics, and social issues are balanced in day-to-day activities.

There are several variables that are especially noteworthy with regard to the teacher-scholar conception. The trend toward granting districts greater freedom to determine curricula and instructional approaches is based on the belief that local officials and teachers can make educational experiences more relevant to local needs and wants. In turn, such decisions are expected to improve student outcomes. Even though superintendents are not likely to decide curriculum and instruction matters unilaterally, they will be expected to be highly competent in the knowledge base of the teaching profession—a prerequisite permitting them to evaluate instructional decisions made by others within the school district. However, expectations for superintendents to be teacher-scholars are also enlarged by the movement toward teacher professionalization and the uncertainty surrounding schools of the future. Technology, for example, already has vastly changed how information is accessed and used in many schools. As new curricula are adopted and as new school buildings are erected—especially in smaller-enrollment school districts having a limited number of administrators—the superintendent's knowledge of pedagogical research and theory is crucial. Likely to emerge are new images or role expectations for superintendents. These might include being coach and facilitator to principals and teachers—directly assisting them with their personal practices.

The conception of superintendent as business manager has changed substantially over the years, but management clearly remains a fundamental aspect of the position. It is often tempting to suggest that managerial skills are incidental to administration, but in truth, they are not. School districts are multimillion dollar enterprises, and many superintendents fall into public disfavor if they are perceived as incompetent managers. Issues such as budgeting, facility development, transportation, and control of pupil conduct remain highly visible aspects of public education. Most states continue to require a substantial amount of graduate study in management-related areas of school administration, reflecting both the expectations of the public and the realties of operating a complex public institution.

As the United States becomes a more diverse society, both conflict and politics become more intense in public education. A recent study of urban superintendents, for example, revealed that both competition for inadequate resources and poverty among families of schoolchildren were critical problems faced by these administrators (Kowalski, 1995a). In many larger school systems, community power structures are changing, there is growing uncertainty regarding who will actually control public education, and multiple—and often conflicting—reform agendas have surfaced. If anything, these conditions have augmented past expectations that the superintendent should be able to work effectively in political settings and to resolve conflict that reduces the productivity of the school district.

However, political behavior continues to have negative connotations for many in the profession. A study of four females who left the superintendency in the early 1990s, for example, found that they almost always used the term *politics* negatively when talking about their administrative experiences (Tallerico, Poole, & Burstyn, 1994). Frequently, political behavior has been cast as the antithesis of professional behavior, leading some to believe that politics has no place in school administration. In truth, political behavior is a common element of decision making in democratic institutions. Over the past decade, greater emphasis has been given to the moral and ethical dimensions of decision making that occur largely within a political context. If current policy trends toward deregulation and decentralization continue, superintendents also will be expected to market school districts within a competitive environment. This task requires managerial, communication, and political skills.

The conception of superintendent as social scientist also has changed considerably, largely because perspectives of social science have changed. Today's practitioners are still expected to be quite knowledgeable in areas such as organizational theory, motivation, and communication. But the theories they use in practice are no longer treated as infallible principles that can be applied across all institutions with equal degrees of effectiveness. Hence, social science remains relevant to practice, but the context in which it is studied is being altered.

> The challenge of the twenty-first century is clear. Social science theory must become more refined, useful, and situationally oriented. Organizational theory must explain rational, nonrational, and irrational elements of behavior, as well as environmental constraints on organizational life. (Hoy & Miskel, 1996, p. 23)

Alone, social science theories have limited value to superintendents. But when these theories are integrated with the professional knowledge base of teaching, the contexts of communities, schools, and people, and prevailing political conditions, they provide invaluable guides to practice.

In the final analysis, superintendents are expected to fulfill, albeit to different degrees, each of the four conceptions discussed in this chapter. More important, they are expected to make transitions among these roles as conditions in their work environment and society change. Despite lingering misconceptions, the days of the authoritarian superintendent are over. No superintendent is likely to succeed by imposing a personal vision on a school district; a critical mass of support makes meaningful change more probable (Lezotte, 1994). In the current climate of uncertainty, "leadership requires deep convictions, strong commitments, and clear ideas about directions for changes in the form and content of schooling" (Starratt, 1996). Superintendents must not only be able to bring diverse groups together, they must provide these groups with direction, facilitate their efforts, and build support for the goals they establish.

Joseph Murphy (1995) identified three emerging trends within the professional knowledge base of school administration. They include (1) a greater emphasis on ethics and values, (2) deeper understandings of the social contexts of schooling, and (3) acceptance of the craft dimensions of practice. Each is serving to refine concepts of ideal practice. A growing number of scholars within the profession (e.g., Griffiths, 1995) are calling for traditional subjects, such as organizational theory, to be studied from multiple perspectives. The purpose is not to train practitioners to apply the best technical solutions, but rather to educate a new generation of practitioners who will be able to apply theoretical and craft knowledge in a contextual manner. Commenting on professional preparation, Robert Donmoyer (1995) noted the following:

> . . . our seminal question should be a pedagogical rather than an epistic one. We should not be asking: What is our knowledge base? The question, though intellectually interesting, is ultimately unanswerable and, hence, a distraction. Instead our primary

Figure 7–2
Factors influencing the integration of role expectations

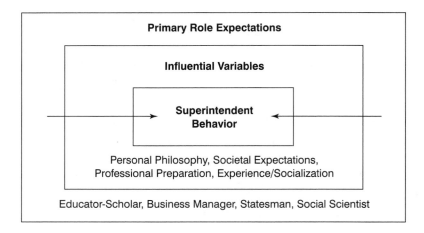

The superintendent's world of practice is not defined by static problems and pre-determined solutions, but rather by uncertainty and change.

> question should be: What sorts of experiences should our students have; what experiences will best prepare them for the complex, idiosyncratic, affect-laden world they will encounter when they attempt to do administrative work in educational settings? (p. 93)

The superintendent's world of practice is not defined by static problems and pre-determined solutions, but rather by uncertainty and change.

The degree to which individual practitioners incorporate each of the four roles into their own behavior is determined by several critical variables (see Figure 7–2). The more readily recognized include individual philosophy, societal expectations, and previous professional experiences (socialization). Another important, but frequently ignored variable, is professional preparation. Among the hundreds of institutions educating prospective superintendents, there is substantial variance in curricula, instructional approaches, enrollment requirements (full-time or part-time), and faculty philosophies. Consequently, orientation to practice is less uniform than in other professions (e.g., medicine).

FOR FURTHER REFLECTION

The purposes of this chapter were to review the historical development of four distinct conceptions of the superintendency and to place these conceptions within the context of modern practice. Both ideal and real roles of administrators are shaped by an intricate mix of public expectations, professional preparation, socialization in school settings, and past practice. This is why understanding the evolution of the superintendency is so essential for practitioners.

As you consider what you read in this chapter, answer the following questions:

1. Prior to the 20th century, what academic preparation was completed by most individuals who became superintendents? Did the content and extent of their professional preparation affect their perceptions of their jobs?

2. When courses and degrees in school administration emerged in the early 1900s, why did many professors and superintendents desire to establish administration as a profession separate from teaching?

3. In the area of organizational theory, what is meant by *assumptions of rationality*? To what extent has the study of social science changed in the area of professional administration?

4. What is meant by an androcentric bias in educational administration?

5. Should superintendents be prepared to be politicians? Why or why not?

6. What is meant by *craft knowledge*? How is craft knowledge acquired in school administration?

7. Is it realistic to believe that a modern-day superintendent can successfully meet expectations in all four roles? Explain your answer and its implications for superintendents.

8. In your opinion, which conceptions have become more important in the past 5 years? Which have become less important?

9. Considering the superintendents with whom you have worked, how do you characterize them according to the four conceptions presented in this chapter?

10. Recently, several large school districts have employed superintendents who have no professional background or academic preparation in education. They have come from the world of business and economics. What arguments can you make to either defend or attack the decisions of the school boards to hire such individuals?

11. As you look to the future, which conceptions do you believe will be dominant in the next decade?

12. The literature in recent years has included a number of articles about teacher professionalization. What does the term *teacher professionalization* mean? How could teacher professionalization affect the role of superintendents?

13. What is your conception of the ideal superintendent? What experiences in your life have contributed to this conception?

CASE STUDY

Dr. Nancy Jones was beginning her 8th year as superintendent of Marsh Creek School District, a school system with 2,350 pupils located in a small midwestern city. Prior to assuming this position she was a 3rd grade teacher for 13 years and an elementary school principal for 5 years in a different school system. Largely because she devoted much of her time visiting schools and working in the areas of curriculum and instruction, she was perceived in the community to be an instructional leader. She openly admitted that responsibilities such as budgets, transportation, and food services were managed by her assistant superintendent, Jack Mason.

Before the current school year, the 7 school board members had given Nancy glowing evaluations. They praised her dedication to academic programs, her positive relationships with teachers and the teachers' union, and her friendly, candid leadership style. These evaluations were also influenced by the fact that students in the district had done quite well on the state achievement tests. Even though Nancy had little involvement in financial matters, and even though she maintained a low profile in the community, the board saw her as an outstanding educational leader.

During the last year, three critical changes occurred in Marsh Creek. Simmons Manufacturing, the largest industry in the community, closed its plant. In addition to nearly 600 people losing their jobs, the plant accounted for approximately 15% of the school district's assessed valuation. The business manager predicted a substantial increase in the tax rates for the next fiscal year.

The second change involved the election of 2 new school board members. George Binder owns and operates a small farm; Ken Atwell owns a restaurant in Marsh Creek. They defeated incumbents who had been on the board for 6 years. The school board election occurred just 5 weeks after the announcement concerning Simmons Manufacturing, and the successful candidates campaigned on the promise of not raising taxes.

The third change pertained to the teachers' union. A slate of new officers was elected, vowing to increase the level of teachers' salaries. Salaries in Marsh Creek were about 12% below the state average. Upon taking office, the new president of the teachers' union informed Dr. Jones that collective bargaining would become much more difficult unless she and the board committed to substantial increases in teacher salaries.

Each of these changes affected the mood of Marsh Creek. Many residents were now unemployed; the tax base of the school district had dropped appreciably; teachers were demanding higher salaries; and the 2 new board members were fiscal conservatives committed to holding down taxes. Conflict among the 7 school board members became visible at meetings. A concerned group of taxpayers was attending every school board meeting urging the board to institute budget reductions to offset the loss in assessed valuation. In its initial package of demands, the teachers' union requested a 15% across the board increase in salaries.

Dr. Jones recognized that she was facing serious fiscal problems. At a meeting with her administrative staff, 5 principals and the business manager, she asked Jack Mason to chair a committee to develop a list of potential budget cuts for the next fiscal year. She indicated that she would not become involved in the committee's deliberations so that she could objectively evaluate their recommendations.

The administrators grew increasingly uncomfortable with the task they were given. They thought they had been placed in a "no win" situation. No matter what they recommended, some group would be dissatisfied. Their discomfort was not eased by the fact that Dr. Jones continued to spend much of her time working with curriculum committees and teachers. One principal's comments summarized the feelings of most administrators in the district,

"Sure, she's still doing positive things with teachers while we've been asked to cut things from the budget. I think she ought to get her hands dirty."

Approximately 2 months after the special committee was formed, things only got worse:

- The high school principal and the business manager resigned to take positions in other school districts. Both were scheduled to leave the school district at the end of their current contracts on June 30.

- Talks with the teachers' union had not progressed, and the rhetoric was becoming more hostile. Jack Mason, who had been the board's chief negotiator, recommended that the board appoint someone else to perform this task. This would ensure continuity if a contract had not been negotiated by June 30.

- The 2 new board members openly criticized Dr. Jones for suggesting that budget cuts may not be the solution to the school district's problems. Although she noted that potential cuts were being studied, she argued that tax increases would be in the best interest of the students.

- Several of the principals contacted school board members to complain about having to serve on the budget-cutting committee. They felt they were going to be blamed for eventual reductions.

- Dr. Jones received only 3 applications for the position of business manager; all 3 candidates were inexperienced.

- The budget for the school district had to be developed in July. Mr. Mason said he would help in its preparation, but he told Dr. Jones he would not make decisions about budget cuts.

Deeply concerned by these events, the school board president scheduled an executive session to discuss an evaluation of Dr. Jones. In each of the previous years, Dr. Jones had received glowing evaluations from the board members. While she anticipated that they would be concerned about the financial problems facing the district, she did not expect that they would be critical of her performance. However, at least four of them were. In reviewing her performance over the past year, the board president indicated that (1) she had failed to exert responsible management, (2) she had spent far too much time visiting classrooms, and (3) she should have been working more directly with her administrative staff to identify potential budget cuts. Finally, she was told that her comments about tax increases exhibited an insensitivity to economic conditions in the community. The board president suggested that her lack of involvement in community matters was contributing to a negative image of the school system, especially among the business owners in Marsh Creek.

Dr. Jones was shocked by the evaluation. Not one word was mentioned about her contributions to academic programs. She responded to the board by saying,

"I think you are blaming me for things that are beyond my control. If anything, I have worked harder this year than in the past. The very things you found to be outstanding in the past now seem to be unimportant. This evaluation is a surprise and a disappointment."

Two of the board members expressed continued confidence in the superintendent, but they were clearly in the minority. Dr. Jones was informed that she would not receive a salary increase for the next school year; she was directed to assume leadership of the committee that was studying budget cuts; she was directed to start attending collective bargaining meetings. The board president indicated that Mr. Mason had agreed to continue as the chief negotiator until his departure, but either the superintendent or the new business manager would have to assume this role after June 30. The meeting concluded with the board president making the following statement,

"Nancy, we want you to be successful. We are facing serious problems that require us to move in different directions. I think there is room for compromise on the tax issue. I think most of us can live with a combination of tax increases and budget cuts. But you're not going to have Jack Mason, and that means you are going to have to change the way you spend your time. Even though you have been here a long time, there are many influential people who say they really don't know you as a person. I hope you take all of this to heart. We will help in any way we can."

Issues for Discussion

1. Is it uncommon for a superintendent in a district of this size to devote a majority of time to instructional leadership activities? On what knowledge do you base your answer?

2. Why do you believe Dr. Jones has chosen to allocate her time this way?

3. Do you agree with the judgment that Dr. Jones should be spending more time in the community? How could this have made a difference in the problems she faces?

4. Assess the strategy of creating a committee responsible for recommending budget cuts. Would you have done things differently?

5. To what extent should the school board assume responsibility for the problems presented in this case?

6. Using the four conceptions of the superintendency presented in this chapter (teacher-scholar, business manager, democratic leader, and social scientist), identify role expectations from each that relate to this case. To what extent did the superintendent address these role expectations?

7. If you were Dr. Jones, how would you respond to the evaluation?

8. What additional information would you like to have about this community if you were to advise Dr. Jones about her future actions?

9. Are there any risks for Dr. Jones if she follows the board's directives? If so, what are they?

10. In a district of this size with a full-time business manager, should the superintendent become directly involved fiscal management? If so, in what way?

REFERENCES

Burroughs, W. A. (1974). *Cities and schools in the gilded age.* Port Washington, NY: Kennikat.

Butts, R. F., & Cremin, L. A. (1953). *A history of education in American culture.* New York: Henry Holt and Company.

Callahan, R. E. (1962). *Education and the cult of efficiency.* Chicago: University of Chicago Press.

Callahan, R. E. (1966). *The superintendent of schools: An historical analysis.* (ERIC Document Reproduction Service No. ED 0104 410)

Counts, G. S. (1952). *Education and American civilization.* New York: Bureau of Publications, Teachers College, Columbia University.

Cuban, L. (1976a). *The urban school superintendent: A century and a half of change.* Bloomington, IN: Phi Delta Kappa Educational Foundation.

Cuban, L. (1976b). *Urban school chiefs under fire.* Chicago: University of Chicago Press.

Cuban, L. (1988). *The managerial imperative and the practice of leadership in schools.* Albany, NY: State University of New York Press.

Darling-Hammond, L. (1988). The futures of teaching. *Educational Leadership, 16*(3), 4–10.

Delacy, W. J. (1966). *The social sciences, an aspect of school administrator preparation.* (ERIC Document Reproduction Service No. ED 010 912)

Dewey, J. (1993). Democracy and educational administration. *Planning and Changing, 22*(3–4), 134–140.

Donmoyer, R. (1995). A knowledge base for educational administration: Notes from the field. In R. Donmoyer, M. Imber, & J. Scheurich (Eds.), *The knowledge base in educational administration: Multiple perspectives* (pp. 74–95). Albany, NY: State University of New York Press.

Epp, J. R., Sackney, L. E., & Kustaski, J. M. (1994). Reassessing levels of androcentric bias in Educational Administration Quarterly. *Educational Administration Quarterly, 30*(4), 451–471.

Glass, T. E. (1986). An overview: School administration texts 1820–1985. In T. Glass (Ed.), *An analysis of texts on school administration 1820–1985.* Danville, IL: The Interstate.

Glickman, C. D. (1992). The essence of school renewal: The prose has begun. *Educational Leadership, 50*(1), 24–27.

Griffiths, D. E. (1966). *The school superintendent.* New York: Center for Applied Research in Education.

Griffiths, D. E. (1995). Theoretical pluralism in educational administration. In R. Donmoyer, M. Imber, & J. Scheurich (Eds.), *The knowledge base in educational administration: Multiple perspectives* (pp. 300–309). Albany, NY: State University of New York Press.

Hanushek, E. A. (1995). Moving beyond spending fetishes. *Educational Leadership, 53*(3), 60–64.

Hoy, W. K., & Miskel, C. G. (1996). *Educational administration: Theory, research, and practice* (5th ed.). New York: McGraw-Hill.

Johnson, S. M. (1996). *Leading to change: The challenge of the new superintendency.* San Francisco: Jossey-Bass.

Iannaccone, L. (1990). Callahan's contribution in the context of American realignment politics. In W. Eaton (Ed.), *Shaping the superintendency: A reexamination of Callahan and The Cult of Efficiency* (pp. 135–164). New York: Teachers College Press.

Iannaccone, L., & Lutz, F. W. (1994). The crucible of democracy: The local arena. *Journal of Education Policy, 9*(5–6), 39–52.

Kerchner, C. T. (1979). The impact of collective bargaining on school governance. *Education and Urban Society*, *11*(2), 181–207.

Kowalski, J., & Oates, A. (1993). The evolving role of superintendents in school-based management. *Journal of School Leadership*, *3*(4), 380–390.

Kowalski, T. J. (1995a). *Keepers of the flame: Contemporary urban superintendents*. Thousand Oaks, CA: Corwin.

Kowalski, T. J. (1995b). Preparing teachers to be leaders: Barriers in the workplace. In M. J. O'Hair & S. J. Odell (Eds.), *Educating teachers for leadership and change: Teacher education yearbook III* (pp. 243–256). Thousand Oaks, CA: Corwin.

Kowalski, T. J., & Reitzug, U. C. (1993). *Contemporary school administration: An introduction*. New York: Longman.

Lezotte, L. (1994). The nexus of instructional leadership and effective schools. *School Administrator*, *51*(6), 20–23.

Maxcy, S. J. (1995). *Democracy, chaos, and the new school order*. Thousand Oaks, CA: Corwin.

Melby, E. O. (1955). *Administering community education*. Upper Saddle River, NJ: Prentice Hall.

Milstein, M. M., & Belasco, J. A. (1973). *Educational administration and the behavioral sciences: A system approach*. Boston: Allyn and Bacon.

Murphy, J. (1995). The knowledge base in school administration: Historical footings and emerging trends. In R. Donmoyer, M. Imber, & J. Scheurich (Eds.), *The knowledge base in educational administration: Multiple perspectives* (pp. 62–73). Albany, NY: State University of New York Press.

Murphy, J. T. (1991). Superintendents as saviors: From the Terminator to Pogo. *Phi Delta Kappan*, *72*(7), 507–513.

Owens, R. C. (1998). *Organizational behavior in education* (6th ed.). Boston: Allyn and Bacon.

Razik, T. A., & Swanson, A. D. (1995). *Fundamental concepts of educational leadership and management*. Upper Saddle River, NJ: Merrill/Prentice Hall.

Rudner, R. (1954). Remarks on value judgments in scientific validation. *Scientific Monthly*, *79*, 151–153.

Schon, D. A. (1987). *Educating the reflective practitioner*. San Francisco: Jossey-Bass.

Sergiovanni, T. J. (1991). The dark side of professionalism in educational administration. *Phi Delta Kappan*, *72*(7), 521–526.

Shakeshaft, C. (1989). *Women in educational administration* (updated ed.). Newbury Park, CA: Sage.

Shakeshaft, C., & Hanson, M. (1986). Androcentric bias in the "Educational Administration Quarterly." *Educational Administration Quarterly*, *22*(1) 68–92.

Slater, R. O. (1994). Symbolic educational leadership and democracy in America. *Educational Administration Quarterly*, *30*(1), 97–101.

Spring, J. (1985). *American education: An introduction to social and political aspects* (3rd ed.). New York: Longman.

Spring, J. (1994). *The American school: 1642–1990* (3rd ed.). New York: Longman.

Starratt, R. J. (1996). *Transforming educational administration: Meaning, community, and excellence*. New York: McGraw-Hill.

Tallerico, M., Poole, W., & Burstyn, J. N. (1994). Exits from urban superintendencies: The intersection of politics, race, and gender. *Urban Education*, *28*, 439–454.

Thomas, W. B., & Moran, K. J. (1992). Reconsidering the power of the superintendent in the progressive period. *American Educational Research Journal*, *29*(1), 22–50.

Tucker, H. J., & Zeigler, L. H. (1980). *Professionals versus the public: Attitudes, communication, and responses in school districts*. New York: Longman.

Tyack, D. (1972). The "One Best System": A historical analysis. In H. Walberg & A. Kopan (Eds.), *Rethinking urban education* (pp. 231–246). San Francisco: Jossey-Bass.

Van Til, W. (1971). Prologue: Is progressive education obsolete? In W. Van Til (Ed.), *Curriculum: Quest for relevance* (pp. 9–17). Boston: Houghton Mifflin.

Wagner, R. K. (1993). Practical problem-solving. In P. Hallinger, K. Leithwood, & J. Murphy (Eds.), *Cognitive perspectives on educational leadership* (pp. 88–102). New York: Teachers College Press.

Chapter 8

Leadership in the School District

Key Concepts

✧ Concept of organizational vision

✧ Developing vision for a school district

✧ Long-range planning

✧ Strategic planning

✧ Integrated and linear planning

✧ Contingency planning

✧ Concept of an administrative team

✧ Recruiting and selecting administrators

✧ Building trust

✧ Instructional leadership in the superintendency

✧ Barriers to instructional leadership

A recurring theme in this book is that modern practice in the superintendency has become much more focused on institutional development. Unlike their predecessors who devoted much of their time to managing and maintaining long-standing values and goals, current school superintendents are more likely to be innovators; they are more likely to be risk takers, motivators, and facilitators. In modern practice, leadership has not replaced management; rather, leadership has become a higher priority.

Two points should be noted about the content of this chapter. First, the focus here is on a superintendent's leadership functions in the school district; a subsequent chapter (chapter 11) addresses leadership in the community. Second, not all functions of the superintendency can be neatly categorized as leadership (deciding what should be done) or management (deciding how things should be done). This chapter is devoted to discussing responsibilities that are highly related to school district renewal. The next chapter, on management, more clearly addresses administrative functions, such as fiscal management, personnel management, and facility management.

Central to the superintendent's role of providing leadership within the school district are responsibilities associated with renewing schools to ensure that they are responsive to the emerging needs of society and to individual students. These duties include functions such as visioning, planning, employing an outstanding team of leaders, instructional leadership, and building positive relationships with administrators.

Unlike many chief executive officers in privately owned corporations, superintendents cannot unilaterally chart new missions and objectives. Superintendents assume their roles in an environment framed by an intricate mix of state and local authority, political and economic restraints, student and community needs, and ideals of professionalism and democracy. A superintendent's responsibilities are made even more demanding by contemporary issues, such as poverty, violence, and illegal drugs. As Spencer Maxcy (1995) astutely observed, "Whenever Americans have become overwhelmed by a sense of impending social evil, they have fastened on the schools to meet the attack" (p. xi). Today many policymakers have abandoned the notion that meaningful renewal can occur within a highly bureaucratic framework. By giving greater degrees of freedom to local districts, they have redefined expectations for the superintendent, who is to lead, facilitate, and implement reform.

VISIONING AND PLANNING

Vacancy notices for school superintendencies commonly include some mention of the need for a leadership vision. For example, a brochure seeking applicants might include the following statement: *The school board seeks a superintendent with vision who can lead the district*. Such declarations often reflect a belief that administrators should possess a vision for the future, a vision that would typically include ideas for school restructuring. Statements like these often transmit the message that the school board is seeking a bold, risk-taking, imaginative administrator.

Unfortunately, the emphasis placed on vision in superintendent searches is often associated with unrealistic expectations about a single individual's ability to change a complex, public institution. In a growing number of communities, school boards are under extreme pressure to implement change. In urban districts, for example, board members are faced with dwindling pools of applicants for superintendent positions, greater demands for quality and accountability, and a renewed activism on the part of business leaders (Jackson & Cibulka, 1992). Since board members must face reelection (or reappointment) every three or four years, they often opt to mollify the community by changing superintendents. However, more often than not, this proves to be nothing more than temporary political relief. Even the most knowledgeable and skilled administrators usually find that they are unable to dismantle the existing rigid bureaucracies in their relatively short tenures. In such instances, the promise of school improvement based on the leadership of a visionary superintendent ends up being a mere illusion of change (Kowalski, 1995). This does not mean, however, that vision and planning are not critical functions in school district administration.

What Is Vision?

One of the challenges of professional preparation is to provide prospective practitioners with an ideal model of the role of a superintendent. This is particularly essential with regard to the ethical and moral dimensions of the position. A prospective school administrator's ability to engage in meaningful reflection, for instance, is dependent on having an image of what a good superintendent should do. Likewise, superintendents need a vision for the organizations they head. Leaders cannot purposefully direct individuals, groups, and resources toward specific outcomes unless the desired outcomes have been identified. Vision is simply the mental image of where the organization has been and where it should be in the future.

Often, visions for schools are personal rather than collective. That is to say, they represent one person's view of past, present, and future. Administrators and teachers frequently express personal visions about their workplace. Robert Starratt (1995) noted that this may be done in several different ways:

- by telling a symbolic story, sometimes with mythical characters, sometimes with real characters ("Our school should be like the school run by the three genial giants. One giant taught laughter, one taught forgiveness, and the other taught imagination.")
- in a series of abstract philosophical statements ("Our school should stress functional literacy. That means literacy in our native tongue, literacy with computers, literacy between the sexes, literacy between ourselves and those we might go to war with.")
- through a scenario of everyday events ("An ideal test in our school would like . . . ")
- through the shape of the building ("Our school should have a learning laboratory connected to each classroom.")

Figure 8–1
Preferred elements in a school
district vision

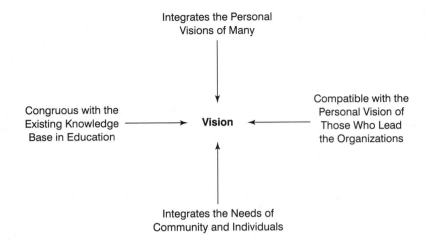

- in terms of structures and programs and systems ("Our school should have continuous pupil progress contracts based on mastery learning and cooperative learning.")
- With images and metaphors ("Our school should be a colorful garden . . . , a great symphony . . . , a treasure hunt . . . , a riverboat.") (pp. 15–16)

Individual visions are important, because collectively these personal messages reveal prevailing values and beliefs. But individual visions, even when they are considered collectively, are not the same as an organizational vision.

An effective organizational vision is more than one person's view of the way things ought to be, and it is more than idle dreaming. Ideally, a school district's vision represents consensus about the future. Most often, it is formalized in a document called a *vision statement*—a one- or two-page narrative that paints a picture of what the school district wants to be at some point in the future (Winter, 1995). To be effective, this statement should be realistic, credible, and attractive to most administrators, teachers, students, and parents; it should set forth a future that is clearly an improvement over prevailing conditions (Bennis & Nannus, 1985). Frequently, vision is a manifestation of culture, a representation of shared values and beliefs about teaching, learning, citizenship, democracy, and life. As a context for adopting change strategies, vision is more effective when it integrates the personal visions of many, reflects the needs of community and individuals, is congruous with the existing knowledge base in education, and is compatible with the personal vision of those who lead the organizations (see Figure 8–1).

The Purpose of a School District Vision

The purpose of leadership is to direct individuals and groups toward attaining intended goals. When new goals emerge, change within the organization is likely to be required. Historically, organizational managers have attempted change by using various approaches. Robert Chin and Kenneth Benne (1985) grouped such approaches into these categories:

1. *Empirical-rational strategies.* Employees are assumed to be rational and motivated by self-interests; they will adapt if the change is shown to be in their best interest.

2. *Normative-reeducative strategies.* Change will occur if employees are led to change their normative orientations to old patterns and develop commitments to new ones. This involves changes in attitudes, values, skills, and relationships as well as new knowledge, information, and intellectual rationales.

3. *Power-coercive strategies.* This is the use of economic or political power to force change.

In all of these strategies, power plays a pivotal role. Most often change in schools has been pursued by either empirical-rational or power-coercive approaches. While these two differ in the types of power exercised, both involve change targets being established by power elites (individuals who possess power and information). In a school district, for example, a superintendent might determine that it is his or her duty and privilege to determine the future. He or she develops new goals and uses various strategies to influence others so that they will work toward attaining these goals.

Top-down change initiatives that impose new goals on teachers and principals are obviously incongruous with concepts such as democratic decision making, professionalism, and schools as communities of learners. Without feelings of ownership, those responsible for implementing change (administrators and teachers) are likely to be indifferent or even adversarial when they perceive that their interests are not being served (Chin & Benne, 1985). Considering the range of principles that should drive public administration (e.g., professionalism, ethical practice, public involvement), visioning should be a process that encourages educators to examine their personal values and beliefs about their work; it should encourage them to study contemporary issues in the profession; it should make them aware of, and sensitive to, community interests and needs. Activities such as these, however, have not been common in public education, largely because schools have been seen as institutions of stability rather than as agencies of change.

William Cunningham and Donn Gresso (1993) noted that vision also is important because it can be the basis for planning (visionary planning). When this occurs, "[t]he visionary model focuses stakeholders' thinking and direction on the ideal school they wish to create. This opposes traditional deficit models that focus attention on correcting the problems that exist within the school system" (p. 75). In essence, a school district vision provides a foundation for planning the future. Not only does a widely supported vision often influence culture and climate, it also programs subconscious thinking about preferred behaviors for goal achievement (Tice, 1980). In essence, the vision becomes a daily guide for employees.

The Emphasis on the Planning Process

Planning has become a more standard part of school administration in the latter half of the 20th century. In part, dwindling resources and greater expectations for services are responsible. Superintendents found that relying on trial and error or serendipity became increasingly problematic as pressures for greater efficiency and productivity intensified. Today a growing number of states are forcing local school districts to engage in long-range planning and to develop specific outcome goals. Often local officials are required to build on state objectives. Even more important, many states have required formal planning as a means to ensure accountability. State planning mandates reflect the generally accepted contention that there is a strong positive relationship between effective leadership and effective school performance, a relationship that is being reinforced by studies of successful change in schools (e.g., Wagner, 1994).

In addition, the popularity of decentralization is elevating the value of planning. While it might seem that concepts such as site-based management would reduce the necessity of having a school district vision and blueprint, the opposite is really true. Greater autonomy usually requires greater coordination because school districts are never really absolved of their responsibilities to provide public education. A summary of issues affecting the importance of school district planning is presented in Table 8–1.

The Essence of Planning

Planning is essentially a mechanism for helping a school district move from its current state to a desired state; it is a tool for integrating vision, mission, and evolving conditions (e.g., new or altered needs). Studies of the most effective schools often reveal that significant improvements cannot be achieved in just one or two years. Rather, they may take as long as a decade. During this extended period, planning becomes the basis for activities and allocation of resources within the school; it provides the long–term perspective of what is to be accomplished (Cunningham & Gresso, 1993).

There are two distinguishable features to planning, consisting of interrelated stages: *process* and *technique*. The former details the sequence of the stages (that is, ordering what is to be accomplished); the latter identifies approaches used at each stage (that is, methods for reaching goals) (Nutt, 1985). Thomas Sergiovanni (1991) described planning as setting goals and objectives and developing blueprints or strategies for their implementation. The two basic features of planning can be addressed in different ways, and this explains the existence of various planning paradigms. Paul Nutt (1985) described a planning morphology consisting of 5 steps:

1. *Formulation.* Interface of existing and visionary states.
2. *Conceptualization.* Breaking the need into smaller components and selecting a paradigm appropriate to the task.

Table 8–1
Examples of issues increasing the importance of school district planning

Issue	Impact
Scarce resources	Political activity between local school districts and other public agencies has increased because of competition for tax revenues; state agencies and officials have become more demanding that public institutions have established goals to justify increased revenues.
Demand for increased services	The growing rate of poverty and other societal conditions result in greater public demands for services; as schools struggle to provide a greater range of services, the use of human and material resources must be planned more carefully.
Internal instability	Employee turnover, especially in top-level administrative positions, has created organizational instability; change cannot be accomplished in 1 or 2 years, so a master plan is needed.
Decentralization	As schools are given greater autonomy to make decisions about curriculum and resources, school district officials become more concerned about coordination and facilitation; the school district plan becomes a coordinating document for individual school plans.
Proven value of planning	Research on effective schools shows that these institutions usually engage in collaborative planning and rely on clearly stated goals produced through a planning process (Purkey & Smith, 1983).
State mandates	Many states have established broad goals that local districts are required to address through local planning documents; some states actually mandate strategic planning and base accreditation on the degree to which local districts attain the goals that were established.
Changing philosophy	Contemporary practitioners are more likely to pursue democratic and professional models for goal setting; formal planning becomes a mechanism for doing this.
Increased accountability	State officials have demanded local officials to be more accountable for the resources they receive; since proper planning includes evaluation, the process provides one avenue for obtaining accountability data.
Lack of consensus regarding purposes of public education	Americans have never fully agreed on the purposes of public education; as states deregulate public education, more decisions about purpose and goals will be made at the local level.

3. *Detailing.* Identifying and refining contingency approaches to meeting needs.
4. *Evaluation.* Identifying costs, benefits, potential pitfalls, and acceptance of identified contingency approaches.
5. *Implementation.* Setting strategies to gain acceptance, identifying implementation techniques.

Nutt's use of evaluation should not be confused with outcome evaluation, that is, actually assessing the impact of the planning document and making evaluative decisions about goal attainment. A depiction of a continuous planning cycle making this distinction is presented in Figure 8–2.

Two terms commonly found in the literature are *long-range planning* and *strategic planning*. Because both concepts address goals that extend beyond one or two years, some authors have treated them as being interchangeable. Other authors (e.g., McCune, 1986), however, have defined them quite differently. When the concepts are separated, long-range planning is viewed as a more closed, restrictive process that is more concerned with the management of resources than with organizational redesign. Strategic planning, on the other hand, is viewed as being more involved with environmental monitoring, broad participation, and vision. Strategic planning commonly refers to proposed actions by which administrators systematically evaluate organizational opportunities and potential impacts of environmental changes in an effort to fulfill the mission of the school district (Justis, Judd, & Stephens, 1985). The word *strategic* stems from military applications in which three elements define the planning task: (1) a clear understanding of the present, (2) a depiction of a desired future situation, and (3) a strategy for organizational adaptation (Stone, 1987).

Common elements of a strategic planning process in a school district include gaining an understanding of changes in the surrounding environment, assessing organizational strengths and weaknesses, developing and implementing specific operational plans, and motivating employees to work toward the operational and long-term goals. Planned change is more likely to be supported if it is gradual and evolutionary. For this reason, the strategic planning approach includes multiple short-term plans. These plans divide the change process into incremental units, commonly called operational or annual objectives (Winter, 1995). Underlying the strategic planning approach is the premise that organizations are never totally in control of their own destiny. This is especially true of public institu-

Figure 8–2
A continuous planning cycle

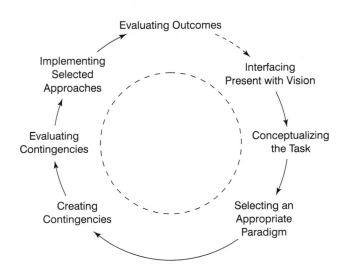

tions, which are continuously being affected by social, economic, political, legislative, and judicial forces. Directions emerge during strategic planning as a result of interfacing institutional strengths with the needs, demands, and potential support of the wider environment (that is, the community and the state) (Verstegen & Wagoner, 1989).

Integrated versus Nonintegrated Planning

Planning paradigms can be broadly categorized as *integrated* or *nonintegrated*. Nonintegrated planning refers to a process carried out in isolation by a limited number of specialists. Some organizations, for example, have planning divisions that devise organizational goals with little or no input from other divisions.

Imagine a company manufacturing automobiles that embraced a long-range plan calling for an increase in the production of luxury models and a decrease in compact models. This goal was part of a plan devised by a small team of internal planners who relied almost entirely on current market conditions to guide their decision. They assumed that the consumer's love affair with big cars would remain constant. Conditions external to the company, however, made this assumption invalid. Changes in import laws, rising fuel costs, and high interest rates pushed consumers toward small, fuel-efficient cars. By not considering these factors, the planners brought their company to the brink of financial disaster.

So, too, local school districts may rely on insulated planning procedures that overlook trends, forecasts, and changing societal conditions. When planning is done in isolation, especially now that there is so much uncertainty about how information and technology will transform the process of education, the effectiveness of the school district plan is compromised.

By contrast, integrated planning treats the school district as a social system, that is, a set of elements standing in relation among themselves and with the environment. Typically, the following information is required for using an integrated, systems approach to planning:

- An accurate depiction of the school district (including philosophy, vision, and mission)
- Identification of the constituent elements of the school district
- Environmental restrictions placed on the school district (e.g., laws, resources)
- Restrictions within the school district (e.g., knowledge and skills, time)
- School district needs and values
- Learner needs and values
- Community needs and values

Warren Schmidt and Jerome Finnigan (1992) noted that most organizations are social systems. As such, they receive inputs, make decisions about operations, and produce outputs. For school districts, inputs are received from both the general environment and from within the organization (that is, values, perceptions of needs, and preferred strategies provided by educators). A depiction of a system model is presented in Figure 8–3. Because a systems approach is holistic and analytical, it is designed to reduce planning errors. However, because critical decisions are made by humans, all planning systems are subject to some measure of error regardless of their degree of sophistication (Banghart & Trull, 1973).

Integrated approaches to planning are preferable for school districts for several reasons. The following are among the more apparent:

- Integrated planning models are more likely to engage a broad base of the organization and community in the planning process.
- Integrated planning models are more likely to incorporate the real needs and philosophies of the community into educational planning.
- Because a variety of people and groups are likely to be involved in an integrated approach, basic disagreements over foundational issues, such as the purposes of education, values, and beliefs, almost always surface. These can be considered and addressed in the planning process.
- Participants in integrated planning are exposed to significant amounts of information; this exposure improves their ability to make informed choices about goals and strategies.
- Persons who are involved in planning often declare ownership of the product; broad-based participation almost always has a positive political effect because both school district and community representatives can claim ownership.

Figure 8–3
A systems planning model

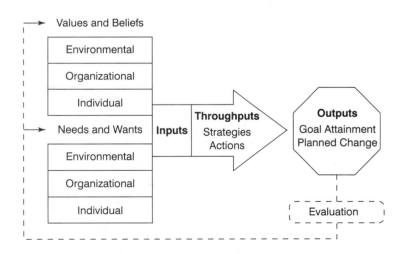

The success of change efforts often hinges on the degree of cooperation from those who are most affected. Both a willingness to change and a commitment to act are essential (James, 1995). These conditions become far less probable when school officials insulate themselves from the general community and subsequently attempt to impose new goals and directions on the schools.

Linear versus Nonlinear Planning

Planning paradigms also are categorized broadly as *linear* or *nonlinear*. Linear models are prescriptive, providing the planner a sequential path to follow. The underlying assumption is that each task builds upon the previous tasks. Those involved in the planning process can devote all of their energy to completing a segment of the planning process before moving on to the next stage. This approach is popular because it provides a rather simple rational recipe, which is readily understood by planning participants.

However, there are several potential problems with linear models. The planning process can stall at a particular stage, causing considerable time delays or even a complete systems failure (that is, planning is abandoned). Because the process is divided into distinct stages (tasks), administrators often appoint different committees or task forces to complete each step. This may be counterproductive since participants gain only a limited amount of information. Linear planning is often associated with bureaucratic thinking because the planning phases are associated with technical expertise and assigned to organizational divisions accordingly. In a large school district, this might mean that one planning stage is completed by the division of instructional services, another by the division of business services, and yet another by the division of community relations.

Nonlinear models are designed to allow various planning tasks to occur simultaneously. The primary purpose is to provide greater flexibility in terms of allocation of time and resources. Advocates of nonlinear planning typically cite two primary benefits:

1. Because of the idiosyncratic nature of institutions and communities, the situation should dictate which element of planning becomes a starting point.
2. A systems break (an unanticipated occurrence) in a linear model forces the planners to start all over; in a nonlinear approach, only one element may need adjusting (Murk & Galbraith, 1986).

Nonlinear models, however, require extensive coordination, and because several planning functions occur simultaneously, resource allocations may be intensified within a single fiscal year. Additionally, nonlinear models can be more demanding of superintendents and other administrators if they are involved in multiple

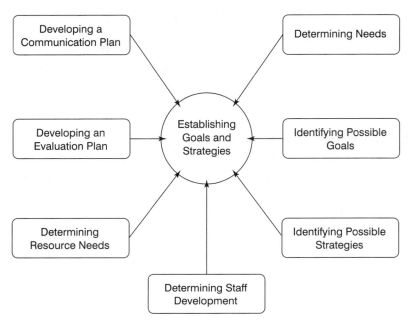

Figure 8–4
A nonlinear planning model

planning functions. This problem is especially common in smaller districts. An example of a nonlinear model is provided in Figure 8–4.

Contingency Planning

Traditional planning models, including strategic planning, are often premised on three assumptions: (1) the future is largely determined by organizational initiatives, (2) administrators know precisely where their organization should be at some point in the future, and (3) administrators know the precise steps that must be taken to move from the current status to the desired state within the specified period of time. Within this frame, long-term goals and related operational (one-year) objectives and strategies are developed. More important, assessment and evaluation are typically based entirely on internal data, that is, data generated within the organization. Problems or a lack of progress usually result in a revision of operational plans rather than a recasting of long-range goals.

Long-term strategic plans based entirely on assumptions that an organization and its leadership can control the future are proving to be of little use. First, decision making is rarely a totally objective, rational process; some degree of chaos can be anticipated (Gunter, 1995; Richards, 1990). Second, information technologies are changing very rapidly, and even a well-conceived plan may become obsolete well before it is fully implemented (Yosri, 1993). Consequently, new paradigms based on the use of contingency futures (that is, multiple scenarios of long-range goals) are becoming more popular. These plans are predicated on the belief that much of the future is not predictable; thus, both environmental conditions and internal operations must be monitored annually. Rather than treating long-term goals as immutable, contingency approaches are based on the assumption that such objectives will need to be adjusted because of evolving conditions. A comparison of a traditional approach and a contingency approach is shown in Figure 8–5. The primary reason why contingency paradigms are so relevant for public schools is that they are based on the interdependency of the organization and the environment. An example of an annual cycle for a contingency planning paradigm is shown in Figure 8–6.

Traditional Model

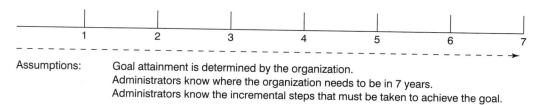

Assumptions: Goal attainment is determined by the organization.
Administrators know where the organization needs to be in 7 years.
Administrators know the incremental steps that must be taken to achieve the goal.

Contingency Model

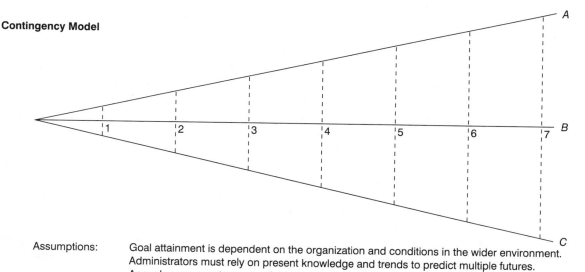

Assumptions: Goal attainment is dependent on the organization and conditions in the wider environment.
Administrators must rely on present knowledge and trends to predict multiple futures.
Annual assessments are required to evaluate contingency goals and operational plans.

Figure 8–5
Traditional and contingency planning models

Figure 8–6
Annual cycle for a contingency
planning model

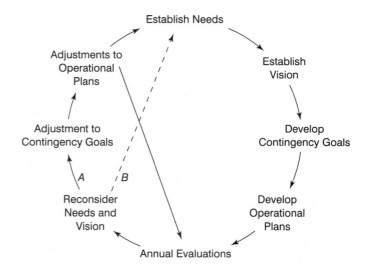

A = needs and vision remain intact
B = needs and vision are redefined

The Superintendent's Responsibilities for Visioning and Planning

The notion of group visioning and planning does not mean that superintendents should not be visionary leaders. Rather, it suggests that it is inadvisable for a newly appointed superintendent to impose a personal vision on a school district—especially when this is done before the superintendent has identified the prevailing climates and cultures in the various schools. Regrettably, myopic managers still cling to the notion that they can accomplish change by unilaterally establishing a vision, transmitting it to employees, and organizing employees according to the vision (Fullan, 1993). Too often such thinking results in the belief that the superintendent's primary role as a change agent remains one of setting the goals and motivating administrators and teachers to work toward them. In contemporary practice, "[t]he major task of the superintendent and other administrators is to create shared visions" (Lilly, 1992, p. 5).

Some might conclude that the ineffectiveness of trying to impose change renders personal conceptions about the future of public education unimportant. To the contrary, a superintendent's personal vision provides a frame of reference for working with other professionals and the community. For example, a leader who sees schools as professional communities in a democratic society usually focuses on the collective potential and energy inherent in educators (Shedd & Bacharach, 1991). For these administrators, personal vision is not a set blueprint for school reform. It is a reference point providing richer meaning to the collective experiences of exploring school district problems, needs, and strengths. Vision and professional knowledge are essential tools for superintendents in handling the inevitable tensions produced by the competing demands of managing, leading, coordinating, and facilitating.

There is also a pragmatic rationale for shared decision making; namely, ownership. The consensus process is more likely to result in strong commitments on the part of those involved to both the evolving vision and the eventual planning goals (Fullan, 1993). A superintendent's prime responsibility in this regard is to build an atmosphere in which stakeholders feel comfortable sharing their values, beliefs, dreams, concerns, and real needs. A true democratic process demands nothing less. This and other examples of responsibilities assumed by a superintendent in the visioning and planning process are found in Table 8–2.

Unfortunately, no one approach to visioning and planning is best suited for all school districts. This is because school districts differ with respect to culture,

Table 8–2
Common responsibilities for the superintendent in visioning and planning

Role	Examples
Creating a proper culture	Assessing the current climates and cultures; altering conditions so that stakeholders feel comfortable sharing philosophy and concerns; placing school reform and change in the context of contemporary conditions.
Establishing a context for visioning and planning	Explaining to the school community the meaning of visioning; detailing the importance of visioning with regard to planning and school improvement; setting parameters for completing the task; establishing small discussion groups allowing for broad participation.
Building a sense of shared responsibility	Establishing visioning and planning as professional and community responsibilities; respecting everyone's dreams and views; setting expectations for involvement.
Providing information	Making data available to those who are involved; linking values, beliefs, and dreams to the professional knowledge base; completing studies (e.g., needs assessments) when necessary; ensuring that valid information is used.
Facilitating the process	Helping others when requested; resolving conflict between individuals and groups; making resources available as needed.
Monitoring the process	Seeing that work is assigned and completed; meeting with subgroups periodically.
Communicating during the process	Keeping the school board, employees, and the general public informed; seeing that communication occurs within the school district and community.
Encouraging others	Keeping individuals on task; providing motivation; helping others to engage in intuitive and critical thinking.
Interfacing school and community	Ensuring that needs of individual students, the schools, and the community are given ample consideration; guiding the process toward the general interests of society and away from the personal interests of powerful individuals.

climate, needs, philosophy, and commitment to school improvement. Even the size of the school system (enrollment, number of schools) can be a factor influencing the effectiveness of a planning approach. Hence, the shaping of an effective renewal strategy is a significant challenge for a superintendent. Commenting on this responsibility, Michael Fullan (1993) astutely observed that a new leader may require as much as one or two years to visit schools, meet with community groups, and study problems before he or she is adequately prepared to lead the change process. He concludes that visioning and planning should occur only after administrators have acquired this necessary information and only after they have worked to build a climate supportive of collaboration.

The superintendent's personal behavior is also symbolically important with respect to school renewal. Unless the top administrator truly believes that programming and services in the school district can and should be improved, meaningful change is very unlikely (Bennis & Nanus, 1985). Employees usually can determine if a superintendent is committed to change; they can sense if a leader really believes in professionalism and democratic administration. For example, both principals and teachers quickly become skeptical of a superintendent who asks for their input and then obviously ignores it. Educators realize that politically motivated administrators may abuse concepts such as teaming and shared decision making to advance their own interests. This is why the symbolic elements of human relations are so critical to establishing trust.

The superintendent's responsibilities also extend to promoting the vision as it evolves from the school community. Even in situations where there is wide-based participation, many may not readily accept the new image for the school district. The effective superintendent acts as a primary facilitator who keeps people focused on the vision and intervenes when the change process appears to be losing coherence (Conley & Goldman, 1994). The term *visionary superintendent* is often used in conjunction with this essential task. James Lewis (1987) described a nonvisionary leader as a person who (1) makes decisions on a day-to-day basis and is consumed with current issues, (2) is formal in dealing with immediate staff and is aloof and critical, and (3) scrutinizes weaknesses in others rather than their strengths. By contrast, visionary superintendents model the values and beliefs underlying a vision; they constantly articulate the shared vision to others; they inspire others and facilitate their efforts.

Overall, the superintendent is much like an orchestra conductor; the task is to elicit peak performance from every musician. To do this, the leader often creates a work environment, arranges assignments, encourages and motivates others, synchronizes work, interprets and evaluates performance (input), and facilitates meeting needs that occur. This concept is quite distinct from the traditional image of the superintendent as the all-knowing, totally objective, totally rational manager who unilaterally determines where the school district ought to be going and coerces others to follow. The contemporary superintendent is more likely to be a designer, teacher, and steward who sets consistent examples that reinforce values and beliefs that he or she shares with others in the school system (Stolp & Smith, 1995).

WORKING WITH ADMINISTRATIVE STAFF

One of the most obvious leadership functions performed by a school superintendent is the assembling of an administrative staff. Both the structure of administrative services and the individuals selected to occupy specific positions have a profound influence on the climate and culture of a school district. In chapter 4, designs for staff configurations were discussed. Here the focus is on three other topics: teaming and autonomy, recruiting and selecting administrative staff, and building trust.

Teaming or Autonomy?

In many areas of American life, competition has been more important than cooperation. This certainly has been evident in certain aspects of public education. Students, for example, have been put in situations where they compete for grades; many rewards, such as admission to a select college, reflect this system. In recent decades, however, social psychologists and educators have sought to identify negative by-products of competition. Ideas such as cooperative learning have been advanced as alternatives. Competition also has been a dominant aspect of school administration. Many policymakers continue to believe that schools (and principals) are more productive when they are forced to compete with one another. Such thinking is evident in reform proposals calling for parental choice and vouchers.

The concept of using administrative teams within school districts is a relatively new idea that enjoyed considerable popularity in the 1960s and 1970s. Essentially, this approach to district administration entails building a team that includes representatives of the central office and school-based administrators (in smaller districts, all administrators may be part of the team). The team engages in shared decision making and coordinates actions with regard to policy implementation, dealing with emerging problems, and responding to emerging opportunities. "Team administration simply refers to genuine involvement—before the fact—of all levels of administration in goal-setting, decision-making, and problem-solving processes" (Duncan, 1974, p. 10). Team management requires superintendents to reconsider bureaucratic notions of management, and it requires them to place more emphasis on conceptual and interpersonal skills (Wynn & Guditus, 1984). Arguments supporting team management are essentially the same as those used to promote all forms of shared decision making. Four sets of assumptions are commonly advanced in the literature:

- Involvement is an ethical/moral right.
- Involvement enhances employee morale and job satisfaction.
- Involvement enhances employee motivation, organizational commitment, and acceptance of change.
- Involvement enhances cooperation and reduces conflict between individual employees and their supervisors (Shedd & Bacharach, 1991, pp. 8–9)

Professionalism is yet another justification for teaming. Principals and central office administrators are highly educated and experienced individuals who can contribute a great deal to school district improvement if they are given an opportunity to do so.

Interest in applying team management in public education has been the result of several forces:

- Larger, more complex school districts (caused by both enrollment increases after World War II and school district consolidation)

- More diversified curricular and extracurricular programs and extended student services (caused by citizen demand for more specialized services for their schools) and efforts to improve school administration (caused by professional and citizen-driven interests in increased quality of services and accountability) (Haynes & Garner, 1977)

- A desire for more democratic procedures and a wider distribution of power (Hadderman, 1988)

- A need for more control and uniform practices (caused by collective bargaining, new civil rights legislation, and court decisions) (Lindelow & Bentley, 1989)

Many school districts during the 1960s and 1970s used the term *team management* to describe their new approach, even if they did not actually apply the concept. Not only did the process fail to produce improvements, it often generated additional stress between the superintendent and the administrative staff. This occurred either because the team members did not understand the nature of the concept or because they did not accept its underlying beliefs and values. In fact, the illusion of consensus decision making sometimes made the participants uneasy.

Among the perceived benefits of using an administrative team are the following:

- Improved decision making as a result of pooling creativity, knowledge, and experiences

- Greater protection for administrators with regard to collective bargaining and enforcement of contracts with teacher unions (Key decisions on these matters could be reached by consensus.) (DuVall & Erickson, 1981)

- Increased commitment to implementing policy and regulations (because the team is highly involved in developing policy recommendations and regulations)

- Higher morale among administrative staff members

- Improved communication and knowledge (Participation on the team makes administrators better informed and induces communication among the administrative staff members.)

- Less of a likelihood that administrators will unionize and form their own collective bargaining units

- Increased sensitivity to school district needs (Administrators are more likely to look beyond the needs of their own positions.)

- Improved trust and confidence among administrators and between the board and administration (Brooks, 1978)
- Improved coordination of services
- Increased administrative efficiency (Lindelow & Bentley, 1989)

Actually achieving these benefits usually requires sound leadership from the superintendent, the formal endorsement of the school board, and the personal commitment of the team members (Hadderman, 1988).

The most prevalent concern among superintendents about the administrative team concept relates to tensions between power and accountability. Some superintendents feel that consensus decision making allows group members to be influential without having a corresponding level of legal responsibility. Richard Wynn and Charles Guditus (1984) made the following observation regarding this concern, "Those decisions or actions that are reached through consensus impose a collective moral responsibility upon all who participate in them" (p. 168). The team concept functions best when professionalism rather than the bureaucratic notion of legitimate power is the guiding principle. Stress between participation and accountability also may be reduced by an understanding that the superintendent may occasionally exempt certain issues from the consensus process. This can be done either by informing the team that a particular decision will be made in the superintendent's office or by referring an issue to the team while reserving the right to veto any decision the group might make (Wynn & Guditus, 1984).

Another problem associated with administrative teams can occur when there is a high level of cohesion (the degree to which group members value their affiliation in the group). The difficulty involves in-group pressures to maintain cohesion by reaching unanimous decisions (Bernthal & Insko, 1993). Noted psychologist Irving Janis (1972) labeled this tendency *groupthink*. When it occurs, an administrative team adopts a collective pattern of thinking that directly affects its ability to make sound decisions. In addition to cohesiveness, conditions associated with groupthink include insulation from other elements of the organization and external environment (community), a lack of methodical procedures for identifying and evaluating alternative solutions, highly directive leadership within the group, and little hope of identifying a solution better than one proposed by the group leader (Janis & Mann, 1977). As a result team members fail to engage in critical thinking and critical evaluation (Manz & Neck, 1995); insufficient attention is given to considering alternative courses of action, risks associated with the proposed action, available information that could enlighten the ultimate decision, and the development of contingencies in the event the selected solution fails (Janis & Mann, 1977).

Negative behaviors associated with groupthink can be avoided if superintendents create a climate that encourages and rewards open and candid discussions. Such an environment prompts team members to offer divergent views on problems and opportunities to express their true concerns and opinions. The group seeks to attain an accurate assessment of its limitations, and discussions of collective doubts are encouraged. In addition, the group recognizes and values the uniqueness of each member (Neck & Manz, 1994).

The size of the administrative team involved in the decision-making process is another critical issue in certain districts. Like most committees, these groups can become too large, resulting in inevitable communication difficulties. One possible remedy is to have a representative team (representatives of central office and school-based administrators). This group would be responsible for the bulk of decision making, but the entire administrative staff would meet periodically to be briefed or to participate in very critical issues.

The renewed interest in decentralization and deregulation raises a number of significant questions about team management in school districts. For instance, some administrators may see site-based management as being incompatible with administrative teaming. The same is true for policymakers who want greater school autonomy in order to intensify competition among schools. However, in truth, the two concepts of decentralization and team management can coexist: if the domains of authority and power between central administration and individual schools are properly identified, the administrative team can devote its energies to district matters. In addition, policy related to school autonomy is likely to be studied on a continuous basis as in-district experiences and state laws and regulations evolve. Teams can be involved in that process. Also, autonomy is not synonymous with power (Hanson, 1996), and many principals in decentralized districts may prefer to function in an environment where there is collegiality and cooperation among school district administrators.

Central to the issue of building an administrative team are the superintendent's leadership style and the prevailing culture of the school district. Sharing power and risk taking do not come naturally for some administrators; in some school districts, teachers and administrators have been socialized to accept highly centralized authority. In addition, the trend toward establishing school councils needs to be considered. Shared power at the school level is likely to raise questions as to why principals are the only school-based professionals who participate on a school district leadership team. Partly because there are so many potential benefits to teaming, creative superintendents can be expected to anticipate and overcome these concerns. For example, some forward-thinking superintendents may examine effective practices and prepare principals and assistant principals to work in an environment of controlled conflict and to take risks (Meadows, 1990). Other superintendents may opt to include teacher leaders on the district administrative team as a means of bridging the gap between the school district and individual schools; some may network the school district team with individual school teams. In summary, current reform trends suggest that superintendents will make important decisions regarding the organization and functioning of administrative staff, especially with regard to determining how central office administrators function in relation to building-level administrators.

Recruiting and Selecting Administrative Staff

Clearly, one of the most important leadership functions of a school superintendent involves selecting an administrative staff. While there is a management dimension to this responsibility (determining how the employment process will function), decisions related to recruiting and selecting key personnel also entail leadership (determining what needs to be done and for what reasons). This is especially true in school districts attempting to produce planned change. Effective practice in this area begins with *position analysis*. That is, the superintendent (or designees in larger districts) thoroughly studies a position prior to beginning the recruitment or selection activities. This process helps to determine whether current job descriptions and less formal expectations remain valid; it also serves to justify the need for the position—a task that is becoming increasingly important in most school systems because of inadequate financial resources.

Recruitment of administrative applicants is becoming a more difficult process for at least four reasons:

1. Federal and state laws governing employment practices affect the entire search process. The responsibilities of the employer fall into the following categories: (1) advertising positions, (2) interviewing candidates, (3) selecting a candidate, and (4) verifying a candidate's legal status (Allred, 1987).

2. Many communities have become increasingly diverse, resulting in the need to recruit female and minority administrators who can serve as role models. While the number of women preparing to become administrators has increased in recent years, there remains a critical shortage of African American and Hispanic applicants (Banks, 1995; Kowalski & Reitzug, 1993).

3. School reform initiatives have served to broaden participation in employment practices. While this is laudable, the fact remains that conflict is more likely. There may be multiple views regarding both applicant qualifications and recruitment procedures.

4. Many school districts, especially in urban and rural areas, have experienced a decline in the number of applicants for administrative positions.

Superintendents have responded to the challenges of administrator recruitment in varying ways. Some have forged formal relationships with universities that permit aspiring school leaders to complete internships and practica in their school districts. Others have developed extensive recruitment networks, often with the assistance of special consultants. In some rural districts experiencing difficulty attracting applicants, superintendents have resorted to preappointing in-district candidates (that is, promising an administrative job to a teacher as a means of keeping the individual in the school district) (Muse & Thomas, 1991). Several urban districts have established programs for prospective administrators. In the Fort Wayne (Indiana) Community Schools, for example, aspiring administrators apply to such a program and receive assessment, counseling, and training and staff development.

The selection phase in the employment process for administrators also has become more complex. In addition to the legal, educational reform, and social diversity issues already mentioned, superintendents face fundamental political and leadership questions. Should applicants from within the school district be given preference? Should school board members be able to influence selection decisions? Should applicants with outstanding leadership qualities be selected when it is apparent that their values and beliefs are not congruous with the existing or intended culture? Because of such questions, employment decisions present unique challenges. A list of potential considerations is provided in Table 8–3.

Two issues relating to the selection of administrators are especially important. The first entails decisions about participation in the selection process. A growing number of districts are electing to use search committees for both the paper screening and interviewing phases. The committee approach, common in higher education, reflects a preference for professionalism, shared decision making, and democratic administration. Clearly, there is a certain degree of symbolism related to using search committees, which can have a positive effect on employee morale and commitment. However, the process also may result in problems if it is not properly structured. Three critical questions should guide the superintendent in this matter:

- Can participation in the selection process be broadened while ensuring that relevant laws and policies will be obeyed?
- Do the participants in the selection process possess the knowledge and skills required to complete the task?
- Will the use of search committees have a negative effect on applicant pools?

Most often search committees function in an advisory role to the superintendent, particularly when the positions in question are based in the central office.

The second issue relating to selection of administrators involves attempts to assess candidates. This is commonly done in two ways: assessment center data and competency test data. Assessment centers began to appear in the mid-1970s (the National Association of Secondary School Principals started using this process in 1975). Participants engage in simulations requiring them to exhibit skills associated with practice. Their performance is evaluated by a panel of assessors who observe the simulations. There is little evidence about the extent to which superintendents rely on assessment center data to make employment decisions (Miklos, 1988).

Some districts require applicants to take one or more competency tests; these may be administered by the school district or a testing agency. Often such examinations focus on basic skills (e.g., writing, mathematics). While the outcomes provide another piece of information about a candidate, they ought not be the sole criterion for selection because administrative positions require a range of qualifications (Reitzug, 1991). There is a proclivity in employment decisions, perhaps because of the potential of legal challenges, to rely primarily on criteria

Table 8–3
Factors affecting the superintendent in the selection of administrative staff

Factor	Implications
Congruence between multiple criteria and position analysis	Recruitment and employment are made more fair and effective when multiple criteria, all of which are linked to position analysis, are used to assess and evaluate candidates.
Legal requirements	Employment practices must comply with national and state laws; such laws include equal opportunity, licensure, and other related issues.
Policies and regulations	Employment practices must comply with state and local district policies and regulations; such policies and regulations could include commitments to affirmative action, the posting of notices, and other related issues.
Past practices	The roots of operational bias are commonly found in the culture of the school district; the effectiveness of recruitment and selection may be diminished if a superintendent radically changes practices that are supported by many employees and the school board (e.g., changing procedures for receiving applications).
Cultural fit/qualification	Often candidates show great promise as innovative leaders even though they do not espouse values and beliefs consistent with the school district's culture. Superintendents must balance building strong cultures and maintaining a climate that encourages change.
Internal/external candidates	While a superintendent's preferences with regard to recruiting candidates from within and outside the school district may be based on a myriad of considerations, employees and the general community usually speculate about and draw conclusions from searches that are restricted to either internal or external candidates; for example, a superintendent's preference for external candidates is often interpreted by the public and employees as being indicative of an intention to impose change; a preference for internal candidates is often interpreted as indicative of an intention to maintain current practices or to reward loyalty and service.
Participation in the process	Increasingly, superintendents are using search committees with regard to administrative vacancies; issues regarding this matter include identifying participants (e.g., other administrators, teachers, other employees, board members, representatives of the community), specific tasks assigned to the committee, and the responsibilities and authority granted to the committee.
Assessment data	Increasingly, superintendents are infusing assessment data in the evaluation of job applicants; issues regarding this matter include the nature of the assessment and the weight that will be given to such data.
Diversity	Beyond discrimination laws and commitments to affirmative action, the superintendent needs to consider issues regarding the recruitment and potential employment of racial and ethnic minorities; the importance of this issue is especially obvious in urban school districts.

that are easiest to measure (e.g., academic degrees, experience, test scores) (Place & Kowalski, 1993). However, when this occurs, a number of critical issues, such as a candidate's disposition toward treating teachers as professionals, may not be incorporated into the decision-making process.

Even today there is evidence that many school districts do not have an established program for recruiting and selecting administrative staff (e.g., Roach, 1997). Practices vary markedly. In some districts, school boards take the precept literally that they hire the superintendent and that then the superintendent hires every other employee. In other districts, school board members interview candidates for administrative positions and may even make the actual selection without input from the superintendent. In effect, the employment of administrative staff has become less routine and less uniform across school districts. It is an area in which the superintendent's leadership has become essential.

Building Trust

Trust means that an "individual holds a firm belief in the reliability, truth, strength, or authenticity of a person or thing" (McBride & Skau, 1995). Historically, superintendents who embraced the principles of scientific management showed little concern for creating or maintaining trusting relationships with subordinates. In fact, several underlying assumptions of classical theory led managers to rely on fear and monetary rewards as motivators. These assumptions are exemplified in the following three beliefs: (1) managers who establish personal relationships with subordinates lose objectivity and thus are unable to render fair and rational judgments about subordinates; (2) individuals are inclined to dislike work, and they require close supervision and direction; and (3) workers are motivated by economic needs and other self-interests (Hanson, 1996). In the context of school renewal, these notions have been shown to be counterproductive to creating a climate in which teachers and administrators treat one another as professionals and work in the spirit of community.

Trusting relationships are built upon respect, confidentiality, consistency, risk taking, honesty, sincerity, and openness (McBride & Skau, 1995). The moral and ethical dimensions of practice, as noted previously with regard to team administration, provide a framework for trusting relationships among professional colleagues. Case studies of successful school renewal efforts often show that the superintendents were able to erect an atmosphere of trust before moving forward with the planning process (e.g., Paula, 1989). Describing what he called "renaissance school administrators," James Lewis (1987) wrote, "They trust their school people by giving them autonomy, freedom and intrapreneurialship" (p. 282).

The importance of the superintendent's building relationships of trust with administrative staff and others is best understood in the context of school district culture and meaningful renewal. Reform requires a culture and climate conducive to change; cultures and climates conducive to change are distinguished by high levels of trust. In effective school systems, superintendents become role models for the intended culture; they become symbolic leaders. In all types of organizations, symbolic leaders "place a much higher level of trust in their fellow employees" (Deal & Kennedy, 1982). Noted leadership expert Stephen Covey (1992) identified low trust as one of the chronic problems in organizations. He noted that it cannot be eradicated unless the top leader possesses both integrity and competence.

INSTRUCTIONAL LEADERSHIP

The superintendent's role of instructional leadership is central in many discussions about the superintendency in journal articles and books, yet this concept remains a poorly defined and poorly researched construct (Ginsberg, 1988). Recognizing this fact, Fenwick English (1992) wrote the following:

> In fact, the words "instructional leadership" have been used so often in connection with principals and superintendents, that they have become a cliché, and have even become the subject of much sniggering from the critics of school administration. (p. 223)

The reasons for this situation are twofold. First, there are multiple definitions of instructional leadership. Some superintendents argue that everything they do involves leadership and instruction; other practitioners see instructional leadership as a very precise, active role separate from political and managerial functions. Second, many superintendents remain only remotely involved with what occurs in classrooms. Consequently, instructional leadership is often treated as a mock role expectation; that is, it is accepted as an ideal, but largely ignored in reality. In part, this may explain why there has been very limited research on this critical area. Both ambiguity and indifference contribute to the fact that there are few data that help define more precisely what constitutes effective practice in the area of instructional leadership.

Understanding Instructional Leadership

In simple terms, instructional leadership often is used to describe leadership activities in the areas of curriculum planning and development (Knezevich, 1984). Allan Glatthorn (1990) identified the following activities as being associated with curriculum leadership: (1) the development of a long-term curriculum evaluation and renewal calendar, (2) shared decision making and clear role expectations, (3) development and alignment of curricular goals, (4) written curriculum guides and scope-and-sequence charts, (5) the development of quality courses, (6) correlation of fields of study, (7) an alignment process ensuring congruence between what is intended and what actually occurs, and (8) staff development. Samuel Krug (1992) summarized a five-factor taxonomy for describing instructional leadership: (1) defining mission, (2) managing curriculum and instruction, (3) supervising teaching, (4) monitoring student progress, and (5) promoting a positive instructional climate. Some of these functions are obviously more relevant for principals than they are for superintendents.

In recent years, instructional leadership has assumed a broader meaning to include functions such as staff development, diagnosis of problems, assessment of student learning, the integration of technology into classrooms, and preparing school personnel to use emerging instructional paradigms. John Daresh (1991) characterized instructional leadership as a form of proactive administrative behavior. He defined proactive behavior as an awareness of personal beliefs, and understanding of organizations, a view of instructional leadership as an ongoing process, a sensitivity to alternative perspectives, a consistency in personal performance, and the ability to understand people.

Instructional leadership is commonly discussed in the contexts of school reform and research into effective schools. Studies often cite instructional leadership as a central element of school effectiveness. However, William Greenfield (1987) observed the following:

> [D]espite these claims by education reformists and researchers, the connection between leadership and school effectiveness is not clear, and more important, the concept of instructional leadership provides school administrators and policymakers with few useful insights about the actual nature of leadership in schools. (p. 1)

As with many facets of school administration, there is no recipe for instructional leadership—no foolproof road map that a superintendent can follow. One superintendent may spend an inordinate amount of time visiting classrooms; another may devote hours each week to curriculum planning. What is common to activities in instructional leadership is a commitment to improving teaching and learning. Here, instructional leadership is considered to include all responsibilities of the superintendency that are associated with the role of teacher-scholar, a conception of a superintendent's role that was discussed in the previous chapter.

Instructional Leadership in the Context of a Superintendent's Work

Taher Razik and Austin Swanson (1995) argue that to qualify as an instructional leader, superintendents would have to spend at least as much time with teaching and learning as they do with policies, rules, and regulations. However, in many school districts, this clearly is not the case (Wimpelberg, 1987). The size of school district may be a contributing factor. Superintendents in very small systems, largely because there are few employees and few attendance centers, have had a greater opportunity than other superintendents to be involved in instructional leadership (Schmuck & Schmuck, 1989). In districts with large enrollments, superintendents are likely to be mired in political problems, and they have central office personnel to whom they can delegate responsibilities for instruction supervision.

Few superintendents, regardless of district size, openly reject the argument that they should be instructional leaders. They frequently perceive that this ideal role is made unattainable because collective bargaining, politics, and board relations consume most of their time and energy (Trump, 1986). There is also a question as to level of importance that school boards actually place on the superintendent's role in instructional leadership. Actual behaviors suggest that board members focus heavily on managerial and political issues, causing the superintendent to be extremely attentive to the same issues. In a mid-1990s study, for example, a group of urban superintendents was asked if their boards expected them to be instructional leaders; 28% said always, 53% said occasionally, and 18% said rarely or never (Kowalski, 1995).

Studying the behavior of superintendents in effective school districts, Joseph Murphy and Philip Hallinger (1986) concluded that these administrators exhibited direct educational leadership in two ways. First, they provided direction for the development of school district goals and the subsequent formation of specific school objectives. Second, they actively monitored the implementation of curriculum, supervised and evaluated principals, and were involved in the review of student achievement data. Often, instructional leadership is viewed as primarily a principal's responsibility. However, research is revealing that superintendents can use their positions in the formal organization to improve instruction through staff selection, principal supervision, setting of instruction goals and monitoring their attainment, financial planning, and consultative management practices (Bjork, 1993). Looking at several districts with demonstrated improvement in student achievement, Edward Pajak and Carl Glickman (1989) found that these districts had created a climate for professional dialogue, provided instructional supervision, and relied on multiple forms of leadership. They concluded that the superintendent and central office staff were key facilitators with respect to school improvement. Simply by allocating resources, superintendents can have a significant effect on teaching practices (Gamoran & Dreeben, 1986).

Discussing possible relationships between effective school districts and superintendent leadership, Lawrence Lezotte (1994) noted, "People follow effective leaders because they share the leaders' dreams, not because they are afraid of what would happen to them if they did not follow them" (p. 22). A superintendent's most direct influence in instructional matters typically takes place with principals. This may occur in three ways: (1) directive influence (determining what a principal should do, plan, or decide); (2) restrictive influence (controlling a principal's time, resources, or actions); and (3) formative influence (helping to shape a principal's attitudes, values, and motivations) (Hord, 1990). In the past, many superintendents believed that they had to dictate structure and closely supervise others to see that the structure was properly used. That is to say, they relied on directive and restrictive forms of influence when issuing commands to principals. Today the effective practitioner relies much more heavily on normative influence to help principals build learning communities.

In many respects, instructional leadership is the construct that binds all leadership activities of a superintendent. It spans visioning, planning, selection of an administrative staff, professionalism, community building, staff development, and program evaluation. Unless a superintendent is involved in determining what should be done (1) to improve student learning, (2) to make student learning more relevant, and (3) to make the educational system more accountable to the general community, he or she is not functioning as an educational leader. The leadership

Figure 8–7
The framework for a superintendent's leadership role in the
school district

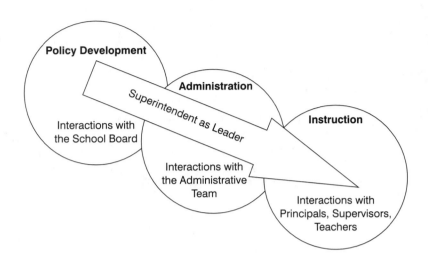

Policy Development

Administration

Superintendent as Leader

Instruction

Interactions with
the School Board

Interactions with
the Administrative
Team

Interactions with
Principals, Supervisors,
Teachers

of the superintendent is a central force linking policy making, administration, and instructional activities. The superintendent is the one person who is actively engaged in decision making in these three domains (see Figure 8–7).

Unfortunately, the road to instructional leadership is strewn with obstacles. The task requires commitment, trust building, and time. To overcome the obstacles, a superintendent must first value instructional leadership. This means that the individual is up to date with current research on effective schools and understands the relationship between district leadership and student outcomes. Second, a superintendent must be committed to democratic learning and learning communities. This means providing leadership for shared visions, empowering teachers to work creatively and professionally, and utilizing formative influences to motivate others.

FOR FURTHER REFLECTION

This chapter examined the leadership roles of the superintendent within the school district. The quest for school renewal has placed added emphasis on change initiatives, causing functions such as visioning, planning, and evaluation to become more essential. Decisions about administration that include staff selection, setting a climate of cooperation, and building trust are also key to effective practice. Likewise, the illusive goal of instructional leadership remains a prominent role expectation for superintendents, especially in a political environment that is tilting toward decentralization and deregulation.

As you consider what you read in this chapter, answer the following questions:

1. What is the difference between visioning and planning?

2. School boards often seek superintendents who are "visionary leaders." What do these words mean to you?

3. What are the advantages and disadvantages of integrated and nonintegrated planning?

4. What are the advantages and disadvantages of linear planning and nonlinear planning?

5. What are the advantages and disadvantages of using an administrative team concept?

6. In smaller school districts, an administrative team often includes all school-based and central office administrators. Do you think this is a good idea? Why or why not?

7. Assume you are superintendent in a district that is too large to include all administrative personnel on the administrative team. However, you want to establish such a team. What options could you pursue?

8. In interactions you have had with school superintendents, what have they done to gain your trust?

9. Often superintendents who use consensus to reach administrative decisions are accused of being weak. How would you respond to this charge?

10. What is your image of a superintendent as an instructional leader? What specific role expectations do you include?

11. Should school district size (enrollment) have any bearing on expectations for a superintendent to be an instructional leader? Explain the reasons for your answer.

12. Assume you were advising a school board that was preparing to interview candidates for the superintendency. What questions would you recommend that they ask about the following: (a) visioning and planning; (b) selecting and developing administrative staff; (c) instructional leadership?

13. Do you believe that the average superintendent has been adequately prepared to be a leader as well as a manager? Has the average superintendent been adequately prepared to be an instructional leader?

CASE STUDY

Dr. Raymond Bernelli was preparing to leave town for a final interview for the superintendency of the Oak Meadow School District. If the experience proved to be fruitful, he would be assuming his 4th superintendency in 16 years. In each of the 3 districts where he had served as the chief administrative officer, new programs were successfully implemented with the enthusiastic support of administrators, teachers, and the community. Because of these successes, he had acquired a reputation as a visionary leader, a change agent, and an innovator.

And his standing among superintendents regionally and nationally did not go unnoticed by search consultants.

The Oak Meadow School District is located in a suburban area of a large midwestern city. The following demographic statistics serve to describe this system:

- The overall enrollment is 22,386.
- The average annual family income is the highest in the state.
- The average teacher salary is the second highest in the state.
- The average annual expenditure per pupil is second highest in the state.
- Eighty-three percent of the high school graduates enroll in 4-year institutions of higher education.
- The racial-ethnic composition of the school district includes a 5% African American population and a 3% Hispanic population.

When Dr. Jacob Eddelman announced his retirement as superintendent after having served in the position for 13 years, the school board was inundated with inquiries about the position. They employed Dr. Rita Morales, a nationally known search consultant, to assist them with finding a new leader. Together the board and Dr. Morales looked at more than 125 applications. They selected 6 finalists for initial interviews; 2 of them were invited to come back to the district for second interviews.

The 7-member school board reflected the composition of the community. By occupation, three were business executives, one was a surgeon, one was an attorney, one was a housewife, and one was a retired electrical engineer. All were college graduates. The board president, Ronald Barrin, was a vice-president of a brokerage firm. He was the senior board member in terms of service, having been on the board for 17 years.

During the first interview, Dr. Bernelli was asked a number of questions about his career and his philosophy of education. He elected to tell the board members about the specific programs that had been implemented in each of the 3 districts in which he had served as superintendent. All 7 board members were impressed with these accomplishments, as they were with his personal appearance, communication skills, and self-confidence. After the first round of interviews, he was clearly the leading candidate.

The second interview took place in the board room. All board members were again present; however, Dr. Morales was not. After about 15 minutes of informal discussion, Mr. Barrin asked two very direct questions:

"Dr. Bernelli, we obviously were impressed by all the accomplishments you outlined in your previous interview. While this is not a district seeking a total makeover, many of us feel that some new ideas would be healthy. Quite frankly, that is one reason why we are so interested in you. You are a person with vision; you're not afraid of change. You have had several weeks since our last meeting to reflect on our school system. My questions are, What ideas would be at the top of your list? What changes are you likely to pursue if we hire you for this job?"

Without hesitation, Dr. Bernelli responded, "I don't know." For the first time during the meeting, everyone could sense a degree of tension. After about 30 seconds of silence, Mr. Barrin spoke.

"Maybe I didn't ask the questions very clearly. Let me try again."

But before he could restate them, Dr. Bernelli interrupted him, "I think I understood your questions. Perhaps I should explain my answer. To provide an intelligent answer, I would need to know a great deal more about your school district. I would need to spend time working with administrators, teachers, other employees, students, and even the community."

One of the other board members asked, "Don't you think there are certain needs and programs that are applicable to all school districts? Aren't there certain school reform initiatives we ought to be pursuing? Aren't there governance and education improvements that would be beneficial regardless of our community and existing programs?"

"Perhaps," Dr. Bernelli responded, "but effective change requires specificity. More important, I don't believe in top-down approaches to change. This is an outstanding school district with outstanding educators. I believe in the collective power of your employees. They have been here; they know the students; they know the community. Future initiatives ought to evolve from our working together. Before we forge a vision or long-range goals, I need to learn a great deal about where this district has been, where it is, where most people want to see it go."

One of the board members asked, "How long would this take?"

"Maybe 1 or 2 years," he responded. "This is a large district."

Sensing a general concern about the direction of the interview, Mr. Barrin said, "I think you are trying to tell us that you believe in collaborative leadership." Dr. Bernelli nodded that this was correct.

The board president continued, "Dr. Eddelman, our retiring superintendent, has a reputation for getting things done. He is not a dictator, but he certainly doesn't fear making decisions. He respects other opinions, but he also is the type of leader who doesn't let things linger. I guess what is puzzling to me is how you were able to accomplish so much in the past if you relied on this collaborative approach."

Dr. Bernelli thought for a moment before speaking. "I guess it would be easy for a new superintendent to come in and change some things rather quickly—especially while he or she is still on a honeymoon with the school board and staff. I prefer to deal with change in an evolutionary way. What I think may be good today may be irrelevant tomorrow. My job is to bring good people with good ideas together. In each of my previous superintendencies, I took at least 1 year to learn the territory before seeking to develop a vision or a strategic plan. In fact, in each successive job, I took a little longer. Maybe that's because the districts got larger—or maybe it's because I became more convinced that I needed to know a great deal before I started to tinker with programs and organizational patterns. There are times when a superintendent has to act very quickly and decisively. Maybe there are problems here I don't know about. But from what I have perceived so far, there is no reason why I should come into this district and impose my vision and my goals. I don't have the crystal ball. The reason why I was successful in each of my superintendencies is not because I had the right vision or the right goals; it was because I was able to lead the school community on a change journey. My contributions were encouragement, coordination, facilitation, and professional insights."

Issues for Discussion

1. Assess Dr. Bernelli's philosophy about change from (a) a professional perspective, (b) a political perspective, and (c) a managerial perspective.

2. Board members are likely to react in different ways to Dr. Bernelli's comments. What might be some of the perceptions they draw of this administrator?

3. Is it reasonable to expect a school board to wait 1 or 2 years before a new superintendent identifies some priorities for organizational change or program improvement? Why or why not?

4. Is it possible for a superintendent to be both decisive and collaborative?

5. What are the potential dangers of relying on consensus building for school renewal?

6. From what you read in this case, do you consider Dr. Bernelli to be a visionary leader? Why or why not?

7. What is your personal impression of Dr. Bernelli? Would you like to be an assistant superintendent working under his supervision? Why or why not?

8. What clues are provided in the case regarding the school board's perceptions of an ideal superintendent?

9. Does the tenure of the retiring superintendent have any relevance to issues of school district change?

REFERENCES

Allred, S. (1987). Recruiting and selecting new school employees. *School Law Bulletin, 28*(4), 13–18.

Banghart, F. W., & Trull, A. (1973). *Educational planning.* New York: Macmillan.

Banks, C. A. (1995). Gender and race as factors in educational leadership and administration. In J. A. Banks (Ed.), *Handbook of research on multicultural education* (pp. 65–80). New York: Macmillan.

Bennis, W. G., & Nanus, B (1985). *Leaders: The strategies for taking charge.* New York: Harper & Row.

Bernthal, P. R., & Insko, C. A. (1993). Cohesiveness without groupthink: The interactive effects of social and task cohesion. *Group & Organization Management, 18*(1), 66–87.

Bjork, L. G. (1993). Effective schools—effective superintendents: The emerging instructional leadership role. *Journal of School Leadership, 3*(3), 246–259.

Brooks, M. (1978). Management team builds trust between board, superintendent. *Thrust for Educational Leadership, 8*(2), 10–11.

Chin, R., & Benne, K. D. (1985). General strategies for effecting changes in human systems. In W. G. Bennis, K. D. Benne, & R. Chin (Eds.), *The planning of change* (4th ed.) (pp. 22–43). New York: Holt, Rinehart, and Winston.

Conley, D. T., & Goldman, P. (1994). *Facilitative leadership: How principals lead without dominating.* (ERIC Document Reproduction Service No. ED 379 728)

Covey, S. R. (1992). *Principle-centered leadership.* New York: Simon & Schuster.

Cunningham, W. G., & Gresso, D. W. (1993). *Cultural leadership: The culture of excellence in education.* Boston: Allyn and Bacon.

Daresh, J. C. (1991). Instructional leadership as a proactive administrative process. *Theory into Practice, 30*(2), 109–112.

Deal, T. E., & Kennedy, A. A. (1982). *Corporate cultures: The rites and rituals of corporate life.* Reading, MA: Addison-Wesley.

Duncan, R. (1974). Public Law 217 and the administrative team. *Indiana School Boards Journal, 20*(2), 9–12.

DuVall, L. A., & Erickson, K. A. (1981). School management teams: What are they and how do they work? *NASSP Bulletin, 65*(445), 62–67.

English, F. W. (1992). *Educational administration: The human approach.* New York: HarperCollins.

Fullan, M. (1993). *Change forces: Probing the depth of educational reform.* New York: Falmer Press.

Gamoran, A., & Dreeben, R. (1986). Coupling and control in educational organizations. *Administrative Science Quarterly, 31*(4), 612–632.

Ginsberg, R. (1988). Principals as instructional leaders: An ailing panacea. *Education and Urban Society, 20*(3), 276–293.

Glatthorn, A. A. (1990). *Supervisory leadership: Introduction to instructional supervision.* Glenview, IL: Scott, Foresman.

Greenfield, W. (1987). *Instructional leadership: Concepts, issues, and controversies.* Boston: Allyn and Bacon.

Gunter, H. (1995). Jurassic management: Chaos and management development in educational institutions. *Journal of Educational Administration, 33*(4), 5–20.

Hadderman, M. L. (1988). *Team management.* (ERIC Document Reproduction Service No. ED 292 217)

Hanson, E. M. (1996). *Educational administration and organizational behavior* (4th ed.). Boston: Allyn and Bacon.

Haynes, A. F., & Garner, A. E. (1977). Sharing administrative decision making. *Clearing House, 51*(2), 53–57.

Hord, S. M. (1990). *Images of superintendents' leadership for learning.* (ERIC Document Reproduction Service No. ED 355 652)

Jackson, B. L., & Cibulka, J. G. (1992). Leadership turnover and business mobilization: The changing political ecology of urban school systems. In J. G. Cibulka, R. J. Reed, & K. W. Kong (Eds.), *The politics of urban education in the United States* (pp. 71–86). Philadelphia: Falmer Press.

James, J. (1995). Negotiating the grand canyon of change. *The School Administrator, 52*(1), 22–29.

Janis, I. L. (1972). *Victims of groupthink.* Boston: Houghton Mifflin.

Janis, I. L., & Mann, L. (1977). *Decision making: A psychological analysis of conflict, choice, and commitment.* New York: The Free Press.

Justis, R. T., Judd, R. J., & Stephens, D. B. (1985). *Strategic management and policy.* Englewood Cliffs, NJ: Prentice Hall.

Knezevich, S. J. (1984). *Administration of public education: A sourcebook for the leadership and management of educational institutions* (4th ed.). New York: Harper & Row.

Kowalski, T. J. (1995). *Keepers of the flame: Contemporary urban superintendents.* Thousand Oaks, CA: Corwin Press.

Kowalski, T. J., & Reitzug, U. C. (1993). *Contemporary school administration: An introduction.* New York: Longman.

Krug, S. E. (1992). Instructional leadership: A constructivist perspective. *Educational Administration Quarterly, 28*(3), 430–443.

Lewis, J. L. (1987). *Re-creating our schools for the 21st century.* Westbury, NY: J. L. Wilkerson Publishing.

Lezotte, L. (1994). The nexus of instructional leadership and effective schools. *School Administrator, 51*(6), 20–23.

Lilly, E. R. (1992). *Superintendent leadership and districtwide vision.* (ERIC Document Reproduction Service No. ED 343 222)

Lindelow, J., & Bentley, S. (1989). *Team Management.* (ERIC Document Reproduction Service No. ED 209 736)

Manz, C. C., & Neck, C. P. (1995). Teamthink: Beyond the groupthink syndrome in self-managing work teams. *Journal of Managerial Psychology, 10*(1), 7–15.

Maxcy, S. J. (1995). *Democracy, chaos, and the new school order.* Thousand Oaks, CA: Corwin Press.

McBride, M., & Skau, K. G. (1995). Trust, empowerment, and reflection: Essentials for supervision. *Journal of Curriculum and Supervision, 10*(3), 262–277.

McCune, S. D. (1986). *Guide to strategic planning for educators.* Alexandria, VA: Association for Supervision and Curriculum Development.

Meadows, B. J. (1990). The rewards and risks of shared leadership. *Phi Delta Kappan, 71*(7), 545–548.

Miklos, E. (1988). Administrator selection, career patterns, succession, and socialization. In N. Boyan (Ed.), *Handbook of research on educational administration* (pp. 53–76). New York: Longman.

Murk, P. J., & Galbraith, M. W. (1986). Planning successful continuing education programs: A systems approach model. *Lifelong Learning, 9*(5), 21–23.

Murphy, J., & Hallinger, P. (1986). The superintendent as instructional leader: Findings from effective school districts. *Journal of Educational Administration, 24*(2), 213–236.

Muse, I. D., & Thomas, G. J. (1991). The thinning ranks of rural school administration: The principalship in trouble. *Rural Educator, 13*(1), 8–12.

Neck, C. P., & Manz, C. C. (1994). From groupthink to teamthink: Toward the creation of constructive thought patterns in self-managing work teams. *Human Relations, 47*(8), 929–952.

Nutt, P. C. (1985). The study of planning process. In W. G. Bennis, K. D. Benne, & R. Chin (Eds.), *The planning of change* (4th ed.) (pp. 198–215). New York: Holt, Rinehart, and Winston.

Pajak, E. F., & Glickman, C. D. (1989). Dimensions of school district improvement. *Educational Leadership, 46*(8), 61–64.

Paula, N. (1989). Key player in school reform: The superintendent. *The School Administrator, 46*(3), 8–11.

Place, A. W., & Kowalski, T. J. (1993). Principal ratings of criteria associated with teacher selection. *Journal of Personnel Evaluation in Education, 7*(4), 291–300.

Purkey, S. C., & Smith, M. S. (1983). Effective schools: A review. *Elementary School Journal, 83*(4), 427–452.

Razik, T. A., & Swanson, A. D. (1995). *Fundamental concepts of educational leadership and management.* Upper Saddle River, NJ: Merrill/Prentice Hall.

Reitzug, U. C. (1991). Administrator competency testing: Its status for the '90s. *NASSP Bulletin, 75*(539), 65–71.

Richards, D. (1990). Is strategic decision making chaotic? *Behavioral Science, 35*(3), 219–232.

Roach, J. A. (1997*). Principal involvement in teacher selection: Practices and attitudes among elementary school principals.* Unpublished doctoral dissertation, Ball State University.

Schmidt, W., & Finnigan, J. (1992). *The race without a finish line: America's quest for total quality.* San Francisco: Jossey-Bass.

Schmuck, R. A., & Schmuck, P. A. (1989). *Being superintendent of a small-town district.* (ERIC Document Reproduction Service No. ED 316 380)

Sergiovanni, T. J. (1991). *The principalship: A reflective practice perspective* (2nd ed.). Boston: Allyn and Bacon.

Shedd, J. B., & Bacharach, S. B. (1991). *Tangled hierarchies: Teachers as professionals and the management of schools.* San Francisco: Jossey-Bass.

Starratt, R. J. (1995). *Leaders with vision: The quest for school renewal.* Thousand Oaks, CA: Corwin Press.

Stolp, S. W., & Smith, S. C. (1995). *Transforming school culture: Stories, symbols, values and the leader's role.* Eugene, OR: ERIC Clearinghouse on Educational Management.

Stone, S. C. (1987). *Strategic planning for independent schools.* Boston: National Association of Independent Schools.

Tice, L. (1980). *New age thinking for achieving your potential.* Seattle, WA: The Pacific Institute.

Trump, J. M. (1986). *What hinders or prevents superintendents from working on instructional improvements?* (ERIC Document Reproduction Service No. ED 284 366)

Verstegen, D. A., & Wagoner, J. L. (1989). Strategic planning for policy development: An evolving model. *Planning and Changing, 20*(1), 33–49.

Wagner, T. (1994). *How schools change: Lessons from three communities.* Boston: Beacon Press.

Wimpelberg, R. K. (1987). The dilemma of instructional leadership and a central role for central office. In W. Greenfield (Ed.), *Instructional leadership: Concepts, issues, and controversies* (pp. 100–117). Boston: Allyn and Bacon.

Winter, P. A. (1995). Vision in school planning: A tool for crafting a creative future. *School Business Affairs, 61*(6), 46–50.

Wynn, T., & Guditus, C. W. (1984). *Team management: Leadership by consensus.* Upper Saddle River, NJ: Prentice Hall.

Yosri, A. (1993). Say good-bye to strategic planning. *Computerworld, 27*(35), 33.

Chapter 9

Management of the School District

Key Concepts

✧ Responsibilities for fiscal management

✧ Planning and managing school facilities

✧ Managing the employment process

✧ Evaluating personnel

✧ Structuring and managing compensation programs

✧ Managing personnel records

✧ Functioning with employee unions

✧ Controlling student records

✧ Special education and student personnel services

✧ Working with the school district's attorney

✧ Managing auxiliary services

uperintendents are often criticized for being preoccupied with the political and managerial aspects of their work. Such denouncements are usually based on the belief that administrators spend far too little time providing leadership for educational programs. As noted earlier in this book, a preoccupation with management science in the early decades of the 20th century was associated with (1) public concerns for efficiency, (2) a desire on the part of school administrators to establish an identity separate from teachers, and (3) a desire on the part of school administrators to appease business leaders. More recently, the public's demand for "accountability and cost-effective management in public schools revived the cult of efficiency in education during the 1960s and 1970s" (Tyack & Cuban, 1995, p. 115).

While management is considered to be less important than leadership, the management function remains an inescapable reality in the superintendency. Robert Starratt (1990) characterized the school administrator as an actor who plays two parts: manager and leader. In one, the superintendent makes and enforces rules, controls fiscal resources, strives for objectivity and rationality, and standardization. In the other, he or she focuses on philosophy, purpose, and school improvement. This dual identity continues to produce conflict for superintendents. While the image of the superintendent as the professional manager fits taxpayer expectations, this role frequently serves to distance the superintendent from other education professionals—an issue that has become even more critical because of school reform (Sergiovanni, 1991). Contemporary superintendents who seek to guide school renewal cannot afford to choose between the public and those in the education profession; positive relationships with both are essential. The challenge, therefore, is to balance these two broad responsibilities. This is most likely to be accomplished by those practitioners who understand that while management is an essential part of the superintendency, leadership constitutes the central core of this position (Sergiovanni, Burlingame, Coombs, & Thurston, 1992).

MANAGING FINANCES AND FACILITIES

There are two problems commonly encountered in any discussions of management as part of the work of superintendents. The first relates to arguments that leadership and management cannot be neatly separated. For example, decisions about budgets and school building design clearly have an impact on instructional leadership. Second, it is difficult to neatly divide managerial responsibilities into exclusive categories. Payroll functions, for instance, are relevant to both business management and personnel management. Keeping these concerns in mind, this chapter is structured to present those areas of practice that are most commonly perceived as managerial. In this first part, the focus is on the critical issues of money and school buildings.

Fiscal Management

The most visible management role performed by a superintendent relates to finances. Partly because a substantial portion of school revenues come from local taxes (although the percentage has decreased substantially in many states as a result of finance reforms) and partly because many budgetary decisions are still made by local school boards, business operations come under close scrutiny from both state officials and taxpayers. However, this is an area of responsibility in which many superintendents feel inadequately prepared for practice (McAdams, 1995). In part, this lack of confidence may be associated with the fact that in some states, superintendents are not required to complete academic courses in the economics of education and school business management. In addition, the scope of financial responsibilities is vast, and many of the topics related to fiscal management simply are not covered in some advanced graduate programs.

The actual role performed by a superintendent in the area of financial management is highly dependent on the size of the school system. In districts with small enrollments, that is, those with less than 2,000 students, superintendents often serve as their own business managers. This means they actually prepare budgets, handle purchasing, and the like. However, even in the largest districts where this is not true, board members and the public expect the superintendent to be knowledgeable in the area of school finance and capable of applying this knowledge in the day-to-day operations of the district.

Business management within public education is a complex responsibility for at least two reasons. First, there are many functions that need to be performed—each requiring specific information and skills. Second, the execution of these functions is framed by state laws and regulations that are less than uniform across the United States. So, for example, a superintendent must not only know how to prepare and manage a budget, he or she must also be aware of ever changing laws and regulations that establish parameters for these tasks within a given state. Table 9–1 shows responsibilities of business management that are of concern to superintendents; these responsibilities do not include facility management because this is treated as a separate topic in this chapter. In smaller school districts, several of these functions can consume a great deal of a superintendent's workday. For this reason, they require more focused attention.

Fiscal Planning

School reform activities contributed to an increased emphasis on comprehensive planning at the school district level. The primary focus for this process is typically instructional programs; however, providing the necessary personnel, buildings, equipment, and materials is also involved. In this respect, school finance is an integral part of systems planning. On an annual basis, the development of a school district's budget is preceded by four critical tasks: (1) identifying needs, (2) establishing goals, (3) organizing objectives, and (4) building a program to meet the objectives (Burrup, Brimley, & Garfield, 1996).

Table 9–1
Responsibilities within fiscal management

Responsibility	Explanation
Fiscal planning	Pertains to long-range planning about revenues and expenditures, especially to integrating these considerations into comprehensive strategic plans.
Budgeting	An annual process of developing a document that details program needs, estimated costs of programs, and estimated revenues.
Accounting	A process that determines the fiscal condition of a school district; usually mandated by state law. The process serves as both a measure of accountability and a source of public information.
Debt management	Entails estimates of debt capacity, the structuring of debt, payment on debt obligations, and other matters associated with indebtedness of the school district.
Auditing	A process mandated by state law that serves as a means of determining the financial status of a school district and determining whether transactions have been executed in compliance with existing laws and regulations. Audits can be internal or external, and some form of external auditing is usually required.
Purchasing	An ongoing process of procuring necessary equipment and materials for the operation of the school district; includes specific functions such as preparing bids, cost analysis, and recommendations for board action.
Inventory management	Controlling and storing equipment and materials that will be used at some future date.
Materials distribution	Disseminating equipment and materials from storage areas to specific sites as such materials are requisitioned.
Risk management	Involves the procurement and management of insurance policies protecting the school district and its property. Specific functions include developing specifications, obtaining competitive bids, selecting insurance carriers, and actual management.
Salary and wage management	A function that includes record keeping and the dissemination of checks to employees; also includes management of fringe benefit programs (e.g., insurance, retirement).

Budgeting

Ideally, a school district's budget is a compilation of three separate plans as illustrated in Figure 9–1. While the three plans (often referred to as the educational plan, the expenditure plan, and the revenue plan) may be developed autonomously, they are integrated in the budgeting process. Despite the fact that the educational plan ought to provide the foundation of the budgeting process by addressing both philosophy and specific objectives, it is the element that is most frequently ignored. When this oversight occurs, the product is a *mechanical budget*—a document that focuses solely on the revenue-and-expenditure process carried out to comply with state law (Hack, Candoli, & Ray, 1995).

Figure 9–1
Three elements of a school district budget

In many school districts, budgeting has been treated as the exclusive domain of the superintendent and school board; teachers and principals have had little or no input. This almost always results in an administration-dominated and highly centralized budget (Hack et al., 1995). As school reform makes decentralization and recognition of teacher professionalization more common, superintendents who attempt to dominate the budget process are likely to face increasing opposition. This is because the purpose and process of budgeting typically change as a result of reforms such as site-based management.

Properly developed, annual budgets can serve different purposes. These include the following:

- As a planning resource
- As a document that communicates educational intentions to the broader community
- As a legal justification for expending public dollars
- As a control mechanism that guides decisions involving revenues and expenditures
- As a guide for evaluating fiscal performance (Hartman, 1988)

As both the economic (allocation of scarce resources) and political (competition for scarce resources) dimensions of school district administration intensify, a superintendent's management skills in each of these areas become more critical. Even in the largest school systems, the public expects the superintendent to be the person ultimately responsible for coordinating the budgeting process. To meet this expectation, a superintendent must be able to integrate knowledge pertaining to topics such as policy development, state financing politics, taxation, planning, and budget management.

Accounting and Auditing

Whereas a budget provides a plan for administrative decision making, accounting and auditing are functions designed to ensure efficiency and effectiveness in fiscal operations. The purposes of an accounting system for school systems have been identified as the following:

- Protecting public funds from losses as the result of carelessness, inappropriate expenditures, theft, embezzlement, or malfeasance on the part of administrators
- Providing a systematic process for interrelating fiscal expenditures with attainment of educational goals
- Meeting the legal requirements of state and other governmental units
- Providing school patrons with fiscal information (Hack et al., 1995)

In addition, accounting procedures provide a decision-making tool for educators and school board members. During a budget cycle, information produced by the accounting process facilitates budget control (that is, being able to make decisions within the established financial parameters specified in the budget).

In general, the superintendent's responsibility is to guarantee that the accounting process is properly executed and supervised. This includes ensuring the following:

- Prescribed accounting procedures conform with legal mandates and governmental regulations.
- Various functions are assigned to workers who are properly prepared to execute their responsibilities.
- Appropriate records are maintained.
- Records are adequately protected against loss and damage.
- The work of one employee serves as a check on the work of another employee.
- All involved employees have property surety bonds.
- Cash receipts are properly handled.
- Safety practices are used for check writing and recording financial transactions.
- Two or more individuals must share the responsibility of dispersing funds.
- Results of the accounting process are properly communicated to taxpayers (Drake & Roe, 1994).

In essence, proper control of an accounting system serves two critical purposes: (1) it is a mechanism for properly recording financial transactions and (2) it is a means of supplying adequate safeguards against errors or the misuse of public funds.

Auditing is an extension of the accounting process; it serves to verify the accuracy and completeness of financial transactions as they relate to the general budget and specific accounts within it (Hack et al., 1995). Generally, audits can be classified as internal (conducted by school district officials) or external. The external audits can further be divided into two groups: required examinations by specified auditors (e.g., by state-appointed auditors) and examinations performed by independent third parties retained by school district officials (e.g., an audit by an independent accounting firm). Internal audits are often used to provide information for the superintendent, school board, or larger community. Because they are not usually mandated, those conducting the process have greater degrees of freedom determining its content and procedures. External audits, especially when mandated by state law, are much more structured. Year-end, external audits usually include the following elements:

- A study of school board minutes in conjunction with financial transaction to determine if proper approvals were obtained
- Verification of revenue receipts of all types
- Verification of expenditures via examination of requisitions, purchase orders, vouchers, and canceled checks
- A review of journal and ledger entries
- Reconciliation of bank statements, accounts, and investments
- A review of subsidiary documents (e.g., deeds, inventory statements, trusts, sinking funds) (Burrup et al., 1996)

In many states, the audit also includes specific judgments regarding the degree to which the school district's financial transactions comply with state laws and regulations.

Over the past few decades, the trend has been to require more stringent and frequent auditing procedures. In many states, higher demands for accountability have led to "open door" or "sunshine" laws that require public officials to report financial data more comprehensively and frequently. Within many school districts, trends toward decentralization and participative decision making also have contributed to increased emphasis on financial reporting (Hack et al., 1995). Only a small percentage of school district audits reveal serious errors and potential wrongdoing; far more commonly, these reports verify good practice, efficiency, and observance of laws and regulations (Burrup et al., 1996). As such, they are a source for building public confidence.

Debt Management

School districts, just like families, incur periodic debts that may be either short-term or long-term obligations. Short-term debts (commonly considered to be one year or less) usually involve loans secured to address financial emergencies created by cash flow problems (e.g., late tax payments). These obligations account for about one fourth of all debt in the municipal markets (that is, debt incurred by governmental agencies). Long-term debts are more commonly associated with capital development projects (e.g., new school buildings, renovations, land acquisition) or the expenditure of large sums of money for equipment (e.g., purchase of school buses or computers).

The administrative responsibilities associated with debt management have always been complex simply because of the nature of the task and the idiosyncratic facets of state laws. Functions such as estimating tax impact, determining advantageous structures for debts, securing loans, and selling bonds exemplify this fact. Debt management also has been made more intricate by changes in federal and state tax laws that restrict arbitrage (investing bond proceeds at a higher rate of interest than is being paid by the issuer of the bonds) and the sale of municipal bonds (Rebore & Rebore, 1993).

Risk Management

Risk management is a process by which administrators make decisions that reduce the school district's exposure to financial loss. It is the "total overview of establishing the best possible manner of minimizing potential risks while protecting the public assets of the school district and taxpayer" (Thompson, Wood, & Honeyman, 1994, p. 479). The scope of potential risks within a school district is quite broad. Possible losses range from law suits over student accidents to the destruction of buildings by fire or tornadoes. Today risk management is considered to be more than purchasing insurance and filing claims; a much greater emphasis is being given to preventive measures. This trend is the result of both the escalating costs of insurance and expectations of insurance carriers that clients will take proactive steps to prevent losses.

There are four primary techniques that superintendents may use to control risk:

- Avoiding exposure to risk or getting rid of exposure if it exists (e.g., removing playground equipment that presents a danger)
- Creating policies and practices that prevent losses (e.g., requiring periodic inspections of buildings)
- Taking steps to lessen the financial impact of losses that cannot be prevented (e.g., taking steps to reduce the potential for severe damage in bus accidents)
- Transferring the legal and financial risk to another party (e.g., requiring someone who uses the school to provide his or her own insurance) (Hack et al., 1995)

Beyond taking measures relating to prevention, schools have two basic choices with respect to losses: officials can contractually transfer risk to another party (e.g., buying insurance policies), or they retain the risk and pay for losses from fiscal resources available to the school district. Since most school districts are not in the financial position to do the latter in many areas of operation, the task of purchasing and maintaining insurance policies has become a more time-consuming task for school district administrators.

Even though many districts assign risk management to a person other than the superintendent, experts agree that a risk management program's effectiveness is affected by the superintendent's support (Burrup et al., 1996). This is because so many areas of risk prevention require district-wide coordination. Consider the following examples of contributions relating to risk management that can be made by a superintendent, even in very large school districts:

- The identification of risk is a critical first step to building an effective program. The superintendent can commission a comprehensive study involving a committee that includes representatives of all segments of the school community. The product can be reviewed annually to ensure accuracy.

- The risk management program will not function well unless it is assigned to a capable individual and given an adequate budget. Both of these decisions are likely to be made by the superintendent.

- Prevention is often based on support programs. For example, a superintendent may initiate a wellness program as a means of reducing employee health insurance claims.

- Prevention is also enhanced by effective policies that protect the school district from risk. For example, a superintendent may recommend revisions of policy relating to the use of school buildings during evenings and weekends.

- Implementation of a risk management program is dependent on effective two-way communication between the school district and the community and between individual schools and central administration. The superintendent is often instrumental in developing and maintaining effective communication.

Purchasing and Inventory Management

An ongoing fiscal function in all school districts is the purchasing of equipment and materials. Because public funds are involved, this responsibility is controlled by laws, state regulations, and local district policies. Collectively, these forces often mandate practices in the following areas:

- *Competitive bidding.* Many states require school districts to receive sealed bids for purchases that exceed a certain amount; laws also may require acceptance of the "lowest and best bid."

- *Requisitions.* School districts commonly require employees to fill out a requisition form and/or purchase order for procuring supplies or equipment.

- *Filing and paying claims.* Transactions between school districts and vendors usually require the use of specified procedures and forms; the superintendent or a designee presents claims periodically to the school board for approval as prescribed by state law.

While such restrictions may hinder the flexibility of purchasing agents, they are deemed necessary to protect the public's interests.

Related to the purchasing function is inventory management. Because savings can be realized with large purchases and because some supplies and equipment are needed for immediate delivery, many school districts maintain centralized warehouses. For smaller districts, decisions about the extent of warehousing are determined by space availability within the school district and the reliability and delivery capabilities of vendors. Other issues that are associated with purchasing or warehousing include the following:

- Determining the amount of space needed for warehousing
- Developing a plan for the distribution of supplies and equipment from the school district's inventory to individual school sites
- Providing proper security and inventory control for the warehouse or central storage area
- Determining the types of supplies and equipment that will be assigned to decentralized storage (that is, storage in the individual schools)
- Weighing leasing options as an alternative to purchasing large-money items
- Disposing of surplus and salvage materials
- Determining minimum and maximum quantities for stored material

Effective purchasing and inventory programs promote buying economies, prevent duplication of purchases, reduce theft, facilitate cost analysis related to purchasing decisions, and promote evaluation of products purchased.

Regardless of who functions as the purchasing agent, the superintendent has the responsibility to see that the program functions effectively and efficiently. This includes requiring objectivity in purchasing decisions, vendor competition, and analysis and evaluation of the existing program. Perhaps most important, the superintendent should ensure that the purchasing and inventory program exists to serve the educational process. That is to say, the ultimate success of the program is predicated on the degree to which it actually meets the needs of principals, teachers, and students. The achievement of this goal is enhanced by involving school-based personnel (principals and teachers) at three stages: (1) drafting the specifications for equipment and material, (2) participating in product demonstrations, and (3) evaluating product effectiveness after use.

Purchasing activities have the potential for conflict of interest—or at least the appearance of one. The conflict would be between the school district's interests and a public official's pecuniary or personal interest. This problem is both legal and political. In some states, statutes require all public employees and board members to disclose possible conflicts. Actually determining what constitutes a conflict, unfortunately, is no simple matter; courts in different states have issued very dissimilar rulings in this matter (Hack et al., 1995). Consequently, superintendents ought to consult with the school district's attorney to ascertain the existing laws governing the matter and to identify persons who may have a potential conflict of interest.

Salary and Wage Management

The responsibility for managing payroll and fringe benefit programs is complex, and even in this era of technology, it can require a considerable amount of attention. Because of the nature of school districts, compensation programs vary from one employee group to another. As an example, professional staff receive annual contracts that stipulate salaries (a set amount of money to be paid for a certain period of time); other employees are usually paid on the basis of hourly or daily wages (Rebore & Rebore, 1993). In addition to issuing checks and maintaining records, this general responsibility also entails a considerable amount of planning and legal monitoring.

Salary and wage management is closely tied to the personnel function in school districts. For example, policies and practices pertaining to structuring compensation programs and fringe benefit packages are typically personnel functions. Decisions in these areas can affect employee morale, generate political tensions (e.g., in collective bargaining situations), or result in legal problems (e.g., errors in making payroll deductions). Generally, the structure of a salary and wage program is shaped by multiple forces, the most prevalent of which are these:

- Organizational philosophy
- State and federal laws
- Existing master contracts with unions
- Employment conditions in the geographic area (that is, prevailing wages, unemployment rates)
- Common practices in other school districts in the state

Facility Management

School buildings constitute a sizable investment of public funds, and the development and maintenance of these structures constitute another broad area of management responsibility for school superintendents. Over the past 2 or 3 decades, a number of factors have heightened the interest of both taxpayers and educational administrators in this area of school administration. Consider the following examples:

- Studies conducted in the late 1980s, indicated that at least 25% of the nation's school buildings were in poor physical condition, and thus, inappropriate as learning environments (e.g., Lewis, 1989). By the mid-1990s, this percentage increased to about one third (General Accounting Office, 1996).
- Many school districts in the United States have been affected by population shifts; in some geographic regions (e.g., Florida), most districts are growing rapidly, requiring new facilities to be added annually. In other areas (e.g., parts of the industrial Midwest, some rural communities), districts have lost considerable enrollment, resulting in the closing of schools.
- Technology has served to redefine appropriate learning environments for elementary and secondary schools (Kowalski, 1995).
- Issues of equity (that is, requiring a reasonably equal fiscal output from taxpayers) continue to be raised in many states with regard to capital development projects. This is especially true in states that do not provide some form of state equalization for funding the cost of school buildings (Thompson et al., 1994).

- Approximately one fifth of the states still require virtually all capital outlay costs to be funded by property tax revenues—a situation that heightens the political tensions surrounding facility projects.

- In an environment characterized by scarce public resources, communities are demanding greater utilization of school buildings and more efficiency in their management.

- School reform has generated many new programs that have implications for educational environments. Expanded school years and increased high school graduation requirements are prime examples of ideas that often require building modifications (e.g., air conditioning, additional science labs).

Collectively, issues such as these have made school facility management a more essential activity in the work lives of superintendents.

Investments in capital outlay for projects related to school facilities require both extensive planning and substantial community support. Basil Castaldi (1994) divided the superintendent's responsibilities in the area of developing school facilities into three broad tasks: (1) developing a long-range plan, (2) building support for the plan, and (3) planning specific facility projects. In many school districts, superintendents are choosing to involve citizens in both long-range planning and the planning for specific projects. While inclusive planning can generate conflict, it usually engenders a sense of ownership and pride among the involved citizens. Often these taxpayers help school officials garner wider community support for facility projects. Their involvement also is likely to produce a more accurate assessment of needs and a wider range of potential solutions.

Public approval for facility projects is required in many states; this is obtained either by referenda or by some form of petition process. Three obstacles often stand in the way of approval: (1) many citizens believe that the property tax, used to fund school building in many states, is unfair; (2) many taxpayers see school buildings as being relatively unimportant to student learning; and (3) there is a general political mood in the country favoring tax relief. Such conditions may make it extremely difficult for superintendents and school boards to obtain political support for capital projects. These difficulties are compounded in districts in which the vast majority of taxpayers have no member of the immediate family enrolled in the schools; in some communities, 80% or more of the taxpayers fall into this category. Given these conditions, planning for school building projects has become inextricably linked with public relations. The involvement of a broad base of the community and school district in the needs assessment phase often is pivotal in securing public approval.

Once projects gain approval, other managerial responsibilities emerge for a superintendent. Foremost are decisions about the project planning team, including criteria for selecting individuals who will be team members. Planning teams include architects, and often other professional services (construction managers, educational planning consultants, financial consultants, and bond counsels) are also included. A superintendent's decisions about planning are shaped by personal and professional values about shared decision making, about the importance of learning environments, and about the degree to which function should dictate form (that is, the extent that programs should influence the design of school buildings).

In addition to gaining support and planning for building projects, superintendents also have oversight responsibilities for facility maintenance. This duty spans many managerial activities such as the following examples:

- Providing an organizational structure for maintenance and custodial services
- Ensuring that maintenance and custodial employees have relevant job descriptions
- Ensuring that maintenance and custodial employees are properly supervised and their job performance is objectively evaluated
- Evaluating the program of maintenance services with respect to supporting educational programs
- Providing adequate human and material resources so that the goals of educational programs can be reached
- Encouraging the preparation of manuals and other documents that enhance program effectiveness
- Promoting values and beliefs within the school community about the importance of maintaining proper learning environments
- Creating a two-way communication process between central office administrators and principals, which facilitates effective maintenance services

The superintendent has the ultimate responsibility for seeing that learning environments are adequate, efficient, flexible, adaptable, healthful, and safe.

Aspects of facility maintenance have changed substantially in the past 3 decades. For example, technology has resulted in more sophisticated mechanical, electrical, and air-control systems. In addition, modern schools are designed to provide students and staff with access to information via computers and other technologies that integrate voice, data, and video, and the Internet is now available to staff and students in many schools. When buildings were less sophisticated, superintendents often elevated skilled maintenance personnel to the top administrative position in this department (e.g., the director of buildings and grounds). They were able to do so because the position did not require a professional license or certificate, and the building environments were less complex. In the early 1980s, for example, just over 67% of all such directors in the United States did not possess a college degree (Abramson, 1981). Many superintendents are now opting to employ individuals who are highly educated in either technology or management areas (e.g., engineers or persons who possess degrees in business management) (Kowalski, 1989).

PERSONNEL MANAGEMENT

Even small school districts are relatively large organizations. A school system with only 1,500 students, for example, could have over 100 employees—far more employees than would be found in many small businesses. People readily recognize that personnel management includes functions such as payroll, fringe benefits, and retirement plans. Less acknowledged, however, is the fact that personnel management can have a direct influence on the quality of instruction within a school district. John Seyfarth (1996) noted that (1) employee selection, induction, and staff development influence teacher knowledge and motivation; (2) the work environment, compensation programs, grievance policies also affect teacher motivation; and (3) personnel evaluation serves to inform and remind employees of the school district's expectations.

While the direct involvement of the superintendent in personnel management is largely determined by the size of the school district and size of the administrative staff

> . . . goals of the personnel function are basically the same in all school systems—to hire, retain, develop, and motivate personnel in order to achieve the objectives of the school district, to assist individual members of the staff to reach the highest possible levels of achievement, and to maximize the career development of personnel. (Rebore, 1995, p. 11)

Organizing the Personnel Function

The actual role of a superintendent in personnel management may range from having general supervisory responsibilities for subordinate administrators who manage the program to being directly responsible for performing most or all of the specific functions. Regardless of how responsibility is fixed, several general principles should be observed in all types of school systems:

- All employees should be considered in organizing the program; personnel management is not a responsibility that only pertains to professional staff.
- Because personnel management is so broad, duties are commonly shared between central office and building administrators and among divisions within the central office. One of the key facets of successful programming is determining which operations should be centralized and which should be decentralized.
- Because responsibilities are shared among a number of administrators, it is important to identify and communicate specific role expectations to those who assume personnel duties and responsibilities.
- Duties and responsibilities ought to be designated on the basis of knowledge, skill, and experience (Castetter, 1992).

These principles illustrate the complexity of personnel management.

A superintendent assumes primary responsibility for four specific tasks relating to personnel programs: (1) policy development, (2) policy implementation, (3) general control of the program, and (4) improvement of the program (Castetter, 1992). In order to ensure a proper level of accountability, the superintendent should maintain adequate two-way communication with persons who are assigned to manage the various personnel functions. Interactions between and among these administrators should include discussions of problems and needs and the development of recommendations for program improvement.

Decentralization of school district governance sparks new questions regarding policy, program control, and program improvement for areas such as employment, staff development, and performance evaluation. How much autonomy can and should be given to individual principals and school-based governance councils to select new employees? What legal risks are incurred if decentralized decision making leads to processes or outcomes that do not conform with state law or school district policy? Primarily because of such legal concerns, complete decentralization of personnel management (that is, executing the responsibility entirely at the individual school level) is unlikely. Technology, however, makes it more possible for personnel management to be a shared responsibility between central office and school-based administrators (e.g., information can be shared in real time via networked computers).

Elements of a Personnel Program

School district size always has been an influential factor with regard to personnel management. As districts became larger, decision making and management became more complicated. For example, growth in the number of employees usually meant that work roles became more specialized and that employees were divided into categories (e.g., professional and nonprofessional). As this occurred, one or two employees in the business office could no longer perform all the necessary record keeping and transactions. A separate division of personnel management became more common.

In addition to the increasing size of districts, the personnel function also has been made more demanding by two other critical developments:

1. Schools, like other professionally dominated organizations (that is, organizations in which a majority of the employees are professionals), have a need to facilitate activities that lead to improved employee performance. This necessity is driven primarily by the constant development of new knowledge and the corresponding need for professionals to improve their skills and knowledge. For example, the microcomputer already has changed the way many teachers and administrators perform their responsibilities.

2. Personnel administration has had to respond to a growing number of federal and state laws affecting employment practices and the treatment of employees. Topics of such legislation have included equal opportunity, sexual

harassment, and age discrimination. Either directly or indirectly, federal and state employment laws have contributed to a pattern of centralized authority within school districts. Fear of not being in compliance with complex laws often motivates superintendents to reduce margins of error by reducing the participative nature of employment-related decisions.

Collectively, the increased size of school districts, the dynamic nature of the educational process, and new laws have made the personnel function an intricate responsibility—and one that continues to be a fundamental responsibility for superintendents.

Every administrative activity that touches an employee is arguably related to personnel management. This area of administration is divided into four primary categories:

1. *Employment practices.* The employment process spans recruitment, selection, and job placement issues.
2. *Human resources development.* This category encompasses activities pertaining to assessing staffing needs, induction, staff development, and employee assistance programs.
3. *Employment management.* This encompasses performance evaluation, record keeping, and compensation programs.
4. *Employee relations.* Employee relations pertains to responsibilities such as collective bargaining, grievances, and litigation.

Examples of specific functions, grouped under these headings, are shown in Table 9–2.

Working with Unions

When collective bargaining gained a foothold in public education in about the 1960s, many superintendents were unprepared and thus reluctant to engage in the process (Campbell, Cunningham, Nystrand, & Usdan, 1990). This was especially true with respect to teachers, because an obvious by-product of unionization was conflict among educators. Prior to teacher unions, both administrators and teachers commonly held membership in the National Education Association (NEA) and that organization's state affiliates. Stress also developed between superintendents and principals, because building administrators frequently had little involvement in negotiating contracts with teacher unions, yet they were almost always affected by the results. In some larger urban districts, principals themselves unionized to protect their interests.

About 85% of the states either require or permit school boards to engage in collective bargaining with employee unions (Lunenburg & Ornstein, 1991). In some states, collective bargaining legislation applies only to select employee groups (e.g., to teachers but not other employees). Twenty-two states have public

Table 9–2
Elements of personnel management

Category	Specific Functions	Examples
Employment practices	Needs assessment	Determining the number and types of positions needed
	Recruitment	Posting vacancies and securing applicants
	Screening applicants	Evaluating both written materials and job interviews
	Selection	Procedures for making employment decisions
	Contracting	Issuing employment contracts
	Evaluating outcomes	Determining effectiveness of employment practices
Human resources development	Induction	Providing orientation and adjustment to the school and to the work role
	Staff development	Workshops, seminars, professional leaves
	Performance evaluation	Formative and summative evaluation, clinical supervision
	Assistance programs	Employee assistance programs for special problems
Employment management	Record keeping	Maintaining personnel files
	Payroll	Working with fiscal management to provide necessary information for compensation
	Fringe benefit programs	Managing insurance, vacation, sick leave, and other types of employee benefits
	Legal problems	Working with attorneys to resolve legal problems affecting employees or the school district
	Environment control	Assuring healthy and safe work environments for employees; providing accommodations for employees with disabilities
	Employee severance	Retirement, layoffs, reduction-in-force, and dismissal decisions
Employee relations	Employee morale	Providing social activities such as picnics, group trips, and opportunities for travel
	Collective bargaining	Negotiating contracts with employee unions
	Grievance management	Handling formal and informal employee complaints

employees relations boards charged with the responsibility of implementing relevant laws and providing third-party services for mediation, fact finding, and arbitration (Rebore, 1995).

Throughout much of the 1970s and 1980s, attention to union-related matters became a time-consuming activity for superintendents. In some districts, there are as many as 6 or 7 employee unions—each having a collective bargaining agreement with the school board. Just the implementation of these documents (e.g., handling grievances) may require an inordinate amount of the superintendent's time and energy. Even more disconcerting is the fact that many of these matters generate tensions, making effective positive relationships between the superintendent and employees more difficult.

Unions and School Reform

Increasingly, policymakers and scholars are questioning the relationship between unionism and reform in public education. The evidence as to whether collective bargaining has been good or bad for public education is often conflicting. Critics of the process, for example, have argued that unions foster greater levels of centralization, as well as animosity between administrators and teachers. By contrast, proponents suggest that collective bargaining has forced boards and superintendents to be less bureaucratic and more attentive to real problems in the schools (Shedd & Bacharach, 1991).

Today many administrators and local union officials recognize that collective bargaining has generated a number of by-products that have been detrimental both to the image of schools and to school improvement. Consequently, they have been searching for more productive processes. Two alternatives to traditional bargaining that have gained popularity in recent years are *collaborative bargaining* and *consensus bargaining*. Unlike conventional negotiations that almost always placed teachers and administrators in an adversarial relationship, these concepts are designed to build trust and to redirect official union-employer contact toward shared decision making. Collaborative bargaining seeks to focus on real problems that are affecting the operations of schools; consensus bargaining strives to promote rational solutions by reducing emotion and extreme positions (Misso, 1995). In essence, these alternative approaches are intended to create "win-win" situations, allowing both the school board and union to claim victories.

New concepts for bargaining, however, have not eliminated concerns about dealing with unions. Some labor relations specialists have warned school officials that collaborative approaches often lead people to become infatuated with the process rather than objectively evaluating outcomes. Further, they have pointed out that the greatest successes with collaboration have been achieved in wealthy school districts, where ample resources have been available to mollify union leaders (Harrington-Leuker, 1990).

Conflicts between educators who see themselves as professionals and the bureaucratic organizations in which they work are certainly not new. Myron Lieberman (1986) explained that teacher unionism was a product of feelings of helplessness; others characterized teacher unionization as a justifiable quest for autonomy (e.g., Newman, 1990). However, even after several decades in which unions have become an integral part of public elementary and secondary education, many teachers remain ambivalent about belonging to them. Such feelings are being intensified by reform initiatives that seek to make teachers true professionals, that is, to give them greater autonomy in practice. The empowerment of individual teachers is in many ways incompatible with the strategy of collective power traditionally espoused by unions. Whether new approaches such as collaborative bargaining will reduce tensions and problems remains uncertain. In the meantime, many superintendents continue to face the reality of performing two seemingly contradictory tasks: being politically effective in the area of union management and building the trust and confidence of teachers as an instructional leader and change agent.

The Superintendent's Direct Role in Collective Bargaining

Regardless of what type of approach is being used for bargaining with employee unions, one essential question must be answered: Should the superintendent be involved directly in negotiating contracts? Across the country, many superintendents—especially those who work in small school districts—serve as chief negotiators or they sit at the bargaining table as members of the board's team. Often the superintendent's involvement is predicated on the size of the school district or the superintendent's experience (Sharp, 1989). In smaller districts, school boards may be reluctant to employ a chief negotiator because (1) they do not want to alienate the union, (2) they do not want to spend the money to hire such a person, and (3) they want to clearly identify the superintendent as a key figure on the management team.

The likelihood of the superintendent being at the bargaining table is increased in those districts that opt for collaborative approaches. In large part, this is because the superintendent is probably most responsible for gaining the necessary level of confidence and trust from both the school board and the union (Attea, 1993). However, many experts urge caution. Critics of the superintendent being directly involved at the bargaining table argue that this role endangers relationships with teachers and pulls the superintendent away from more essential leadership functions (Ficklen, 1985). Some observers (e.g., Pennella & Philips, 1987) argue that superintendents can be more effective if they are providing leadership behind the scenes. If they are viewed by teachers as tough-minded negotiators, superintendents' effectiveness in other areas is likely to be eroded.

There is no simple answer to the question of direct involvement of superintendents in collective bargaining. Each school district is unique with respect to past practices, union relationship, philosophy, needs, culture, milieu, and resources. In those districts where collaborative bargaining has been productive, the superintendent's direct involvement may be desirable and beneficial. However, in other situations where the more traditional, adversarial approach still prevails, caution is in order. It is extremely difficult to be a hard-nosed bargaining agent one day and a trusted professional colleague the next. While the overt hostility associated with union-related issues has diminished in many school districts in recent years, the challenges generated by these matters continue to require the superintendent's direct attention.

SPECIAL EDUCATION AND STUDENT PERSONNEL SERVICES

Two areas of responsibility for public school districts that have grown substantially in the past several decades are special education and student personnel services. Legislation for individuals with disabilities requires school districts to provide a wide range of programs and accommodations to serve the special needs of students. In addition, societal and economic changes have combined to create new pressures for increased services to be provided to students in addition to basic programming. In some districts, for instance, there is a need to accommodate children who were affected by the drug use of their mothers. These types of problems often affect both special education and student personnel services. In some districts, these two functions may be combined, but more generally, they are considered separate services.

Special Education Services

Historically, public schools have been required by state statutes or regulations to provide services to students with disabilities. However, in the 1970s, the scope and descriptions of these services were broadened substantially by the passage of three pieces of federal legislation: (1) the Rehabilitation Act of 1973, (2) Public Law 93–380 in 1974, and (3) Public Law 94–142 in 1975 (Lunenburg & Ornstein, 1991).

Public Law 94–142, the Education for All Handicapped Children Act, required states to adopt policies that ensure public schools provide a free appropriate education based on the needs of individual students. Such services could include classroom instruction, physical education, home instruction, and instruction in special institutions (residential care facilities, hospitals). The most discussed aspect of programming was the concept of *least restrictive environment* (originally called *mainstreaming* but more recently referred to as *inclusion*). This facet of the law specified that children with disabilities are to the maximum extent possible to be educated with children who do not have disabilities and that removal of a special needs student from the regular classroom can occur only when the nature or severity of the handicap makes education in the regular classroom unsatisfactory.

In considering litigation in the area of special education, the courts have rather consistently exhibited a preference for enforcing the concept of inclusion (Berger, 1995). In addition, school districts are required under this law to provide related services for students with disabilities, which might include special accommodations for transportation and recreation; developmental, corrective, or support services such as therapy (speech, language, occupational, physical, psychological); and diagnostic and evaluative medical services and counseling (Campbell et al., 1990).

The requirements placed on school districts were made quite specific by Section 504 of the Rehabilitation Act, as amended in 1974. This legislation stated that schools could not exclude a student from participation in programs on the basis of the student's handicapping condition. To do so would constitute discrimination. Provisions extended rights to areas such as accessing school buildings. The Handicapped Act Amendments of 1990 gave Public Law 94–142 a new title, the Individuals with Disabilities Act. This legislation officially changed basic terminology by substituting the term *disability* for *handicap* (LaMorte, 1996).

Compliance with the numerous laws protecting the rights of students with disabilities has become a complex matter for school superintendents. There are many facets of the topic that are covered in separate school administration courses such as law, finance, and school facility planning. Here, two responsibilities are examined because they directly affect the superintendency. The first pertains to the organization of services; the second focuses on legal issues.

Today most school districts belong to joint ventures, often called special education cooperatives. These entities became common after the 1970s federal legislation regarding students with disabilities for three primary reasons: (1) most school districts could not afford to operate low-incidence programs, (2) many superintendents could not afford to employ a separate director of special education, and (3) the number of students qualifying for special programs increased dramatically. In some states, school districts with a sufficient enrollment base to justify low-incidence programs and the employment of special support personnel (e.g., psychologists and psychometrists) may opt to have their own programs and not to be part of a joint services agreement. The legal and operational dimensions of joint services ventures were discussed earlier in the book. A superintendent is expected to be sufficiently knowledgeable of the laws and prevailing conditions to advise the school board on policy matters pertaining to the structure and organization of special education services.

The second matter, legal problems, often catches newly appointed administrators by surprise. In particular, they underestimate the amount of time that will be consumed by parental complaints, hearings, and lawsuits involving special education. Such disputes usually center on decisions made in developing the individualized educational program for students with disabilities (called the IEP), interpretations of the IEP with regard to programming, suspension or expulsion of students with disabilities, parental dissatisfaction with programming decisions (especially as related to inclusion), and placement in special schools or institutions (e.g., placement of a student in a hospital, which will require substantial financial payments by the school district).

A guide for critical issues pertaining to special education is outlined in Table 9–3.

Table 9–3
Key considerations with regard to special education

Responsibility	Examples of Critical Questions
Program organization	What options exist with regard to providing services? What are the advantages and disadvantages of membership in a joint services venture? What factors may change organizational structures? If the school district becomes part of a joint services venture, what authority/role will the school district have in the governance of the joint services entity?
Supervision of services	How will programming be supervised? How much supervision must or should be provided by the superintendent?
Personnel management	How many individuals will be directly employed by the school district? How many will be employed by the special education cooperative? What legal issues are raised in the area of employment (e.g., tenure status of teachers who work in the district but are employed by the cooperative)?
Adjudicating problems	What role will the superintendent play in disputes? What policies need to be developed with regard to adjudicating problems for students with disabilities?

Student Personnel Services

One of the commonly overlooked areas of management in a school district relates to student personnel services—an aspect of school district operations that supplements basic programming for students. Generally, this area of responsibility includes administrative and supervisory functions concerned with enrollment-related issues (e.g., admission, registration, classification) and issues of student services (e.g., development of abilities, interests, and needs) (Knezevich, 1984). In smaller school districts, these duties are often dispersed among the available personnel, with much of the responsibility being shouldered by building-level administrators. In larger districts, it has become common to centralize many of these functions. This typically is accomplished by making student personnel services a subdivision of instructional services or by establishing a separate department within the central office (e.g., setting up a division of student personnel services headed by a director or assistant superintendent).

There are no universally established boundaries for student personnel services. For example, some districts include special education in this division; however, this is no longer the norm. The most common elements of pupil personnel administration are listed below:

1. *Attendance services.* Included here are matters pertaining to student enrollment and attendance. This could include legal matters governing residency, verification of pupils' ages, compliance with state laws and district policy

concerning attendance, maintenance of attendance records, and the preparation and filing of required attendance reports.

2. *Services for the economically disadvantaged.* Administration of federal assistance programs such as Title I and Head Start are often housed within student personnel services in large school systems. Responsibilities include the development, management, and evaluation of relevant programs.

3. *Guidance and counseling services.* With the expansion of counseling services in schools, greater attention is being given to providing coordination and support from the central office. Common services include standardized testing programs (including interpretations of state-mandated achievement tests), support for building-level counselors and teachers, a referral service for serious problems, and resources for vocational and academic counseling.

4. *Administration of pupil conduct.* Although most student discipline issues are handled at the level of the individual school, central administration commonly becomes involved in certain activities. These might include (1) providing suspension and expulsion hearings; (2) dealing with legal matters pertaining to student conduct; (3) policy analysis and evaluation; (4) consultation services for administrators, teachers, parents, and students; and (5) staff development.

5. *Student health services.* The primary purposes of this function are (1) the assessment and diagnosis of student health problems; (2) compliance with state laws and district policies relative to health screening tests (e.g., vision tests); and (3) wellness programs and preventive measures.

6. *Social work.* Largely because of expanding social and economic problems, many school districts are employing social workers. These professionals usually address student needs associated with poverty, dysfunctional families, child abuse, and community-based problems.

In some school districts, speech and hearing therapy and psychological services also may be included under student personnel administration; more commonly, these functions are provided within the scope of special education programs.

Most superintendents find that the area of student personnel services is demanding greater attention for several reasons:

- A growing number of students in America are living in poverty.
- Principals and school-based counselors are often too busy to deal with emergency situations.
- An increasing portion of the school district budget is being allocated to these services.
- There is growing acceptance of the concept of full-service schools. That is, educators are acknowledging that schools cannot ignore social, physical, psychological, economic, or emotional problems that prevent students from learning.

- When services have not been coordinated, additional stress on the school district results. With responsibility dispersed among various staffs, districts have found it extremely difficult to respond to opportunities (e.g., potential federal grants) and changing needs (e.g., intervention programs for gang-related violence).

- Without some form of centralized coordination, larger school districts find that it is extremely difficult to provide adequate supervision of these programs. If all social workers function independently as school-based personnel, for example, coordinating and balancing their caseloads may be impossible.

Challenges for a superintendent are probably greatest in those districts not sufficiently large to merit a separate division for pupil personnel services. In these situations, the superintendent must answer the following questions:

- Which services need to be provided?
- Who will be delegated the responsibility for providing the services?
- How will the services be funded?
- How will supervision be provided?

WORKING WITH THE SCHOOL ATTORNEY

The management of legal issues in public education is yet another responsibility that has expanded markedly in the last half of the 20th century. School districts routinely employ or retain the services of an attorney to handle a variety of issues ranging from the acquisition of property to lawsuits. Several essential issues pertaining to the superintendent's relationship with the school attorney are examined in this section. They are (1) options for legal services, (2) the selection and evaluation of a school district attorney, (3) compensation options for attorneys, and (4) the actual role of the attorney.

Virtually all decisions regarding employing a school attorney are framed by values and beliefs about this position. In some instances, in choosing an attorney to retain, school boards place far more emphasis on the fact that a lawyer be a taxpayer in the district than they place on his or her knowledge and experience in area of school law. In part, this is because superintendents and school boards often see the school attorney playing a restricted role involving only routine matters of general law. If unusual problems occur, these district officials are prepared to retain special assistance from external sources such as the state school board's association or from a law firm with lawyers specializing in particular school problems (e.g., in labor relations). At the other end of the spectrum, there are superintendents and school board members who believe that most legal problems are not routine. For that reason, they prefer to employ a school attorney who has an established reputation in this specialization. These school officials pay little or no attention to the attorney's place of residence since it is likely that they will have to go outside the local community to obtain the expertise they desire. Other issues that school boards ought to consider in selecting a school attorney include accessibility to the attorney, the attorney's availability to attend school board meetings, and the attorney's general workload.

The process for selecting an attorney varies across school systems. In some districts, school board members see this task as their responsibility; they may not even consult with the superintendent regarding opinions about possible appointees. In other districts, the superintendent plays the dominant role in the selection process; the board merely formalizes the superintendent's selection by approving his or her recommendation for the appointment. Most commonly, however, the selection of a school attorney is a shared responsibility. Both the superintendent and board realize that the attorney's performance will affect them and the welfare of the entire school community.

School attorneys may be compensated in various ways. A decision on this matter may be restricted by state statutes and regulations—that is, some states may limit the options that may be used. The following alternatives have been used by school districts across the United States:

- An *annual retainer.* This is a fixed amount per year for which the attorney is expected to perform normal and customary duties; typically a retainer does not cover items such as defense in lawsuits or bonding issues.

- *An hourly rate*

- *A combination of retainer and hourly rate.* The retainer provides services up to a specified number of hours of service per month; additional time is billed at an hourly rate.

- *Employment of an attorney on a full-time basis.* The attorney is a regular employee of the school district, with a specified annual salary.

The last option, full-time employment, is not feasible for most districts. Some districts employ several attorneys, with one being designated officially as the school district's attorney of record. In some instances, school districts retain a firm rather than an individual, and the assignment of an attorney is based on the problem being handled.

The actual role assumed by the school attorney is perhaps the most critical issue for the superintendent. Since World War II, the courts have assumed an increasingly aggressive role in shaping educational policy (Kirp & Jensen, 1986; Tyack, James, & Benavot, 1987). This has resulted in a blurring between making policy for school districts versus making a legal analysis of a policy. To be more precise, many attorneys often establish the spirit and language of school board policy rather than rendering an opinion about the legal ramifications of a proposed or enacted policy. In a study conducted in Indiana, Joseph

McKinney and Thelbert Drake (1995) found that school attorneys were heavily involved in policy making. Since these attorneys brought their own values and biases to the process, their involvement raises fundamental questions about the interrelationship among the superintendent, school attorney, and school board with regard to setting district policy. Assume, for example, that a school district is contemplating a new policy regarding student expulsion. Does the attorney develop the policy and present it to the school board for approval? Or does the attorney advise the superintendent so that the superintendent can integrate legal input in forming his or her final recommendation to the school board?

In addition to policy making, a superintendent's association with the school attorney involves matters relating to administering the district on a day-to-day basis. Not only do the interventions of the courts influence laws, state regulations, and district policies, they also serve to place controls on rules and regulations promulgated and enforced by principals and superintendents. In some districts, most legal interpretations provided by the school attorney relate to enactment and enforcement of rules and regulations associated with board policies.

An atmosphere of openness, candor, and trust between the superintendent and attorney obviously facilitates good management. Ideally, their relationship is like an effective partnership. They respect each other's philosophy, knowledge, and responsibility.

SUPPORT SERVICES

In a small town or rural area, the public school system is commonly the largest transportation and food service provider. Unfortunately, many taxpayers do not realize the amount of management that is required to make these operations run smoothly. The purpose here is to highlight the superintendent's responsibilities for these important support functions.

Student Transportation

Central to providing a system of student transportation are two questions: How will the function be organized within the school district? How will the services be provided?

The first question relates to administrative responsibility. Except for the smallest school districts, it is likely that the superintendent will have someone designated as a director or coordinator for pupil transportation. In larger school systems, the operation is often placed under the general supervision of the chief school business official. The responsibility of coordinating a transportation program generally requires two types of knowledge and skills: managerial and technical. The former relates to areas such as budgets, personnel management, routing, insurance, and policy management; the latter pertains to functions such as writing specifications for purchasing buses or replacement parts, maintenance operations, and supervision of maintenance personnel.

In determining how services will be delivered, superintendents in most states are faced with several choices. These are outlined in Table 9–4. In essence, the choices can be reduced to the options of ownership and contracting for services. Advocates of private contracting (e.g., Lieberman, 1986) point out that both management responsibilities and labor-related problems can be reduced with this option. Skeptics argue that for-profit companies are often insensitive to student and parent input and more prone to cut corners that may affect safety. In addition, contracting may generate political problems in the local community, especially if a number of employees are displaced (Saks, 1995). Rural districts have often used the option of individual contracts. Farmers, for example, find driving a school bus a good way to augment their income. While the school district saves money because it does not have to purchase or maintain buses, the operating costs may be high unless there is some reasonable level of competition among bidders for the established routes.

Experts generally agree that neither purchasing nor contracting is necessarily superior. The appropriate choice depends on the particular conditions in a school district. Critical considerations for weighing the feasibility of using private contractors to provide school transportation programs are shown in Table 9–4.

Table 9–4
Options for operating a transportation system

Option	Explanation
District ownership and maintenance	The district purchases all of its own buses and maintains the fleet with district employees; only major mechanical problems may be contracted out for services.
District ownership and contracted maintenance	The district purchases all of its own buses but enters into a contract with a private company for maintaining the fleet.
Partial ownership and partial contracting	The school district owns some buses but enters into contracts with private parties or companies for other routes; generally, the school district maintains its own buses and contractors are responsible for maintaining their buses.
Complete contracting by routes	The school corporation develops bus routes and advertises for bids from private contractors; under this option, the school district has no capital outlay; individual contractors buy and maintain their own buses.
Complete contracting with one firm	Rather than contracting with multiple providers by individual routes, the school district enters into a single contract with a company that provides total transportation services; under this option, the school district has no capital outlay.

Figure 9–2
Considerations relating to contracting for transportation services

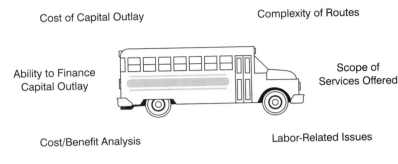

Prevailing State Laws

Cost of Capital Outlay

Complexity of Routes

Ability to Finance
Capital Outlay

Scope of
Services Offered

Cost/Benefit Analysis

Labor-Related Issues

Potential Political Ramifications

The choice of district ownership versus contracting prompts key questions such as the following:

- Does state law permit both district ownership and private contracting? If so, are the laws written in a manner favoring one option over the other?
- To what extent does existing policy and past practice restrict the degrees of freedom the superintendent may have in choosing between ownership and contracting?
- To what extent will ownership require additional management services from district administrators?
- Are there differences in liability costs between contracting and ownership?
- What purposes are served by the transportation program? For example, are buses also used for field trips, athletic events, or community activities?
- How much usage will the buses have in one year?
- What is the intended life span of a bus?
- How often will the buses need to be serviced? What level of maintenance will be required?
- What political issues are involved? For example, districts that have been using individual private contractors may find considerable political opposition to a change to school district ownership.
- What is the school district's capacity to incur debt for purchasing buses? State finance laws and economic conditions in individual districts vary markedly; while some districts may find it economically advantageous to purchase buses, others may find this option to be impractical.
- How does ownership compare with contracting with regard to operational costs, insurance, and maintenance?

The responsibility of managing a transportation system has been made even more complex by federal and state legislation protecting the rights of individuals with disabilities. In this context, transportation has been defined to include (1) travel to and from school and between schools; (2) travel in and around school buildings; and (3) specialized equipment (such as specially designed buses) that may be required to transport those with disabilities. Both direct costs for such services (e.g., mileage, taxi fares) and indirect costs (e.g., tolls, parking fees) must be assumed by school districts (Bluth & Hochberg, 1994). Because many students with disabilities are educated in schools other than the one they would normally attend and because some students with disabilities cannot be transported on regular school buses, a myriad of special considerations must be handled.

Some taxpayers apply inappropriate criteria when judging the effectiveness of student transportation programs. Most notably, they use efficiency and economy, and not safety and convenience, as primary assessment criteria (Zeitlin, 1989). This tendency has become even more prevalent as fewer taxpayers have children enrolled in the schools and as school districts face the problem of providing expanded services with dwindling resources. The real challenge for the superintendent is to simultaneously do the following: (1) ensure safety, (2) be responsive to student, school district, and community needs and wants, and (3) apply sound principles of business management.

Food Services

Almost always, superintendents delegate the general supervision of food services to another employee. Even so, there are several policy-related matters that must be addressed. These include establishing proper criteria for operations, determining the scope of services provided, and establishing an appropriate format for delivering services.

With regard to criteria, superintendents should strive to balance the goals of nutrition, consumer wants, and efficiency. Effective programs are able to show positive outcomes in all three areas. Superintendents typically rely on state guidelines and professional advice to determine the quality of meals provided, and they rely on principals to provide input on consumer satisfaction. The issue of efficiency falls more directly on the shoulders of central office administration. In the past, many superintendents have treated food services programs with a polite indifference; if the programs did not have a serious deficit, they were left alone. Often overlooked were long-term operating costs such as large-equipment items. Proper management requires (1) adequate supervision to ensure productivity, (2) the maintenance of cost controls, (3) cost-benefit analysis, and (4) a reinvestment of resources to fund necessary improvements (Boehrer, 1993). The issue of supervision is especially noteworthy. In most schools, head cooks or cafeteria directors have the general responsibility to provide first-level management. However, for the most part, they never have received management training to perform these duties (Anderson & Durant, 1991). They typically need basic skills in purchasing, inventory management, record keeping, performance assessment, and accounting.

With respect to the scope of services provided, almost all school districts provide lunch programs for students. In recent decades, federal programs for disadvantaged students and local district initiatives have resulted in additional services. The most notable addition has been breakfast for some or all students. Also under the scope of services are issues related to offering student choice. For example, some schools have added salad bars and à la carte lines to encourage more students to participate in the lunch program. In some communities, school food-related facilities are also used for social activities, club meetings, and the like outside of the regular school day. All of these extensions have policy implications.

As in transportation, private contracting also has become an issue in the food services area. However, the potential for political problems associated with switching from a district-operated format to outside providers is often greater. This is because food services have commonly operated on a more decentralized basis; that is, each school operates its own program. Under such conditions, cafeteria employees are seen as a part of neighborhood schools. When their jobs are threatened, negative reactions from parents are very likely. Choosing a private company to operate food services within a school district may be prompted by several factors. For example, union-related problems, a lack of managerial staff, or consumer preferences may sway the superintendent and board in this direction. Another reason simply has to do with management itself. Between 1989 and 1993, nearly 300 school districts dropped out of the National School Lunch Program (a federally subsidized program) because of growing competition from fast food providers and because of the complex nature of rules and regulations attached to the program (Van Wagner, 1995).

Even if school districts decide not to opt for contracting, the superintendent may face questions about satelliting. Under the satellite concept, there is a central location for food preparation. Satellite food programs became popular in the 1960s and 1970s as a cost-saving measure. During that period, many districts were erecting new schools. Using the satellite concept helped reduce capital outlay expenses since full kitchens did not have to be replicated. Proponents of the concept also argue that there (1) are operational cost savings, that is, fewer employees are needed because food preparation is done in large volumes; (2) is an increasing level of quality in the food; and (3) is more standardization in the product served (Van Egmond-Pannell, 1983). However, despite these claims, some school officials question the value of satellite programs. Some school districts could find that transportation and other costs equal or exceed cost savings; other districts may reject the concept for political reasons (e.g., the schools prefer to maintain a totally decentralized system).

FOR FURTHER REFLECTION

This chapter identified major managerial responsibilities facing the modern school superintendent. Two other chapters address leadership responsibilities (chapter 8 and chapter 11). The primary duties described here included the following: finance, facilities, personnel, working with the school attorney, special programs, student personnel services, transportation, and food services.

As you consider what you read in this chapter, answer the following questions:

1. Have management functions become lower priorities for school superintendents in the past 10 to 15 years? What is the basis for your answer?

2. Are superintendents adequately prepared to manage the fiscal matters of a school district? What evidence do you have to support your position on this matter?

3. In larger school districts, superintendents often are able to employ a business manager or assistant superintendent for business. If you were a superintendent, what qualifications would you establish for this job? What would be your relationship with this staff member?

4. What problems do superintendents commonly encounter in the area of facility planning? Are these problems becoming more or less complex?

5. Assume you were the superintendent of a small district enrolling 1,000 pupils in 3 schools. Which elements of personnel administration are you likely to manage yourself? Which aspects would be delegated to others?

6. What issues are likely to be raised about personnel selection in school districts that decentralize governance (e.g., as is the case with site-based management)?

7. What is consensus bargaining? To what extent does this concept affect views regarding the role that should be played by the superintendent in the collective bargaining process?

8. Why has special education become a management concern for many superintendents?

9. What responsibilities are commonly included in student personnel services? What factors are causing this to become a higher priority for many districts?

10. Who should select the school attorney?

11. What role should a school attorney play in policy development?

12. One of the major decisions superintendents make about student transportation programs relates to the option of private contracting. What are the possible advantages and disadvantages of having such a contract for a school district?

13. What are the advantages and disadvantages of using a private contractor to provide food services in a school district?

14. What is a satellite food program? What criteria might you use to judge whether such a program is feasible in your school system?

CASE STUDY

Over the past 7 years, the Dalton Township School District has increased about 20% in enrollment. Currently, there are about 1,750 students in grades kindergarten through 12. This growth has presented a number of challenges for the district's superintendent, John Zeemer. When he entered this position 5 years ago, John had expected the district's enrollment to remain stable, but the construction of an electronics factory in a neighboring community sparked a number of new housing starts in Dalton Township. Enrollment projections completed in the last year indicate that the student population is expected to continue increasing for the next 10 years at about 3% to 5% annually.

One of the most obvious problems facing the superintendent and school board is overcrowded conditions in the school buildings. The 2 elementary schools and the junior-senior high school are operating at about 105% to 120% of designed capacity. Last year the board approved the construction of a third elementary school; this year, a commitment was made to renovate and enlarge the junior-senior high school building. Prior to becoming a superintendent, John had never been involved as an administrator in a school construction project. Over the past 16 months, he learned just how much of his time would be consumed with this one responsibility.

Getting the community and school board to recognize the need for a third elementary school was the superintendent's first challenge. Despite several years of steady growth, most school board members preferred to take a "wait and see" posture toward school construction because they were skeptical that the growth would continue for a prolonged period. John spent many hours preparing presentations for the board and community groups showing the already-crowded conditions in the schools.

After the school board accepted John's recommendation to build a new elementary school, many other tasks had to be addressed. There were interviews related to selecting an architect; a planning committee was formed; state laws and regulations had to be reviewed. John was able to attend to all of these emerging responsibilities only because he delegated more and more of his routine work to the 3 other persons who worked with him in the school district's central office and to the 3 principals.

Ever since the school district was formed approximately 45 years ago, the superintendent has been the only professional employee in the central office. The 3 other persons who work with him are—

- Ruth Mayfield (bookkeeper and treasurer for the district)
- Deloris Evers (secretary to the superintendent)
- Norma Fetcher (secretary and receptionist)

In addition to her general office responsibilities, Norma also helps coordinate transportation services; Deloris maintains all the records for the food services program. In the past year, the superintendent has asked the principals to take greater responsibility for several personnel functions, including teacher selection; Ruth had to assume much of the responsibility of planning the district's annual budget. The strain on the employees was becoming apparent to John.

Now faced with starting the facility project at the junior-senior high school while the construction of the new elementary school had not started, John was appropriately concerned about how he was going to get everything done. Prior to the building programs, he had tried to spend about 25% of his time being an instructional leader; that no longer was a feasible goal. John also is the chief negotiator for the school board, and although relationships with the teachers' union are positive, this task still consumes a good bit of his time. Last week Ruth Mayfield told the superintendent that this year would be her last—she was going to retire. His secretary also has been hinting at the possibility of doing the same.

Stress was beginning to affect John. He was not sleeping well; he only used 5 of his 24 vacation days last year. In general, he really was not enjoying his job as much as he had in past. The hours were getting longer, and the conflict was more pervasive. And John was increasingly troubled by the fact that he had to delegate more work to others. The principals were beginning to complain that they had insufficient time to observe teaching and to get involved in critical instructional matters.

John realized that matters would only get worse in the next year. The enrollment again was projected to increase; the two ongoing building programs would consume much of his time; he would have to replace 1 and possibly 2 of his key staff members in the central office. He began to develop a list of possible actions that might alleviate some of the stress. At the top was the goal of creating a new position for an assistant superintendent. However, politically, he was unsure the board would support the idea. The two building projects will increase the district's tax rate by about 30%. Additional state revenues for enrollment growth were barely adequate to fund new teaching positions and necessary equipment and materials. Hence, adding an assistant superintendent—even at a modest salary—would necessitate a tax increase for the operations budget.

Issues for Discussion

1. Identify and evaluate possible actions other than adding an assistant superintendent that John might consider in addressing his problem.

2. Do you believe that the size and nature of the central office staff in this district are typical for a school district with 1,700 students and 3 or 4 attendance centers?

3. If you were in John's position, what arguments could you present to the school board to add an assistant superintendent?

4. If you received approval to add an assistant superintendent, how would you reconfigure work in the central office?

5. One of the aspects of this case relates to greater management responsibility being delegated to principals. In districts where there are no other professional personnel in the central office other than the superintendent, is there typically an adverse effect on the ability of principals to function as instructional leaders?

6. Assume that John knows that a majority of the board will not support a recommendation to add an assistant superintendent. Does he have an ethical or professional responsibility to make the recommendation anyway?

7. Assess the fact that the superintendent is the board's chief negotiator in the bargaining process with the teachers' union. Should he use this current problem as an opportunity to relinquish this role? Why or why not?

8. Do superintendents in small districts generally spend more time managing than do superintendents in large districts? What evidence do you have to support your response?

9. If you were the superintendent, how would you respond to the following comment from a school board member? "Just be patient. The building programs will be over in year or two, and these enrollment increases are only temporary. Everything will be back to normal before you know it."

10. What aspects of a school facility project are likely to consume the most time with respect to a superintendent in a smaller school district?

REFERENCES

Abramson, P. (1981). The superintendent of buildings and grounds: His job, his status, his pay. *American School and University*, *54*(2), 66–71.

Anderson, K. M., & Durant, O. (1991). Training managers of classified personnel. *Journal of Staff Development*, *12*(1), 56–59.

Attea, W. (1993). From conventional to strategic bargaining: One superintendent's experience. *School Administrator*, *50*(10), 16–19.

Berger, S. (1995). Inclusion: A legal mandate, an educational dream. *Updating School Board Policies*, *26*(4), 1–4.

Bluth, L. F., & Hochberg, S. N. (1994). Transporting students with disabilities: Rules, regs and their application. *School Business Affairs*, *60*(4), 12–17.

Boehrer, J. M. (1993). Managing to meet the bottom line. *School Business Affairs*, *59*(11), 3–8.

Burrup, P. E., Brimley, V., & Garfield, R. R. (1996). *Financing education in a climate of change* (6th ed.). Boston: Allyn and Bacon.

Campbell, R. F., Cunningham, L. L., Nystrand, R. O., & Usdan, M. D. (1990). *The organization and control of American schools* (6th ed.). Upper Saddle River, NJ: Merrill/Prentice Hall.

Castaldi, B. (1994). *Educational facilities: Planning, modernization, and management* (4th ed.). Boston: Allyn and Bacon.

Castetter, W. B. (1992). *The personnel function in educational administration* (5th ed.). New York: Macmillan.

Drake, T. L., & Roe, W. H. (1994). *School business management: Supporting instructional effectiveness*. Boston: Allyn and Bacon.

Ficklen, E. (1985). Whoa there! By stationing the superintendent at the bargaining table, you could be gunning for trouble. *American School Board Journal, 172*(5), 32–33.

General Accounting Office (1996). *School facilities: America's schools report differing conditions*. Report to congressional requesters. (ERIC Document Reproduction Service No. ED 397 508)

Hack, W., Candoli, I., & Ray, J. (1995). School business administration: A planning approach (5th ed.). Boston: Allyn and Bacon.

Harrington-Lueker, D. (1990). Some labor relations specialists urge caution. *American School Board Journal, 177*(7), 29.

Hartman, W. T. (1988). *School district budgeting*. Upper Saddle River, NJ: Prentice Hall.

Kirp, D., & Jensen, D. (1986). *School days, rule days: The legislation and regulation of education*. Philadelphia: Falmer Press.

Knezevich, S. J. (1984). *Administration of public education: A sourcebook for the leadership and management of educational institutions* (4th ed.). New York: Harper & Row.

Kowalski, T. J. (1989). *Planning and managing school facilities*. New York: Praeger.

Kowalski, T. J. (1995). Chasing the wolves from the schoolhouse door. *Phi Delta Kappan, 76*(6), 486, 488–489.

LaMorte, M. W. (1996). *School law: Cases and concepts* (5th ed.). Boston: Allyn and Bacon.

Lewis, A. (1989). *Wolves at the schoolhouse door: An investigation of the condition of public school buildings*. Washington, D.C.: Education Writers Association.

Lieberman, M. (1986). *Beyond public education*. New York: Praeger.

Lunenburg, F. C., & Ornstein, A. C. (1991). *Educational administration: Concepts and practices*. Belmont, CA: Wadsworth.

McAdams, P. (1995). Everything you always wanted to know about the superintendency, but were afraid to ask. *NASSP Bulletin, 79*(570), 86–90.

Misso, J. D. (1995). Consensus bargaining: A step toward rational thinking. *School Business Affairs, 6*(12), 26–28.

McKinney, J. R., & Drake, T. L. (1995). The school attorney and local educational policy-making. *West Education Law Quarterly, 4*(1), 74–83.

Newman, J. W. (1990). *America's teachers*. New York: Longman.

Pennella, M., & Philips, S. (1989). Help your board negotiate: Stay off the bargaining team. *Executive Educator, 9*(4), 28–29.

Rebore, R. W. (1995). *Personnel administration in education: A management approach* (4th ed.). Boston: Allyn and Bacon.

Rebore, W. T., & Rebore, R. W. (1993). *Introduction to financial and business administration in public education*. Boston: Allyn and Bacon.

Saks, J. B. (1995). Exercising your options. *American School Board Journal, 182*(10), 38–40.

Sergiovanni, T. J. (1991). The dark side of professionalism in educational administration. *Phi Delta Kappan, 72*(7), 521–526.

Sergiovanni, T., Burlingame, M., Coombs, F., & Thurston, P. (1992). *Educational governance and administration* (3rd ed.). Boston: Allyn and Bacon.

Seyfarth, J. T. (1996). *Personnel management for effective schools* (2nd ed.). Boston: Allyn and Bacon.

Sharp, W. (1989). *The role of the superintendent and school board in collective bargaining*. Paper presented at the annual meeting of the Midwestern Education Research Association, Chicago.

Shedd, J. B., & Bacharach, S. B. (1991). *Tangled hierarchies: Teachers as professionals and the management of schools.* San Francisco: Jossey-Bass.

Starratt, R. J. (1990). *The drama of schooling, the schooling of drama.* Bristol, PA: Falmer Press.

Thompson, D. G., Wood, R. C., & Honeyman, D. S. (1994). *Fiscal leadership for schools: Concepts and practices.* New York: Longman.

Tyack, D., & Cuban, L (1995). *Tinkering toward utopia: A century of public school reform.* Cambridge, MA: Harvard University Press.

Tyack, D., James, T., & Benavot, A. (1987). *Law and the shaping of public education 1785–1954.* Madison: University of Wisconsin Press.

Van Egmond-Pannell, D. (1983). Satelliting school lunch production. *School Business Affairs, 49*(11), 20,42–43.

Van Wagner, L. R. (1995). Fed up. *American School Board Journal, 182*(5), 39–41.

Zeitlin, L. S. (1989). Pupil transportation and fiscal responsibility. *School Business Affairs, 55*(4), 35–39.

Chapter 10

Being an Effective Communicator

Key Concepts

✧ The superintendent in an information age

✧ One-way and two-way communication

✧ Organizational communication

✧ Obstacles to effective communication

✧ Attributes of effective communication

✧ Listening and nonverbal communication

✧ Communication networks

✧ Being an effective communicator

✧ Working with the media

Since we live in an age of information, it is not surprising that many proven leaders have been characterized as effective communicators. Interacting with people, both within and outside of the school district, has always been an essential part of the superintendency. However, the importance of this aspect of the job has been increased by recent societal changes that place a premium on the timely exchanges of information. In addition, modern technologies have heightened expectations that public officials will be more attentive and responsive to constituent needs. Over the past 4 decades, the development of information technology has provided an invaluable tool for meeting these expectations and for improving organizations (Lucas, 1996). So whether it is using the Internet to obtain the latest data on educational initiatives or using technologies that integrate voice, video, and data to communicate with the community and build goodwill, an ever-increasing number of school superintendents are realizing that communication has become a key facet in effective practice.

IMPORTANCE OF COMMUNICATION

In the early 1980s, futurist John Naisbitt (1982) outlined 10 trends that he saw reshaping American society. Among them were 3 that are affecting public education rather directly:

- *Transition to an information society.* Both curriculum and instructional technologies are changing as schools focus less on preparing students to work in a manufacturing society.
- *The creation of a global economy.* Government officials, business leaders, and others who influence public policy see a connection between American dominance in the world and the quality of public education.
- *Movement from hierarchies to networking.* The increasing value of information is prompting a reconsideration of the traditional administrative structure of school districts.

In large measure, these trends have helped to frame reform agendas over the last 2 decades; they have pushed administrators to seek new approaches to identifying and solving problems; they have forced school districts to invest in new communication systems. Although communication is "complex, subtle, and ubiquitous" (Hoy & Miskel, 1996, p. 341), those who aspire to be educational leaders must be knowledgeable about the nature of communication and proficient in using it. Anything less is apt to create problems for the contemporary superintendent.

Understanding the Concept of Communication

Broadly defined, communication is the process of imparting information or knowledge. The process includes a sender, a receiver, a sent message, a time dimension, a medium, and an outcome (Kowalski & Reitzug, 1993). The process can be categorized according to (1) status, (2) form, (3) action, and (4) flow (see Figure 10–1). Here is a description of each category and how it can be related to a school context.

1. The *status* of a communication is commonly classified as being either formal or informal. Formal actions are initiated and sanctioned by the formal organization (that is, the school district or an official subdivision of the school district); informal actions are initiated by individuals outside of their formal roles or by informal groups (e.g., a teacher evaluating the principal's performance in a conversation with other teachers).

2. There are two basic *forms* of communication: verbal and nonverbal. Verbal communication uses words to convey messages; it may be oral or written. Nonverbal communication occurs in the presence of another but does not rely on the use of words; for example, this kind of communication might involve conveying feelings through gestures.

3. In terms of the category of *action,* parties to a communication process act either as senders or as receivers; in interactive exchanges, they move between the two roles.

4. The *flow* of communication can be described as either one-way or two-way. One-way communication is almost always a top-down approach in which supervisors convey selected messages on an "as needed" basis to subordinates; two-way processes involve both horizontal and vertical communication that can be both top-down and bottom-up.

Richard Schmuck and Philip Runkel (1994) described three basic types of communication, which they labeled (1) unilateral, (2) directive, and (3) transactional. The first two categories are forms of one-way communication. In unilat-

Figure 10–1
Categories of communication

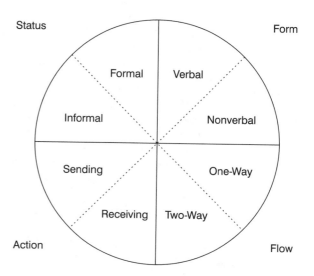

eral communication, a message is terminated with the message being sent. That is to say, the initiator of the message typically does not know whether the message was received or understood by the receiver. In a school district, newsletters from the superintendent, announcements from central administration, or memoranda are examples of unilateral communication. Directive communication involves a face-to-face exchange in which the receiver acknowledges receiving and understanding the message. An example is a superintendent telling a principal to start complying with a district regulation on student conduct; the principal is merely expected to listen and accept the message. Transactional communication is a two-way process. There is an exchange of information and ideas between or among the parties.

Early studies of communication in organizations were based on linear models that concentrated on the one-way flow of messages. Such studies reinforced beliefs that only one-way channels were necessary or appropriate. The limitations of these models eventually became evident, and interactional paradigms were developed—that is, models that took into account the critical importance of feedback and focused on reciprocal exchanges (Harris, 1993). Individuals who function in organizations quickly learn that communication is not handled uniformly by managers. School districts are no exception; administrators exhibit a wide range of behavioral differences with respect to transmitting and receiving messages. These differences may be associated with the quantity of information provided, the quality of information provided, the channels used to communicate, the timeliness of transmitting information, and directional flow of information. Most of us recognize the administrative skills necessary for using one-way channels—skills such as being able to write a good memorandum or being able to give a good speech. Less obvious are skills necessary for using two-way communication—skills such as listening, decoding nonverbal messages, and resolving conflict (O'Hair & Spaulding, 1996).

Within the realm of classical theory, communication was defined as the "transmission of information" (Hanson, 1996, p. 223). Thus, highly bureaucratic organizations have relied largely on one-way, top-down messages in which content is restricted to the employee's prescribed assignments. More precisely, one-way channels served five functions: (1) to provide job instructions, (2) to provide job rationale, (3) to explain established procedures, policies, and practices, (4) to provide performance feedback, and (5) to inform employees of the organization's mission and goals (Katz & Kahn, 1978). High-ranking officials who rely on one-way channels conclude that there is no reason to receive information from subordinates. This pattern of behavior is exemplified by the superintendent who discourages employees from providing input and who routinely does not share general information about issues such as long-range planning, fiscal conditions, and policy disputes.

The evolution of organizational theories had a profound effect on the ways in which managers treated communication. The human relations movement brought to the fore issues such as motivation and transactional exchanges; emphasis was placed on both the sender and receiver. Within the context of open systems theory, communication has been defined as "the exchange of messages and meaning between an organization and its environment as well as between its network of interdependent subsystems" (Hanson, 1996, p. 224). Given the nature of school districts, the view embodied in the open system is most relevant. Superintendents should not only be concerned about the quality and quantity of information exchanges between subsystems in the district; they also should be concerned with information exchanges between the district and the community.

Each school district is a unique entity because of its culture, climate, leadership strategy, leadership style, and prevailing needs, and these factors are in constant evolution. Thus, understanding the communication process in any given district requires an examination of such variables. E. Mark Hanson (1996) noted that a true understanding of how we communicate with each other is predicated on our awareness of three dimensions:

> (1) the process of sending and receiving messages through specific channels; (2) the formal and informal impediments and facilitators of the process; and (3) the multivariate social, political, cultural, and economic environments that surround and permeate every aspect of the communication process. (p. 224)

Noted public relations specialist Albert Holliday (1996) described educational communication within political and rational perspectives:

> Educational communication has two components. The first is the political aspect. This deals with laying the groundwork for staffing, facility, and programming needs so that the public will adequately fund schools. The second is the rational aspect. This deals with interrelationships of educators, students, parents, and others in the community. In this area, partnerships and parent-volunteer contributions exemplify enhancements that can make a school outstanding. Both components—the political and the rational—though different in purpose call for similar attitudes and skills on the part of administrators. School leaders must be able to build consensus among staff and the citizenry with regard to relevant goals and approaches to achieving them. They must value sharing, asking, and discussing more than telling. (p. iv)

This definition of educational communication is especially meaningful for school officials who see public schools as democratic institutions seeking to empower professional employees and seeking to engage in meaningful renewal.

Effective Communication in a School District

All organizations are affected by the quality of communication within them. Communication is the basis for a broad range of functions such as planning, instructional delivery, enforcement of policy and regulations, and socialization. In school districts, communication should promote clarity and understanding to facilitate goal attainment (Hoy & Miskel, 1996). The critical nature of communication in public education can be summarized in two broad categories. First, superintendents must use communication to galvanize support among policymakers and taxpayers and to persuade them to endorse and enthusiastically support the district's initiatives (Howlett, 1993). Second, the highly technological information age requires superintendents to facilitate the work of other educators; for example, helping principals and teachers "to reach diverse groups of students and their parents" (O'Hair & Spaulding, 1996, p. 157). These two purposes serve to frame the importance of effective communication in the modern school district. As resources become increasingly scarce, and as policymakers and taxpayers become increasingly skeptical about the productivity of public education, the superintendent's ability to use communication in its broadest form has become essential. Current policy initiatives such as school choice, vouchers, and charter schools seek to place public schools in more competitive situations. As this occurs, the ability of a district to use modern communication systems is likely to influence both public perception of schools and the quality of services they provide.

Previous attempts to change the course of public education, such as those following the Russian launching of the first satellite *Sputnik* in the 1950s and those following the publishing of *A Nation at Risk* in the early 1980s, serve to inform current practitioners about the realities of trying to reinvent public institutions. In particular, previous reform efforts revealed the inadequacies of both rational/scientific models and political models of organizational change; neither exposing educators to new knowledge via staff development nor imposing intensification mandates produced lasting change. Past efforts to reconceptualize schools have led a growing number of reformers and policymakers to conclude that cultural paradigms are central to producing desired and necessary levels of change.

Cultural models focus on values, norms, and symbolic behavior. As previously discussed in chapters 3 and 4, this approach is being pursued by leaders who seek to make schools more democratic, more responsive, and more professional—a challenge that is highly dependent on information and the behavior of individuals who have access to information. For example, accurate exchanges about problems and ideas become more essential as decision making becomes more inclusive. Teachers cannot function as true professionals unless they are able to engage in communication with other professionals and unless they have access to relevant databases. Likewise, teacher empowerment remains a meaningless idea if superintendents are unable to properly use communication to convey the values and beliefs that underlie this concept (Geddes, 1993). This is why communication is a central issue in school renewal; it is both a means for re-creating culture and climate and a reflection of the prevailing culture and climate.

In a cultural model for change, the symbolic nature of the superintendent's behavior becomes a focal point. Administrators who demand openness and two-way communication from others but who exhibit the opposite behaviors themselves are likely to be judged more by their acts than by their words. More specifically, effective communication becomes more likely if the superintendent and other leaders are themselves effective communicators. These individuals serve as models of ideal behavior.

Charles Conrad (1994) observed, "Cultures are communicative creations. They emerge and are sustained by the communicative acts of all employees, not just the conscious persuasive strategies of upper management. Cultures do not exist separately from people communicating with one another" (p. 27). Stephen Axley (1996) described the bond between culture and communication this way: "Communication gives rise to organizational culture, which gives rise to communication, which perpetuates culture" (p. 153). This association implies that communication cannot be understood sufficiently by reducing it to a loop of linear steps or by focusing research exclusively on the transmissions between senders and receivers (Katz & Kahn, 1978). Instead, investigators need to treat communication as a process through which members of an organization express their collective inclination to coordinate beliefs, behaviors, and attitudes. Put more simply, communication is a course of action that people in a school or district use to give meaning to their organizational lives by sharing perceptions of reality. A negotiated order evolves from both internal and external interactions among individuals and groups, and this interplay occurs in the informal as well as formal organization. When viewed from this social system standpoint, communication is a process that shapes, transmits, and reinforces a socially constructed culture (that is, a set of shared dimensions that form the assumptions, values, and artifacts of a particular organization) (Mohan, 1993).

Within the framework of a cultural change model, problem solving requires administrators to identify how individuals perceive reality so that this information can be used to erect mutual understandings about a school's purposes and practices. This objective is unlikely, however, in situations where administrators employ communication practices, either consciously or unconsciously, that restrict the debate of values, discourage conflict, and limit access to information (Deetz, 1992). Regrettably, managers in many organizations continue to treat information as power, and they restrict access to it as a means of protecting personal power (Burgess, 1996). Superintendents who fall into this category are incapable of actualizing the primary function of transformational leadership—shaping and developing new norms in the school (Carlson, 1996).

The reciprocal relationship between culture and communication is especially noteworthy with respect to the symbolic frame of administration. When administrators appropriately recognize that organization does not precede communication but is supported by it, they are more inclined to view organization as an effect of communication (Taylor, 1993). This puts a different viewpoint on critical leadership attributes. For example, credibility and trust (essential characteristics of leaders who assume the role of change agent) are not produced by structure or programs; instead, they spring from human interactions. Unless leaders accurately evaluate the effects of communication on underlying assumptions and unless they properly dissect the language of a school, they probably cannot determine the extent to which culture facilitates or obstructs change (Kowalski, 1998).

COMMON BARRIERS AND EFFECTIVE ACTIONS

Various categories have been used to identify and describe barriers to communication. For instance, some authors have used verbal and nonverbal classifications (e.g., Sigband & Bell, 1989). In such dichotomies, nonverbal obstacles relate to issues such as interpretation, cognition, and prejudice; verbal obstacles focus on the use of language. Others have elected to discuss barriers within organizational and theoretical frames (e.g., Hanson, 1996; Razik & Swanson, 1995). In this context, barriers are commonly associated with attributes of the organization or attributes of individuals. Organizational barriers are rooted in the prevailing culture, climate, or organizational dimensions. In a district with a long history of collective bargaining problems, for example, teachers may mistrust information provided by administrators; consequently, they develop informal networks and rely on one another for information. Individual barriers relate to abilities, knowledge, and specific behaviors. For example, a principal with poor writing skills sends teachers an ambiguous memorandum concerning directions for ordering instructional materials. Rather than achieving its purpose, the memo serves to confuse the teachers.

Although barriers are found in all school districts, some superintendents are able to overcome them, both organizationally and personally. In large measure, this is due to a superintendent's ability to identify obstacles and his or her willingness to deal with them. Fundamental to both tasks can be a philosophical perspective promoting democratic decision making and a climate of openness toward subgroups in the district and toward the community at-large.

Barriers to Communication

What constitutes a barrier to communication is shaped by beliefs about power and authority in school districts. Today it is commonly accepted that leaders in public institutions ought to be engaging in two-way communication. They should be exchanging information with people in the district and the community. The purposes are to make the schools responsive to real needs and to provide services that enhance community development. Barriers to two-way communication are presented in two categories: organizational obstacles and personal obstacles.

Organizational Obstacles

The culture, climate, and other attributes of an organization may create impediments that deter accurate and timely exchanges of information. Among the most common are the following:

- *Size of the school district.* One of the most easily understood problems relates to school district size. Large districts often have more difficulty engaging in two-way communication than do small districts. Factors such as the number of attendance centers, the number of employees, and the geographic size of the school district may restrict the superintendent's ability to communicate (Hanson, 1996).

- *Strict adherence to a chain of command*. In hierarchical organizations, effort is made to have every employee reporting to a single supervisor. The purpose is to provide tight control and supervision and to reduce ambiguity relative to job responsibility. This bureaucratic principle has been commonly applied in school districts. For instance, school principals in a district of 4,000 students may report to an assistant superintendent; because of this organizational arrangement, contact between them and the superintendent may be minimal—and the level of contact between the superintendent and teachers is probably even lower (Kowalski & Reitzug, 1993).

- *Information overload*. This problem refers to people being inundated with information to the extent that they are unable to engage in effective two-way communication. It can occur at all levels of a school district. In a small district, a superintendent may be responsible for virtually every function; his or her desk is covered with mail from government officials, purchase orders, parental complaints, and so on. Teachers also may suffer this problem as they receive countless messages from central office personnel, the principal, the department chair, parents, and students (Lunenburg & Ornstein, 1991).

- *Information filtering*. Especially in districts in which communication passes through multiple levels (e.g., messages follow a path of superintendent to assistant superintendent to principals to teachers to students to parents), information is often filtered. That is, at each stage the message is altered. This can be a purposeful act, such as a subordinate selectively editing so that his or her supervisor does not receive certain information; or filtering can occur because of encoding or decoding errors. Filtering can occur in either top-down or bottom-up processes (Lunenburg & Ornstein, 1991).

- *Selective perception*. Often information provided by a school district is not received in the manner intended. Employees, students, or parents extract only bits and pieces in order to interpret the communication to their liking (Hanson, 1996). An example is a principal who receives the district's annual report and only reads the positive material pertaining directly to his or her school. Selective perception may be especially troublesome in districts with weak cultures (i.e., districts in which teachers and administrators hold varying values and beliefs about their work, about children, and so on), because people pay attention to information that is congruent with their beliefs.

- *Closed climate*. Organizational climates are often described on a continuum ranging from open to closed. Organizations with closed climates attempt to repel external interventions. A school district that avoids community input exemplifies this type of organization. As schools attempt to move toward more democratic governance and as they attempt to build symbiotic relationships with their communities, a closed posture toward information exchanges constitutes an obvious obstacle to effective communication.

- *Insensitivity to diversity*. In many cities, public school officials communicate with people of multiple and diverse cultures. If they do not understand these cultures or if they are unwilling to adjust their communication to each to meet the needs of different audiences, two-way exchanges are quite unlikely.

Personal Obstacles

In addition to organizational barriers, a superintendent's effort to be an effective communicator may be blocked by personal characteristics. Among the most common are the following:

- *Poor listening skills*. Superintendents who have poor listening skills are typically unable or unwilling to receive information from others. When someone is speaking, they may daydream, become impatient, jump to conclusions, or nonverbally express a lack of interest. Poor listeners are often bypassed by others. That is, people discern that a person is a poor listener and they decide to communicate around the individual (O'Hair & Spaulding, 1996). This condition usually reduces a superintendent's effectiveness; for example, employees may bypass the superintendent and communicate directly with board members.

- *Poor encoding or decoding skills*. Superintendents need to communicate with diverse groups. For instance, they often engage in information exchanges with persons who have different levels of education and cultural perspectives. Their ability to transmit a message about an educational problem with equal effectiveness is crucial. Doing so requires both encoding (e.g., putting ideas into words) and decoding (e.g., interpreting messages from others). Being able to interpret a principal's body language during a performance evaluation conference is an example of a decoding skill.

- *Lack of credibility*. Both a superintendent's reputation and a history of honest interactions establish a record of credibility. Once credibility is lost, "it is difficult, if not impossible, to regain within the organization where the loss occurred" (Razik & Swanson, 1995, p. 243). Obviously communication within a school district suffers immensely when people decide that they do not believe the superintendent's words are accurate.

- *Lack of trust*. Trust within organizations is "built very slowly and in small increments, is established more by deeds than by words, and is sustained by openness in interpersonal relations" (Schmuck & Runkel, 1994, p. 127). If employees feel they are being used or manipulated or if they feel that the superintendent does not act in their best interests, communication is not likely to flow in a productive manner.

- *Elitism*. Some superintendents isolate themselves from the general community, choosing to communicate solely with power figures or other influential citizens. Others possess an attitude that their practice should be directed exclusively by professional knowledge; hence, the views of parents or other taxpayers are judged to be unimportant.

Organizational and personal barriers prevent effective communication and result in problems, such as poorly informed decisions, an uninformed public, rumors, and distorted messages. Two-way channels of communication must be planned and nurtured.

Attributes of Effective Communication

Leaders in organizations spend about 70% of their waking moments engaged in some form of communication (Irmsher, 1996). Competence in this critical area obviously influences overall job performance. There are many attributes that may contribute to an individual's communication effectiveness; most are behaviors that can be learned. Among them are six that are especially relevant to superintendents; they are displayed in Figure 10–2.

Listening Skills

Listening is a complex task that extends beyond the moment of receiving a message. In large measure, poor listening skills are associated with a lack of mental processing (e.g., decoding and committing to memory). While the average person speaks at a rate of approximately 150 words per minute, people generally have the capacity to listen at a rate of over 1,000 words per minute. The difference results in idle time during which the mind is apt to wander (Robbins, 1976). Mary O'Hair and Angela Spaulding (1996) discussed the following activities that are associated with the development of good listening skills:

- *Understanding and committing to the listening process.* The individual should know that listening entails more than hearing the message; understanding the message and remembering the message also are critical. A commitment to all three elements is a first step toward becoming a good listener.
- *Listening between the words.* To receive a message as it is intended, a person must listen between and beyond the words transmitted. This requires interpretations of how things are said (e.g., tone of voice, loudness), as well as interpretations of what is actually being said.

Figure 10–2
Critical communication competencies for superintendents

Listening Skills	Credibility	Understanding Nonverbal Communication
Communicating in Context	Resolving Conflict	Creating a Climate for Two-Way Communication

- *Improving memory.* Using information properly often relies on a person's memory. The development of long-term memory involves linking new stimuli to stored information. Such linkages allow the receiver to remember information and reflect on it at a later time.

- *Clarifying messages through second-guessing.* Second-guessing is a form of skepticism; listeners can review and analyze the message in an effort to filter out slanted or prejudiced views. While this process may not be necessary in all communications, the skill is necessary when listeners have reason to doubt the veracity of the information received.

- *Using excess thinking time productively.* Good listeners utilize the gap between the speed at which a message is heard and their capacity to receive the message to interpret what is being transmitted; rather than daydreaming, they think about the logic of the message, seek to verify what they hear, think about questions, provide feedback to the speaker, and so on.

- *Adopting mental guidelines.* Good listeners are able to relate new information to old information; they engage in reflection to identify key points to evaluate, process, and use information (pp. 164–168).

The integration of hearing, decoding, and remembering is essential to being a skilled listener.

Studies of communication in organizational settings report that individuals are aware of listening-related behaviors such as attentiveness, nonverbal behavior, attitudes, memory, and overt responses (Lewis & Reinsch, 1988). A person who routinely exhibits good listening skills is seen as respectful, interested, and concerned (Burbules, 1993). Even so, many administrators are unaware that their listening skills are constantly being assessed by individuals with whom they communicate. Leaders in business communication are convinced that listening comprehension is a learned behavior; as such, they are urging business schools to teach listening skills and encouraging companies to provide training in this area for executives at all levels (Spinks & Wells, 1991). Listening skills are especially important to school administrators. Everything a superintendent does is dependent on the accuracy and adequacy of information he or she possesses—and most of this information is accessed through oral communication (Blumberg, 1989).

Credibility

One major expectation of leaders is that they are able to motivate people to achieve organizational goals. This task becomes virtually impossible in situations in which people view communication from the leader with suspicion. More directly, leaders cannot effectively lead if they lack credibility. Credibility, however, is not an attribute acquired merely through experience or academic study; rather, it is something that a leader earns over a period of time (Kouzes & Posner, 1993). It is associated with two characteristics: expertness and trustworthiness (Hoy & Miskel, 1996).

The perceived competence of a superintendent in matters of curriculum and teaching, for example, plays a significant role in determining whether teachers and principals see the superintendent as a credible instructional leader. Perceptions of competence may be affected by reputation, but in most instances they evolve from interactions. Individuals interpret the superintendent's communications and behaviors with respect to judging his or her professional competence. Administrators who fly by the seat of their pants eventually are unmasked by their colleagues.

John Gardner (1988) identified trustworthiness as an essential quality for those who engage in leadership in any type of organization. Trust in human relationships evolves over time and is nurtured by positive experiences. In drawing a distinction between managers and leaders, Warren Bennis (1989) observed that managers do things right, while leaders do the right things. Doing the right things has both an organizational and personal dimension. Organizationally, leaders are expected to make decisions about what issues need to be addressed; personally, doing the right thing has a moral and ethical connotation. For example, it means telling the truth, modeling appropriate behavior, and having faith in others. James Kouzes and Barry Posner (1993) provided a self-evaluation guide for being trustworthy based on four key questions:

- Is my behavior predictable or erratic?
- Do I communicate clearly or carelessly?
- Do I treat promises seriously or lightly?
- Am I forthright or dishonest? (p. 109)

Credibility is earned through honesty and professionalism. Just one incident of being caught in an untruth can destroy credibility.

Understanding Nonverbal Communication

Messages are not always transmitted in words. Nonverbal communication is often symbolic and occurs at an unconscious level. Rolling our eyes when we do not believe something or folding our arms when we are closed to an argument are examples. While these gestures may be more powerful than words, they are not always detected or understood. Nonverbal communication may serve several functions:

- a way of expressing emotions (e.g., excitement, disappointment)

- an avenue for conveying interpersonal attitudes (e.g., sincerity, openness)

- an avenue for presenting one's personality to others (e.g., aggressive, introverted)

- an extension of verbal communication (e.g., reinforcing words, substituting gestures for words) (Argyle, 1988)

E. Mark Hanson (1996) noted that nonverbal communication can occur through five media:

1. *Distance:* How far we stand from someone suggests something about our relationship to them. Distance may reflect status or intimacy. If a physical object such as a desk stands between the individuals, an authority relationship is heightened.

2. *Dress:* Our clothes say much about how we want to represent ourselves—conservative, rich, laid-back, mellow, unconcerned. Our manner of dress alone can create tensions, just as someone who wears a three-piece suit in a slum classroom.
3. *Physical contact:* Shaking hands, clasping both hands, kissing on the cheek, and embracing all reflect varying degrees of friendship.
4. *Facial expressions:* The frown, yawn, smile, and raised eyebrow all have almost universally recognized meanings.
5. *Gestures:* Although some gestures have almost universally recognized meaning, such as shaking the head for yes or no, others are tied to a particular culture or are even unique to an individual. The emotion of our thoughts can often be read in our hand gestures just as they can in our eyes. (p. 232)

Dress is an especially important issue for school superintendents. Clothing conveys many messages about how we see ourselves and how we associate power with position (Harris, 1993). For some, dressing as an executive serves a dual purpose: it enhances self-confidence, and it serves to inform others that superintendents possess more legitimate power than other employees in the school district.

Given the vast amount of time superintendents spend interacting with others, an understanding of nonverbal behavior is essential to being an effective communicator. Without this knowledge, an administrator may be unable to control transmitting unintended messages and unable to decode clues provided by others.

Communicating in Context

Exchanges of information can be influenced by contextual factors that interfere with communication, even to the extent that a message is completely distorted (Hoy & Miskel, 1996). In school districts, these contextual barriers could include factors such as prejudice, ethnic diversity, gender differences, and even organizational climate. In a highly closed school system, for instance, the superintendent may routinely ignore information about changing community demographics. Rather than acquiring and assessing data related to these transitions, the superintendent continues to rely on internal conversations with a select group of subordinates to make decisions about student needs. By learning to communicate in context, a superintendent is able to avoid these obstacles.

Gender and ethnicity are two of the most important contextual variables influencing the quality of communication. Women and men, for instance, often display different communication behaviors (Shakeshaft, 1989). This fact is especially relevant in public education because in the typical school district, most employees are women and the superintendent is a man.

Superintendents in many communities also need to cultivate culturally diverse communication patterns, allowing them to maintain meaningful interactions with all segments of the school district and the larger community. Communication styles for both verbal and nonverbal communication are culturally acquired (Weaver, 1995). In order to communicate appropriately with another culture, a person needs to have some understanding of verbal and nonverbal behaviors in that culture (Varner & Beamer, 1995). A sensitivity to communicating in various cultural contexts already has had a profound influence on leaders in the business community; ethnic and cultural diversity among employees and competition in a global economy have prompted them to better understand the relationships between culture and communication (Boiarsky, 1995).

Time is also an important contextual variable. When information is provided too soon or too late, the quality of the communication system suffers (O'Hair & Friedrich, 1992). Many of us have experienced a situation in which we are informed of an opportunity that could benefit either the school district or students (e.g., submitting a grant proposal), but we receive the information so late that we cannot properly respond. Such communication errors often lead to criticism and resentment.

Resolving Conflict

Conflict is inevitable in all types of organizations. While communication can take place without conflict, "conflict cannot occur without some type of communication" (Harris, 1993, p. 396). In many school districts, superintendents spend a significant portion of their time dealing with tensions that form and grow as a result of social interactions. Consequently, conflict and communication are inextricably linked because communication behaviors both contribute to conflict and become a vehicle for resolving conflict (e.g., building cooperation).

Organizational conflict may be related to a number of factors. The more common with respect to schools are the following:

- *Incompatible goals.* For example, teachers and administrators have different goals for student discipline.
- *Scarce rewards.* For example, employees feel that their work is not recognized and rewarded appropriately.
- *Interference or opposition.* For example, a group of employees opposes a proposed change.
- *Disagreement or controversy.* For example, teachers and administrators hold different views as to why a program is not working as expected (Harris, 1993).
- *Scarce resources.* For example, teachers fight over art materials because there is not enough to satisfy everyone's needs.
- *Perceived injustices.* For example, parents feel that discipline measures were too harsh.
- *Misperception.* For example, principals erroneously believe that the superintendent does not trust them.
- *Unrealistic expectations.* For example, school board members demand that students score 15% higher on the state achievement tests (O'Hair & Spaulding, 1996).

For much of the first half of the 20th century, managers viewed all conflict as being counterproductive. More recently, however, scholars have determined that it can be functional as well as dysfunctional (Robbins, 1976). For example, when a group of teachers complains about procedures for purchasing instructional materials, the administration may feel discomfort, but the teachers' collective action forces an open discussion of the issue, which ultimately leads to improved purchasing practices. In this instance, the conflict (dissatisfaction with the existing purchasing regulations) proves to be functional because it is a catalyst for organizational improvement. The line separating functional and dysfunctional conflict, however, is neither clear nor precise (Robbins, 1976). The ultimate value of conflict for the organization is predicated on the quality of management that is applied. If superintendents view tensions as consistently unproductive, the result is likely to be avoidance of conflict or accommodation, neither of which are appropriate leadership responses. By contrast, there are good reasons for superintendents to encourage and foster goal-oriented conflicts (Bolman & Deal, 1991). These tensions can improve decision making and be a step leading to desired change.

A superintendent's communication behaviors can produce conflict and determine the ultimate value of conflict to the school district. For example, actions such as repressing information, providing too much information, being ambiguous, issuing threats, or deviating from normal channels of communication usually results in stress or conflict (Robbins, 1976). The productive management of conflict is impossible if an administrator has little understanding of organizational communication. This includes (1) a comprehension of the dynamics of organizational conflict, (2) an understanding of the context in which conflict is communicated, and (3) the ability to structure cooperative communication via strategies that facilitate conflict resolutions (O'Hair & Spaulding, 1996).

Creating a Climate for Two-Way Communication

A superintendent's ability to emerge as a great communicator also is dependent on building a climate within the district that facilitates the two-way communication process. The first step to achieve this goal is an analysis of the existing climate. At least four primary dimensions of the current environment for communication need to be addressed:

1. Context, that is, how organizational communication occurs
2. Intentions, that is, the purposes of organizational communication
3. Logistics, that is, the channels and networks through which communications flow
4. Consequences, that is, outcomes of the communication process (Hanson, 1996)

Data obtained from this analysis provide a baseline for reshaping climate; it allows the superintendent to identify gaps between "what is" and "what is desired."

A productive climate also is dependent on the philosophical dispositions of the superintendent. Does he or she really value community input? Are principals and teachers truly expected to state their feelings openly? Leaders who want open, learning organizations must create conditions that permit them to "listen fully and accurately to all voices, both negative and positive (Sharpe, 1996, p. 61). Unfortunately, this does not occur in many districts. Rather, employees perceive themselves as being essentially isolated, both from administration and from one another. This lack of communication often reinforces feelings that input is not valued, and it has encouraged teachers to rely on formal coalitions (e.g., unions) or informal groups for information and power. These circumstances are particularly alarming in light of evidence suggesting that communication is critical to both teacher job satisfaction and career commitment (Shedd & Bacharach, 1991). Edgar Schein (1992) observed "The learning culture must be built on the assumption that communication and information are central to organizational well-being and must therefore create a multichannel communication system that allows everyone to connect to everyone else" (p. 370). Both the expanding presence of technology and the evolving strategies for school renewal encourage superintendents to shape the environment for communication.

COMMUNICATION NETWORKS

In every school district, there are established patterns or channels through which communication flows. "A network is composed of a specific body of individuals who are interconnected as links in the communication flow" (Hanson, 1996, p. 227). These may be formal in that they are sanctioned by the school district and intended to facilitate the goals of the district. For example, many districts have had policies requiring communication to follow an established "chain of command." In these organizations, principals are expected to communicate with teachers, assistant superintendents communicate with principals, and so on. The formal communication network is often made apparent by a district's organizational chart. Some authors differentiate formal networks from informal networks by referring to them as "channels" (e.g., Harris, 1993).

Communication in school systems does not occur exclusively through formal channels. Informal networks also exist (e.g., grapevines); these are neither sanctioned nor recognized by the formal organization. "These networks emerge as a result of formal networks and are formed by individuals who have interpersonal relationships, who exchange information across reporting chains, and who disregard formal status and timing" (Shockley-Zalabak, 1988, pp. 47–48). In closed organizations, that is, school districts relying on restricted one-way communication and avoiding interactions with the larger environment, informal networks often flourish because employees are left out of normal information loops. An illustration of how formal and informal networks differ is shown in Figure 10–3.

Many administrators adhere to the adage that "knowledge is power." Accordingly, the networks they design and support usually reflect personal philosophies toward schools and communication. Three factors are especially important in the

Formal Network

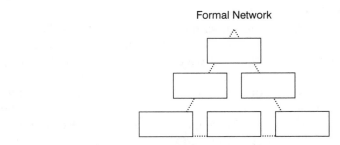

Developed and controlled by the formal organization; typically
designed to conform with the established chain of command.

Informal Network

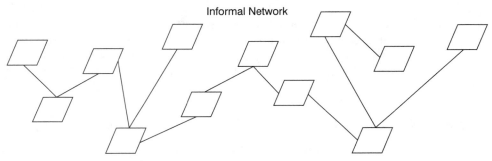

Developed by individuals and groups to exchange
information by bypassing the formal network.

Figure 10–3
Formal and informal communication networks

design of networks: (1) centralization, (2) organizational shape, and (3) level of
information technology (Hoy & Miskel, 1996).

1. Centralization involves concentrating power and information at the top levels of
   a school district. For example, a superintendent would have the greatest
   amount of information. Organizations that remain highly centralized tend to
   become dysfunctional in periods of uncertainty and rapid change (Nonaka &
   Takeuchi, 1995). This is particularly noteworthy with respect to school reform.
   As school districts continue to be pressured to apply decentralization theory, the
   communication characteristics of centralized governance need to be eradicated.

2. The second factor, organizational shape, is determined by the number of layers within a school district. In very large districts, for instance, there may be
   five or six layers of administration. Often these layers are constructed without any direct thought given to how they will determine formal communication networks or encourage the development of informal networks.

3. The final factor, technology, has become increasingly apparent because of the
   prominence of computers and the expansion of the "information highway."
   In some school districts, every teacher already has a computer that is linked

to the Internet and networked to teachers and administrators throughout the school district. Hence, technology already has become a primary determinant of how people communicate in many schools and districts.

Communication networks also may be described and understood by examining three properties:

1. *Symmetry.* This means the extent to which information is distributed equally and there is a two-way give-and-take of information in the organization.
2. *Strength.* This refers to the frequency and length of interactions.
3. *Reciprocity.* This refers to the extent of agreement among organizational members about their networks (Shockley-Zalabak, 1988).

In a school district in which communication flows downward and infrequently, the formal network is likely to be asymmetrical, weak, and non-reciprocal. That is to say, there is a concentration of information at the top level of the district, communication flows in one direction (from the top to the bottom), and employees are highly uncertain about their roles in the network.

In developing formal networks, superintendents should give ample consideration to five issues:

1. *Inclusiveness.* This refers to the extent to which the communication loop includes all sectors of the school district.
2. *Transmission.* This refers to the extent to which messages remain unaltered or are modified at each level of the network.
3. *Feedback capacity.* This refers to the extent to which the network encourages/permits feedback to the initial communicator.
4. *Efficiency.* This means the speed and degree of accuracy of transmitted messages.
5. *Organizational fit.* This refers to the extent to which the network is congruous with the needs and goals of the district (Katz & Kahn, 1978).

Most important, these factors should be weighed in designing line and staff relationships within the school system because such decisions almost always determine formal channels of communication.

Employee dependence on informal networks usually breeds communication problems. The most effective measure to deter rumors, false information, and misinterpretations is the creation of formal two-way channels that provide employees continuous access to information and the capability of horizontal and vertical communication. In this information age, both school employees and the community will develop their own means for obtaining information if they are excluded from the school district's formal communication loop. Contrary to what some might conclude, technology alone does not rectify problems involving information access; both organizational climate and culture may preserve the status quo even when new technologies are introduced. If information is to be used to nurture professionalism, shared governance, and school-community relations, the fundamental beliefs of the school district and the work environment, including formal communication channels, must support these goals.

In addition to fashioning appropriate channels of organizational communication, a superintendent also should be skilled in knowing how to use those channels. For instance, there are times when face-to-face discussions are better than sending a memorandum (O'Hair & Friedrich, 1992). There are also occasions when the grapevine can be used to augment the formal network. In open systems, interactions between the formal and informal networks become less distinctive. This is especially true if there is substantial linkage among the subsystems within an organization and between the organization and the wider environment.

WORKING WITH THE MEDIA

Long before the United States moved into an age of information, superintendents recognized that the media performed a critical function with respect to public education. Reporters from the various media assume the role of describing and interpreting the actions of both the school district and superintendent to the general community; as such, they often have the power to shape public opinion. However, while contact between a superintendent and representatives of the local media is a certainty in all types of school districts, the nature of those relationships should not be expected to be uniform. In large measure, it is the superintendent's attitudes and behaviors that determine whether reporters will be a positive or negative force in shaping public opinion.

In the past, many administrators have been inclined to avoid reporters. For some, keeping a low profile appeared to be prudent behavior; others feared that they would be treated unfairly. Over time, however, most superintendents exhibiting an avoidance behavior discovered that they really could not hide from the media. Because the business of public education should be conducted openly and candidly, those who assume the leadership of school districts should be prepared to build and maintain effective relationships with the media. Thus, rather than assuming bureaucratic postures that restrict information, they should treat the media as a valuable resource for providing, accessing, and exchanging information.

Creating a Positive Perspective

A first step to building a positive relationship with the media involves creating a program for this purpose. Richard Wallace (1990) suggested three key indices of effective programming that can be applied to the superintendency:

1. Superintendents have realistic expectations of the media.

2. Media relations become personalized so that the superintendent knows the reporters and the reporters know the superintendent.

3. Superintendents maintain some degree of control regarding access to the media and the types of messages that are transmitted.

To accomplish these goals, administrators must know something about journalism, journalists, and local media markets.

One way superintendents can help prepare themselves and other administrative staff members to be effective communicators is to invite several local reporters to attend administrative meetings to discuss (1) the role of local media in relation to public education; (2) the reporters' specific responsibilities as journalists in relation to school issues; and (3) what radio, television, and print media consider as news. This is also a time when administrators and reporters can share role expectations. Providing training to staff on communication issues is another approach that may be used to improve communication. This alternative may be especially effective in situations in which administrators routinely encounter confrontational reporters (Walker, 1990). A less formal technique that superintendents often use to familiarize themselves with local journalists and media markets is to schedule periodic lunches with reporters or news directors. Each party usually benefits from this type of relaxed contact. These informal contacts can be especially helpful to new superintendents who want to make a positive impression on reporters (Nebgen, 1993).

Positive relationships with media almost always begin with the belief that the press can be an ally in communicating the school district's messages (Shaw, 1987). This attitude obviously influences decisions regarding the quality and quantity of information the school district exchanges with other agencies and the manner in which information is made available. It also affects operational decisions concerning policy and regulations for handling public information (e.g., will the school district have a public information official?). In essence, the superintendent's disposition toward working with the media usually determines whether there is a comprehensive plan for media relations and what the content of that plan is.

Guidelines for Practice

In addition to building goodwill and developing a written plan, superintendents need to concentrate on day-to-day behaviors that also shape media relations. Listed below are several guidelines for practice.

- *Learn to deal with negative news.* Negative news in public education is unavoidable. Whether it is a press release about statewide test scores or a story about a parent suing the school district, superintendents have to be prepared to deal with unflattering stories. There are three criteria that should guide administrative responses to negative news: (1) admitting there is a problem is better than trying to cover up, (2) the impact of negative news is usually softened when the superintendent informs the public that there is a course of action to deal with the problem, and (3) the plan of action is communicated to the public in language that is understood by reporters and the public (Hennessey & Kowalski, 1996).

- *Never lie to the media.* While it may be tempting to lie to the media, mistruths have a way of coming back to haunt those who tell them. Any gain from misleading the media is apt to be temporary; good reporters are able to find the true story (Posner, 1994). It simply is foolish to do anything that undermines integrity and credibility—being honest is the best policy (Ordovensky, 1986).

- *Concentrate on getting the school district's story to the media.* Superintendents often lament that the media is not interested in positive stories about public education. In truth, many stories promoted by school district officials simply do not lend themselves to newspaper articles or television news broadcasts. Superintendents are more likely to succeed in getting positive stories in the news if they have an understanding of how local media operate (Conners, 1988). Additionally, timing is often a critical variable. Reporters, for example, may exhibit increased interest in certain stories if they are working on a series of articles focusing on the same topic (e.g., getting a reporter to use a story about a new discipline program while the reporter is developing a series of articles on pupil conduct in local schools). Likewise, reporters may show greater interest in stories generated by the school district during slow news periods (Hennessey & Kowalski, 1996).

- *Act swiftly to correct errors.* Mistakes in news stories are certain to occur. When they do, the superintendent should act swiftly to provide corrections. This is especially true if the error was caused by information provided by the school district. When the mistake is attributable to a reporter's sloppiness or misinterpretations, the problem should be discussed with the individual responsible or with the individual's supervisor. The media should know that the superintendent is monitoring stories for accuracy (Hennessey & Kowalski, 1996).

- *Be cautious about speaking "off the record."* In general, superintendents should avoid speaking off the record. First, this term means different things to different people. Once information is made public, arguments about meaning and intentions do little to ameliorate the situation (Frohlichstein, 1993). A superintendent must decide whether he or she has a trusting relationship with a reporter; also, the superintendent needs to weigh carefully whether there is any advantage to holding conversations off the record.

- *Avoid using educational jargon.* A key to communication is transmitting a message in language that is clearly understood by the receiver. Many reporters have no specific training that prepares them to cover education. Keeping this mind, administrators should take care to avoid using terms that are not readily understood by the reporter or by the general public.

- *Avoid the option of "no comment."* In the eyes of many reporters and the public, a response of "no comment" conjures up ideas of guilt. Clearly, there are issues that should not be discussed openly with the media (e.g., a sensitive personnel matter). In such instances, it is preferable for the superintendent to explain why he or she cannot provide an answer to a reporter's question at a particular point in time.

- *Maximize the potential of technology.* Computers, e-mail, fax machines, and other technologies provide new opportunities for school districts to communicate with the media in a timely manner. In this age of information, superintendents will need to make full use of these tools to prepare press releases, respond to crises, and provide concise and useful information to the media in a timely manner. The ability to exchange information rather rapidly allows administrators to be more accommodating of the deadlines that often set the parameters for a reporter's work.

- *Be a role model for the board members, administrators, and other employees.* The superintendent should set the tone for media relations in the school district. Many practitioners overlook the symbolic nature of their behavior. If a superintendent avoids media contacts or talks about reporters negatively, district employees are likely to emulate these behaviors.

Preparing for Television

At one time, only large-city and suburban superintendents had to be concerned about appearing on television. The cable television industry and local access channels now have put most school districts into direct contact with this medium. A growing number of school districts have live or taped broadcasts of their board meetings; superintendents are appearing more frequently in news interviews and public interest shows. Growing interest in covering public education on television is also attributable to expanded local news broadcasts. Many stations, especially in larger markets, broadcast three to four separate news shows daily; these may span as many as 5 hours of daily broadcasting. This permits reporters to cover a wide range of local stories.

Appearing on television for the first time can be an anxiety-producing experience for some administrators. Being prepared is the best protection against having a negative or humiliating experience. Among the factors that should be considered are the following:

- *Dress properly.* A superintendent ought to look like he or she does every day in the office (Ordovensky & Marx, 1993).

- *Seek credibility.* Believability often depends on whether viewers see you as a real person (Hennessey & Kowalski, 1996). It is a mistake to try to be someone you are not.

- *Be prepared.* Prepare answers to anticipated questions; suggest questions that the reporter might ask you (Ordovensky & Marx, 1993).

- *Be confident.* Avoid appearing defensive; look at the interviewer; politely ask for adequate time to complete your answers (Parker, 1991).
- *Be direct.* Often time is limited. Choose words carefully; place issues in context; use audiovisuals to emphasize your points (Hennessey & Kowalski, 1996).
- *Maintain control.* Remain calm; take charge by being able to use related questions to make points; avoid repeating hostile questions (Parker, 1991).

Administrators should be aware of the fact that the encounters with television reporters can have a different tone from encounters with newspaper reporters. Because of the nature of television, reporters may be more confrontational—more apt to ask direct and controversial questions (Walker, 1990). Hence, being properly prepared for television also entails anticipating this type of behavior.

Maintaining Relationships

One of the problems many superintendents face is the rapid turnover of reporters who are assigned to cover education. Often this task is given to relatively new, inexperienced reporters who have little or no understanding of the inner workings of public education. Each time a new reporter is assigned to cover the school district, the superintendent should make it a priority to provide the new person with an orientation to the school district and try to build a relationship with the reporter. The positive aspect of reporter turnover is that it prompts the superintendent to reassess associations with the media periodically. Such reconsiderations are less likely, however, when reporters remain in their assignments for prolonged periods. In these instances, the superintendent needs to make a conscious effort to evaluate media relationships annually. One way to do this is through meetings with reporters, either one-on-one meetings or meetings that include several reporters.

The maintenance of positive media relationships requires the superintendent to look beyond personal contacts with reporters. It also requires an evaluation of how other employees and school board members interact with the media. Effective communication is facilitated by a philosophy that values openness and candor on the part of every person in the school district (Lober, 1993). This does not mean that school board members and employees ought to communicate constantly with reporters; rather, it suggests that all representatives of the school district should operate as a team providing accurate information when it is their responsibility to do so.

Finally, positive relationships with the media are likely to be sustained if superintendents keep their work with reporters in proper perspective. In every school district, there are both positive and negative stories; there is cause for both praise and criticism (Shaw, 1987). "When confronted with negative press, school officials ought not bury their heads in the sand or run for cover. Nor should they concentrate on making excuses. Rather, they should attempt to manage the conflict" (Hennessey & Kowalski, 1996, p. 223). To do so, superintendents often have to admit that problems exist; more important, they should be prepared to offer meaningful solutions to the problems. When leaders are forthright and when they have plausible ideas, they may be able to use conflict to build support for the school district and for themselves.

FOR FURTHER REFLECTION

Both school reform and life in an information age have contributed to the need for superintendents to be outstanding communicators. As Kristen Amundson (1996) aptly pointed out, "Communicating positively may be an educator's only recourse to build solid relationships with the community based on mutual respect" (p. 3). In today's dynamic environment, superintendents must do more than object to criticism and refute claims that schools are ineffective. They must step forward with a positive agenda; they must be able to communicate clear, concise, and positive ideas for school renewal. In addition, superintendents need to take positive actions within the school district to ensure that communication channels allow employees to access and use information to improve their practice.

As you consider what you read in this chapter, answer the following questions:

1. How has transition to an age of information heightened expectations that superintendents can be effective communicators?

2. What is the difference between one-way and two-way communication?

3. What is the relevance of two-way communication with respect to interactions within a school district? With respect to interactions between a school district and the wider community?

4. Distinguish between formal and informal communication networks in a school district. Why is each formed? How is each formed?

5. Considering the school administrators with whom you have had contact, what positive communication behaviors have you observed on their part? What negative behaviors have you observed?

6. Assess the relationship between the media and the public schools in your community. Is it positive or negative? What factors did you consider in arriving at an answer?

7. Assume you are a newly appointed superintendent in an unfamiliar community. What steps would you take to acquaint yourself with local reporters?

8. How can modern technologies contribute to a superintendent's performance as a communicator?

9. How can you assess your abilities as a communicator?

10. What factors are associated with being a good listener?

CASE STUDY

The Turner Public School District is a relatively small and predominately rural system consisting of 2 elementary schools and a junior-senior high school. The total enrollment is just under 1,300 students. Support for education is exhibited in a number of ways, including well-maintained and modern facilities, a relatively high tax rate, and per-pupil spending that places the district in the top 20% in the state.

After the recent retirement of a superintendent who had been in office for 14 years, the board employed Dr. Francine South to lead the district. Dr. South had been serving as the director of technology in a large district in the same state. She had a total of 18 years of experience in education, including 5 years as a principal and 4 years as a director of technology.

Within the first 3 months after starting her job in Turner, Dr. South obtained a large grant from a private corporation to purchase additional computers for the schools and to create a computer network in the district. While the school system had been investing in computers and while a computer lab had been established in each school, many teachers did not have personal computers. The grant provided additional computers to be placed in each classroom, including a personal computer for each teacher. The network connected all professional employees to one another through their computers. The school board, the teachers' union, and the community uniformly applauded Dr. South's efforts in making these things possible.

After the new computers and the network were installed, Dr. South conducted a workshop for teachers and administrators regarding the use of these technologies. She emphasized that communications within the district could now be executed more efficiently and rapidly. At the workshop, she also announced that she would be distributing a newsletter via the network every Monday morning. This one- or two-page document was designed to share information and announcements that would be of interest to professional employees—it would also serve to exhibit the potential of this communication network. Among the other opportunities that were emphasized were a school district data bank, which allowed employees to access certain information, such as student records. In concluding the workshop, Dr. South expressed her thoughts on the importance of establishing a two-way communication process in the school district.

After several months, Dr. South became concerned about the degree to which the employees were not taking advantage of the network. She based this concern on the following observations:

- She continued to receive memoranda or telephone calls rather than e-mail messages from principals and teachers.
- Management problems indicated that some of the announcements made in the weekly newsletters were not reaching their intended audience (e.g., announcements about payroll changes).

- The principals continued to use memoranda to request information that could be retrieved through their personal computers.

The superintendent raised these concerns at a meeting with the 3 principals. Two of the principals quickly indicated that they were not sure why the network was not being used to a greater degree. They seemed surprised by the superintendent's concern over this issue. The third principal, Melvin Barns, usually was the spokesperson for the principals. He offered a different response to the superintendent's concern.

"Except for one or two younger teachers, I don't think my staff feels comfortable using the computer to send mail or to receive mail. At our elementary school, people are close. We depend on one another for information. The computer seems so impersonal. I ask my secretary to print out your newsletter for me every Monday. I prefer to read things from paper. Occasionally, I ask teachers if they have read the newsletter. My guess is that some do not. So, I try to share key points from the newsletter when I have the opportunity to do so."

One of the other principals then asked Dr. South, "Do you get many e-mail messages from teachers?"

The superintendent responded that she had received two or three every week. The principals looked at one another, and Mr. Barns again spoke for the trio.

"We are a little concerned about teachers bypassing us and sending messages directly to you," he said. "This is much easier to do with the computer. We have had a long-standing practice in this district of respecting the chain of command. To put it bluntly, we're concerned that teachers can now access information without going through us. What types of messages or questions do you get from teachers?"

"They are primarily comments about items in the newsletters," Dr. South answered. "Several teachers, for example, have offered suggestions about ways that we can improve the textbook selection process. If these communications focused on an administrative issue in your school, you can be sure that I would talk to you about them."

"But that's just it," Mr. Barns responded. "Where do you draw the line between what is an administrative problem and what is not? Textbook adoption is an issue that involves us. If teachers are making suggestions about changing the process, shouldn't we be part of the discussion?"

Dr. South explained that the communication involved suggestions and information sharing, not actions. She noted that any eventual change in policy and regulations for something like textbook selection would involve open discussions among all parties who have a direct interest in the eventual decision. However, she sensed that her comments failed to ease the principals' concerns.

After the meeting, Dr. South thought about her discussion with the principals. Even though she had an open and frank discussion with them, her primary question about the network remained unanswered. She still was not sure of the extent to which it was being used; she was puzzled why some teachers were apparently choosing not to read the weekly newsletters. She also thought about the principals' behavior. Why did they not take advantage of e-mail? Why were they concerned about teachers sending messages to her?

Issues for Discussion

1. Do you think that Dr. South is being premature in judging that the principals and teachers are not taking advantage of the network? What is the reason for your opinion?

2. What are some of the possible reasons why employees might not take advantage of this communication tool?

3. Can you identify any organizational barriers that may prevent the network from working as planned? What are they?

4. Should Dr. South have taken a different approach to preparing employees to use the network? If so, what should she have done?

5. Assess the principals' concerns about teachers' being able to communicate directly with the superintendent. If you were a principal in this district, would you feel the same way?

6. One of Dr. South's goals is to create a two-way communication process. Do you think she is relying too much on the computer network to achieve this goal? Why or why not?

7. How can a superintendent guard against the impersonal nature of communicating via computers?

8. What, if any, judgments can you make about the formal and informal communication networks in this school district?

9. Is it a good idea to give school board members access to the school district computer network? Why or why not?

10. In what ways does a superintendent's leadership style affect the ways in which he or she communicates with administrative staff members?

11. In your opinion, did the superintendent move too quickly to implement technology for communication purposes?

REFERENCES

Amundson, K. (1996). *Telling the truth about America's public schools*. Arlington, VA: American Association of School Administrators.

Argyle, M. (1988). *Bodily communication* (2nd ed.). London: Methuen.

Axley, S. R. (1996). *Communication at work: Management and communication-intensive organization*. Westport, CT: Quorum Books.

Bennis, W. (1989). Why leaders can't lead. *Training and Development Journal, 43*(4), 35–39.

Blumberg, A. (1989). *School administration as a craft*. Boston: Allyn and Bacon.

Bolman, L. G., & Deal, T. E. (1991). *Reframing organizations: Artistry, choice, and leadership*. San Francisco: Jossey-Bass.

Boiarsky, C. (1995). The relationship between cultural and rhetorical conventions: Engaging in international communication. *Technical Communication Quarterly, 4*(3), 245–259.

Burbules, N. C. (1993). *Dialogue in teaching: Theory and practice.* New York: Teachers College Press.

Burgess, J. C. (1996). *Corporate culture: Friend or foe of change?* Paper presented at the Academy of Human Resource Development, Minneapolis.

Carlson, R. V. (1996). *Reframing and reform: Perspectives on organization, leadership, and school change.* New York: Longman.

Conners, A. J. (1988). Let's hear about the good stuff: School community relations. *Clearing House, 61*(9), 399–402.

Conrad, C. (1994). *Strategic organizational communication* (3rd ed.). Fort Worth, TX: Harcourt Brace College Publishers.

Deetz, S. A. (1992). *Democracy in an age of corporate colonization.* Albany: State University of New York Press.

Frohlichstein, T. (1993). Dealing successfully with media inquiries. *NASSP Bulletin, 77*(555), 82–88.

Gardner, J. W. (1988). Leader-constituent interaction. The heart of the matter. *NASSP Bulletin, 72*(511), 61.

Geddes, D. S. (1993). Empowerment through communication: Key people-to-people and organizational success. *People and Education 1*(1), 76–104.

Hanson, E. M. (1996). *Educational administration and organizational behavior* (4th ed.). Boston: Allyn and Bacon.

Harris, T. E. (1993). *Applied organizational communication: Perspectives, principles, and pragmatics.* Hillsdale, NJ: Lawrence Erlbaum.

Hennessey, A., & Kowalski, T. J. (1996). Working with the media. In T. Kowalski (Ed.), *Public relations in educational organizations: Practice in an age of information and reform* (pp. 210–225). Upper Saddle River, NJ: Merrill/Prentice Hall.

Holliday, A. E. (1996). Foreword. In T. Kowalski (Ed.), *Public relations in educational organizations: Practice in an age of information and reform* (pp. iii–iv). Upper Saddle River, NJ: Merrill/Prentice Hall.

Hoy, W. K., & Miskel, C. G. (1996). *Educational administration: Theory, research, and practice* (5th ed.). New York: McGraw-Hill.

Howlett, P. (1993). The politics of school leaders, past and future. *Education Digest, 58*(9), 18–21.

Irmsher, K. (1996). *Communication skills.* (ERIC Document Reproduction Service No. ED 390 114)

Katz, D., & Kahn, R. (1978). *The social psychology of organizations* (2nd ed.). New York: John Wiley.

Kouzes, J. M., & Posner, B. Z. (1993). *Credibility: How leaders gain and lose it, why people demand it.* San Francisco: Jossey-Bass.

Kowalski, T. J. (1998). The role of communication in providing leadership for school restructuring. *Mid-Western Educational Researcher, 11*(1), 32–40.

Kowalski, T. J., & Reitzug, U. C. (1993). *Contemporary school administration: An introduction.* New York: Longman.

Lewis, M. H., & Reinsch, N. L. (1988). Listening in organizational environments. *Journal of Business Communication, 25*(3), 49–67.

Lewis, P. V. (1975). *Organizational communications: The essence of effective management.* Columbus, OH: Grid.

Lober, I. M. (1993). *Promoting your school: A public relations handbook.* Lancaster, PA: Technomic.

Lucas, H. C. (1996). *The T-form organization: Using technology to design organizations for the 21st century*. San Francisco: Jossey-Bass.

Lunenburg, F. C., & Ornstein, A. C. (1991). *Educational administration: Concepts and practices*. Belmont, CA: Wadsworth.

Mohan, M. L. (1993). *Organizational communication and cultural vision: Approaches and analysis*. Albany: State University of New York Press.

Naisbitt, J. (1982). *Megatrends: Ten new directions for transforming our lives*. New York: Warner Books.

Nebgen, M. (1993). Getting to know you: Planning for success as a new superintendent. *People and Education, 1*(4), 344–354.

Nonaka, I., & Takeuchi, H. (1995). *The knowledge-creating company*. New York: Oxford University Press.

O'Hair, D., & Friedrich, G. W. (1992). *Strategic communication business and the professions*. Boston: Houghton Mifflin.

O'Hair, M. J., & Spaulding, A. M. (1996). Institutionalizing public relations through interpersonal communication: Listening, nonverbal, and conflict-resolution skills. In T. Kowalski (Ed.), *Public relations in educational organizations: Practice in an age of information and reform* (pp. 157–185). Upper Saddle River, NJ: Merrill/Prentice Hall.

Ordovensky, P. (1986). Dealing with the media: Honesty is the best policy. *NASSP Bulletin, 70*(494), 35–37.

Ordovensky, P., & Marx, G. (1993). *Working with the news media*. Arlington, VA: American Association of School Administrators.

Parker, J. (1991). *Accessing the media*. (ERIC Document Reproduction Service No. ED 339 337)

Posner, M. A. (1994). Read all about it. *Case Currents, 20*(1), 8–13.

Razik, T. A., & Swanson, A. D. (1995). *Fundamental concepts of educational leadership and management*. Upper Saddle River, NJ: Merrill/Prentice Hall.

Robbins, S. P. (1976). *The administrative process: Integrating theory and practice*. Upper Saddle River, NJ: Prentice Hall.

Schein, E. H. (1992). *Organizational culture and leadership* (2nd ed.). San Francisco: Jossey-Bass.

Schmuck, R. A., & Runkel, P. J. (1994). *The handbook of organizational development in schools and colleges* (4th ed.). Prospect Heights, IL: Waveland Press.

Shakeshaft, C. (1989). *Women in educational administration* (2nd ed.). Newbury Park, CA: Sage.

Sharpe, M. (1996). What school administrators need to understand. In T. Kowalski (Ed.), *Public relations in educational organizations: Practice in an age of information and reform* (pp. 58–72). Upper Saddle River, NJ: Merrill/Prentice Hall.

Shaw, R. C. (1987). Do's and don'ts for dealing with the press. *NASSP Bulletin, 71*(503), 99–102.

Shedd, J. B., & Bacharach, S. B. (1991). *Tangled hierarchies: Teachers as professionals and the management of schools*. San Francisco: Jossey-Bass.

Shockley-Zalabak, P. (1988). *Fundamentals of organizational communication*. New York: Longman.

Sigband, N., & Bell, A. (1989). *Communication for management and business* (5th ed.). Glenview, IL: Scott, Foresman.

Spinks, N., & Wells, B. (1991). Improving listening power: The payoff! *Bulletin of the Association for Business Communication, 54*(3), 75–77.

Taylor, J. R. (1993). *Rethinking the theory of organizational communication: How to read an organization*. Norwood, NJ: Ablex.

Varner, I., & Beamer, L. (1995). *Intercultural communication in the global workplace.* Chicago: Irwin.

Walker, K. B. (1990). Confrontational media training for administrators: Performance and practice. *Public Personnel Management, 19*(4), 419–427.

Wallace, R. C. (1990). Greet the press! *School Administrator, 47*(7), 1–17, 19.

Weaver, G. R. (1995). Communication and conflict in the multicultural classroom. *Adult Learning, 6*(5), 23–24.

Chapter 11

Leadership in the Larger Community

Key Concepts

✧ A superintendent's leadership role in school and community relations

✧ Creating dialogue about the purposes of education

✧ Informing the community about education

✧ Building and maintaining community support for public education

✧ School district partnerships

✧ A superintendent's personal involvement in community activities

A superintendent's role in providing leadership beyond the school district is associated with political realities and professional responsibilities. In the political framework, superintendents are commonly seen as public property (Blumberg, 1985; Kowalski, 1995). As such, their behavior is constantly scrutinized. Any impropriety may become a scandal. However, taxpayers do not only see superintendents as public servants; they also view them as public resources. In this light, many citizens believe that the responsibilities of the position extend beyond managing the school district to include activities such as attending public functions and speaking at them and serving on the boards of various civic groups (Lober, 1993). Board members and school district employees also routinely expect superintendents to be active in community matters, especially with regard to being a forceful politician who is able to compete with other governmental leaders for scarce resources.

A superintendent's responsibility to be a leader outside of the school district is framed within the conceptions of the superintendent as teacher-scholar and as democratic leader. Specific obligations include (1) building a symbiotic relationship between the school district and the community, (2) informing the public of educational needs, (3) bringing people together to create visions and goals, (4) interpreting educational goals to the public, and (5) building support for school initiatives. As policy making shifts toward the local level as a result of deregulation and decentralization, these responsibilities become increasingly important.

This chapter explores three primary topics related to the superintendent's leadership in the larger community. The first entails leadership for positive school-community relations; the second relates to the growing popularity of partnership programs; the third pertains to the superintendent's involvement in community service.

LEADERSHIP IN SCHOOL-COMMUNITY RELATIONS

In states that exert a high degree of control over public education, school boards and superintendents often function primarily as regulators. That is to say, their primary responsibilities pertain to ensuring that laws, policies, and regulations developed at the state level are followed appropriately at the local district level. However, as policy making shifts to the local level, success in the superintendency becomes more dependent on leadership than on management. In this context, not only do superintendents play a pivotal role in facilitating the task of deciding what should be done, they also are accountable for building and maintaining public support for the schools. This responsibility of a superintendent, commonly addressed under the topics of *public relations* or *school-community relations*, has three fundamental components:

1. To *inform* the public (e.g., about intentions, processes, and outcomes)
2. To *persuade* the public (e.g., to modify attitudes and opinions that are based on misperceptions)

3. To *integrate* the actions and attitudes of the school organization with those of the community (e.g., to ensure that the values and purposes driving the school district are congruous with the values and beliefs in the larger community) (Cohen, 1987)

To properly perform these duties, superintendents must engage in honest, open, consistent, fair, and continuous two-way communication with the community. Their efforts should produce credibility, confidence, goodwill, and social harmony (Seitel, 1992). This responsibility requires an understanding of the political context of contemporary practice, especially as it relates to public perceptions and values about education.

The Issue of Purpose

Despite intense rhetoric that suggests the contrary, the public schools remain one of the most democratic institutions in American society (Amundson, 1996). Local school boards still retain sufficient authority to make significant decisions that affect students, employees, and the entire community. These decisions are not made in a vacuum; they are influenced by pressure groups and powerful individuals who have their own agendas for elementary and secondary education. Public beliefs about the role of schools in our society are critical; these convictions influence community values and ultimately educational policy. This fact becomes quite evident when diverse purposes for education are analyzed in light of the reform agendas that have been proposed over the past 2 decades.

Reform is certainly not a new issue in public education. Throughout the 20th century, there have been recurring cycles during which the public has demanded school improvement. These periodic expressions of dissatisfaction are associated with several realties about the structure of American society. First, reform has often been pursued at the national and state levels—largely because centralized initiatives are easier to initiate. However, these top-down efforts rarely have been successful in eradicating the problems they hoped to address. Second, the proposed solutions often reflect a narrow perspective of schools. This has resulted in the promotion of solutions that are usually too simplistic to solve the real problems. Third, the problems faced by public education are directly linked with the persistent dilemma of pursuing seemingly conflicting metavalues (Cuban, 1988).

To elaborate, education policy has been, and continues to be, guided by five values: liberty, equality, adequacy, efficiency, and fraternity. Tensions between liberty and equality—ethical values derived from the doctrine of natural rights—are especially important with respect to analyzing school reform policy. While liberty pertains to the right to act without undue restriction, equality refers to the state of enjoying reasonably equal social, political, and economic rights (Swanson & King, 1997). The simultaneous influence of these metavalues is visible in both policy and laws. For example, court decisions in school finance litigation often reveal a determination to maintain an equilibrium between the principles of liberty and equality (Burrup, Brimley, & Garfield, 1996). Kern Alexander and Richard Salmon (1995) noted the following:

> Equality and economic freedom are ultimately intermingled and highly interdependent. The role of the state in fostering care, protection, and equality as balanced against individual freedom and liberty forms the primary ground on which political philosophy is argued and tested at the polls, in the legislatures, and in the courts of this nation. (p. 134)

Tensions between liberty and equality are becoming ever more visible in school reform initiatives because the unresolved issues of purpose are central to improving education. For example, school choice and vouchers are ideas intended to increase liberty. Critics of these ideas charge that allowing parents to select schools—and especially using tuition vouchers in either public and private schools—promotes racial and economic segregation. Proponents counter that a student does better in a school that complies with his or her family's values and philosophy. Tensions over such reform ideas reflect the problem of not having a set of universally accepted purposes for public education. As metavalues are pursued, they rekindle basic tensions. School finance, the quintessential example of conflict between two educational metavalues, continues to be debated in the courts, even after more than 30 years of litigation (Whitney & Crampton, 1995).

Less abstract differences regarding the purposes of education have been discussed during the most recent cycle of reform initiatives. Four have been particularly prominent:

1. Promoting the intellectual attainment of students
2. Shaping good citizens in the interest of a better society
3. Preparing students for the workforce
4. Fostering lifelong learning skills (Armstrong, Henson, & Savage, 1989)

In addition to values and beliefs, directions for public schools also are shaped by changing societal conditions. Drug abuse, technology, poverty, and the changing nature of work are but a few of the factors in this category. Collectively, values and societal circumstances combine to form individual perceptions of what schools should be accomplishing—and more important, they become the basis for reform agendas.

Americans have always been unable to agree on specific purposes for public schools (Spring, 1990), and there is little doubt that this condition has been primarily responsible for the past failures of top-down, centralized reform initiatives. The lack of a national consensus regarding what is expected of public schools often leads to a situation in which powerful individuals or groups are able to advance their narrow views as being representative of society (Tesconi, 1984). Much of what was attempted during the 1980s, for instance, was predicated on erroneous assumptions that schools were unproductive simply because students were lazy and teachers were incompetent. David Clark and Terry Astuto (1994) correctly observed that many of these efforts would have been dismissed as ridiculous had they not been vigorously supported by powerful advocates. By the end of the 1990s, many policy analysts discerned that "one size fits all" educational mandates that ignored vast differences among communities and learners had done little to improve our schools. In light of these failed experiences, Clark and Astuto (1994) concluded, "No one can reform our schools for us. If there is to be authentic reform in American education, it must be a grassroots movement" (p. 520).

Appropriately, reform efforts since the early 1990s have been tilting toward deregulation and decentralization—strategies intended to increase the relevance and effectiveness of change-related policies. However, as noted earlier in this book, the concept of directed autonomy serves to remind us that state governments and the courts will exercise their responsibilities to ensure that increased freedoms at the local level do not result in an unequal, inadequate, or inefficient system of public education. In addition, meaningful renewal is unlikely unless educators commit themselves to openly discussing the purposes of education among themselves and ultimately with the community at-large (Sarason, 1996).

If local districts are to engage effectively in school renewal, three critical issues need to be understood by the community:

1. There is a need to recognize that the diversity of opinion regarding the purposes of education is no less important at the school district or school level than it is at the national or state level. Taking the matter to the local level merely makes it more likely that these differences can be identified accurately and that subsequently understanding these differences can become a basis for building consensus concerning education goals. While citizens disagree about what may be the most important educational purpose, opinion polls often reveal that there is majority support for five or six rather common goals (e.g., Elam, Rose, & Gallup, 1996). This fact adds credence to the workability of the strategy of seeking consensus at the local level.

2. There is a need to recognize that local policies and regulations regarding school improvement should be made within a framework of legal requirements and state political expectations (e.g., that school districts will be accountable for student outcomes). Increased liberties do not diminish the importance of other metavalues, such as equality, adequacy, and efficiency.

3. There is a need to recognize that school boards and superintendents are responsible for ensuring that all students in a local district receive reasonably equal educational opportunities. Thus, individual schools are unlikely to receive total freedom to set their visions and long-range plans.

The responsibility for explaining these issues, first to the school board and employees and then to the broader community, belongs to the superintendent. In addition, it is the superintendent who is most likely to play the central role of creating and facilitating a format allowing a democratic debate to take place. In many communities, it will be difficult, and possibly politically uncomfortable, for the superintendent to articulate these issues. Likewise, bringing people with differing philosophies to the table to discuss the goals of education is certain to generate higher levels of conflict. However, unless these issues are addressed, school renewal at the local level is improbable.

Keeping the Community Informed

Inertia in public education is often blamed on obstacles that prevent school districts from implementing change. An unsuitable building that cannot be adapted to new needs and an inadequate budget are examples of barriers that educators and general public readily understand. Less obvious are barriers to understanding and barriers to acceptance. The former include a lack of understanding of key concepts or purposes for change; the latter include rejection on the part of those who have the power to influence implementation (Connor & Lake, 1994). The need to promote public understanding and acceptance of educational programs has increased in a society in which nearly 80% of taxpayers do not have children enrolled in the elementary and secondary public schools. Another problem for superintendents to face is that since the 1950s, there has been an erosion of confidence in public education. "Rather than being held in high esteem, public education now is viewed by many as unproductive and fiscally excessive" (Kowalski, 1995, p. 11). Consequently, superintendents must work to reverse this perception. To do this, they must inform the public of what the schools are really trying to do; they must persuade the public that these initiatives positively affect individuals and society. Most important, they must exhibit that the school district is in harmony with the community.

In addition to facilitating democratic discussions of the purpose of education, the superintendent's leadership role in the community extends to informing the public of agreed-upon goals, instructional and curricular decisions related to those goals, and student outcomes that allow goal attainment to be evaluated. A first step in this direction entails identifying various publics who should receive this information. A superintendent can accomplish this task by developing a list of key communicators such as parents, government officials, and business leaders. Both the school board and administrative staff should review the list before it is finalized to ensure its completeness and accuracy.

Another facet of a superintendent's leadership in school-community relations involves deciding what needs to be communicated to the various publics. Clearly, informing the community of shared visions, goals, and outcomes becomes an overriding responsibility in a policy-making arena requiring direct citizen support (e.g., for change ideas, for tax increases). In large measure, this is true because both deregulation and decentralization result in a dispersing of power and knowledge (Murphy, 1994). While superintendents always have been expected to educate the public about the school district's goals, role expectations related to this task are changing in many districts. Rather than informing the public of personal agendas and personal decisions, superintendents are more likely to be communicating shared decisions, outlining the importance of community support for those decisions, and providing outcome data that allow the public to assess the school district's effectiveness.

Increasingly, superintendents also find themselves having to share research-based data that relate to school improvement. For example, districts considering the formation of site-based councils may find it advantageous to share empirical data on the concept. The National Institute on Educational Governance, Finance, Policymaking, and Management (1997) offers the following suggestions for disseminating such information to policy audiences:

1. Information should be distributed in a timely manner.
2. Information should be succinctly and clearly written; summaries are better than long reports.
3. Information should be provided in a form that accommodates the intended audiences. Audiotapes, for example, may be preferred by busy individuals.
4. Information should be objective, accurate, and fairly reported.

Unfortunately, school districts have not been prone to thinking, planning, executing, and evaluating services from viewpoints outside of their organizations (Topor, 1992). Many superintendents continue to be oriented toward internal reference groups (e.g., other administrators in the district, board members), and consequently, they devote much less time to community-based interactions than their counterparts in private industry typically give to interactions outside their organizations. Moving to continuous, two-way communication requires both an appropriate philosophy and an appropriate strategy to change traditional behaviors.

Building and Maintaining Community Support

Communities are unique entities that differ substantially with respect to engagement in political activity and support for public education. Thus, no one recipe is universally effective for building and maintaining community support for public education. Instead, superintendents are wise to devise their own plans based on the uniqueness of the community, the specific needs of a school district, and a congruence between educational and community values.

Citizens often expect to have substantial input and influence over educational decisions for two very practical reasons. First, they pay taxes to support schools; second, they have a stake in public education. In addition, people in America are inherently political. Many do not respond passively when they are excluded from educational decisions. When their individual voices are ignored, they are likely to gather into groups and form associations. To gain even greater political leverage, they may form coalitions (West, 1985). In addition, those who are ill informed or who perceive they are being excluded from school matters become prime targets for misinformation from those who oppose change or increased fiscal support (Ledell & Arnsparger, 1993). However, one of the most significant findings from the various reform reports is that stakeholders typically have little involvement in decisions that affect them (Patterson, 1993).

School reform expert Philip Schlechty argues that restructuring creates expectations that superintendents become active in influencing stakeholder decisions (Brandt, 1993). Some superintendents, however, may have negative feelings about assuming this role. For them, influencing others has connotations of using sales pitches, engaging in arm twisting, and using other public relations gimmicks; they tend to define persuasion narrowly and negatively. According to Philip West (1985), persuasion is a relatively complex concept that needs to be understood at both its lowest and highest levels:

> At its lowest level persuading may be identified as propaganda and attempts to distort or deceive. It is reporting good news but concealing bad and preaching by word and not by deed. At its highest level it is akin to educating in the most palatable manner in order to motivate people to act in their best interests. It is skillfully organizing a message to get a much needed point across. (p. 28)

Clearly, it is the highest level of persuading that is consistent with the moral and ethical responsibilities of a superintendent as a professional educator and community leader. To a large extent, this responsibility merely means telling the public the truth (Amundson, 1996). However, to fulfill this seemingly simple task, superintendents must have the data that present the truth; they must be willing to correct others when they present incorrect data—even when these others are powerful individuals and groups.

In large city districts, the superintendent needs direct assistance in gaining community support. Some of that assistance can come from other district employees and school board members; it can also come from opinion leaders. These are individuals who "often serve as key sources of information about issues, and, in an informal sense, frame issues for discussion, debate, and action" (Ledell & Arnsparger, 1993, p. 9). Opinion leaders usually make themselves known. They attend school-related meetings; they exhibit an interest in education; they are good organizers who are respected by others; they are well-informed and ask relevant questions (Ledell & Arnsparger, 1993).

Whether school districts will be able to capitalize on the current window of opportunity to have greater autonomy over school reform depends on several issues. Among them are the following:

- The degree to which the community is given an opportunity to interact with educators to reach consensus on the purposes of education
- The degree to which these interactions reduce a meaningful vision and goals
- The degree to which the community supports the vision and goals
- The degree to which the community receives accurate information about progress toward goal attainment
- The degree to which community support is sustained over long periods of time

There are many signs that policymakers and other power elites are becoming increasingly intolerant of ineffective leaders who fail to produce real school improvement (Sarason, 1996). Their displeasure could actually move public education in the direction of less, rather than greater, autonomy. However, the issue of public dissatisfaction is not the sole reason why superintendents need to give greater attention to community support. Others include (1) reduced resources; (2) an increasing percentage of taxpayers who do not perceive themselves receiving a direct benefit from schools; (3) shifting educational needs and priorities; and (4) continued reliance on property tax revenues (which often means voter approval for tax increases). Because of such conditions, superintendents are expected to gain responsive and representative community participation, identify emerging issues and needs, and abort issues that are counterproductive to school reform (West, 1985). Thus, leadership for change includes building good-will in the community and gaining public support.

An organized approach for a superintendent to accomplishing these leadership tasks is strategic marketing. Strategic marketing in education has been defined as including the planning, implementation, and control of programs designed to create voluntary exchanges of values and beliefs between the schools and targeted segments of the school district's population (Kotler & Fox, 1985). Essentially, the process spans three key functions: (1) obtaining accurate information (needs and values); (2) developing relevant programs; and (3) building public support for the programs. Each of these functions prompts the superintendent to engage and inform the public. In addition, superintendents "have an obligation to protect the schools from being manipulated by special interest groups who seek to misinform the general public or advance a narrow agenda" (Ledell & Arnsparger, 1993, p. 35).

BUILDING PARTNERSHIPS

The growth of school partnerships parallels public disfavor with education. Generally, partnerships are joint ventures involving two or more organizations working together to reach common goals. These relationships may or may not be based on a formal contract. An example is a manufacturing company that provides technology resources to a local district because it desires to hire computer-literate high school graduates.

In 1983, only 17% of the nation's schools had such compacts; by 1989, this percentage more than doubled to 40% (Marenda, 1989). By 1990, the United States Department of Education estimated that there were over 140,000 partnership nationwide in just one category—partnerships between schools and businesses (Rigden, 1991). In large measure, the popularity of partnerships is attributable to several factors, which are outlined in Table 11–1. They include economic, political, demographic, and philosophical issues that prompt superintendents to pursue formal associations with other organizations.

Table 11–1
Factors associated with the growing popularity of school partnerships

Factor	Implication
Demographics	America is becoming a more diverse society; a growing number of students are living in poverty. These conditions increase the need and demand for services in public schools. Partnerships can support some of these services.
Economics	Many public school districts simultaneously face increased demands for services and dwindling resources. Hence, partnership ventures are often forged as a means to overcome deficiencies in resources.
Social implications	The consequences of educational failures have shifted from the individual to society. In an information age and global economy, there are few jobs for those who do not succeed in school. Each student who fails to get an appropriate education becomes a concern for the community, state, and nation.
Politics	Gaining the support of community power structures or a majority of taxpayers is becoming increasingly difficult. Three issues—public skepticism about the quality of public education, a growing resistance to taxation, and the fact that a decreasing number of taxpayers have children enrolled in the public schools—are largely responsible. Partnerships are seen as a way to build bridges to those citizens who have become disconnected from schools.
Philosophy	Many superintendents believe that real improvement in schools becomes more likely in environments where there is a symbiotic relationship between schools and community.

Defining the Partnership Relationship

Relationships between school districts and other agencies are often described by different terms, which may or may not reflect actual differences in the nature of the relationships. These associations are commonly described by four terms that reflect varying levels of commitment and legal obligations between the parties (see Figure 11–1).

1. The weakest linkage is *networking*. Organizational networks may be formal or informal, and they often are formed solely to facilitate communication (e.g., sharing information, statistics). Members commonly are freestanding participants (that is, the organizations retain autonomy) (Harris, 1993).

2. Organizational *coordination* almost always is based on a formal agreement. For example, a school district and a community college execute a coordination agreement designed to avoid duplication of adult education programming. The two organizations sacrifice little autonomy and continue to function as parallel education providers. There is only a minimal level of contact between agency leaders (Loughran, 1982).

Figure 11–1
Levels of school district linkage with other organizations and agencies

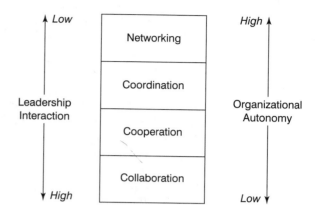

3. Institutional *cooperation* is the next level of commitment and obligation. Generally, some degree of autonomy is sacrificed. One party to the agreement operates the programs in question with the cooperation and support of one or more other agencies. There is greater contact among leaders than is the case with either networking or coordination. Most joint ventures in special education and vocational education exemplify cooperative ventures. One district serves as the legal agent for the cooperative, and other members provide financial support for the services they receive.

4. *Collaboration* designates ventures in which participating organizations commit to a common goal and sacrifice considerable autonomy in affected areas of operation. Power and authority are shared; leaders in the participating organizations often have considerable contact with one another. Collaborative arrangements are usually quite formal in that they are based on written agreements designating purpose, goals, contributions, and so on.

While each of these four levels of linkage may be called partnerships, they clearly represent different concepts of working together. Precise understandings are made even more difficult by the fact that schools enter partnerships with different types of groups and agencies. The most widely publicized relationships have been between schools and businesses. Common examples of partnership activities include tutoring programs, field trips and special activities, donations (supplies, equipment), student jobs, summer jobs for teachers, loaned executives, and resource persons to speak to classes (American Association of School Administrators, 1988). The National Alliance of Business (1987) defined six levels of potential interaction:

1. *Level I—Policy.* These alliances are designed to shape new policy or modify existing policy by influencing state or national legislation.

2. *Level II—Systematic educational improvement.* Groups work together to identify areas needing reform and make joint efforts over a long period of time to seek improvement in those areas.

3. *Level III—Management assistance.* Business partners provide school administrators with management support and business expertise over a broad range of management areas.

4. *Level IV—Training and development.* Business partners provide opportunities for educators to update skills and learn about labor markets, industrial/business operations, workplace needs, and career opportunities.

5. *Level V—Classroom activities.* Business volunteers serve as guest instructors or entire classrooms visit business sites.

6. *Level VI—Special services.* These are short-term projects, student-specific activities, or resource allocation to assist schools with a specific need or problem.

Some business leaders unfortunately believe that they have little to gain by interacting with school administrators. For them, partnerships with schools have nothing to do with improving their leadership skills or broadening their understanding of public institutions. Instead, the linkages are justified in terms of influencing the education of potential future employees and of gaining positive media exposure in the community. Business leaders have tended to ask two questions about partnerships with schools: (1) How can business improve public schools? and (2) How can public schools respond more directly to the needs of employers? Both questions fail to take into consideration the needs and interests of students (Wise, 1981).

School districts also establish formal relationships with other educational institutions, most notably colleges and universities. These ventures may be related to the commitment on the part of many institutions of higher learning to general service to the community (e.g., helping to improve community life by improving the public schools), or they may be pragmatic linkages serving mutual needs (e.g., joint programs in teacher education). Commonly, partnerships between school districts and universities take four forms:

1. Program assistance (e.g., advanced placement courses for high school students)

2. Programs and services for educators (e.g., staff development for teachers and administrators)

3. Curriculum and assessment projects (e.g., conducting program evaluation, assisting with the design of evaluation systems)

4. Sharing educational resources (e.g., consultants, sharing technology) (Pitsch, 1991)

Other partnerships involving school districts are community based. These might include linkages with parents (who serve as volunteer aides or on special task forces), volunteers (for special school projects), local government, churches, or other service agencies. In some cities, for instance, the public schools have joined forces with churches, hospitals, and mental health agencies to provide services to troubled students (e.g., pregnancy counseling, therapy for behavior disorders). Recreation programs and adult education programs are two of the most established areas of school-community collaboration.

More recently, partnerships have been categorized according to goals and intentions. Three categories are commonly used for this purpose: (1) program enhancement, (2) new programs, or (3) reform-related programs. While the first two involve adjustments to the current school program, the third entails more significant and sweeping changes to schools and districts. Reform-related partnerships are usually rooted in a mutual conviction that school improvement cannot be achieved without restructuring. A three-tiered approach for categorizing school partnerships—based on intentions, nature of school partners, and scope of projects—is shown in Figure 11–2.

Intention of Partnership

Program Enhancement	New Program	School Reform
Improving or expanding an existing program (e.g., new software for a computer class)	Adding a new program to the existing structure/curriculum (e.g., adding a mathematics program)	Significant changes to the structure and/or curriculum of the school (e.g., moving to a decentralized, shared governance system)

Partners

Business/Industry	Community	Other Schools
A joint venture with a private, profit-seeking organization (e.g., partnership with a local bank)	A joint venture with agencies, groups, or individuals who are not engaged in business or industry (e.g., partnership with parents, city government)	A joint venture with other education organizations (e.g., a partnership with a university)

Type of Partnership

Adopt-a-School	One-Way, Project Driven	Limited, Two-Way	Full, Two-Way
Resources are given to the school for general purposes; school does not provide resources to the partner.	Resources are given to the school for a specific project that is of interest to the partner; school does not provide resources to the partner.	Resources are given to the school for one or more projects; school responds by meeting a need of the partner.	Resources are exchanged over a broad area of programs; mutual benefits become a focal point for programming.

Figure 11–2
Categorization of school partnerships

Critical Decisions About Partnerships

The literature abounds with success stories about school partnerships; less known is the fact that many of these projects fail to live up to their potential. A study of 133 schools in one of the nation's largest districts, for instance, found that only 8 of 450 partnership projects with local businesses had led to instructional change (Miron & Wimpelberg, 1989). Pressured by the demands of a global economy, many business leaders in the 1980s presumed a cause-and-effect relationship between education and prosperity (Wynne, 1986). At the same time that they were publicly criticizing schools, many were assuming a more active role with local schools and encouraging their colleagues to do so. Hence, many of the partnerships spawned in this environment were based on unrealistic and narrow goals flowing from the conclusion that education was responsible for America's declining dominance in world markets. These collaborative efforts were prone to failure because they were ill conceived or improperly supported.

To avoid the potential pitfalls of collaboration, superintendents should raise a series of essential questions before any agreement is reached. Factors that drive these questions and the range of possible decisions are shown in Table 11–2.

Of greatest importance are the following questions:

- *Compatibility of organizational cultures.* To what degree does a school district and a potential partner possess similar cultures? To what extent are their cultures strong or weak (that is, whether there is wide acceptance of basic values or not)? Unless cultures are reasonably compatible, excessive conflict may deter goal attainment (MacDowell, 1989).

Table 11–2
Issues associated with forming school partnerships

Factor	Range of Possibilities	Desired Condition
Compatibility of organizational cultures	Incompatible to compatible	Reasonably compatible cultures
Relationship between risk and experience	Low to high	Previous successful experiences for high-risk projects
Needs foci	Organizational to individual	A balance between organizational and individual needs
Benefits received	One-sided to mutual	Mutual benefits
Communication among partners	One-way to two-way	Continuous two-way communication
Partnership goals	Rigid to flexible	Sufficiently flexible goals to allow for periodic adjustments
Organizational coupling	Loose to tight	Sufficient coupling to enhance cooperation and conflict management
Duration of the relationship	Short-term to long-term	Long-term relationships
Resource commitments	Minimal to substantial	Fairly substantial commitments

- *Relationship between risk and experience.* To what extent is risk involved? Have the partners worked together before? Do potential partners have previous experiences with these types of ventures? It is often advisable to build on previous successes, and it is advantageous to begin with a project that is likely to succeed (Page, 1987).

- *Needs foci.* Will the partnership projects focus solely on organizational needs? If so, what problems will be created? Are there ways to simultaneously address organizational and individual needs? Balancing the needs of the organization and individuals is most likely to produce interest and personal commitments in any projects.

- *Benefits received.* Is the partnership designed so that only one partner is the beneficiary? If so, how might this condition negatively affect goal attainment? Are there ways of pursuing mutual benefits? When schools are the sole beneficiaries, projects tend to be short-lived. Each potential partner should be encouraged to answer the question, "What's in it for me?" (Page, 1987).

- *Communication among partners.* Will communication be restricted to the school district giving information to the partner? Or will the partner be exchanging messages with the school district? Without active exchanges of information, one or more of the partners may become disinterested or form faulty conclusions about the project's effectiveness.

- *Partnership goals.* Are the goals long-term and rigid? Are there provisions for adjusting goals based on short-term outcomes? Setting rigid long-term goals prevents periodic adjustments for unanticipated problems or outcomes. All parties should agree on the goals before the project starts (MacDowell, 1989).

- *Organizational coupling.* To what extent will the partners sacrifice autonomy? To what extent will the partners be required to share power, decision making, and responsibility? Without coupling, organizations are likely to protect interests and authority to the extent that the project might be negatively affected.

- *Duration of the relationship.* What is the time frame for the partnership? Does the association have an opportunity to grow and prosper—or will it be terminated at a specified time regardless of outcomes? Because most change in public education requires time and patience, the most productive partnerships tend to be long-term ventures.

- *Resource commitments.* Will each partner be contributing resources? Will these resources be material or human? Are necessary resource allocations identified and understood? Without fairly substantial commitments of human and material resources, partners find it easy to withdraw when problems are encountered.

It is far better to ask and answer these types of questions before a relationship with other organizations is formalized. Unfortunately, this does not always occur. Often educational administrators seize what they think are golden opportunities to gain resources without adequately considering the long-term repercussions of doing so.

Why Partnerships Fail and Succeed

Given the unique nature of school districts as well as of their potential partners, there are a myriad of reasons why joint ventures succeed or fail. Nevertheless, experience and observation provide insights into recurring issues that appear to influence the ultimate fate of school partnerships. Among the many stumbling blocks, five have proven to be especially troublesome. They are identified in Figure 11–3 and explained below.

1. *Turf protection*, which refers to the tendency of organizations or divisions of organizations to protect authority, has long been recognized as a source of conflict within bureaucratic-like organizations. In the realm of partnerships, jurisdictional disputes often emerge with respect to autonomy—that is, the degree to which a school district or partner must surrender autonomy. One example of this problem was visible in a joint venture between a school district and a community college. Existing side by side in the same city, the two institutions agreed to collaborate in the area of adult education. Conflict emerged when administrators disagreed over ultimate control of curricular and scheduling decisions. While the officials recognized the benefits of working together, neither side was willing to sacrifice autonomy to accomplish this goal. Turf protection also can emerge in partnerships with business. Here schools are often confronted with aggressive executives who attempt to use their clout to control key educational decisions.

2. Partnerships also fail because of *insufficient planning* and *ambiguous direction*. These arise for two main reasons. First, superintendents or principals are often impetuous, entering partnerships with little forethought about end products and the means for reaching those goals. The ideal is to aim for long-term relationships that have incremental objectives (Gardner, 1990). Second, administrators may enter partnerships without giving adequate time and attention to comprehensive planning; critical issues are either ignored or insufficiently studied.

Figure 11–3
Common reasons why partnerships fail

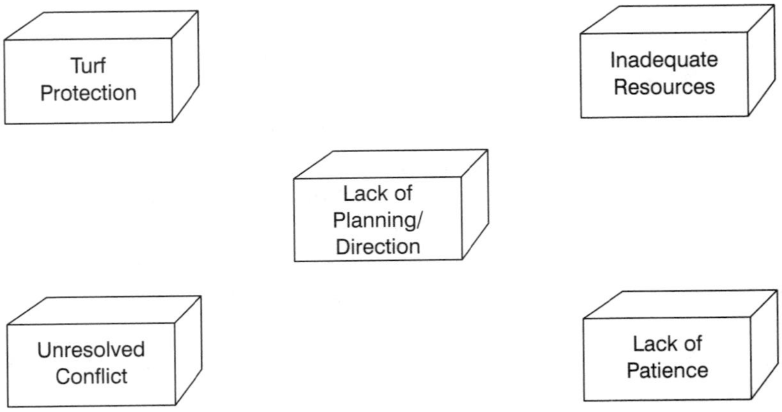

3. A more obvious reason for failure relates to *inadequate resources*. An example of this barrier was obvious in a project between a school district and a local manufacturing company. The primary goal was to provide summer jobs to high school juniors and seniors. The company wanted the school district to provide an after-school training program that would prepare students for future work experiences. The project ran into difficulty when funds could not be secured to pay instructors for the training program. Equally dysfunctional are situations in which administrators and teachers are asked to perform the work created by a partnership without receiving additional compensation or released time.

4. *Unresolved conflict* is almost always associated with the unwillingness of partners to address tensions that are inevitable in their joint ventures. A drug counseling project between a school district and local mental health agency exemplifies this barrier. Tension was generated because the school counselors and staff at the agency disagreed with respect to counseling approaches. Rather than attempting to resolve their differences, they worked around each other. Eventually, the project fell apart because of a lack of communication.

5. A final problem deserving attention involves time parameters. Many business executives are accustomed to seeing short-term results in their programs. For example, they want to see signs of increased sales within 6 to 18 months from the time that they improve a product. Accordingly, those who become engaged in school partnerships often exhibit *a lack of patience*. They do not understand that the fruits of education may require many years of nurturing. Unless this is adequately explained at the front end of project, partners may become impatient and withdraw from the joint agreements.

Success, too, can be attributed to many different factors. The more prominent ones are identified in Figure 11–4. There is a synergistic element to these factors. That is to say, they become more effective when they occur collectively. Put simply, the more of these elements that are present, the more likely the partnership will be successful. Brief explanations are provided for each of these recurring attributes related to success.

- *Partners receive recognition*. To a certain degree, partnership ventures represent a transactional process; each partner expects to gain something. In the case of one-way, restricted ventures, the school district's partners often seek positive publicity. Thus, school officials need to take the necessary steps to ensure that all partners receive recognition.

- *Employees are supportive*. Projects are often developed without employee involvement. This mistake can be disastrous. In effective projects, enthusiasm and support are usually visible among administrators, teachers, and others who have direct responsibilities in the work involved for the project.

- *Periodic progress reports are provided*. Anyone who invests time and money wants some feedback regarding progress. Hence, a prescribed system of

Figure 11–4
Common reasons why partnerships succeed

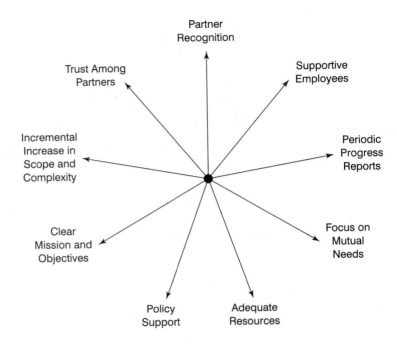

communication should provide periodic reports to the partners; a minimum of three or four reports a year is recommended.

- *Mutual benefits are at the core of the partnership.* While many arguments can be made for schools accepting handouts, one-way partnerships often fail to live up to their full potential. Ventures predicated on mutual interests and mutual gains are more likely to endure. A key to effective partnerships is establishment of an intersection of educational interests—a point at which partners are able to justify the commitments they make to each other (Wise, 1981).

- *Adequate resources are in place.* Clearly, partnerships will not achieve their intended outcomes unless necessary resources are available.

- *Policymakers are supportive and involved.* Enduring partnerships often require adjustments—adaptations to unforeseen problems or emerging needs. This quality is more likely in partnerships in which key policy figures are involved in the project. For example, a school board member can serve on the advisory committee for the project.

- *Mission and objectives are clear and understood.* Those engaged in the partnership should be able to identify the mission and objectives with the same degree of clarity. Resolving misunderstandings about intentions can be extremely counterproductive once a partnership is in effect.

- *Scope and complexity should increase incrementally.* Like all relationships, partnerships require time to become stronger. Often it is best to begin with simple projects. This allows the partners to experience success and to build on that accomplishment. The best partnerships often reveal this evolutionary pattern of growth.

- *Trust is central to the relationship.* Because the most effective partnerships are two-way ventures and because two-way ventures almost always require interdependency, trust is an essential ingredient. Over time, partners who trust each other are more likely to rely on transformational rather than transactional exchanges to set their goals.

While all the above factors may be essential in given situations, trust is undoubtedly the most powerful and pervasive ingredient in successful collaboration.

Despite the immense popularity of school partnerships, there has been very little formal research on this topic. In part, this is due to the fact that it is extremely difficult to isolate outcomes that are directly attributable to collaboration; it is especially difficult to determine the effects of partnerships on student outcomes (Cobb & Quaglia, 1994). Because collaboration is often sparked by economic and political forces, evaluation of such projects concentrates on resource acquisition and public relations. For example, projects may be deemed successful simply because schools received additional equipment or because positive publicity was generated for the partners. From a political perspective, however, partnerships are valuable simply because they serve to bring the school and the community closer to each other.

A SUPERINTENDENT'S PERSONAL INVOLVEMENT IN THE COMMUNITY

Four different conceptions of the superintendency (teacher of teachers, business manager, democratic leader, and applied social scientist) were reviewed in chapter 7. Stresses commonly produced by these competing role expectations continue to capture the attention of researchers and practitioners. One common area of conflict pertains to expectations that superintendents simultaneously should be professional leaders and effective politicians. Unmistakably, there is a certain degree of incompatibility between requiring a superintendent to have a specific level of education (and hence, a specified professional knowledge base) and requiring a superintendent to acquire political support from nonprofessionals for critical education decisions. Arthur Blumberg (1985) referred to this issue as the political dilemma of being a nonelected public official. That is, nonelected officials face a certain degree of role conflict in their work because they are both professionals and political figures. Blumberg cited several reasons why the superintendency was unique among such nonelected official positions:

- Superintendents lead institutions to which some of the most deeply held values in the American tradition are attached.
- Superintendents assume their jobs as supposed experts, yet their expertise is dependent on their ability to develop a supportive constituency among the school board, community, and professional staff.

- School districts are composed of people who often have equal or more expertise in education than the superintendent.

Even though superintendents may be highly educated and highly experienced, they rarely are able to make decisions outside of a political context.

The need to gain public acceptance and support is one compelling reason why superintendents should assume leadership roles in their communities. Being an active member of a service club, serving on city and county boards, and attending public functions regularly permit the superintendent to learn the history, values, and politics of the community. These activities also provide forums for communicating; they allow the superintendent to provide information (e.g., about school programs, emerging needs), as well as to receive information. Often persons not directly connected to the schools are opinion leaders; and unless superintendents become active in the larger community, they may not be able to cultivate their support.

Community involvement also allows a superintendent to identify various publics. This task is particularly important in larger, heterogeneous communities. In urban districts, for example, school boards are often composed of individuals who represent single constituencies (Kowalski, 1995). Unless the superintendent has ongoing interactions with all of these publics, personal relationships with board members may suffer. In addition, contact with various publics serves a multitude of purposes including the following:

- Being able to get a better perspective of real needs and expectations of the community
- Being able to establish an identity and working relationship with a broad base of citizens
- Being able to engage in two-way communication
- Being able to secure support for resources and reform

Involvement within the community is also linked to the fact that the superintendent is the visible head of the school district. Because of this role, superintendents find themselves interacting primarily with adults, unlike teachers and principals who spend more of their time interacting with students. "Much of what the superintendent does in these meetings is symbolic; the superintendent represents the schools to the community" (Sergiovanni, Burlingame, Coombs, & Thurston, 1992, p. 321). Thus, it is extremely important for a superintendent to be active in the community, to have access to power structures, and to have positive relationships with influential individuals who make up the power structures.

Maintaining high visibility in the community has become an even more important issue for superintendents because of educational reform. Public schools have a myriad of stakeholders, and these stakeholders often want a voice in major proposed changes. Because many patrons are not well informed about what is occurring in the schools, they are likely to accept misinformation (Ledell & Arnsparger, 1993). If no concerted effort is made to provide them with accurate data, they are not likely to support proposed reforms—especially if the changes are linked to tax increases. A superintendent can exercise leadership for school reform by pursuing activities such as these:

- Having a series of meetings involving a broad cross section of the community
- Inviting reform opponents to face-to-face meetings
- Keeping focused on what the community wants and expects from public schools
- Getting patrons to visit schools (Ledell & Arnsparger, 1993)

In addition, face-to-face contacts with elected officials, business leaders, clergy, and other influential community members allow a superintendent to take advantage of informal communication networks across the community.

While there are many potential benefits associated with a superintendent maintaining a high profile in the community, several caveats need to be considered. In most school districts, superintendents are expected to spend a good portion of their time dealing with internal matters. That is, they are expected to manage the day-to-day problems of the school district. If a superintendent spends too much time away from the office, this may be viewed negatively in certain contexts. Effective superintendents balance their time and set priorities; much of their contact with community groups occurs outside of the regular school day.

Interacting with power structures can be a highly political activity. On occasion, a superintendent may need the support of influential citizens. Such contacts, while advantageous to the school district, can place an administrator in a compromising position. For example, in exchange for supporting a school bond issue, a person may request that the superintendent provide overt support for a political candidate, endorse certain programs, or provide preferential treatment for a relative who is seeking employment in the school district. Usually such transactions are not blatant attempts at receiving favors; they occur after relationships have developed naturally over time and the requests may be quite indirect. A superintendent may soon discover that it is not easy to work effectively in political arenas while maintaining high ethical and moral standards. There are, however, hundreds of skilled practitioners who are able to achieve this balance. They do so by placing the interests of the school district above personal interests, by being honest and candid in their communication, by avoiding illegal and unethical deals, and by honoring their responsibilities inherent in being a public official in a democratic society.

FOR FURTHER REFLECTION

This chapter examined the leadership role of the superintendent in the wider community. These responsibilities span providing an effective school-community relations program, partnerships with other groups in the community, and a superintendent's personal involvement in community activities.

As you consider what you read in this chapter, answer the following questions:

1. Public relations has become a higher priority for many school districts. What factors have contributed to its rise in importance?

2. School districts have multiple publics. What measures can a superintendent take to identify such publics and communicate with them?

3. In most communities, multiple purposes for public education are identified by taxpayers. How does this fact relate to the superintendent's responsibility to provide leadership in the community?

4. What are the advantages of schools entering into partnerships with business? With other educational agencies?

5. What common problems can superintendents expect with regard to building and maintaining effective partnerships?

6. Do you believe that the size (enrollment) of a school district influences the amount of time a superintendent spends with community activities? Why or why not?

7. Based on your experiences with superintendents, do they devote a considerable portion of their time to being visible within the community? What is the basis for your response?

8. Assume you were interviewing for your first superintendency. A board members asks you, "Are you an educator or a politician?" How would you respond?

9. Many taxpayers are not well informed about what is occurring in the public schools. In part, this is because a high percentage of them no longer have children enrolled. In addition to traditional newsletters and occasional press releases, how can superintendents reach out to establish meaningful communication with these individuals?

10. Should superintendents ever become involved in supporting candidates for a school board election? Why or why not?

CASE STUDY

Brighton, the home of Southeastern State University, is a community with about 13,000 residents. The public schools enroll 2,600 students at six attendance centers. Over the years, the school district and university have maintained a positive relationship that focused largely on teacher education. Education students at the university have access to the local elementary and secondary schools for classroom observations and student teaching. George Bascum, the superintendent of the Brighton school district, himself a graduate of Southeastern, serves on the university's Alumni Board.

Two years ago, when Dr. Sandra Walker was named president at Southeastern, the relationship between the university and school district changed. Having been an elementary school teacher and dean of education, President Walker had a particular interest in developing a partnership with the local schools. Although the two institutions had been collaborating for years, no formal agreement defined their activities. The dean of Southeastern's school of education, Dr. Elizabeth O'Ryan, was urged by the new president to formalize the relationship. At first, Dean O'Ryan was reluctant to do so because she felt that the current situation had worked well for both parties. President Walker, however, wanted a relationship that would allow the university faculty to take a more direct role in school reform efforts. She explained her position to Dean O'Ryan as follows:

"While our current level of involvement with the public schools is essential, I am thinking about doing more than just placing our students in their district to do classroom participation and perhaps student teaching. The quality of our teacher education programs depends on having access to schools that are using 'cutting edge' ideas. Without a formal agreement for collaboration, it will be difficult for our faculty to become involved in school improvement. I am thinking about a real partnership—one in which their staff and ours work side by side to reconstruct the schools. To do this, I think we need a formal partnership. I've outlined some key points for such an agreement. You need to contact Mr. Bascum and discuss the proposal. If he is reluctant, I'll become involved. I would prefer, however, that the two of your work things out."

Dean O'Ryan met with the superintendent several days after being instructed to do so. She shared President Walker's interest in developing a formal partnership. She then outlined basic elements for the agreement.

- The partnership would begin with two pilot schools (one elementary school and one secondary school).
- At each of these schools, a planning committee would consist of (1) the school principal, (2) two of the school's teachers, and (3) three professors appointed by Dean O'Ryan.
- The planning committee would identify specific needs and projects associated with school reform. The school district and university would work collaboratively to implement these initiatives. There would be no cost to the school district for university personnel.
- School district personnel serving on the planning committee or directly involved in partnership initiatives would be eligible to receive a 50% reduction in tuition for any graduate courses they would take at Southeastern.
- The planning team would determine how teacher education students could participate in the newly developed programs.

Superintendent Bascum reacted cautiously to the university's proposal. "I'll have to discuss this matter with the school board, but I see a great deal of opportunity here. You know, many residents are urging us to develop closer ties with Southeastern. There may be ways that we can save resources by working together."

Dean O'Ryan responded, "We have many resources in this community. We should work together to ensure that the schools in the community provide the very best education for students. Your students and teachers will benefit, and our faculty and teacher education students will be able to receive highly relevant experiences. It's a win-win situation."

Mr. Bascum was not totally convinced that the partnership was a good idea. After Dean O'Ryan left, he immediately went to see Peter Jones, his assistant superintendent. He outlined the proposal and asked, "What do you think?"

"Well, there are possible benefits and possible problems," Jones answered. "What if we get into situations where the committee becomes divided? How can we get anything done if the votes are evenly split? And what happens if our teachers and administrators don't like the ideas that come out of these committees? But on the other hand, we may have no choice but to play ball with them. We could have real political problems if we reject their offer."

The pair decided that the idea should be presented to the school board at the next meeting. Their intention was to share the idea and see how the five board members reacted. There were several reasons why they believed the board would not respond favorably:

- Two of the board members had previously complained about university personnel wanting to influence school district policy. Just 2 weeks ago, for example, one of them complained to Mr. Bascum about "pushy professors who wanted to run the school district."

- Several professors had written letters to the editor of the local newspaper in the past year criticizing either the school district's discipline policies or the school's curriculum. The board had reacted rather negatively to these letters.

- Only one of the five board members was employed by the university. Barbara White, director of food services in the dormitories, had shown no previous interest in developing joint programs with the university.

- The board members generally felt that the schools were very good, and they were cautious about "pursuing change just to be in vogue."

However, after outlining the details of the proposal, Mrs. White immediately made a motion to approve the partnership concept. Brian Debow, a farmer and one of the 2 board members who previously voiced concerns about university employees trying to influence policy, argued against the motion. He asked the board to delay action on the matter. Mrs. White countered that the partnership was an opportunity to discuss new ideas and that it should be started as soon as possible. Another board member asked Mr. Bascum how he felt about the proposal. He said that although there had been little time to consider it, it basically looked like a great opportunity for the school district. After about 20 minutes of discussion, the board voted 4 to 1 to approve the partnership proposal.

The local media reported the board's action the next morning. A live interview with President Walker aired on the local radio station at 7:30 A.M. She expressed optimism about collaborating with the school district, and she congratulated the superintendent and school board for having approved the agreement. The morning newspaper carried a front-page article announcing the partnership. The article described it as "a positive example of public institutions working together." Unfortunately for Mr. Bascum, most school employees found out about the partnership from these sources; many were surprised and concerned that the matter had not been discussed within the school district.

That afternoon Mr. Bascum met with the principals in his office. He first apologized for the way the partnership was announced. He told the principals, "I wish we would have had more time to discuss this, but I really thought the matter would be tabled by the school board. This would have given us the opportunity to examine the partnership proposal more closely. That didn't happen." After sharing the details of the proposal—the same details outlined by Dean O'Ryan and approved by the school board—he asked if any of the principals wanted to have their schools serve as pilot sites. Only one elementary principal volunteered, and she was the least experienced of the group. Neither the middle school nor high school principal wanted to participate. After the superintendent stated that it was necessary for one of the schools to become involved, the middle school principal reluctantly agreed to cooperate.

The initial meeting of the planning teams at both schools occurred approximately 1 month after the school board had acted to approve the partnership. The school personnel entered the first meeting expecting to engage in general discussions about current practices and possible ideas for improvement. Instead, they were surprised when the professors distributed a proposal calling for the consideration of three specific programs: site-based management, cooperative learning, and differentiated staffing. The professors suggested that these programs have been proven to be effective in a number of schools, and, thus, they provided possible starting points. One professor serving on the elementary school planning team noted, "I'd love to have my students see these programs operating in real schools."

The school representatives at both schools became more apprehensive after their initial meetings with the professors. They were especially concerned that there might be a "hidden agenda." Even though no decisions were made during the first meeting, the school personnel felt they were already put on the defensive; they had to provide reasons why these programs were not good starting points. Their sentiments quickly spread through their schools via informal communication channels. Rumors emerged about the purposes of the project and the amount of control that the university would now exercise over the schools. One rumor was that the university was trying to turn the two participating schools into laboratory schools. The principals of these sites started to receive a myriad of questions and complaints; they wasted no time in informing Superintendent Bascum of that fact.

At the next committee meetings at both the middle school and elementary school, the professors were asked why they had selected these three programs. The same answer was given at both schools—the programs were tied to successful reform ventures in other public schools. The professors also pointed out that it would be helpful if both schools pursued the same initiatives. In addition, they denied accusations that there was a hidden agenda in the partnership. The professors urged the school representatives to present their own ideas about possible programs; however, none was offered.

After just two meetings, the planning teams were clearly divided. The school personnel were highly suspicious of the university's motives, and the professors generally viewed the school representatives as unwilling to look at new ideas. Both teams decided to wait two weeks before having their third meeting.

The two principals of the partnership sites met with Mr. Bascum after the second meetings. This time they were more emphatic, pointing out that the partnership had become a disruptive force in their buildings. The superintendent knew that collaboration was likely to generate conflict; however, he was astonished it occurred so quickly. Based on the information he received from the principals, he concluded that some form of intervention had to occur before the teams met again. He went to see Dean O'Ryan after his meeting with the principals. He shared the concerns that had emerged among the teachers. He told her, "I'm getting messages from my principals that the planning team meetings are not going well. There is some feeling on the part of our representatives that there is a hidden agenda—that the university is trying to take control of these two schools. For example, they feel that the professors have already decided which projects will be pursued."

Dean O'Ryan responded, "Our representatives merely offered three ideas as starting points for discussion. They feel your principals and teachers immediately became defensive; rather than offering their own ideas, they continued to question our motives." The two agreed that the problem required their intervention. Dean O'Ryan suggested that the two of them attend the next planning meeting at each school. "We have to convince everyone that there is no hidden agenda; we have to create an atmosphere of openness and flexibility. If not, this project will fail. And if it does, we all look bad."

Superintendent Bascum agreed with Dean O'Ryan's suggestion. They would try to reduce tensions by ensuring the participants that the only goal was to improve both the school programs and the university's teacher education program.

However, when he returned to his office, Mr. Bascum went to see his assistant superintendent. He told Mr. Jones about his meeting with Dean O'Ryan and then said, "This thing is really backfiring on us. We have had good relationships with Southeastern, and this partnership thing may destroy that. Teachers are starting to think they are being used as guinea pigs; the principals are claiming that the partnership is causing a great deal of conflict."

Mr. Jones responded, "I think we need to find a way out. And the quicker we do that, the better. This is a lot of trouble we don't need. I never thought the board would buy into this—at least not right away. Maybe we can convince everyone to put this on the back burner for a year or so."

"No, we can't do that," Superintendent Bascum responded. "We made a commitment and we have to stand by it—at least for a reasonable period of time. How would it look if we backed out now? What would the board say? We would probably get criticized heavily in the media. No, we can't just quit at this early point, and stalling for a year is no better alternative. After all, maybe the professors are correct; maybe our people are being too defensive."

A letter, signed by both Superintendent Bascum and Dean O'Ryan, was sent to the 12 members of the planning teams. In it, the pair indicated that they would be attending the next meeting to discuss the intentions of the partnership and to answer questions about unfounded rumors. The day after that letter was delivered, Mr. Bascum received letters signed by virtually all of the teachers at the two schools requesting that the school district withdraw from the partnership—at least until the faculties at the two schools had an opportunity to discuss the potential of such a partnership among themselves. He also received a letter from the president of the teachers' union criticizing him for having entered the partnership without consulting the union. He sat at his desk and read each of the letters a second time. He also looked at several telephone messages from school board members indicating that they had received complaints about the partnerships. He then stared out of his office window and contemplated what he should do next.

Issues for Discussion

1. Evaluate the decision of the superintendent to take the proposal to the school board so quickly. What matters should have been investigated before the proposal was taken to the school board?

2. Did the superintendent have any alternatives to taking the proposal to the school board? If so, what were they?

3. Discuss the intended purposes of the partnership as outlined by President Walker. To what extent did these purposes contribute to the conflict?

4. Is it common for school personnel to be apprehensive about working with university personnel? What information or experiences contribute to your conclusion?

5. This chapter presented information about effective school partnerships. Evaluate the actions of the institutional leaders in this case based on that information.

6. Can this partnership be saved? If so, what actions are needed?

7. Fear of public criticism is one reason why the superintendent does not want to retreat from the partnership. Do you believe that fear is warranted? Why or why not?

8. Would it have been helpful for the school district and university to start with a small project that was likely to succeed? Why or why not?

9. If you had been the superintendent, would you have discussed the proposal with the teachers' union prior to taking it to the school board?

REFERENCES

Alexander, K., & Salmon, R. G. (1995). *Public school finance*. Boston: Allyn and Bacon.

American Association of School Administrators (1988). *Challenges for school leaders*. Arlington, VA: Author.

Amundson, K. (1996). *Telling the truth about America's public schools*. Arlington, VA: American Association of School Administrators.

Armstrong, D. G., Henson, K. T., & Savage, T. V. (1997). *Teaching Today: An introduction to education* (5th ed.). Upper Saddle River, NJ: Merrill/Prentice Hall.

Blumberg, A. (1985). *The school superintendent: Living with conflict*. New York: Teachers College Press.

Brandt, R. (1993). On restructuring roles and relationships: A conversation with Phil Schlechty. *Educational Leadership, 51*(2), 8–11.

Burrup, P. E., Brimley, V., & Garfield, R. R. (1996). *Financing education in a climate of change* (6th ed.). Boston: Allyn and Bacon.

Clark, D. L., & Astuto, T. A. (1994). Redirecting reform: Challenges to popular assumptions about teachers and students. *Phi Delta Kappan, 75*(7), 512–520.

Cobb, C., & Quaglia, R. J. (1994). *Moving beyond school-business partnerships and creating relationships*. (ERIC Document Reproduction Service No. ED 374 545)

Cohen, P. M. (1987). *The public relations primer: Thinking and writing in context*. Upper Saddle River, NJ: Prentice Hall.

Connor, P. E., & Lake, L. K. (1994). *Managing organizational change* (2nd ed.). Westport, CT: Praeger.

Cuban, L. (1988). Why do some reforms persist? *Educational Administration Quarterly, 24*(3), 329–335.

Elam, S. M., Rose, L. C., & Gallup, A. M. (1996). The 28th annual Phi Delta Kappa/Gallup poll of the public's attitudes toward the public schools. *Phi Delta Kappan, 78*(1), 41–59.

Gardner, A. L. (1990). *School partnerships: A handbook for school and community leaders*. (ERIC Document Reproduction Service No. ED 331 899)

Harris, T. E.(1993). *Applied organizational communication: Perspectives, principles, and pragmatics*. Hillsdale, NJ: Lawrence Erlbaum.

Kotler, P., & Fox, K. (1985). *Strategic marketing for educational institutions*. Upper Saddle River, NJ: Prentice Hall.

Kowalski, T. J. (1995). *Keepers of the flame: Contemporary urban superintendents*. Thousand Oaks, CA: Corwin.

Ledell, M., & Arnsparger, A. (1993). *How to deal with community criticism of school change*. Alexandria, VA: Association for Supervision and Curriculum Development.

Lober, I. M. (1993). *Promoting your school: A public relations handbook*. Lancaster, PA: Technomic.

Loughran, E. L. (1982). Networking, coordination, cooperation, and collaboration. *Community Education Journal, 9*(4), 28–30.

MacDowell, M. A. (1989). Partnerships: Getting a return on the investment. *Educational Leadership, 47*(2), 8–11.

Marenda, D. W. (1989). Partners in education: An old tradition renamed. *Educational Leadership, 47*(2), 4–7.

Miron, L. F., & Wimpelberg, R. K. (1989). School-business partnerships and the reform of education. *Administrator's Notebook, 33*(9), 1–4.

Murphy, J. (1994). *The changing role of the superintendency in restructuring districts in Kentucky.* (ERIC Document Reproduction Service No. ED 374 519).

National Alliance of Business (1987). *The fourth R: Workforce readiness.* Washington, DC: Author.

National Institute on Educational Governance, Finance, Policymaking, and Management (1997). *Meeting the information needs of educational policymakers.* Washington, DC: U.S. Government Printing Office.

Page, E. G. (1987). Partnerships: Making a difference over time? *Journal of Career Development, 13*(3), 43–49.

Patterson, H. (1993). Don't exclude the stakeholders. *School Administrator, 50*(2), 13–14.

Pitsch, M. (1991, September 11). School-college links seen as fundamental to education reform. *Education Week, 11*(2), 1, 12–13.

Rigden, D. W. (1991). *Business-school partnerships: A path to effective restructuring* (2nd ed.). New York: Council for Aid to Education.

Sarason, S. B. (1996). *Revisiting "the culture of the school and the problem of change."* New York: Teachers College Press.

Seitel, F. P. (1992). *The practice of public relations* (5th ed.). New York: Macmillan.

Sergiovanni, T. J., Burlingame, M., Coombs, F. S., & Thurston, P. W. (1992). *Educational governance and administration* (3rd ed.). Boston: Allyn and Bacon.

Spring, J. (1994). *The American school: 1642–1990.* (3rd ed.). New York: Longman.

Swanson, A. D., & King, R. A. (1997). *School finance: Its economics and politics* (2nd ed.). New York: Longman.

Tesconi, C. A. (1984). Additive reform and the retreat from purpose. *Educational Studies, 15*(1), 1–10.

Topor, R. (1992). *No more navel gazing.* Mountain View, CA: Topor & Associates.

West, P. T. (1985). *Educational public relations.* Beverly Hills, CA: Sage.

Whitney, T. N., & Crampton, F. E. (1995). State school finance litigation: A summary and analysis. *State Legislative Report, 20*, 1–16.

Wise, R. I. (1981). Schools, businesses, and educational needs: From cooperation to collaboration. *Education and Urban Society, 14*(1), 67–82.

Wynne, G. E. (1986). School-business partnerships: A shortcut to effectiveness. *NASSP Bulletin, 70*(491), 94–98.

Chapter 12

Work Lives, Stress, and Adjustments

Key Concepts

✧ Duties and responsibilities of superintendents

✧ Time requirements

✧ Nature of the work

✧ Rewards and frustrations expressed by superintendents

✧ Occupational stress

✧ Work and personal health

✧ Perceived and real levels of stress in the superintendency

✧ Common reasons for stress

✧ The healthy and unhealthy effects of stress

✧ Balancing one's private life with the superintendency

Even though the superintendency is the most visible job in public education, relatively little is known about the daily work lives of those who occupy the position. Noting the lack of research about superintendents, Robert Crowson (1987) wrote, " . . . the superintendency is a position strangely awash in contradictions and anomalies and, frankly, a distinct puzzle to those who seek to make a bit of conceptual sense out of this intriguing job" (pp. 49–50). This situation is partially explained by the fact that school districts and superintendencies differ significantly. For instance, the daily work schedules of a large urban district superintendent and a small rural district superintendent may reveal very little in common. Research is also made extremely difficult because both personal and situational variables found in the work are multifaceted and difficult to control.

The overall purposes of this chapter are to provide a profile of the work lives of superintendents and to review the commitments that they often must make to complete the work. With regard to understanding what superintendents do on a daily basis, the chapter explores (1) time demands, (2) the nature of work, (3) common rewards and frustrations, and (4) potential changes in work activities. Changes in the nature of the position are examined in the context of stress and personal growth.

WORK LIVES OF SCHOOL SUPERINTENDENTS

While most educators readily understand that the work of the superintendent differs from the work of principals and other administrators, the nature of the distinctions are not always clear. Superintendents, as well as many other central office administrators, spend much of their time in meetings with other adults. In this, there is some similarity with the role of principals, who spend time interacting with adults but who also spend much of their time interacting with students. The work of superintendents has a symbolic aspect; they function as official representatives of the school district (Sergiovanni, Burlingame, Coombs, & Thurston, 1992). In some school districts, much of a superintendent's contact with other adults occurs outside of the office and even outside of the school district (e.g., attending professional meetings, attending legislative sessions). And unlike many other employees, the superintendent's day may not be clearly defined by a beginning and ending time.

Time Requirements

How much time does the average superintendent spend on work-related issues each day? The answer often depends on both the individual and the specific position. However, it is not uncommon for these administrators to devote more than 65 hours per week to their work. This is certainly true if functions such as banquets, athletic events, and community meetings are included. A recent study of urban superintendents established that the average workweek was 73 hours (Kowalski, 1995). Veteran superintendent, Daniel Domenech (1996), noted,

"Twelve-hour workdays are the rule, and we often are expected to be at our best during board of education meetings, after we already have put in a full day" (p. 41). No doubt there are superintendents in all types of districts who devote less time to their work, but it is generally unrealistic to believe that the responsibilities of the position will require less than 50 to 60 hours per week.

Superintendents commonly spend two to three evenings per week on job-related activities. In larger school districts, a superintendent may even meet with the school board as often as twice per week. Meetings or special events, such as the dedication of a new school building or a graduation ceremony, frequently occur on weekends. With so many potential activities, superintendents may discover it is difficult to find time for personal and family activities. Studies of first-year superintendents (e.g., Pavan, 1995) often reveal that time management emerges as a crucial issue for them. One big-city superintendent described his previous day's work in a log he was keeping:

5:00 to 5:15 A.M.:	Drank a cup of coffee and read the morning paper—in my office
5:15 to 5:45 A.M.:	Went through my mail from the previous day and did paperwork
5:45 to 6:45 A.M.:	Finished a speech for a breakfast meeting that day
7:15 to 9:00 A.M.:	Attended a breakfast meeting; delivered my speech
9:00 to 9:30 A.M.:	Drove across town to attend a chamber of commerce board meeting
9:45 to 10:30 A.M.:	Attended chamber meeting
10:30 to 10:45 A.M.:	Returned to my office
10:45 to 12:00 P.M.:	Met with the secondary principals' group
12:00 to 1:45 P.M.:	Met with several staff members individually; returned approximately 12 phone calls
1:45 to 2:00 P.M.:	Drove to the teachers' union offices
2:00 to 4:15 P.M.:	Met with board of directors of the teachers' union (not a pleasant meeting)
4:15 to 4:30 P.M.:	Held postmortem of meeting with union officials with two staff members who attended the meeting with me
4:30 to 4:45 P.M.:	Drove back to my office
4:45 to 6:15 P.M.:	Returned more telephone calls and met with several staff members
6:15 P.M.:	Left the office for home
6:30 to 7:30 P.M.:	Had a drink and ate dinner with my wife
7:30 to 8:30 P.M.:	Prepared speech to be delivered to administrators and supervisors the next day

| 8:30 to 9:30 P.M.: | Returned several more phone calls, read the paper, watched the news on TV |
| 10:15 P.M.: | I collapsed! |

Such a demanding schedule is fairly typical for superintendents of larger school districts. Superintendent in these settings may be asked to serve on a dozen or more boards of directors—a time-consuming but usually worthwhile commitment.

While the job is extremely demanding, superintendents enjoy a luxury not readily available to other educators; they typically are able to exercise control over their time. That is, they can select which activities will receive their immediate attention. Because of this flexibility, time management is an invaluable asset. Effective practitioners, for example, often rely on weekly plans based on priorities to guide their daily schedules. Unfortunately, some administrators attempt to cope by simply working longer or working faster—alternatives that are likely to result in errors and fatigue. And while exerting extra energy may work briefly, sustained behavior of this type is likely to result in weariness or even more severe mental and physical problems.

There are certain aspects of work that cannot be changed to reduce the demands on a superintendent's time. The size of the school district, a long-standing organizational culture, and available resources are examples. Thus, time management requires superintendents to manage themselves within the confines of contextual parameters. This involves three general tasks: (1) studying how time is spent(that is, getting to know one's behavior through keeping a log or diary); (2) evaluating time allocation in light of priorities and emerging issues (that is, interpreting how time is spent in relation to pressing needs and outcomes); and (3) planning and building a time schedule for future work (that is, devising a time management schedule) (Rees, 1986). Other time management strategies suggested for administrators include the following:

- Establishing priorities for your time
- Being brief in your communication
- Clustering tasks into time blocks (e.g., allocating 5 hours per week to visit schools)
- Setting deadlines and remaining focused so that issues or problems do not linger
- Delegating selected activities to others
- Learning to say no to avoid becoming overcommitted
- Scheduling quiet time for yourself
- Learning to plan your time (Hartley, 1990)

Time management is an effective means for preventing stress because it helps to reduce uncertainty in an executive's work (Quick, Nelson, & Quick, 1990).

Mental and physical stamina are also important in the superintendency. Many who enter the position may not fully understand the potential for stress, even when time is managed reasonably well (Domenech, 1996). Studies of superintendents frequently reveal that the job negatively affects family life (e.g., Kowalski, 1995; Sharp & Walter, 1995). And because needs and conditions do not remain static, even highly experienced superintendents should periodically assess and adjust their time management plans.

Nature of the Work

The typical job description for a school superintendent is extremely broad, including duties that span virtually every phase of operations of the school district. This is to be expected since the chief executive officer is ultimately responsible for everything that occurs. Descriptions of administrative work are usually discussed within two frameworks. The first is a social context, identifying the degree to which administrators interact with others. In these depictions, the administrator's work is described in terms of meetings and encounters with parents, employees, board members, and so on (e.g., Frase & Hetzel, 1990; Walton, 1973). The second framework is based on role expectations. Here administrative behavior is discussed with respect to varying duties and responsibilities that are attached to the position (e.g., Kowalski & Reitzug, 1993).

From a social perspective, the superintendent's job is highly symbolic. The superintendent is the one individual who is most readily identified with the school district. Thus, other people continuously assess and evaluate the superintendent's internal and external interactions. Speeches before service clubs, testimony before a legislative committee, and informal conversations with parents exemplify situations in which the superintendent formally and symbolically represents the philosophy and programs of local public education (Sergiovanni et al., 1992). In this age of reform, patrons and employees are particularly observant; they may rely more on what they see in the superintendent's behavior than the words that are communicated to them. Therefore, if a superintendent is committed to building a truly democratic school environment, he or she "must be able to articulate that ideal in terms that teachers, students, and parents find understandable, practical, and exciting" (Slater, 1994, p. 100). For many practitioners, the social aspect of practice constitutes a major portion of work. That is, much of the average day is spent in communicating with people. After studying work behaviors, Jon Morris (1979) characterized school administration as taking place in a highly verbal environment. He concluded that the preference for face-to-face verbal communication patterns over more formal modes (e.g., written memos), and the overall use of verbal information was different in school districts than in other types of organizations.

Role expectations for superintendents fall broadly into eight categories, which are displayed in Figure 12–1. Perhaps the most prevalent is the *representing* role. For this position, the responsibility has both formal and informal elements (Blumberg, 1985). During the average week, the superintendent may be

Figure 12-1
Role expectations for superintendents

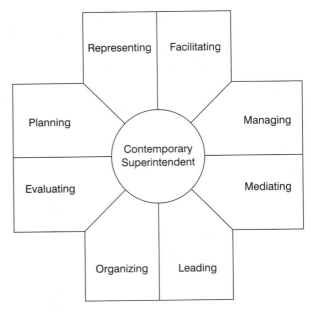

the official representative of the school district at civic functions on numerous occasions. Examples include attending a city council meeting, being present at the dedication of a new library, or testifying before a county commission. The superintendent continues to be an official representative of the school district at informal functions. A superintendent's conduct at an athletic event or a party is not separated from his or her formal role. A recent study of Illinois superintendents indicated that private lives do indeed get considered when formal evaluations are conducted by school boards (Maloney, 1996).

Two other responsibilities that are gaining in prominence are *facilitating* and *mediating*. The popular principles of decentralized authority and teacher empowerment are largely responsible. Success in a school district is often associated with the delivery of instruction and positive student outcomes. Appropriately, there is a growing interest in the professional literature on the ways that administrators can influence this process (e.g., through staff development). Administrators are more likely to work effectively with teachers if professional relationships prevail. In many districts, this means that the adversarial roles produced by collective bargaining must be overcome. The increased demand for mediation is related to the reality that both the need for change and insufficient resources create tensions and conflict. In site-based management, superintendents may be required to settle jurisdictional disputes between schools and the district. In general, it is far more difficult to develop consensus than it is to dictate solutions to disagreements. Larry Cuban (1988) noted that the ability to resolve emerging conflict has become an essential characteristic of the effective superintendent. The remaining role expectations in Figure 12-1—*planning, organizing, leading, managing*, and *evaluating*—have been discussed in previous chapters.

How do superintendents characterize the nature of their own work? A study of urban superintendents revealed that the position is perceived as being hectic, demanding, and exciting. In addition, the respondents characterized their jobs as being very high in status, highly rewarding, and highly interactive (Kowalski, 1995). When superintendents talk about their work, they repeatedly mention the importance of being able to get along with other people. This attribute is becoming even more important as school districts get less bureaucratic.

The nature of work can also be described through superintendents' perceptions of what is expected of them. Thomas Glass (1992) asked a national sample of superintendents in all types of districts about the primary expectations that school boards held for them: being a general manger was ranked first, human relations skills was ranked second, instructional leadership was ranked third, and knowledge of finance and budgets was ranked fourth. However, when these data were analyzed on the basis of school district enrollment, the pattern changed for smaller districts. In both the very smallest districts (those with fewer than 300 pupils) and the smaller districts (300 to 2,999 pupils), knowledge of finance and budget was ranked first and general management was ranked second. Such findings support the contention that in smaller districts, a greater emphasis is placed on managerial skills.

Surprisingly little information has been collected with respect to where superintendents do their work. A recent study of urban school chiefs indicated that the greatest portion of the day was spent in their own offices (the average for the group was 48%). Another 20% of the work took place at other locations in the central office; 12% took place in the district's school buildings; and only about 6% of the time was reported outside of school district property (Kowalski, 1995). It should be noted, however, that the range of responses was quite large. For instance, one superintendent reported spending 75% of his work time in his own office, while another reported spending only 20% of his time there. In general, it appears that superintendents exhibit considerable differences with respect to where they spend their work time.

Rewards and Frustrations

What do superintendents see as the most rewarding and frustrating parts of their jobs? Obviously opinions on this matter vary somewhat, but there are certain factors that tend to recur when superintendents discuss their work. Commenting on life in the superintendency, one highly experienced superintendent wrote this:

> Nobody ever said public life was devoid of frustrations—or that every member of the general public, all staff, each board of education member, every parent, all town officials, all students, and every other person and groups of persons with whom school leadership is in professional contact will always be intelligent, insightful, open, empathetic, tolerant, emotionally secure, flexible, well motivated, or any other way you'd prefer them to be. (Cattanach, 1996, p. 337)

In essence, this superintendent points out that any educator who seeks this office ought to realize that a certain amount of frustration is unavoidable. However, numerous positive factors prompt many practitioners to remain in this challenging leadership position.

A survey conducted by the *Executive Educator* magazine found that despite the long hours and stress, most administrators expressed contentment with their jobs (Boothe, Bradley, & Flick, 1994). A national study of superintendents revealed similar findings; approximately two thirds of all superintendents indicated they would still choose the superintendency as a career if they had a chance to start over in life (Glass, 1992). Similarly, approximately two thirds of the superintendents noted that they found considerable self-fulfillment in their work (Glass, 1992). A more recent study of superintendents in Illinois and Massachusetts yielded similar results (Sharp & Walter, 1995). So in spite of the long hours and demanding challenges, it is clear that many who enter the position have no regrets.

In part, the relatively high level of job satisfaction among superintendents probably relates to an intrinsic motivator: these are people who are deeply committed to helping others. When asked what they like about their jobs, superintendents often identify items such as developing new programs and empowering others to be more effective (e.g., Wallace, 1992). More specifically, they say things like these: "I want to help the instructional staff to do their best." "I want to create opportunities for students to succeed." "Especially in these times, I think I can make a difference in building a better school district." A study of Canadian superintendents revealed that satisfaction with work was most associated with (1) the work itself, (2) positive feedback about performance, (3) problem solving, and (4) seeing a project successfully implemented (Holdaway & Genge, 1995). The fruits of a superintendent's labors, unlike those of a teacher, are often highly visible and discernible in a relatively brief period of time. For example, a sense of accomplishment may come from a newly developed strategic plan or a newly constructed school building. And even though superintendents often say that they experience personal satisfaction from being able to help students, teachers, and principals, there has been little research examining the superintendent's influence on academic achievement in school districts (Hart & Ogawa, 1987).

Some superintendents also identify legitimate power and prestige to be rewarding elements of the job (Kowalski, 1995). More so than other school district employees, they are able to assume the role of change agent; they often believe that they have more power than others to influence the "bigger picture." Commenting on his career as a superintendent, Richard Wallace (1992) noted that he entered the position to test his hypothesis that a superintendent could be a true instructional leader. Such comments are associated with the understanding that the superintendency typically provides greater latitude for an individual to make personal decisions about work assignments (e.g., which managerial tasks can be relegated to others). A recent study of aspiring administrators found that the most powerful motivator for becoming a superintendent was the ability to exercise power and control over organizations (Daresh & Playko, 1992). And contrary to what many might believe, many superintendents perceive the status and prestige of their position to be relatively high (Glass, 1992). Superintendents are usually well known in their communities; they receive considerable exposure in the media; and they are often among the highest-paid public officials in their communities. Yes, extrinsic rewards such as salary and fringe benefits are seen by many practitioners as a significant reward. As noted earlier in the book, superintendents are routinely the highest-paid employee in their organizations—and in some instances, the salary gap between the superintendent and the next-highest-paid employee is substantial. In addition, superintendents frequently receive more lucrative fringe benefit packages than those provided for other employees.

In any examination of the potential frustration associated with the position, it is important to note that individuals differ in their reactions to common problems and needs. For example, some are optimists, others are pessimists; some are extroverts, others are introverts. In addition to such personal differences, frustrations may also be related to the type of district in which a person is employed. Superintendents in larger districts, for example, may express frustrations that are considerably different from those voiced by small-district leaders.

A group of urban district superintendents identified the following common frustrations:

- A general lack of fiscal resources
- The political nature of the position
- Unrealistic workloads
- An inability to get things done quickly
- Apathetic students and staff
- School board meddling in administration
- Elitism and racism (Kowalski, 1995)

Two of these issues—adequate funding and politics—appear to be frustrations that are common to superintendents in all types of districts.

Feelings of disappointment with respect to funding may relate to either adequacy or equity or both. That is, superintendents may be discouraged by a lack of adequate fiscal resources or by an inequitable distribution of resources. The concern for adequate funding is not unique among American superintendents; in a recent study, Canadian superintendents identified adequate funding as their greatest concern and equity of funding as the second greatest concern (among 70 concerns) (Webber, 1995).

Politics has long been a troublesome issue for school administrators. However, the nature of political issues and the context in which these tensions occur vary across school districts. In large urban settings, competition for resources with other governmental units may result in overt hostility; mayors in these cities may try to exert considerable control over administrative and school board actions (Kowalski, 1995). In other districts, political influence may come more directly from school district or state agencies (e.g., positions taken by the admin-

istrative staff, mandates from the state department of education without sufficient resources for implementation) (Shelton, Beach, & Chissom, 1989). However,
regardless of origin and context, many practitioners find the political nature of
the position to be frustrating.

While certain issues—such as a lack of resources, excessive political activity,
or a lack of political support for tax increases—may bother most superintendents, those working in small rural districts often face several unique frustrations. These may include low salaries, the inability to escape managerial duties
because of a lack of support personnel, and the effort required to offer sufficiently comprehensive programs. Practitioner frustrations in small districts also
may be due to the fact that some individuals enter these jobs as a stepping-stone
to the position they really desire (e.g., a suburban or larger-city district). A lack of
fulfillment for these administrators is especially likely if they find themselves with
no professional support staff in the central office. This condition restricts their
freedom to concentrate on issues of greatest interest.

Talking about their greatest frustrations, superintendents often describe
dilemmas that involve conflicting interests among the school district, employees,
and students (Kowalski, 1995). This type of discomfiture is readily evident in
most teacher strikes. Administrators are placed in the middle of competing interests, and inevitable questions emerge. Should drastic measures be taken to keep
the schools open? Do teachers really deserve to be paid higher salaries? Conflict
of this type sparks a myriad of legal, professional, moral, and ethical questions.
And because such battles often produce winners and losers, they are very taxing
on the person who has to make the ultimate recommendations to the school
board; namely, the superintendent. Virtually every problem that makes its way to
the superintendent's desk can affect the community, the school district, students,
and employees—and unfortunately, the interests of these parties are often not
compatible. It is not uncommon for superintendents also to be frustrated by the
unrealistic expectation that they can act unilaterally to reconstruct a school district. Jerome Murphy (1991) aptly noted that top-down, dictatorial approaches to
change are ineffective; school improvement, according to him, is more likely to
be produced by a diverse group of well-educated superintendents who understand that special interests must be balanced with the general welfare of the
community. However, many school boards across the country continue to search
for superintendents who supposedly possess a secret formula for school
improvement.

UNDERSTANDING AND RESPONDING TO STRESS

Occupations can be described along a continuum from stressful to nonstressful.
On this scale, the superintendency is almost always portrayed as a high-stress
job. In reality, it is more accurate to depict the position as demanding. Many
administrators are able to do their jobs over prolonged periods without any serious effects to their physiological or psychological health. On the other hand,

some may experience burnout in a relatively short period of time. These differences are partially explained by contextual conditions of work; that is, not all superintendencies are equally stressful. There are, however, certain pressures and complications that are common to the job, and those who aspire to this position should realize that no superintendency is stress free. Decision making and conflict management, for example, are responsibilities that are not going to disappear (Ramsey, 1996).

To a greater extent, differences in the effects of stress are explained by a person's tolerance and coping skills. An individual who has a relatively high tolerance for stress and who has learned to rely on positive adjustments to stress is often able to deal with extremely challenging situations, even over a prolonged period of time. This is why an understanding of one's tolerance level and an awareness of positive and negative coping behaviors are important for anyone aspiring to the position.

Work and Health

Most health professionals recognize that work can be a primary contributor to poor health. In some instances, the connections are obvious; coal miners, for example, are often at great risk of developing lung problems. Less recognized are the combined influences of social, biological, and psychological forces. Illnesses such as heart problems, strokes, and cancer are now routinely linked to unhealthy lifestyles and stress (Wood & Wood, 1996). For this reason, many health professionals are using a biopsychosocial paradigm to study how lifestyle may contribute to health or illness. Here are aspects of the model:

1. Within the social component, negative influences include loneliness, feelings of exploitation, and violence.
2. In the biological component, negative influences include a lack of physical activity, poor diet, or existing disease or injury.
3. In the psychological component, negative influences include depression, stress, and poor coping skills (Green & Shellenberger, 1990).

When a number of these negative conditions exist simultaneously, they place the individual at greater risk of serious health problems. The superintendency may produce some of these negative health conditions. At the social level, for instance, the position can make a person feel lonely and isolated. At the biological level, the hectic pace and sedentary nature of work may result in poor eating habits and a general lack of physical activity. However, it is at the psychological level that risks may be the greatest. Leadership and management require decision making, and this responsibility alone can produce a considerable level of anxiety and stress. Not all superintendents, however, are adversely affected by these circumstances; some actually experience satisfaction from being challenged.

Nature of Stress

Stress in humans has been defined as a nonspecific response of the body to a demand (Selye, 1976). Any demand, whether it is associated with family life, occupation, or societal conditions, affects the individual. Even though this is true, not all individuals are equally affected. The severity of stress is partly determined by the specific demand and partly by the individual (Coleman, 1960). This explains why a specific demand may have a dramatically different effect on two individuals in the same position. Imagine two superintendents working in neighboring school districts; both receive less than favorable performance evaluations. One reacts by making a commitment to improve her performance; the other is emotionally devastated and opts to resign his position. Stressors (that is, adjustment demands) also differ in degree. For instance, the death of a spouse or parent is almost always much more stressful than getting in an argument with someone at work.

The actual sources of stress in the superintendency vary. Most often stressors are related to conflict, a common occurrence in leadership positions in complex organizations. For instance, having to choose between two competing positions is a task that is likely to recur throughout a school administrator's career. Other stressors stem from the unpredictable nature of some responsibilities. When a key staff member suddenly resigns or when school board members change their position on a key policy matter, a superintendent can be caught off guard. Feelings of not being in control also produce stress for some practitioners. As chief executive, the individual feels responsible for all aspects of operations. When students perform poorly on state tests or when teachers go on strike, the administrator may be disheartened by factors that seem unmanageable. Finally, stress can be caused by catastrophic events. A school building destroyed by a tornado or an automobile accident that results in the death of several high school students are examples of crises that administrators may have to face.

Problems of adjustment are commonly classified as *frustrations* (the thwarting of a motive), *conflict* (contradictory goals or means that vie with each other), and *pressure* (perceived demands) (Coleman, 1960).

1. Examples of frustrations often voiced by superintendents are not having sufficient resources, a lack of public support, and apathy. Frustration also may stem from not accomplishing goals.

2. As already noted, conflict is pervasive as a result of the nature of the superintendency and occurs both within and between groups (Hanson, 1996). For example, administrators often have to make financial decisions between competing needs such as raising teacher salaries or buying new computers.

3. Pressure can come from within ourselves or from others. Inner pressures are related to personal aspirations and ego ideals; outside pressures obviously

are generated by others (e.g., a spouse who expects a partner to increase salary substantially by moving to progressively larger school districts).

Multiple factors contribute to the severity of a stressor in any given situation. Among the more important are duration (the extent to which the stressor perseveres), the importance of the need not being met, self-efficacy (self-confidence), personal competence to deal with stress, unfamiliarity (the degree to which the person understands and has previously experienced this type of stressor), suddenness (the unexpected emergence of a stressor), and the individual's tolerance (Coleman, 1960). In addition, the level of stress is increased when the individual encounters multiple stressors simultaneously. An administrator, for example, may experience the cumulative ill effects of multiple problems, whereas any one or two of the problems in isolation would not be unduly taxing. In this regard, many small problems occurring at the same time can be more stressful than one large problem to which the superintendent can give his or her total attention. Finally, stressors that are unpredictable and uncontrollable tend to be more stressful than those that are predictable and controllable (Wood & Wood, 1996).

Walter Gmelch and Forrest Parkay (1995) defined the stress cycle as having four stages: (1) stressors (that is, issues that generate stress); (2) perceptions (that is, how the individual appraises the stressor); (3) responses (that is, how the individual reacts to the stressor); and (4) consequences (that is, the intensity and long-range negative effects). Other authors (e.g., Lazarus & Folkman, 1984) have similarly described stress as occurring in four stages: (1) there is a potentially stressful event; (2) the mind or body evaluates the stressor as being threatening or benign; (3) the mind or body selects coping mechanisms; and (4) there is a stress reaction (that is, physiological, emotional, and behavioral responses). The degree of stress depends on one's perception of the adjustment demands. If the individual's perception is accurate and if he or she has the personal resources to respond appropriately, the stressor is unlikely to harmful. On the other hand, misperceptions and discrepancies between personal resources and the adjustment demand can lead to ineffective responses.

Clearly the ultimate effects of stress can be quite damaging. Under severe pressure, superintendents may experience problems such as a loss of energy, a loss of concentration, anxiety, or exhaustion. When reasoning is hampered, administrators may be inclined to behave uncharacteristically and to do things that they later regret. When it is uncontrolled, stress reduces the body's resistance, producing greater risk of exposure to physical illness.

Burnout is a popular term used to connote a significant decline in productivity because of excessive levels of stress. It typically occurs in stages and is characterized by four conditions:

1. Some degree of physical and emotional exhaustion
2. Socially dysfunctional behavior (e.g., isolating oneself from others at work)

3. Psychological impairment (e.g., developing negative feelings about oneself)
4. Organizational inefficiency (e.g., not doing one's work) (Cedoline, 1982)

The symptoms also have been described in this way:

- The development of negative emotions (e.g., frustration, depression)
- The emergence of interpersonal problems (e.g., moodiness, emotional withdrawal, excessive irritability)
- The development of health problems (either emotional or physical)
- A decline in work performance
- The development of feelings of meaninglessness (e.g., feeling that work is pointless) (Potter, 1993)

As these symptoms indicate, burnout is a serious condition. Some writers, however, have used the term rather loosely to indicate less severe effects of working in stressful situations.

Common Stressors and Levels of Stress

Unquestionably, the school superintendency can be a highly stressful position for some individuals. The very nature of the job creates all types of frustrations, conflict, and pressure. Larry Cuban (1988) labeled conflict the DNA of the superintendency. However, a large number of practitioners are able to spend decades in the job without showing any signs of personal damage. In truth, practitioners are usually quite divided in their opinions regarding the stress level of their work. National studies sponsored by the American Association of School Administrators in 1982 and 1992, for example, showed that superintendents were almost evenly divided over this issue. In 1992, less than 1% characterized the job stress-free; nearly 8% said there was little stress; about 42% said there was some stress; another 42% said there was considerable stress; and just under 8% said there was very great stress (Glass, 1992). Also noteworthy is the fact that these results were extremely similar to those obtained in 1982. In the aftermath of *A Nation at Risk* published in 1983, public dissatisfaction with education seemed to reach a high point. Nevertheless, superintendent opinions about stress in 1992 were amazingly similar to those voiced 10 years earlier. In general, studies often find that administrative roles are perceived as only moderately stressful (e.g., Wiggins, 1988). Moreover, those in the job often disagree about which types of school districts produce the greatest amount of stress. Some working in small-town districts argue that their work is the most stressful because there is little or no support staff and every taxpayer knows who you are. Others working in large districts argue that the intense politics of working in urban areas and being at the helm of a large bureaucracy is even more stressful (Goldstein, 1992).

Top executives in all types of organizations are exposed to stressful situations, which can be categorized as either organizational demands or personal demands. Within the organizational frame, stressors may be produced by (1) interpersonal demands (e.g., having to deal with certain people or groups); (2) informational demands (e.g., not having adequate information to make an important decision); and (3) external environment demands (e.g., state directives to do certain things). In the personal frame, stressors may be related to (1) internal demands (e.g., high self-expectations); (2) family demands (e.g., a spouse who is pushing a partner to increase earnings); and (3) friends and community (e.g., conflict with neighbors) (Quick et al., 1990).

Although research has cast some light on the question of perceived levels of stress, rather strong differences of opinion persist in the literature about the general level of stress experienced by all school administrators. Jim O'Connell, executive director of the 741-member New York State Council of School Superintendents, noted, "Stress is becoming a greater liability of the job than ever before. I've never seen it tougher" (Goldstein, 1992, pp. 9–10). Others who have studied the demands of the superintendency take exception with such judgments. Michael Milstein (1992), for one, has challenged the contention that administrative work is highly stressful; he has argued that the case for "administrator burnout" has been exaggerated. Examining the work lives of superintendents, he cited poorly designed research studies and generalizations as ample cause to question whether the job is really unduly stressful for most practitioners. A study of big-city superintendents seems to provide support for this position. Working in what many consider to be the most difficult of situations, only 18% of these urban school executives thought the job had been harmful to their health (Kowalski, 1995).

Walter Gmelch (1996), who also has written extensively on the topic of stress in school administration, observed, "Stress intrigues and plagues superintendents and scholars alike" (p. 32). He recognized that while 1,000 articles have been written about the strains of school administration since 1966, many of them were anecdotal in nature and mythical in content. Among the myths he identified are the following: (1) stress is harmful; (2) stress should be avoided; (3) the higher up in the organization, the greater the stress; (4) stress is a male-dominated phenomenon (that is, stress is more commonly experienced by males); (5) superintendents experience excessive stress (p. 33). He, like Milstein, takes the position that stress in superintendency appears to be moderate.

What types of adjustment demands are most common in administrative work? Although conflict is part of the job, many of the stressors identified by practitioners actually fall into the category of frustrations. This is illustrated in Table 12–1, where common stressors identified by Anthony Cedoline (1982) and Gmelch (1996) are examined with respect to possible implications and type of adjustment demand. In certain districts, superintendents are especially troubled by confrontational school boards (conflict) and dissatisfied constituents (pressure) (Goldstein, 1992). Another adjustment demand that faces many new superintendents relates to role change. In particular, individuals who move directly

Table 12–1
Selected stressors commonly identified by administrators

Stressor	Possible Implications	Type of Adjustment Demand
Lack of sufficient resources	Inability to perform in a desired manner	Frustration
Lack of support from public or superiors	Lowered aspirations; apathy; creation of substitute goals	Frustration
Excessively high self-expectations	Working too hard; developing feelings of inadequacy	Pressure
Work overload/excessive paperwork	Ignoring some responsibilities; increase of work errors	Frustration
Collective bargaining	Indecision, anxiety; divided loyalties	Conflict
Lack of clear direction	Role ambiguity; confusion	Conflict/frustration
Federal and state laws	Feelings of being unduly controlled; perceptions of low value to work	Frustration/pressure
Lacking control	Feelings of being unable to control students, faculty, or schools; competing demands for political decisions	Frustration/conflict
Evaluating others	Excessive tension; disputes regarding outcomes	Conflict
Meeting all student needs	Role ambiguity; facing competing demands for services; indecision	Conflict/frustration
Gaining public approval/support	Resistance to external demands; attempting to do too many things at the same time; excessive political behavior	Pressure
Making decisions affecting others	Tension over competing demands; ethical/moral concerns	Conflict

Note: These stressors are not presented in any particular order of importance.

from a principalship to the superintendency often find the necessary adjustments to be greater than anticipated. While much of the day is still consumed meeting with people, the new superintendent finds that the nature of the problems and the types of people change. Also, many who enter the superintendency are individuals who set high personal goals. A study of superintendents in Maine, for instance, found that self-induced pressures were a primary stressor for those administrators (Eastman & Mirochnik, 1991).

Healthy and Unhealthy Effects of Stress

Adjustment demands to stress can be constructive (*eustress*) or destructive (*distress*) (Saville & Kavina, 1982). For example, conflict can lead a superintendent to become more highly involved in an issue—an experience that may produce a positive outcome for the school district and enhance the superintendent's self-confidence. Stressors often raise awareness and draw the individual's attention to important matters. "Stress becomes a problem when it ceases to be a healthy stimulus, but instead creates a burden the individual cannot handle without harmful effects" (Cedoline, 1982, p. 2).

Studies of occupational stress have identified four types of distress as especially prevalent:

1. *Time distress* (e.g., feeling that you are overwhelmed by deadlines and that you simply cannot get everything done on time)
2. *Anticipatory distress* (e.g., being anxious about your work, dreading the next catastrophe)
3. *Situational distress* (e.g., feeling threatened because you constantly face situations that you cannot control)
4. *Encounter distress* (e.g., having to face people you consider unpleasant or unpredictable) (Albrecht, 1979)

Contrary to what many believe, stress cannot be totally avoided. Hence, the challenge is not to steer clear of stressful situations, but rather it is learning how to manage stressors appropriately. While the demands of the job often cannot be controlled or manipulated, the administrator is able to influence his or her perception of the stress, attitudes about stress, and coping techniques for dealing with stress (Gmelch, 1996). This is why understanding the nature of stress is so important for persons in the superintendency.

Many responses to stress occur at the unconscious level; the individual acts on the basis of acquired habits without even thinking about appropriateness or consequences of his or her actions. Excessive consumption of alcohol or overeating exemplify negative coping mechanisms that people often use unconsciously when they are confronted with stress. As a first step to avoiding such behavior, experts advise individuals in potentially stressful jobs to gain an awareness of their own level of tolerance and an awareness of negative habits. Second, the individual needs to establish a repertoire of effective responses "equally balanced in the social, physical, intellectual, entertainment, managerial, personal, and attitudinal categories" (Gmelch & Parkay, 1995, p. 61).

Coping mechanisms also have been described as being either problem-focused or emotion-focused. In the former, the responses are targeted at the source of stress. That is, the person tries to reduce, modify, or eliminate whatever is generating the stress. In the latter, the responses are targeted at the emotional impact of the stressor. That is, the person tries to reduce any psychological pain associated with problems (Wood & Wood, 1996).

The superintendency can be an extremely lonely position. Some individuals who have opted for isolation in the position have been influenced by the bureaucratic notion that fraternization with employees prevents objectivity and erodes legitimate authority. Unfortunately, many practitioners have been socialized to accept this idea. The deficiency of this management strategy becomes apparent in times of high stress, occasions when it is extremely helpful to have trusted allies within the school district in whom to confide. While many administrators rely on family and friends to provide such support, this type of assistance may be insufficient when critical situations involve intense organizational conflict (e.g., a teachers' strike).

Stress management can be learned. In addition to seeking social support, the average person can do many things to combat common psychological stressors. Physical activity is one of the most effective outlets for mental stress. Other suggestions include regular exercise, a balanced diet, using caffeine and alcohol in moderation, learning to be patient, and taking time to step back from the job to relax (Wood & Wood, 1996). A personal plan for stress management requires the individual to identify stressors and responses to them. It also necessitates an understanding of options, so that responses can be evaluated in the context of other possible behaviors. Lastly, it requires a flexible approach, allowing the individual to make necessary adjustments since neither stressors nor responses to them are constant (Quick et al., 1990).

In summary, stressful conditions in the practice of school administration are inevitable. The key to effective performance is to use such situations to one's advantage or at least to manage them so that the damage they produce is not debilitating. Not managing stress properly may be related to the following: (1) a lack of knowledge about oneself, (2) a lack of knowledge about stress, (3) an indifference toward managing stress, (4) misperceptions about actual stressors, and (5) the selection of inappropriate coping techniques. It is important to keep in mind that one's perception of a stressor is more critical than the stressor itself (Lazarus & Folkman, 1984). Examples of the five deficiencies are shown in Figure 12–2. Even though the stressfulness of the superintendency has probably been exaggerated, the position is sufficiently demanding to require effective coping skills.

Problem	Example
A lack of knowledge about yourself	Not knowing your own stress tolerance
A lack of knowledge about stress	Not knowing the causes or potential effects of stress
An indifference toward managing stress	Believing you have the savvy and/or strength to overcome any amount of stress
Misperceptions about actual stressors	Blaming others for nervousness or tension rather than engaging in introspection
The selection of inappropriate coping techniques	Resorting to unhealthy habits (e.g., overeating, excessively consuming alcohol)

Figure 12–2
Common problems related to coping with stress

BALANCING WORK AND PRIVATE LIFE

Many who consider becoming superintendents ask themselves if they can still have a private life if they choose this career. There is little doubt that key public officials sacrifice a great deal of their privacy when they seek and enter office in this era when information is readily available and exchanged. Earlier in this book, discussion of the superintendent as public servant highlighted the fact that many superintendents are under the public's constant scrutiny. In many respects, school districts are like a theater, and the superintendent is cast in the lead role. How a superintendent plays this role depends on several factors including "one's understanding of the script, interactions with an audience, and awareness of personal style and values" (Deal, Lison, & Deck, 1993, p. 28).

Two studies of superintendents (Blumberg, 1985; Kowalski, 1995) indicated that the superintendency is almost certain to effect one's private life (most often, family life or personal health). A study of Canadian superintendents found that the greatest negative effect on personal life was reduced time to spend with family (Holdaway & Genge, 1995). Even so, it is difficult to discern a common response among practitioners about the effect of the job on their personal life. Some superintendents bring their work home; they share problems with their spouses. Others make concerted efforts to shield their families from their work (Blumberg, 1985). A study of urban superintendents—administrators who are certainly before the public eye constantly—indicated that individual personalities and philosophies contributed to different perceptions about the effects of work on family life. "Although some of the superintendents lamented the fact that their private lives were nonexistent and although a few said the job had taken an extensive toll on their personal health, there were those who liked being in the limelight" (Kowalski, 1995, pp. 118–119).

In addition to considering personal dispositions toward working as a public official, aspiring superintendents also should think about community context. Small rural communities may not tolerate certain behaviors that are acceptable elsewhere. For example, school administrators in some small towns encounter problems if they are seen drinking alcohol in a restaurant; they are chastised if they use profanity in a casual conversation. Social, economic, cultural, and religious variables determine acceptable behavior, and while certain types of communities are similar, they are never identical. Another variable to consider would be a community's expectations for involvement in community life. Not only may some school boards insist that the superintendent live in the community, they also may demand that he or she be visibly active in community life.

In weighing the potential effects of work on private life, an aspiring superintendent needs to answer questions such as the following:

- What are my personal values and beliefs about privacy?
- Are my values and beliefs compatible with the realities of the superintendency?

- Given my family and personal life, in what type of community would I be most comfortable?
- What sacrifices am I willing to make?

The spouses and children of superintendents also are affected by the demands of the job and community standards. Accordingly, they deserve an opportunity to share in critical discussions on these matters.

While it may seem apparent that a demanding public job will affect one's personal and family life, many who enter the position overlook this fact (Domenech, 1996). True, there are plenty of superintendents who maintain high job performance without any damaging effects to their private lives. For some, this outcome is a matter of serendipity. That is, they are lucky to have a supporting family and lucky to be in a community where demands are realistic. More often, however, superintendents have to plan carefully if they want to balance work and personal interests. Some, for example, try to involve family members in school-related activities, such as attending dinners or conferences. Others plan vacations or quality family time—and they refuse to let unanticipated problems interfere with those plans. This is often accomplished by being able to use support staff effectively, that is, by reducing one's personal involvement in less important and less urgent tasks.

FOR FURTHER REFLECTION

This chapter examined several critical issues surrounding practice in the superintendency.

One purpose was to provide an understanding of what superintendents do in their jobs—a topic that has not been widely discussed in the literature. Another was to explore the issue of stress. The intention was to provide a balanced discussion of the tensions and strains that are inherent in the position and to show that the effects of stress differ among practitioners. Lastly, the chapter addressed the need to balance work and personal life.

As you consider what you read in this chapter, answer the following questions:

1. In your experience, do superintendents appear to spend any more time on the job than do principals? Give examples.
2. What is meant by time management? How is this accomplished?
3. What do you see as the greatest potential rewards of the superintendency?
4. Many practitioners identify a lack of resources as a major frustration. Do you agree or disagree with the contention that schools lack adequate resources to function at a more effective level?
5. What do you consider to be the most stressful elements of the superintendency?
6. How can you determine your tolerance level for stress? Why is it important to have this information?

7. What coping mechanisms could be used to deal with stress in the superintendency?

8. Under what circumstances can stress be positive?

9. In your own community, to what extent does the media cover the actions of the school superintendent? Has this coverage been balanced?

10. What steps can be taken by superintendents to ensure sufficient time for a private life?

CASE STUDY

Albert Davidson was raised in the rural South. He was the oldest of six children and the first member of his immediate family to graduate from high school and college. He was an above-average student and a gifted athlete. After graduating from high school, he attended a state university on a football scholarship; his goal was to be a social studies teacher and football coach. His plans for beginning his teaching career were delayed when he won a National Collegiate Athletic Association scholarship to attend graduate school. He earned his master's degree in history at a large research university, and he entered the teaching profession at the age of 24.

During his first 5 years of teaching and coaching football at a large-city high school in the Northeast, Albert was persuaded by his principal to pursue his principal's license. He attended night classes at a nearby university and completed seven courses in school administration. As soon as he completed the work and was granted a principal's license, he accepted a position as assistant principal at the school at which he was working. Although he missed teaching and coaching, he found administrative work to be rather fulfilling. Much of his time was devoted to working with student discipline and overseeing athletic responsibilities.

Three years passed, and Albert found himself at another career crossroads. One of the professors whom he had met while pursuing his principal's license was encouraging him to return to graduate school on a full-time basis; he was offered a scholarship to pursue a doctoral degree in school administration. Not wanting to lose his services, the school district superintendent countered with an offer to promote him to a middle school principalship. Matters were further complicated by the fact that Albert was getting married to Jackie Miller, one of the teachers at his school. In the end, it was she who convinced him to opt for the graduate school scholarship.

Jackie told him, "The doctorate will open many doors for you. I have a good job, and this will be the best time in our lives for you to go to school. Later, children and other responsibilities are likely to complicate matters."

Albert spent the next 2 years in graduate school. Several months before he completed his degree, he had four job interviews. Two were for high school principalships in large cities; one was for an assistant superintendent's job in a smaller midwestern district; the fourth was for a superintendency in Colburn, a small district just 40 miles from where Albert had grown up. At first, Albert had no intention of applying for superintendencies—he was even a bit apprehensive about applying for central office positions below this level. However, his parents and the Colburn school board persuaded him to interview for the job.

After the four interviews, Albert and his wife decided that the assistant superintendent's job was their first choice. As luck would have it, it was the only position he was not offered. After a great deal of thought, Albert accepted the superintendency.

The Colburn School District has an enrollment of approximately 2,100 students. When the school board announced that it had employed Dr. Albert Davidson as the new superintendent, most residents were quite pleased. Many still remembered him as a star football player from a neighboring county; others were gratified that the district had employed its first African American superintendent.

When they moved to Colburn, Jackie was 4 months pregnant and decided not to continue teaching—at least not for the next several years. While Albert readily adjusted to the community, she found small-town life to be quite different from what she was used to; she had spent her entire life in a large northeastern city. And even though about 50% of Colburn's population were African Americans, she felt out of place. Albert was confident, however, that she would eventually adjust to small-town living.

Albert's job kept him away from home about three nights every week. On Friday nights, he and his wife usually attended a football or basketball game. Albert left for work at 7:00 A.M. and often did not return until 6:00 P.M. or later. Jackie missed teaching, and she was not used to spending so much time alone.

In early January during their first school year in Colburn, Jackie gave birth to a baby boy. By now, Albert was spending more, not less, time at work. In addition, he was increasingly having to make overnight trips to meetings and conferences. Jackie also noticed that he was more irritable than normal; he often did not want to discuss anything that pertained to his job. However, he always tried to spend several hours each week with the baby. At least once each week, he insisted that he and Jackie dine out and have some time to themselves.

As summer approached, Jackie became convinced that she did not want to spend the rest of her life in Colburn. She urged Albert to move back to the Northeast after the end of the coming school year.

One night while she and Albert were eating dinner, Jackie bluntly stated her feelings. "I'd feel a lot better if I knew we were not going to stay here for a long period of time. Eventually, I want to go back into teaching. I don't want to teach in the same district where you are superintendent. If we stay here, I'd have to drive a great distance—that is, if I could even get a job. And I don't want our son being raised in such a small town. I think he would have more opportunities if we lived near a large city."

"Listen, I don't plan to stay here forever," he told his wife. "But I made a commitment to these people. I signed a 3-year contract, and I told them that if things worked out, I'd probably stay 5 or more years. This job is pretty demanding. I wasn't totally prepared when I came here. There were a lot of things I had to learn. I'm spending a lot more time on the job than I imagined. I'm not sure I'm ready to move to a bigger job. And I sure don't want to move backwards to a lower-level job in a larger district. We made sacrifices when I went to graduate school, and we have to make some sacrifices now. Things aren't that bad here."

What Albert did not share with Jackie was his resolve to prove that an African American could be highly successful as superintendent in Colburn. He felt that leaving after 2 years would make it more difficult for another minority person to follow him. And he believed that two of the board members would be delighted if he tucked his tail between his legs and left. However, he could not ignore Jackie's strong feelings about leaving Colburn.

During the first few months of the second school year, Albert experienced his first major dispute with several school board members. The conflict resulted from a disciplinary action against a high school football player. Albert supported the principal's decision to remove the student from the team because he was caught smoking a cigarette in the restroom at school. Two of the board members openly criticized Albert and the principal at the school board meeting. A motion was made to reinstate the student on the football team. It was passed by a vote of 4 to 3.

Two weeks after this incident, one of the elementary schools was destroyed by a fire. Fortunately, the fire occurred on a Saturday and no one was hurt. However, Albert had to find temporary classroom space for nearly 200 students; he had to deal with insurance adjusters; and he had to start plans to replace the school. All of this took him away from normal duties that already consumed his workday.

Albert began having trouble sleeping at night. He lost about 10 pounds over the next 4 to 6 weeks. He now was spending almost every evening on school business. To make matters worse, Jackie started questioning whether Albert should spend his career as a school superintendent.

Throughout his life, Albert had been highly successful in everything he did. Frustration was not something with which he had a lot of experience. It seemed that everything was piling up on him. He started to have doubts about his decision to come to Colburn. More important, he started to question his commitment to being a school superintendent.

Issues for Discussion

1. Assess Albert's decision to accept the superintendency in Colburn. What may have influenced this decision?

2. Not all stress is related to work. What events outside of work described in this case may have been stressful for Albert?

3. Place yourself in Albert's position. Would you not discuss work-related problems with your spouse? Why or why not?

4. Practice in school administration is highly affected by context. What contextual variables contribute to the problems being experienced by Albert?

5. Social support is important for people experiencing stress. What types of social support might be available to Albert?

6. What coping mechanisms might Albert use to deal with his current situation?

7. Is Jackie being fair with Albert by openly stating her negative feelings about living in Colburn? Why or why not?

8. Assess Albert's feeling that he made a commitment to the school board in Colburn. Does he have a legal responsibility to meet this commitment? Does he have an ethical responsibility?

9. Assume you were in Albert's position when he was offered the job in Colburn. Make a list of questions that you would have addressed prior to accepting or rejecting the job.

REFERENCES

Albrecht, K. (1979). *Stress and the manager*. Upper Saddle River, NJ: Prentice Hall.

Blumberg, A. (1985). *The school superintendent: Living with conflict*. New York: Teachers College Press.

Boothe, J. W., Bradley, L. H., & Flick, T. M. (1994). This working life. *Executive Educator*, *16*(2), 39–42.

Cattanach, D. L. (1996). *The school leader in action: Discovering the golden mean*. Lancaster, PA: Technomic.

Cedoline, A. J. (1982). *Job burnout in public education: Symptoms, causes, and survival skills*. New York: Teachers College Press.

Coleman, J. C. (1960). *Personality dynamics and effective behavior*. Chicago: Scott, Foresman and Company.

Crowson, R. L. (1987). The local school district superintendency: A puzzling role. *Educational Administration Quarterly*, *23*(3), 49–69.

Cuban, L. (1988). Conflict and leadership in the superintendency. *Phi Delta Kappan*, *67*(1), 28–30.

Daresh, J. C., & Playko, M. A. (1992). *Aspiring administrators' perceptions of the superintendency as a viable career choice*. (ERIC Document Reproduction Service No. ED 346 564)

Deal, T., Lison, C., & Deck, L. (1993). Exits and entrances. *School Administrator*, *50*(5), 26–28.

Domenech, D. A. (1996). Surviving the ultimate stress. *School Administrator*, *53*(3), 40–41.

Eastman, M., & Mirochnik, D. A. (1991). *Stressed for success: A study of stress and the superintendency*. (ERIC Document Reproduction Service No. ED 336 854)

Frase, L., & Hetzel, R. (1990). *School management by wandering around*. Lancaster, PA: Technomic.

Glass, T. E. (1992). *The 1992 study of the American school superintendency*. Arlington, VA: American Association of School Administrators.

Gmelch, W. H. (1996). Breaking out of the superintendent stress trap. *School Administrator, 53*(3), 32–33.

Gmelch, W. H., & Parkay, F. W. (1995). Changing roles and occupational stress in the teaching profession. In M. O'Hair & S. Odell (Eds.), *Educating teachers for leadership and change: Teacher education yearbook III* (pp. 46–65). Thousand Oaks, CA: Corwin.

Goldstein, A. (1992). Stress in the superintendency: School leaders confront the daunting pressures of the job. *School Administrator, 49*(9), 8–13, 15–17.

Green, J., & Shellenberger, R. (1990). *The dynamics of health and wellness: A biopsychosocial approach*. Forth Worth, TX: Holt, Rinehart & Winston.

Hanson, E. M. (1996). *Educational administration and organizational behavior* (4th ed.). Boston: Allyn and Bacon.

Hart, A. W., & Ogawa, R. T. (1987). The influence of superintendents on the academic achievement of school districts. *Journal of Educational Administration, 25*(1), 72–84.

Hartley, H. J. (1990). Make time to manage your time more effectively. *Executive Educator, 12*(8), 19–21.

Holdaway, E. A., & Genge, A. (1995). How effective superintendents understand their own work. In K. Leithwood (Ed.), *Effective school district leadership* (pp. 13–32). Albany, NY: SUNY Press.

Kowalski, T. J. (1995). *Keepers of the flame: Contemporary urban superintendents*. Thousand Oaks, CA: Corwin.

Kowalski, T. J., & Reitzug, U. C. (1993). *Contemporary school administration: An introduction*. New York: Longman.

Lazarus, R. S., & Folkman, S. (1984). *Stress, appraisal, and coping*. New York: Springer.

Maloney, J. M. (1996). Your private life counts at evaluation time. *School Administrator, 53*(3), 49–50.

Milstein, M. M. (1992). The overstated case of administrator stress. *School Administrator, 49*(9), 12–13.

Morris, J. R. (1979). Job(s) of the superintendency. *Educational Research Quarterly, 4*(4), 11–24.

Murphy, J. T. (1991). Superintendents as saviors: From the Terminator to Pogo. *Phi Delta Kappan, 72*(7), 507–513.

Pavan, B. N. (1995). *First year district superintendents: Women reflect on contradictions between education and politics*. (ERIC Document Reproduction Service No. ED 389 077)

Potter, B. (1993). *Beating job burnout: How to transform work pressure into productivity*. Berkeley, CA: Ronin Publishing.

Quick, J. C., Nelson, D. L., & Quick, J. D. (1990). *Stress and challenge at the top: The paradox of the successful executive*. New York: John Wiley & Sons.

Ramsey, K. (1996). Back to the trenches. *School Administrator, 53*(3), 22–28.

Rees, R. (1986). SOS: A time management framework. *Education Canada, 26*(2), 8–15.

Saville, A., & Kavina, G. (1982). Use stress to improve your job performance. *Executive Educator, 4*(4), 18–19.

Selye, H. (1976). *The stress of life*. New York: McGraw-Hill.

Sergiovanni, T. J., Burlingame, M., Coombs, F. S., & Thurston, P. W. (1992). *Educational governance and administration* (3rd ed.). Boston: Allyn and Bacon.

Sharp, W. L., & Walter, J. K. (1995). *The health of the school superintendency*. (ERIC Document Reproduction Service No. ED 389 067)

Shelton, B. S., Beach, R., & Chissom, B. S. (1989). Perceived political factors related to superintendents' administration of school districts. *Educational Research Quarterly, 13*(2), 11–17.

Slater, R. O. (1994). Symbolic educational leadership and democracy in America. *Educational Administration Quarterly*, *30*(1), 97–101.

Wallace, R. C. (1992). *On exiting the superintendency: An autobiographical perspective*. Paper presented at the annual meeting of the American Educational Research Association, San Francisco.

Walton, H. F. (1973). *The man in the principal's office: An ethnography*. New York: Holt, Rinehart & Winston.

Webber, C. F. (1995). *A Profile of the school superintendency: Issues and perceptions*. (ERIC Document Reproduction Service No. ED 383 111)

Wiggins, T. (1988). Stress and administrative role in educational organizations. *Journal of Educational Research*, *82*(2), 120–125.

Wood, S. E., & Wood, E. G. (1996). *The world of psychology* (2nd ed.). Boston: Allyn and Bacon.

Chapter 13

Personal Development: Decision-Making Skills and Ongoing Professional Growth

Key Concepts

✧ The essential nature of decision making in the superintendency
✧ Models for decision making
✧ Professional growth
✧ Importance of lifelong learning
✧ Reflective practice
✧ Staff development
✧ Continuing education
✧ Mentoring and networking

Joseph Murphy and Philip Hallinger (1987) noted that school reform initiatives in the middle to the late 1980s showed that superintendents can have considerable influence over their districts. A reconsideration of relationships between a school district and the community, a renewed interest in public education, and the belief that meaningful improvements in schools were most likely to occur at the local level created an environment in which district-level leadership became a key reform variable. As a result, policymakers and the general public are now becoming less tolerant of management-oriented superintendents who dedicate themselves to protecting the status quo. Instead, they expect superintendents to be competent leaders who are well informed and capable of bringing educators and the community together so that critical decisions can be made at the local level. Within this context, certain dimensions of the superintendency have assumed added importance. Decision making and professional growth are among them.

While people routinely make decisions in their daily lives, most of them are rather inconsequential. Organizational leaders, by comparison, make dozens of important determinations each day—some of which touch the lives of thousands of people. Decision making at this level is certainly not routine; it requires an understanding of process, context, and alternative actions (Giesecke, 1993). Decisions have even been called "the primary output of all administration" (Baird, 1989, p. 4). And like many aspects of practice, it is both an art and a science. As school districts are given greater degrees of freedom to seek self-renewal, it is increasingly expected that administrators are able to make judgments, settle disputes, and provide direction.

The quest for school reform in a changing world also contributes to the need for educators to engage in continuous learning. Public education, unlike many private organizations, has invested very little in the development of human resources. For much of the 20th century, the lack of attention to this critical issue was not seen as a deficiency by most members of society. In part, this is because the average taxpayer erroneously assumes that educators should have all the necessary knowledge and skills at the time they enter practice. Further, they argue that the public has no responsibility to pay for remedial work for those educators who do not have such skills. However, the current criticisms of public schools appear to be causing many to reconsider this myopic assumption.

The purpose of this chapter is to examine the issues of decision making and professional growth. Each topic is discussed in the context of changing conditions that require superintendents to reconsider definitions of effective practice.

DECISION MAKING IN THE SUPERINTENDENCY

A decision involves a determination made by a person or persons. *Decision making* is a pervasive human activity, and it has been studied extensively in the context of organizational work since the early 1900s. Michael Murray (1986) defined decision making as a process involving the selection of a course of a action from a group of alternative actions. Basically, the process includes problem identification, a search for alternative actions, an evaluation of alternative actions, and the selection of preferred alternatives (Browne, 1993). When a problem requires a series of interrelated decisions, the process may be referred to as *problem solving* (Tallman & Gray, 1990). A *decision-making model* identifies and describes the elements of decision making in a manner that allows different administrators to replicate the process consistently (English, Frase, & Arhar, 1992).

Historically, those who studied school administration were preoccupied with two issues: (1) establishing a rational, scientific process for decision making; and (2) focusing on managerial determination and skills in making decisions. Charles Sharman (1984) noted that most authorities "consider decision making to be the essence of the administrative process" (p. 13). Others (e.g., English et al., 1992) feel that administrators earn their salaries by making decisions on a daily basis.

Over the past 20 to 30 years, interest in this area has clearly shifted toward the more effective use of participative decision-making methods. And rather than concentrating on the idiosyncratic behavior of superintendents, researchers are interested in discovering how administrators influence the ways in which organizations actually approach decision making (Owens, 1998). This influence flows from administrators' personal philosophies and leadership styles. Accordingly, those practitioners who understand decision-making paradigms are more likely to make informed choices and to exhibit consistent behavior when they attempt to guide organizational directions.

Scientific Approaches

Over the years, the practice of applied decision making in education was heavily influenced by John Dewey's scientific method for solving problems. The quest for a rational model was embedded in the principles of scientific management; it was an effort to maximize the economies of action (Giesecke, 1993). Scientific approaches have been referred to as rational decision making, ideal decision making, and normative decision making. But regardless of terminology, these paradigms analyze how the decision-making process *should* occur (Razik & Swanson, 1995). Rationality refers to "a set of skills or aptitudes we use to see if we can get from here to there—to find courses of action that will lead to the accomplishment of goals" (Simon, 1993, p. 393).

In reality, there is no single rational model of decision making, rather there are a number of related models (Zey, 1992). Daniel Griffiths (1959) concluded that most rational models incorporate the following approaches to decision making:

- Recognize, define, and limit the problem.
- Analyze and evaluate the problem.
- Establish criteria or standards by which a solution will be evaluated or judged as acceptable and adequate.
- Collect data.

- Formulate and select the preferred solution and test it in advance.
- Put the preferred solution into effect.

A seven-step model of rational decision making, which basically reflects the above steps, has been suggested by many authors (e.g., Sharman, 1984). This paradigm is shown in Figure 13–1.

Rational decision making relies on logic and science to make impartial choices based on objective analysis (Giesecke, 1993). Among the suggested strengths of this decision-making model are the following:

- It provides rules for a potentially disorderly process.
- It provides a precise process of deductive problem solving.
- It provides predictability, order, technical competence, impersonality, and rationality (Tanner & Williams, 1981).

The popularity of rational models was diminished by concerns articulated by some of the leading theorists in the 1950s and 1960s. Herbert Simon (1960), for example, argued that in order to make objectively rational decisions, an administrator must do all of the following, a set of actions that seem impossible in most situations: (1) view all decision alternatives in panoramic fashion prior to making a decision, (2) consider all consequences that would follow each choice, and (3) assign a value to each alternative and select one alternative from the set. Practitioners too were often skeptical and critical of rational models because they perceived a substantial gap between the ideal and the real. In their world of work, ambiguity and uncertainty were pervasive. For them, problems and needs did not emerge in an orderly linear manner, nor were they resolved consistently in that fashion. Commenting about decision making in schools, Robert Owens (1998)

Figure 13–1
A rational model for decision making

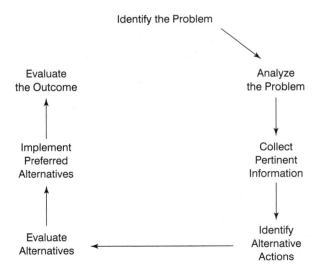

wrote, "[D]ecision making is usually an iterative, ongoing process whereby the results of one decision provide new information on which to base yet another decision" (p. 257).

Rational paradigms often fail to give adequate consideration to philosophical and political variables that result in decisions actually being made outside the parameters of some sort of idealized management world. For example, the power of a teacher's union, a commitment to shared governance, and the restricted power of administrators are examples of conditions that may counteract the intended efficiency of rational decision making. In truth, administrators rarely have complete information, an exhaustive list of alternatives, or totally unbiased dispositions (Browne, 1993). Thus, decisions in school districts are made in the context of mixed motives, ambiguities, and limited information—characteristics of social systems that serve to lessen the potential effectiveness of rational paradigms.

Bounded Rationality Models

As the deficiencies of rational models became known, variations on them emerged. While these were called by a number of different names (such as "bounded" models), they shared the goal of reducing erroneous assumptions about choices and outcomes in decision making. More specifically, they provided substantial modification to earlier models that treated organizations as rational entities, but they did so without eliminating some aspects of the linear process.

Herbert Simon (1997) divided decision making into four phases:

1. *Intelligence activity.* This involves identifying problems.
2. *Design activity.* This consists of identifying possible courses of action.
3. *Choice activity.* This involves deciding on a course of action.
4. *Review activity.* This is the evaluation of outcomes.

In bounded models, the idea of *satisficing* plays a central role. It has been defined as an individual's or organization's tendency to select something less than ideal (Hellreigel & Slocum, 1996). Herbert Simon is credited with coining the term. He noted that administrators do not usually have all the alternatives for a decision on hand; they have to search for alternatives and evaluate them after they are discovered. Rather then sustaining the search and evaluation process until the ideal decision is identified, the decision maker selects an alternative that is reasonably likely to produce acceptable results (Simon, 1997). Hence, decision makers frequently do not choose or consider the most effective alternatives.

Bounded models also differ from the traditional rational models in that decision making is not seen as a value-free enterprise. Instead, five types of biases may be injected into the information processing:

1. *Availability bias.* This is the tendency of individuals who remember an event to overestimate the number of times it occurred.

2. *Selective participation bias.* This is the proclivity of administrators to select information with which they agree and to ignore other information.

3. *Concrete numbers bias.* An administrator may rely on a single personal experience rather than contradicting statistical evidence.

4. *Law of small numbers bias.* This is the proclivity to rely on a few cases as being representative of the larger population, even if they are not.

5. *Gambler's fallacy.* This involves seeing an unexpected number of similar events and concluding that an event not seen is thus more likely to occur (Hellreigel & Slocum, 1996).

In essence, bounded models prescribe an orderly approach to decision making while recognizing that uncertainty, values, competing interests, and biases enter the process.

Other Models

Studies of administrative behavior uncovered widespread discrepancies between the ways in which theorists said decisions should be made and the ways in which they were actually made. This led to the development of descriptive models. Unlike normative models, descriptive models are predicated on the belief that individuals do not always make decisions that are either ideal or rational (Razik & Swanson, 1995). Descriptive models seek to describe actual decision-making processes. Several of the more well-known descriptive paradigms are discussed here.

The Garbage Can Model

Recognizing that many decisions are not made in a linear manner, some scholars have likened the decision-making process to a garbage can that attracts problems, solutions, and participants. The imagery of a garbage can is used to describe choice opportunities (Cohen, March, & Olsen, 1972). These are events that focus attention and create opportunities for change (Hanson, 1996). In schools, this might be the firing of a principal or a serious accident on school property. Decisions reflect the fact that a particular solution and a particular problem floating in the can find a sponsor.

> That is, a participant, or a coalition of participants, decides to use extensive time and energy to promote a particular solution to a specific problem. That participant or coalition may prevail because other participants sponsoring other problems and solutions reduce their participation or drop out from involvement altogether. (Hanson, 1996, p. 144)

Unlike the scientific approach, in which decisions are formulated only after a problem has been identified and analyzed, the garbage can process holds that a solution may actually precede problems. In addition, participation (who is involved in the decision) may be determined more by happenstance than by reason (Kowalski & Reitzug, 1993). Connections among problems, solutions, and participants are not always clear; the organizational environment is often complex; there are numerous variables (e.g., resources) that influence the decision-making process.

Consider an elementary school in which a principal becomes convinced that cooperative learning should be implemented. Knowing that there is likely to be considerable resistance, the principal waits until a choice opportunity occurs. In this example, it happens to be a growing concern about low scores on a state-mandated achievement test. The principal seizes the opportunity to promote cooperative learning because the problem of low scores makes some would-be opponents less likely to be resistant. The principal's proposed solution (cooperative learning) was floating in the garbage can for some time before it was linked to a significant problem.

Superintendents often embrace certain solutions and wait until appropriate choice opportunities arise before they connect those solutions to problems. This method of decision making certainly is not linear, nor is it totally rational. Neither do the decision makers study the complete range of alternative solutions, nor do they know the precise consequences of their decision.

Political Model

Because school districts operate in a political environment and because they are political organizations (Sergiovanni & Carver, 1980), decisions often reflect the realities of competing forces and external interventions (that is, the ability of individuals, groups, or agencies outside of the school district to influence decisions). In the political model, the focus is on bargaining between opposing factions; decisions are negotiated based on the amount of power possessed by opponents. The goals of the school district are often displaced by the goals of the competing interest groups (Estler, 1988).

One depiction of political decision making is the interacting spheres models (see Figure 13–2). Within this paradigm, individuals and groups in schools formally and informally develop their own spheres of influence. Within their individual spheres, power and authority are not routinely contested. However, there also are overlapping areas called contested zones; here decisions are the product of informal and formal negotiation (Hanson, 1996). In a school district, for example, certain functions such as budgeting and transportation management may be centralized; other functions, such as the operation of cafeterias and the employment of substitute teachers, are the exclusive domain of principals. Other issues, such as policy enforcement and textbook selection, may fall in the contested zone. Political decision making occurs at two levels: the determination of spheres of influence and decision making within the contested zone.

Common characteristics of the political model include the following:

- The participants are interdependent (that is, they are making decisions in contested zones).

Figure 13–2
Interacting spheres of decisions
in a school district

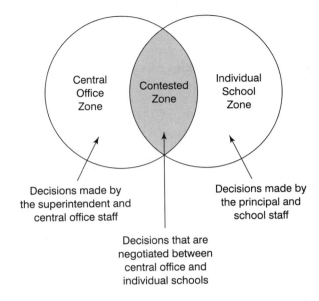

Central Office Zone

Contested Zone

Individual School Zone

Decisions made by
the superintendent and
central office staff

Decisions that are
negotiated between
central office and
individual schools

Decisions made by
the principal and
school staff

- Administrators need to assess the distribution of power throughout the organization to enhance their bargaining strategy.
- Information is critical to providing supporting evidence for proposals.
- Bargaining, coalition building, and incremental strategies are likely to be used in situations where the decisions are deemed to be critical (Giesecke, 1993).

Conflicting goals and a distribution of power often require administrators to seek political solutions to problems, even though this process for decision making can be time-consuming and generate additional conflict.

Consider the earlier example of the elementary school with low test scores. In the context of a political model, the adoption of cooperative learning does not depend on matching this solution to a problem, but rather on bargaining the issue with those teachers who are opposed to implementation. To accomplish the goal, the principal may have to make certain concessions or sacrifices. In this respect, the primary objective of the school (to improve test scores) becomes secondary to special interest goals (the principal's goal of implementing cooperative learning; the teachers' goal of always getting something for making concessions to the principal).

As schools move to site-based management or other forms of decentralized governance, political decision making is likely to intensify.

Moral-Ethical Model

Herbert Simon (1997) shed light on the ethical nature of decision making when he wrote the following:

Decisions are something more than factual propositions. To be sure, they are descriptive of a future state of affairs, and this description can be true or false in a strictly empirical sense; but they possess, in addition, an imperative quality—they select one future state of affairs in preference to another and direct behavior toward the chosen alternative. In short, they have an ethical as well as factual content. (p. 56)

Ethical leadership is very much grounded in values. Values provide the leader with a structured rationale that guides decision making (Hitt, 1990).

One of the most widely recognized writers in the area of ethical leadership in schools is Robert Starratt (1991). His approach—based on the ethical considerations of critique, justice, and caring—was discussed in chapter 3. His work is predicated on the notion that human factors, expressly moral in nature and previously neglected, need to be incorporated into the decision-making processes of a learning community. The role of the leader is to help create a culture in which such a process can flourish. At times, superintendents may put themselves in the other person's shoes; at another times, they might assume responsibility for the social consequences of decisions.

Imagine a superintendent who is faced with making a merit salary decision for a highly experienced principal. Although this principal's performance in the past years has been rated as "above average," this year's evaluation, completed by an assistant superintendent, is in the below-average range. Comments on the evaluation form indicate that the principal frequently left work early, missed numerous meetings, and failed to pay adequate attention to day-to-day managerial responsibilities. Based on these observations, the evaluator recommended that the principal not receive a salary increase for the coming year (salaries for administrators in the district are based entirely on merit). As the superintendent reviews this matter and contemplates making a decision, he knows that the principal's spouse has been seriously ill during the past year. He suspects that this problem is a primary cause for the change in work behavior. The superintendent asks himself pertinent questions and attempts to place himself in the principal's situation before deciding whether to approve the salary recommendation. To what degree should a spouse's illness be a consideration with respect to job performance and salary increases? Would the superintendent have done anything differently if it were his spouse who was seriously ill? Answering these questions provide the superintendent with moral and ethical perspectives that may influence his decision.

Decisions made by superintendents almost always have consequences for students, employees, the school district, and society. In an ethical framework, administrators do not focus exclusively on what is best for the school district or for themselves; they do not make decisions based exclusively on political expediency. Rather, the focus is on fairness with personal concern for the long-term outcomes of the decision. Ethics play an important role in determining the success of all organizations (Hitt, 1990).

Again using the example of the elementary school with low test scores, a decision within the moral-ethical framework would focus on what is best for all who are affected. Should teachers be forced to implement a program they do not accept? Will students merely be pawns in a power struggle between the principal and the teachers? What will be the long-term consequences of implementing this program? These are the types of questions that would guide decisions.

Participatory Model

In the 1920s and 1930s, dissatisfaction with the impersonal nature of rational decision making prompted managers to explore alternatives that would allow organizational members to participate in decisions that affected them and the organization. Participatory approaches are grounded in several values:

1. There is a relationship between participation and increased productivity.
2. Both ethics and human growth are issues that need to be considered by administrators.
3. Decisions in organizations should reflect life in a democracy.
4. Participation raises employee consciousness with respect to their rights (Estler, 1988).

This type of decision making is not without its problems. First, the process is often time-consuming and, therefore, inappropriate for situations demanding quick actions. Second, the process is subject to groupthink—a condition in which participants place more emphasis on group cohesion than on the quality of the decision. Third, high-status participants (e.g., the superintendent) often inhibit the creativity and participation of lower-status participants. Fourth, a dominant personality in the group may be able to control most or all participants, diminishing many of the benefits of having a variety of individuals involved (Ivancevich & Matteson, 1996).

There are a number of perceived benefits associated with participation. These commonly include acquiring a broader perspective of the problem, creating an educational opportunity for employees (by participating, they learn about the organization as well as the problem), and increasing the likelihood that the decision will be accepted and supported (the participants typically develop a sense of ownership). The last point is especially important because the acceptance of a decision can be as important as its quality. In school districts, the involvement of teachers and administrators almost always expands the knowledge base necessary for making an effective decision. For example, instruction-related problems are likely to be addressed more adequately if professionals who work with students are involved. By involving others, an administrator can be more creative and discover new ways of solving problems (Robbins, 1998).

The two prevalent techniques used for making group decisions include consensus and voting. The former is predicated on "win-win" strategies that permit all participants to have a feeling of accomplishment when the final decision is made. When consensus is reached, the product ranks high with respect to acceptance and support. On the other hand, the process frequently requires group members to make concessions, a condition that may result in a less than ideal decision. Voting, by contrast, is quick, easy to execute, and consistent with democratic process. Unfortunately, voting tends to produce winners and losers—a condition that usually creates factions or intensifies tensions between existing factions.

The size of school districts precludes all employees participating in the process of making critical decisions. In selecting participants, Robert Owens (1998) suggests criteria that can be helpful. They include the following:

- *Relevance.* To what extent does the person have a stake in the decision to be made?
- *Expertise.* Can the person make a significant contribution to the decision-making process?
- *Jurisdiction.* Does the individual have the authority to implement the decision?
- *Desire.* Does the person wish to be involved?

When decision groups are put together without considering these criteria or when coordination and facilitation are insufficient, participatory approaches may fail altogether—that is to say, the group disbands without reaching a decision.

Decision Making in Practice

This brief overview of scientific and descriptive models of decision making is intended to provide insight into the gap between ideal and real practice. Whereas scientific approaches are usually linear, well defined, highly structured, and predicated on certainty, descriptive models focus on the ambiguity and uncertainty that actually exists in school districts. They recognize that decision making may reflect politics, ethics, or happenstance.

The challenges of decision making in school administration have been made more complex by continuing attempts to move districts away from bureaucratic-like structures. Participatory decision making, while not a new concept, is receiving much more attention in the context of teacher professionalism and democratic administration. Teacher participation, for example, is justified for several reasons:

1. It will make teaching a more stimulating and professional occupation.
2. It will increase teacher autonomy and thus result in better attitudes and resulting improved performance.
3. As human beings, we should have a right to control our own destiny.
4. Increasing teacher participation in school decision making will expand the scope of expertise that is brought to bear on decisions and, thus, is likely to result in improved decision making. (Kowalski & Reitzug, 1993, p. 204)

While current trends indicate that decision making in school districts will become more decentralized, total decentralization is improbable. Therefore, superintendents need an understanding of different decision-making models, and they must select appropriate models based on distributions of authority and power (i.e., degrees of decentralization).

In summary, superintendents ought not expect to enter practice with a cookbook recipe for decision making. Rather, they should be prepared to enhance and refine their knowledge and skills in this area by constantly observing and critiquing decisions and the processes used to make them. They should be especially cognizant of their own behaviors. They should recognize and cope with extreme political pressures and uncertainty that lessen the effectiveness of scientific approaches. And they should be committed to moral and ethical standards that add yet another dimension to this complex and vexatious task. The effective superintendent adheres to the adage "There is no right way to do a wrong thing" (Blanchard & Peale, 1988, p. 19). Because problems and needs are constantly evolving, the modern practitioner also must be dedicated to continuous learning that will enlighten them about new theories and emerging research. In this respect, decision-making skills are enhanced when superintendents invariably incorporate their own experiences and emerging theoretical insights into their professional knowledge base.

GROWTH AS AN ESSENTIAL ASPECT OF PROFESSIONAL PRACTICE

Debates over the status of school administration have continued since the granting of the first degrees in this field. Today, the label of "professional" is used rather freely in American society to refer to almost any organized occupation (Sergiovanni, Burlingame, Coombs, & Thurston, 1992). Several writers have sought to clarify the status of school administration by dissecting the demands of practice. Arthur Blumberg (1989), for example, argued that school administration was neither a true science (rarely did models and prescriptions fit the problems of practice) nor an art (practice requires more than tacit knowledge and intuition), but rather a craft learned through skillful application and reflection. There are, however, several properties that distinguish school administration from long-standing trades or crafts (e.g., plumbing or tailoring). Several of the more obvious are required academic study, state licensing, and reliance on a theory-based body of knowledge to inform practice.

Those who remain skeptical about whether school administration is a true profession often point to other characteristics to explicate their position. Consider the following conditions that show distinctions between school administration and the most highly established professions, such as medicine and law:

- There is no single national organization for school administrators analogous to the American Medical Association or American Bar Association. Instead, administrators may belong to any number of organizations as discussed earlier in this book.

- States, through licensure programs, have dictated the content of professional study. Social and political factors have influenced licensure (and academic preparation) more than have research and theory (Goldhammer, 1983).

- Admission, retention, and completion requirements in the field are considered very modest. Most who wish to complete academic preparation for the study of school administration are able to do so (Sergiovanni et al., 1992).

- There are over 500 institutions offering courses or degrees in school administration in the United States. There are no standard curricula for academic degrees; licensure requirements often vary markedly among states (Kowalski & Reitzug, 1993).

Because of such issues, arguments over the professional status of school administration are not likely to be resolved in the near future. Nevertheless, many practitioners realize that their work occurs in the context of a profession, and as such, it requires them to be lifelong learners. Most believe that doubts about their status are predicated on political issues and the context of their roles in primarily public institutions, rather than on valid questions about school administration as a discipline or true profession.

Past and Present Emphasis on Professional Growth

David Torres (1991) defined a profession in terms of four essential characteristics: (1) knowledge (e.g., practice rooted in a theoretical and craft knowledge base); (2) regulation and control (e.g., standards of practice used to control entry, licensure, performance); (3) ideology (e.g., shared values of ideal practice); and (4) association (e.g., common purpose, collegiality). Perhaps the most common misperception is that administrators acquire all of their knowledge and skills in prelicensure programs; another is that professional knowledge provides precise, technical solutions for virtually all problems the practitioner will encounter. In truth, preservice education largely acts as a foundation, providing the student with entry-level knowledge and skills.

John Daresh and Marsha Playko (1992) viewed the professional development of school administrators as a broad concept having three components:

1. *Academic preparation.* Academic preparation is acquired largely through traditional university-based courses of study.
2. *Field-based learning.* Field-based experiences include internships and practica.
3. *Professional formation.* This includes personal reflection, mentoring, and personal and professional development (Daresh & Playko, 1992).

Other writers often refer to professional development more narrowly, suggesting that the term is analogous to professional growth after entering practice. In any event, superintendents are required to complete a necessary preservice program in virtually all states. Compliance is ensured through the control of licensing. Professional formation, however, has been largely ignored or undervalued until recently. This is truly unfortunate since professional development entails the gradual expansion of expertise through the integration of professional knowledge and experience—it is the process that usually distinguishes novices from experts (Ohde & Murphy, 1993).

Until the early 1980s professional development for administrators was not viewed as a necessity; consequently, there were no widely held expectations that superintendents engage in continuous learning. Commenting on this fact, Philip Hallinger and Joseph Murphy (1991) wrote, "The absence of norms for professional growth has been reinforced by an administrative culture that promotes a pull-yourself-up-by-the-bootstraps attitude" (p. 516). This situation began to change in part as a response to widespread criticism of educators and calls for school reform. It also changed, however, because most people came to believe that continuous learning can make a difference; that is, it can affect some attitudes and behaviors (Pitner, 1987). However, the value of professional development for superintendents also increased because of a growing awareness that initial preparation was often the product of rigid state requirements and university norms—it did not necessarily reflect the needs of practitioners (Hallinger & Murphy, 1991).

Within the atmosphere of reform, a growing number of states moved to revamp licensing standards, especially as they pertained to granting life licenses. The trend was clearly toward requiring all educators, including superintendents, to engage in periodic learning experiences. Such actions raised fundamental questions about the responsibility for professional growth. Clearly there are many compelling arguments for states to require educators to engage in continuing education. Variables such as changing demographics, globalization, diversity, and the changing family structure reshape the needs of students and society, and educators need to understand and respond to such changes. Some, though, have criticized state-required continuing education as being inherently contradictory to the definition of professionalism (e.g., Ohliger, 1981). These critics argue that lifelong learning is a fundamental and ethical responsibility of a professional.

Elements of Professional Growth

As noted earlier in this book, the practice of school administration is heavily influenced by context. That is, the effectiveness of decisions or other actions is partly determined by the conditions surrounding administrators. This is why a particular action can be highly effective in one setting and terribly inadequate in another. If the context of practice remained constant, administrators would have greater confidence in a set of predetermined actions. In addition, problems do not emerge in a predictable or sequential order; rather, they often come forth as complex and unexpected issues.

Starting up new programs may require a superintendent to acquire considerable knowledge. This includes both content and process knowledge; that is, knowledge of the content of new programs and knowledge of how to implement programs. In the past, practitioners have relied heavily on state-sponsored or organization-sponsored workshops to fulfill this need. Such workshops typically focus on the transmission of new information without any particular concern for integrating the content with the learner's previous knowledge base. As such, the material is not typically studied in the context of the learner's work—a condition that often diminishes the relevance of the learning experience. While traditional workshops will continue to provide one means for professional growth, the modern practitioner is more likely to depend on a wider range of learning opportunities. They may include peer networks, self-directed learning, additional university courses, and work exchanges (e.g., trading roles with persons in other districts for several weeks a year).

Reflective Practice

With respect to compensating teachers in the United States, experience has been the primary criterion. That is, teachers who have the most experience generally make the highest salaries. Further, this custom is based entirely on the quantity of experience; most school districts make no attempt to evaluate the quality of experience (except in rare cases where dismissal becomes an issue). Underlying this mode of compensation is the assumption of a positive correlation between effective practice and experience. While superintendents are not commonly placed on salary schedules, many school board members deem experience to be a salary-related criterion—both because it is quantifiable and because it is consistent with compensation criteria for teachers. Superintendents and teachers usually benefit from experience during the first 1 to 3 years of practice. This is because they learn the culture and climate of their work environment, and they encounter and learn to cope with new and unexpected challenges. After the first few years of practice, however, the behaviors of many educators become fixed. Teachers, for example, often learn to imitate established practices during student teaching and their induction year (Valli, 1992).

Observable behavior is related to personal action theories. An individual superintendent's personal action theories may be influenced by theoretical constructs studied in graduate school and by personal values and beliefs. Such theories are divided into two categories: *espoused theories* (theories that influence what we think and believe) and *in-use theories* (theories that influence what we really do). The former exist at the conscious level and are more likely to be altered as a person gains exposure to new knowledge and unique experiences; the latter often exist at the unconscious level and are usually highly resistant to change (Argyris & Schon, 1974). This is why, for instance, an administrator may overtly take a position against corporal punishment (because everything he has read encourages him to do so) while continuing to paddle students for misbehaving (because he remains personally convinced that it will have a desired effect on the student).

Espoused theories in school administration are influenced by professional study and reinforced by professional standards. Theories-in-use, by contrast, are learned from experiencing life—both inside and outside of the school (Osterman & Kottkamp, 1993). Imagine that a second-year teacher who has not completed a single course in school administration is asked to assume the principalship of her school for one month. It is highly probable that the teacher's behavior will reflect what she has learned by watching principals function as well as her personal dispositions regarding what principals should do. If the principals whom she has observed were good practitioners and if she has defensible values and beliefs about administration, she may function rather well during this short-term assignment. Even so, she probably could not analyze or explain her own administrative behavior. This is because she is merely emulating others without having a real understanding of the behavior. If administrators function at this level, they are almost certain to encounter difficulty as unexpected and unique problems emerge. For example, the administrator may not be able to arrive at novel solutions suited to the particular situation.

More than any other scholar, Donald Schon (1983, 1990) has been responsible for exhibiting that the complexity and ambiguity of practice in all professions require more than technical knowledge. He accomplished this by describing three intermediate zones of practice: (1) *uncertainty* (e.g., problems do not always occur to superintendents as well-informed structures); (2) *uniqueness* (e.g., superintendents often encounter problems that are not discussed in textbooks); and (3) *value conflict* (e.g., when solving problems, superintendents must often choose between positions supported by conflicting values). In addition, he concluded that situations may be problematic in several of these ways at once. For example, a first-year superintendent may have to decide which programs to cut so that necessary budget reductions can be achieved. This superintendent has never had to make such reductions in the past; the outcomes of budget cuts are largely unknown; factions within the school district are lobbying for distinctively different decisions.

Not only does the art of reflective practice serve to place professional preparation in a proper perspective, it also reinforces the importance of context in professional practice. Context analysis is an especially powerful tool for analyzing organizational behavior and determining the learning needs of practitioners (Erlandson, 1992). Schon (1990) differentiated between "knowing-in-action" and "reflecting-in-action." The former is embedded in the socially and institutionally structured context shared by those who enter school administration. The latter represents a type of artistry that becomes important when problems and challenges are unique and less than rational. School administrators, like other professionals, develop an implicit repertoire of techniques and strategies for responding to the demands of their work. Within the context of their action theories, they also develop mental images of likely outcomes that become part of their routine behavior. When things go as expected, they have little need to give further thought to the situation (in fact, experiences such as these serve to verify convictions already embedded in the administrator's tacit knowledge). Occasionally, however, things do not turn out as expected. These surprises may "trigger both reflection in-action and reflection-on-action, causing the individual to reflect on what is causing the unanticipated consequences both as they are occurring and later, after the heat of the moment has dissipated" (Kowalski & Reitzug, 1993, p. 236). This mental activity is not an easy task. Administrators are often unable to identify the components of their work that lead to successful outcomes; many are uncertain as to how their own behavior serves as a barrier to professional growth (Osterman & Kottkamp, 1993). This is because much of their behavior is based on their implicit compliance with the cultural norms of their work environments and their own work habits.

The theory of experiential learning has been defined by David Kolb (1984) as a cyclical process with four distinctive stages: (1) experience, (2) observation and reflection, (3) abstract reconceptualization, and (4) experimentation. In this context, experience provides a basis for learning; but experience alone does not guarantee learning. Learning is accomplished when the practitioner uses the four stages of experiential learning to provide a nexus between theory and the real world of practice. As a model for professional growth, reflective practice focuses on both a continuous restructuring of the professional knowledge base and the improvement of personal performance. This is accomplished by integrating uncertain, unique, and value-laden experiences into personal theories of action. When this is achieved, administrative behaviors involve more than the application of recipes for rational decisions. Performance is predicated on a framework of contextual variables that involve emotions, competing interests, and behavioral regularities common to schools and school districts.

Contrary to what some may believe, reflective practice entails more than casual thoughts about work. It is the application of experiential learning. Superintendents who do not engage in this form of self-learning are likely to become creatures of habit. Reflective practice is a means for avoiding this trap. A superintendent learns to integrate an awareness of personal behavior and the outcomes of personal performance; the product of this artistry results in a continuous redefining and expansion of the professional knowledge base (see Figure 13–3). Accordingly, reflective practice becomes a self-managed program of learning and professional development.

Reflective practice occurs both individually and in groups. For the superintendent, the group reflection typically occurs in planned sessions with other school and district administrators. Some superintendents, for example, hold debriefing sessions the morning after school board meetings. At these sessions, behaviors and outcomes are analyzed and evaluated; the purpose is to improve future performance. Group reflection also may occur in meetings with other superintendents. Roundtable discussions at professional meetings often serve the purpose of allowing administrators to engage in personal reflection by using shared language and concepts to define problems of practice. More important, these encounters may generate strategies for dealing with problems or provide opportunities for storytelling in which superintendents explain their experiences with a given problem (Bolman & Deal, 1992). Even though this form of collective reflection usually arises out of the pragmatic needs of practice, the activity makes an important contribution to professional growth.

The necessity for reflective practice in school administration is rooted in the reality that no graduate school program, regardless of its reputation or faculty, can provide a knowledge base that is consistently effective throughout one's career. It is also grounded in the inescapable fact that the needs of society and the needs of learners are not constant. However, there are many in society and in the profession who continue to believe that professional schools have a responsibility to teach aspiring practitioners everything they will ever need to know as a precondition of graduation and licensure. This view is sometimes voiced by mis-

Figure 13–3
Effects of reflection on the
knowledge base and on artistry

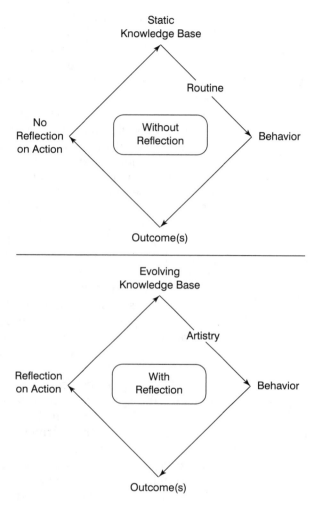

guided administrators who upon completing their preparation programs comment, "Wow, am I glad that is over! I'll never have to read another book or take another class." In truth, professional schools simply prepare students to enter practice; the purposes of preservice studies are usually (1) to provide the individual with sufficient entry-level knowledge and skills, (2) to provide a socialization experience, and (3) to help the individual learn how to develop lifelong learning skills.

Professional growth occurs when administrators are able to capitalize on real work experiences—to use them to give deeper meaning to both theoretical and craft knowledge. Recognizing the importance of lifelong learning, some school administration preparation programs already offer courses and other experiences designed to teach reflective practice skills. Case studies, simulations, and certain types of field experiences are being used for this purpose. In addition, design studios, similar to those used in other professional schools such as architecture, provide an alternative for students to apply classroom knowledge to problems of practice (Hart, 1993). In these experiences, graduate students may spend an extended period of time developing a decision for a real problem that existed in a school district. This is made possible by providing the student with information that was available to administrators who really experienced the problem. Studios also help prepare future practitioners to engage in the process of reflection because they are able to critique their work once it is complete.

Staff Development

Unlike reflective practice, which has become prominent in school administration literature in the past few decades, staff development has been the traditional and most prevalent model for the professional growth of educators. Staff development, however, has multiple meanings. Gary Griffin (1983) provided this concise definition: "any systematic attempt to alter the professional practices, beliefs, and understandings of school persons toward an articulated end" (p. 2). Some authors have defined staff development in ideal terms (that is, what it can or should accomplish); others have focused on the real experiences of school employees. The term also has been used interchangeably with inservice education; however, some authors take exception to this use. Those who do so usually see inservice education as a rather negative practice that

> ... connotes an attempt to pour learning into the heads of participants, as if a funnel could be placed at the top of a person's head and knowledge could be poured in: a "servicing" of people in much the sense that cars or cows are serviced on a regular basis. (Bradley, Kallick, & Regan, 1991, p. 4)

Less harsh distinctions between the two terms are made on the basis of time frames. Inservice is seen as addressing immediate goals, whereas staff development implies a process of growth over time. However, despite objections, many educators continue to use the terms staff development and inservice interchangeably.

Staff development can occur in many locations and in different forms. The most common formats include conferences (state, local, regional), workshops, institutes, seminars, and short courses. The purposes of these programs also are varied; they may relate to national and state initiatives, school district and school goals, individual needs, or a combination of these factors. Sponsorship may be provided by governmental agencies, national and state organizations, regional service centers, school districts, or even for-profit agencies.

The argument for staff development is grounded in two indisputable facts: (1) schools constantly face new needs and challenges and (2) educators must engage in continuing education if they are to remain effective in their practice. Staff development programs offered outside of the school district have been highly attractive to superintendents for several reasons. First, many superintendents prefer learning experiences that include other superintendents. Second, the comprehensive nature of responsibilities facing the superintendent results in a high demand for new knowledge. Every time a new program is mandated by the state, for example, there is a need to obtain implementation or compliance information. Third, many providers target superintendents as likely participants in development programs. This is because superintendents often have greater flexibility and resources to attend staff development functions—especially those that occur outside of their school districts. Fourth, many superintendents view staff development programs as serving a dual purpose: it is a time to learn and a time to spend a few days away from the daily tensions of the job.

However, while traditional forms of staff development arguably provide relevant learning experiences, this approach to professional growth is not without its imperfections. The more prevalent problems are identified and explained in Table 13–1. In general, traditional staff development programs for superintendents have been criticized for being nothing more than snippets of information, often provided unsequentially, without regard for actual implementation and without

Table 13–1
Common criticisms of traditional staff development programs for superintendents

Criticism	Explanation
Programs not directed to the actual needs of the participants	Programs usually focus on general state or school district issues while ignoring the more specific needs of the participant; the contents of the programs have little or no relationship to reflective practice.
Lack of integration and coordination	Superintendents commonly attend programs that are offered by different agencies and presenters; these "one-shot" experiences are unrelated to one another.
Lack of continuity	The programs are typically offered from 1 to 3 days; there is no extension of the learning experience beyond this point.
Lack of participant involvement in program planning	Most of these programs are planned for, not by, superintendents; often participants are uncertain about the value of the activities.
Lack of relevance to critical issues	Some programs may focus on obscure topics that have little relevance to the real work of the participants; such programs merely serve to verify that the superintendent has engaged in some form of staff development.
Poor design and organization	Some programs totally ignore principles of adult learning; presentations are disjointed, boring, and offer little opportunity for learner participation.
Focus on remediation rather than growth	Some programs are designed to disseminate information without any attempt to focus on implementation, practitioner behavior, or organizational improvement.

regard for real needs of educators. Detractors point out that such programs are usually expensive and have little visible effect on outcomes in school districts.

Partly because of the weaknesses associated with traditional forms of administrator staff development, the concept of administrative centers has become increasingly popular over the past few decades (Unikel & Bailey, 1986). Some, such as the Principals Center at Texas A & M University, were encouraged by both practitioner needs and changes in state legislation (Wilmore & Erlandson, 1993). Learning experiences at these sites differ from traditional staff development programs in several noteworthy ways: (1) the learning experiences are often sequenced and span a long-term time frame (e.g., several years); (2) learners play a role in identifying instructional needs; (3) some learning experiences are active; (4) there are opportunities for participants to learn from one another; (5) learning experiences often include applications in the learner's workplace; and (6) learners play a central role in evaluating outcomes and redesigning instructional experiences. In addition, such centers strive to create a context of mutual support and trust that fosters personal and professional relationships among participants (Levine, Barth, & Haskins, 1987).

In summary, staff development programs remain an important component in professional growth. For many superintendents, workshops and special programs are a necessary information resource. Nevertheless, it is quite clear that such learning experiences by themselves are insufficient to meet the challenges of contemporary practice. Accordingly, practitioners need to ask and answer questions such as the following:

- What role should staff development programs play in my personal growth plan?
- How will I integrate reflective practice with the knowledge and skills I receive in staff development programs?
- To what extent do staff development programs address the real needs of my position and school district?
- How much time can I devote each year to staff development programs?

While superintendents may be in a more advantageous position than other district employees to participate in staff development programs, neither time nor resources are unlimited; therefore, choices regarding attendance have to be made. For assessment of the potential value of a staff development program, certain criteria associated with effective learning experiences may prove helpful. These criteria are presented in Table 13–2.

Continuing Education

As used here, continuing education refers to enrollment in university-based courses after the individual has entered practice. Philosophically, the need for such learning experiences can be found in the literature throughout much of the 20th century. In recent years, many states have taken action to reinforce this belief: they have rescinded life licenses for superintendents and made continuing education a requirement for license renewal.

Table 13-2
Criteria for assessing the potential value of a staff development program

Criterion	Questions to Ask
Program is based on real needs	Did the program result from a needs assessment of superintendents? What needs are addressed by the program?
Relevance of focused needs	Does the program address personal needs? Does it address needs of my school district?
Clearly stated objectives	Are there stated objectives for the program? Do I understand the objectives?
Cost-benefit ratio	What are the potential benefits of participation? Are the potential benefits justified in relation to costs?
Integration with other growth activities	How does the program relate to other learning activities in which I am involved?
Nature of instruction	How will the program be conducted? Will instruction conform to the principles of adult learning? Will the instruction be compatible with my preferred learning style?
Quality of instructors	Who will provide the actual instruction? Are the instructors qualified to present the content? Are they sufficiently familiar with practice in the superintendency?
Profile of the participants	Who will be participating in the program? Are these persons with whom I want to share a learning experience? Will I benefit from interaction with the other participants?
Time commitment	How much time will be required to participate? What adjustments must be made to work schedules to allow participation?
Potential for secondary benefits	Will the products of this program be of interest or value to other school district employees? Will I be able to share knowledge and skills with other employees?
Relationship to high priorities	Does the program address major priorities in the school district? In what way can the program contribute to major improvement goals?

Individuals already in practice usually demand high relevance in university courses, an expectation that is generally held by adult learners. In addition, superintendents are preoccupied with the problems and challenges of their practice; as such, they prefer to enroll in classes that integrate theory and practice in some relevant manner. Because many states have changed their licensure laws, departments of educational leadership are paying more attention to developing courses that specifically address the continuing education needs of practitioners.

As professionals, school administrators have a responsibility to continue their education at a more personal level. That is, they are expected to remain current in their profession by reading journals and books that address new knowledge and issues of practice. Some critics of public education (e.g., Sarason, 1996) argue that schools have not improved because they are led by unimaginative individuals who rarely read research in their field. Frequently, superintendents who fail to engage in this aspect of professional growth argue that educational journals and books are too abstract and idealistic to be useful for their work. These individuals fail to recognize that knowledge is not static. Both research and shared experiences contribute to an ever-expanding body of professional knowledge.

Mentoring and Networks

Mentoring has become a popular concept in school administration, and it may occur at the preservice, induction, or inservice phase (Daresh & Playko, 1992). A mentor is one who helps an aspiring or relatively inexperienced professional to develop and advance a career by improving his or her productivity and effectiveness (Shelton & Herman, 1993). The concept, though, is not precisely defined in the literature, and it is often interpreted in varying ways. Most often in school administration, the relationship has been construed as a way of overcoming overt or covert barriers to professional advancement, especially for women and minorities. In the case of the superintendency, the primary barrier has frequently been characterized as "the good ole boys network"—a reference to the position being dominated by white males who have established informal channels of communication and power (Schmuck, 1986).

Typically, mentors have been successful superintendents or influential professors. A mentor's responsibilities usually include advising, communicating, counseling, guiding, modeling, protecting, and promoting skill development. As a means for professional growth, mentoring helps the developing professional to (1) frame issues, (2) identify goals, (3) promote self-directed learning, (4) establish realistic limits, and (5) become empowered to take necessary actions (Daresh & Playko, 1992). If a mentor is truly interested in helping another person, the relationship will be sustained even after the career goal (the superintendency) has been achieved. At this stage, the mentor may serve as a confidant, a confessor, and a personal adviser.

National and state support networks are another vehicle for professional growth, and they are becoming more prevalent. These arrangements may be formal and informal, and they exist to help administrators share information and resources. In many instances, they also exist as professional and political support mechanisms. Networks may be prompted by issues of underrepresentation (e.g., gender, race), organizational commitment (e.g., university alumni clubs), or common personal interests (e.g., a group of superintendents in a given region of a state). Networking, much like mentoring, has been popularized by perceived political and professional advantages. Not only may networking provide assistance for career advancement, it also may serve to eradicate or counteract damaging stereotypes (McGrath, 1992).

Networks also can be a useful tool for professional growth. Through formal meetings (e.g., school study councils or regional service centers), teleconferencing, and informal contacts (e.g., personal telephone calls), superintendents can share problems, discuss effective practices, and otherwise provide counsel to one another. Superintendents often find it helpful to discuss a problem with a peer who is experienced in the area of concern.

A Balanced Approach

The complexity of the superintendency makes professional growth absolutely essential. This need is commonly recognized by school boards, and, consequently, they typically provide superintendents opportunities to attend a number of conferences and workshops. Unfortunately, some practitioners do not take advantage of this privilege or they abuse it—that is, they attend conferences for the wrong reasons. To be beneficial, learning experiences must be sequential and relevant; they should address both organizational and personal needs. Studies of successful practitioners often reveal how these individuals are able to personalize professional development plans to fit the challenges of their work (e.g., Wendel, Hoke, & Joekel, 1996).

After examining the professional development needs of school administrators, Nancy Pitner (1987) identified themes that should guide decisions in this area. The following are especially relevant to superintendents:

- Provide time away from the work setting
- Seek experiences that allow the individual to personalize the learning
- Seek experiences that encourage reflection
- Build on one's experiential base
- Seek experiences that tend to combine personal and organizational needs
- Seek experiences that are cumulative and based on the continuous assessment of skills
- Keep focused on the purpose of professional development

In addition, superintendents should consider learning opportunities that extend beyond formal sessions, allowing new knowledge and skills to be tested in actual work situations.

Professional development also requires time. A superintendent needs to create and maintain a professional development plan to ensure that the scope of the learning experiences and the time allocated to them are adequate. Such a plan ought to be built on a foundation of reflective practice and should include opportunities for staff development, continuing education, networking, and mentorships (see Figure 13–4). In the practice of all professions, there is a need for artistry. Donald Schon (1990) used this concept "to refer to the kinds of competence practitioners sometimes display in unique, uncertain, and conflicted situations of practice" (p. 22). Professional artistry makes it more likely that superintendents will be able to resolve issues of practice that do not fall within the parameters of textbook examples. This attribute evolves from a purposeful melding of one's professional knowledge base, exposure to new research and evolving theories, and experiential learning acquired through daily practice.

Figure 13–4
Professional growth in the super-intendency

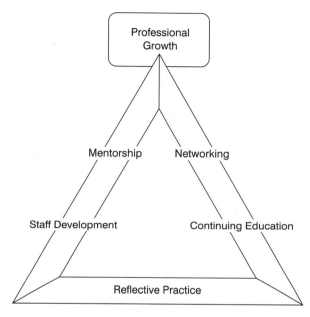

FOR FURTHER REFLECTION

Decision making and professional development are not new topics in school administration. With respect to the superintendency, these two issues have gained added importance over the last few decades. Changing demographic conditions and evolving social, economic, and political problems have caused the priorities for public education to shift. Even more relevant is the fact that the governance structure for public education is also being altered. As states attempt to improve education, school reform initiatives increase the importance of local decision making and heightened expectations for superintendents to be effective leaders as well as managers. Because knowledge is developing rapidly in this age of information and because experience can be an invaluable asset for improved practice, a commitment to lifelong learning is essential in the superintendency.

As you consider what you read in this chapter, answer the following questions:

1. Decision making usually refers to a specific action (a decision) and the process used to arrive at the action. In what ways might process affect the ultimate outcomes of a decision? For example, does it matter whether a decision is made unilaterally or democratically?

2. What problems might a superintendent experience if he or she is totally dependent on rational decision-making models?

3. What are the distinctions between rational decision-making models and bounded rationality models?

4. Is it possible to address political and moral-ethical issues simultaneously in decision making? Why or why not?

5. People often feel more comfortable when they can predict a leader's behavior. Is it better, therefore, for a superintendent to be consistent in decision-making behaviors or is it better for a superintendent to allow context to determine decision-making behaviors?

6. What is the difference between reflection and reflective practice?

7. What is the difference between *reflection-in-action* and *reflection-on-action*?

8. Why is technical knowledge insufficient for practice in the superintendency?

9. Assess your own experiences with staff development programs. Have they been positive or negative? What did you like or not like?

10. In what ways can mentoring and networking contribute to a superintendent's professional growth plan?

11. Why is it best to have a balanced plan for professional development?

CASE STUDY

Nick Jordan has been a superintendent for 24 years, the last 18 in his current position in the Webster Township School District. At age 57, he has not yet decided when he will retire. He has told his administrative staff on many occasions, "I just take it year by year. All I know is that when I retire, it will be from this job."

The Webster Township School District serves a suburb that adjoins a relatively large industrial city and that has a largely blue-collar population. With a stable enrollment of about 4,300 students, the district has a low tax base; there is no major industry, and only a handful of businesses are located in the district. Many of the taxpayers are products of the school system, and most are avid fans of the high school's successful athletic teams. Academically, programming is best described as modest; and only about 30% of the graduates from the high school enter 2 or 4-year institutions of higher education. A majority of the students enter the local workforce without formal education past the 12th grade.

When Nick Jordan came to the Webster Township School District, he followed a good friend and mentor, George Gidapolos. George was Nick's first principal, and it was he who urged Nick to consider a career in administration. George eventually became a superintendent in Webster Township, but he maintained a keen interest in Nick's career. George often told the board members in this district, "When I retire, the man you want to hire is Nick Jordan. He's a solid individual." They heeded the advice.

Nick Jordan firmly believed that he had been successful in every position he had held. During a 2-year experience as a high school principal, he was a finalist for the principal-of-the-year award in his state. As a superintendent, both in his previous position and in Webster Township, he never once was in jeopardy of being fired. He attributed his success largely to two things: common sense and an understanding of people. George was never an especially good student, and he found graduate classes to be boring. When he finished his master's degree and obtained his superintendent's license, he told some close friends, "Now I can go out and learn about the real world of school administration."

Everyone in Webster Township knew that Nick Jordan was a smooth political operator. Outgoing and charming, he related extremely well to the district's patrons. But he also had a reputation as a tough-nosed administrator. Principals, however, appreciated the fact that he always was fair and consistent in his behavior; he didn't play games and he told you what was on his mind. Nick was especially skillful at relating to the school board. He often did things with them socially, and he went out of his way to make sure they always felt comfortable visiting his office. Perhaps Nick's greatest gift was his ability to delegate responsibilities. He had three full-time assistant superintendents to whom he shifted virtually all of the day-to-day operations. This allowed Nick to roam freely about the community and spend considerable time with the school board members.

The newest of the assistant superintendents was Dr. Elizabeth Simmons. Her employment was unusual for two reasons. First, she was the first woman ever to be hired into a position at this level in Webster Township. Second, it had been common practice to promote one of the principals to an assistant superintendency when such positions became vacant. But Nick was willing to forego customary practices because he realized he needed someone who knew a great deal about computers—and Beth Simmons met that criterion. She had been an elementary principal in another state for 14 years. Like Nick, she was outgoing and related well to other people.

Although Beth understood the community of Webster Township, she found life in the school district to be a bit of a culture shock. Her experiences as a teacher and a principal took place in affluent suburban communities. Many of her peer administrators were "upward mobiles" who were either going to graduate school to complete advanced degrees or seeking higher-level jobs. This certainly was not the case in Webster Township. Here most administrators showed little interest in either advanced degrees or in leaving the school district.

As Beth developed a comprehensive technology plan for the district, she also discovered that most principals had little or no knowledge about using computers. When she raised this issue with them, they generally showed no interest in becoming better informed. One principal told her, "Hey, I'm no young teacher. I'm too old to learn new tricks. In 5 or 6 years, I'm out of here. That's why we hired you. I think these computers are a good idea—but probably not for me. Anything you need with respect to implementing the plan, you just ask. But don't ask me to start messing around with a computer after all these years."

The behavior of the principals caused Beth to explore the use of computers in the central office. Outside of the business office, the only persons using computers were the secretaries. Neither the superintendent nor the assistant superintendent for personnel had a computer.

Beth did not expect Webster Township to be on the cutting edge of educational innovation, but neither did she anticipate that the district would be in the dark ages. The absence of technology prompted her to examine the whole issue of professional development—especially as it related to the administrators. What were they doing to remain current? What types of learning experiences were they having? Travel records showed that virtually all of the principals had attended the state and national meetings of their respective principals' associations in the past 2 years. Several also attended workshops sponsored by the state department of education. Superintendent Jordan, however, had restricted his activities to one annual event—the national meeting for school board members. Each year he and the five board members attended. Beth found the lack of professional development to be especially troublesome, since a major part of her job was to enhance instructional leadership roles. She decided to discuss the matter with the superintendent.

After listening to her concerns about the apparent indifference to technology and professional development in the district, Nick responded. "Beth, there are two kinds of people in this world. Those with 'street smarts' and those without 'street smarts.' To survive in this business, you had better be in the first group. I learned a long time ago that being a superintendent is largely a matter of being an effective politician. You don't learn this role in a college classroom or a seminar at Lake Tahoe—at least I didn't. I learned it by getting my hands dirty; by dealing with real people and real problems. Now don't get me wrong, not all of us have to be dealing with conflict and putting out fires. Schools also need people like you. You have special knowledge and skills that our teachers and students need—skills that many of us do not have. But don't assume that principals are incompetent because they don't want to go back to school or because they are not excited about having to learn to use a computer."

Beth argued that all administrators had a responsibility to grow professionally. "I don't know how principals can be effective instructional leaders if they are not modeling what they preach," she told the superintendent. "Every administrator ought to be committed to learning new things, to keeping current in the profession. I realize there is a lot of politics in administration—but there is more than politics."

But Nick was not swayed. "If you want to know how our principals are doing," he told her, "ask the parents—or ask the school board members. In this district, a principal who gets in trouble with parents or board members is not likely to be around very long. No, you shouldn't worry about our principals. Start worrying when they refuse to help you put your plans into effect. Then come and see me, and we will twist a few arms. But don't be concerned because a principal isn't working on a doctoral degree or trying to move to a better job."

Beth returned to her office in disbelief. How could she work to improve instructional programs if the superintendent and principals had so little interest in what she was doing? How could she work in a culture where leaders did not see a need to be lifelong learners?

Issues for Discussion

1. How would you characterize the leadership style of Nick Jordan?

2. To what extent does the community environment contribute to Mr. Jordan's behavior?

3. What do you think the principal meant when he told Dr. Simmons, " . . . that's why we hired a person like you"?

4. Is Dr. Simmons correct in her assertion that the principals cannot be effective instructional leaders if they are not models for effective learning?

5. Many observers would argue that Nick Jordan is a highly effective superintendent. The school board is happy, and most patrons are happy. Do you think he is effective?

6. What steps might Dr. Simmons take to change the attitudes of principals toward professional development?

7. Nick Jordan is described in the case as a tough, but consistent, administrator. Many employees prefer consistent behavior from their leaders. To what extent do you consider consistency to be an asset? A liability?

8. In what ways does the superintendent's personal attitudes and behavior affect other administrators in the district?

9. What is an "upward mobile"? Are these types of administrators more inclined to engage in professional development?

10. Does Superintendent Jordan have a grasp of both the ideal and real roles associated with his position?

REFERENCES

Argyris, C., & Schön, D. A. (1974). *Theory in practice: Increasing professional effectiveness*. San Francisco: Jossey-Bass.

Baird, C. I. (1989). *Managerial decisions under uncertainty*. New York: John Wiley & Sons.

Blanchard, K. H., & Peale, N. V. (1988). *The power of ethical management*. New York: W. Morrow.

Blumberg, A. (1989). *Administration as a craft: Foundations of practice*. Boston: Allyn and Bacon.

Bolman, L. G., & Deal, T. E. (1992). Everyday epistemology in school leadership: Patterns and prospects. In P. Hallinger, K. Leithwood, & J. Murphy (Eds.), *Cognitive perspective on educational leadership* (pp. 21–33). New York: Teachers College Press.

Bradley, M. K., Kallick, B. O., & Regan, H. B. (1991). *The staff development manager: A guide to professional growth*. Boston: Allyn and Bacon.

Browne, M. (1993). *Organizational decision making and information*. Norwood, NJ: Ablex.

Cohen, M. D., March, J. G., & Olsen, J. P. (1972). A garbage can model of organizational choice. *Administrative Science Quarterly, 7*(1), 1–25.

Daresh, J. C., & Playko, M. A. (1992). *Aspiring administrators' perceptions of the superintendency as a viable career choice*. (ERIC Document Reproduction Service No. ED 346 564)

English, F. W., Frase, L. E., & Arhar, J. M. (1992). *Leading into the 21st century.* Newbury Park, CA: Corwin Press.

Erlandson, D. A. (1992). The power of context. *Journal of School Leadership, 2*(1), 66–74.

Estler, S. (1988). Decision-making. In N. Boyan (Ed.), *Handbook of research in educational administration* (pp. 305–319). New York: Longman.

Giesecke, J. (1993). Recognizing multiple decision-making models: A guide for managers. *College & Research Libraries, 54*(2), 103–114.

Goldhammer, K. (1983). Evolution in the profession. *Educational Administration Quarterly, 19*(3), 249–272.

Griffin, G. A. (1983). *Staff development: Eighty-second yearbook of the National Society for the Study of Education* (part 2). Chicago: University of Chicago Press.

Griffiths, D. E. (1959). *Administrative theory.* New York: Appleton-Century-Crofts.

Hallinger, P., & Murphy, J. (1991). Developing leaders for tomorrow's schools. *Phi Delta Kappan, 72*(7), (514–520).

Hanson, E. M. (1996). *Educational administration and organizational behavior* (4th ed.). Boston: Allyn and Bacon.

Hart, A. W. (1993). Reflection: An instructional strategy in educational administration. *Educational Administration Quarterly, 29*(3), 339–363.

Hellreigel, D., & Slocum, J. W. (1996). *Management* (7th ed.). Cincinnati, OH: South-Western College Publishing.

Hitt, W. D. (1990). *Ethics and leadership: Putting theory into practice.* Columbus, OH: Battelle Press.

Ivancevich, J. M., & Matteson, M. T. *Organizational behavior and management* (4th ed.) Chicago: Irwin.

Kolb, D. A. (1984). *Experiential learning: Experience as the source of learning and development.* Upper Saddle River, NJ: Prentice Hall.

Kowalski, T. J., & Reitzug, U. C. (1993). *Contemporary school administration: An introduction.* New York: Longman.

Levine, S. L., Barth, R. S., & Hanskins, K. W. (1987). The Harvard Principals' Center: School leaders as adult learners. In J. Murphy & P. Hallinger (Eds.), *Approaches to administrative training in education* (pp. 150–163). Albany, NY: SUNY Press.

McGrath, S. T. (1992). Here come the women! *Educational Leadership, 49*(5), 62–65.

Murphy, J., & Hallinger, P. (1987). New directions in the professional development of school administrators: A synthesis and suggestions for improvement. In J. Murphy & P. Hallinger (Eds.), *Approaches to administrative training in education* (pp. 245–282). Albany, NY: SUNY Press.

Murray, M. A. (1986). *Decisions: A comparative critique.* Marshfield, MA: Pitman.

Ohde, K. L., & Murphy, J. (1993). The development of expertise: Implications for school administrators. In P. Hallinger, K. Leithwood, & J. Murphy (Eds.), *Cognitive perspective on educational leadership* (pp. 75–87). New York: Teachers College Press.

Ohliger, J. (1981). Dialogue on mandatory continuing education. *Lifelong Learning: The Adult Years, 4*(10), 24–26.

Osterman, K. F., & Kottkamp, R. B. (1993). *Reflective practice for educators: Improving schooling through professional development.* Newbury Park, CA: Corwin Press.

Owens, R. G. (1998). *Organizational behavior in education* (6th ed.). Boston: Allyn and Bacon.

Pitner, N. J. (1987). Principles of quality staff development: Lessons for administrator training. In J. Murphy & P. Hallinger (Eds.), *Approaches to administrative training in education* (pp. 28–44). Albany, NY: SUNY Press.

Razik, T. A., & Swanson, A. D. (1995). *Fundamental concepts of educational leadership and management.* Upper Saddle River, NJ: Merrill/Prentice Hall.

Robbins, S. P. (1998). *Organizational behavior: Concepts, controversies, applications* (8th ed.). Upper Saddle River, NJ: Prentice Hall.

Sarason, S. (1996). *Revisiting "The culture of the school and the problems of change."* New York: Teachers College Press.

Schmuck, P. A. (1986). Networking: A new word, a different game. *Educational Leadership, 43*(5), 60–61.

Schön, D. A. (1983). *The reflective practitioner.* New York: Basic Books.

Schön, D. A. (1990). *Educating the reflective practitioner.* San Francisco: Jossey-Bass.

Sergiovanni, T. J., Burlingame, M., Coombs, F. S., & Thurston, P. W. (1992). *Educational governance and administration* (3rd ed.). Boston: Allyn and Bacon.

Sergiovanni, T. J., & Carver, F. D. (1980). *The new school executive: A theory of administration* (2nd ed.). New York: Harper & Row.

Sharman, C. S. (1984). *Decision making in educational settings.* (Phi Delta Kappa Fastback No. 211). Bloomington, IN: Phi Delta Kappa Educational Foundation.

Shelton, M. M., & Herman, J. J. (1993). Mentoring and shadow consulting: Keys to enhancing novice and veteran school administrator training. *Journal of School Leadership, 3*(6), 666–678.

Simon, H. A. (1970). *The new science of management decisions.* New York: Harper & Row.

Simon, H. A. (1976). *Administrative behavior.* New York: The Free Press.

Simon, H. A. (1993). Decision making: Rational, nonrational, and irrational. *Educational Administration Quarterly, 29,* 392–411.

Simon, H. A. (1997). *Administrative behavior: A study of decision-making processes in administrative organizations* (4th ed.). New York: The Free Press.

Starratt, R. J. (1991). Building an ethical school: A theory for practice in educational administration. *Educational Administration Quarterly, 27*(2), 185–202.

Tallman, I., & Gray, L. N. (1990). Choices, decisions and problem solving. In W. R. School & J. Staw (Eds.), *Annual Review of Sociology* (Vol. 16) (pp. 405–433). Palo Alto, CA: Annual Reviews.

Tanner, C. K., & Williams, E. J. (1981). *Educational planning and decision making: A view through the organizational process.* Lexington, MA: D. C. Heath and Company.

Torres, D. L. (1991). What, if anything, is professionalism?: Institutions and the problem of change. *Research in the Sociology of Organizations, 8,* 43–68.

Unikel, B. W., & Bailey, M. A. (1986). A place where principals can learn. *Principal, 65*(5), 36–39.

Valli, L. (1992). Beginning teacher problems: Areas for teacher education improvement. *Action in Teacher Education 14*(1), 18–25.

Wendel, F. C., Hoke, F. A., & Joekel, R. G. (1996*). Outstanding school administrators: Their keys to success.* Westport, CT: Praeger.

Wilmore, B. E., & Erlandson, D. A. (1993). Planning for professional growth: A process for administrators. *NASSP Bulletin, 77*(551), 57–63.

Zey, M. (1992). *Decision making: Alternatives to rational choice models.* Newbury Park, CA: Sage.

Chapter 14

Becoming a Superintendent

Key Concepts

✧ Selection process for superintendents

✧ School boards working without professional assistants

✧ Search consultants

✧ Considerations before applying for a superintendency

✧ Making an application

✧ Interviewing

✧ Negotiating an employment contract

✧ Importance of career planning

✧ Characteristics of an effective career plan

✧ Building a personal career plan

✧ Special importance of career planning for women and minorities

This final chapter explores four practical issues related to becoming a superintendent. All pertain to matters associated with employment in this position. The first focuses on the common procedures used by school boards to secure a new superintendent; the second examines the value of career plans; the third explores suggested actions for applicants to the superintendency; the fourth pertains to developing a comprehensive and worthwhile employment contract. Individuals aspiring to become superintendents usually have not been prepared to deal with aspects of employment that are essentially unique to the superintendency (Hess, 1989). For example, teachers and administrators in lower-level positions rarely have had interviews with school board members; having to negotiate a contract outside of established salary schedules and union contracts also may be a new experience for them.

A lack of preparedness usually means that first-time applicants have a large number of questions. What should be submitted in the written application? Should school board members be contacted? Is it appropriate to apply for several jobs at the same time? How is the employment contract determined? Unready candidates are either forced to rely on trial and error or to seek counsel from someone more experienced. A lack of information about employment at this critical career point can produce anxiety, and in some instances, it may even cause a person to not apply. In an effort to overcome such problems, this chapter addresses fundamental issues about superintendent selection and concludes with several considerations related to individual career planning.

SUPERINTENDENT SELECTION

Selecting a superintendent is arguably the most important task a school board must perform (Hord & Estes, 1993). In most instances, it is the only time the school board directly controls and executes the recruitment, screening, and selection of an employee. For all other positions, the school district administration exercises these responsibilities (although in some smaller school districts, applicants for professional positions may have to have an interview with school board members). This fact is noteworthy for several reasons. Many board members are inexperienced in employment and personnel administration; many have had no previous experience employing a superintendent. In most states, there is no "common practice" or required procedure that provides boards with a trustworthy method for completing this responsibility. In those cases, boards usually devise their own approach or retain a consultant to advise them. Some choose to involve employees and community representatives on search committees; some insist on public forums allowing any interested party to pose questions to the candidates; some operate in a highly secretive manner with no input or involvement from others.

Scope of Participation

Probably the two most essential decisions school boards make in connection with superintendent searches are their answers to the following two questions: Should the board retain a consultant or search firm to assist with the process? To what extent should school district employees or patrons be involved in the process?

For varying reasons, many school boards opt not to use search consultants. This decision may be based on factors such as finances (e.g., the services are seen as too costly), politics (e.g., taxpayers may resent expenditures for this purpose), self-interests (e.g., board members do not want to share power), negative experiences (e.g., previous experiences with such consultants were unsatisfactory), a perceived conflict of interest (e.g., a feeling that consultants are biased toward certain candidates), a lack of information (e.g., the board does not know that such consultants are available or they are unaware of the nature of services they provide), and a fear of relinquishing authority (e.g., the consultant, and not the board, will select the superintendent). When school boards decide to employ a superintendent without professional assistance, the level of uncertainty for applicants is likely to increase. This is because search consultants tend to follow established patterns and techniques, and they are skilled at preparing vacancy notices and application materials that provide adequate information to potential applicants.

Criteria for superintendent searches are often influenced by a board's experience with the departing superintendent. If he or she is admired and respected, the board may be seeking a clone. In other situations, especially those involving dismissals, the board often pursues candidates whose strengths compensate for the previous superintendent's weaknesses (Johnson, 1996). This tendency also may influence critical decisions about conducting the search. If board members were pleased with the outgoing superintendent, they are likely to repeat the search procedures that were used to hire that individual.

Some school boards are highly effective conducting searches on their own, but others may lose their way because they lack a coherent plan. For example, board members may start a search without having reached consensus about the type of superintendent needed. As the process progresses, they rely on their personal biases and general perceptions rather than on relevant and specific criteria accepted by the entire board. Conflict among board members becomes probable in such situations. Critical tasks that boards may ignore include these:

- Conducting a needs assessment related to the position
- Adequately preparing vacancy notices, brochures, and so on
- Developing an advertising strategy
- Specifying how applications and contacts will be handled
- Determining parameters for the employment contract (e.g., salary range)
- Setting time lines for the selection process
- Determining who will be involved in the search and selection activities

Failure to address any one of these tasks diminishes the effectiveness of a search.

Unfortunately, only a limited number of studies have examined variables that influence school boards when they select superintendents. One such study conducted in Missouri found that candidates' self-presentation skills, the candidates' backgrounds as confirmed by references, and the candidates' interests in student achievement and district educational effectiveness were the three most influential factors (Anderson & Lavid, 1985). Reviewing research in this area, Erwin Miklos (1988) identified the following attributes in candidates as potential influences: character, judgment, personality, physical and mental health, intelligence, sense of humor, open-mindedness, voice, and cultural background. Advanced degrees, especially a doctorate, is another factor that may carry considerable weight in certain situations (Hord & Estes, 1993). The extent to which any of these attributes may affect board decisions is especially unpredictable when the board has not specified selection criteria.

Boards also exhibit considerable variance with regard to involving others in the search process. Some districts have relied on special search committees made up of various segments of the school community; other districts have required final candidates to appear at public forums to state their philosophy and answer questions; and still other districts continue to restrict involvement in the superintendent search to school board members. The board's decision on who is involved in the selection process provides a clear example of a board's philosophy toward governance and decision making; however, it may also reflect a board's interpretation of an outstanding need. Widespread displeasure with the departing superintendent also may encourage a board to broaden involvement as a way to mollify critics in the community.

Search Consultants

Since the early 1980s, there has been a definite trend toward using professional consultants to assist school boards with superintendent searches. At least six conditions have been responsible:

1. Many school boards lack in-house expertise in this area.
2. Some boards have been criticized for previous searches.
3. Superintendent searches can consume an inordinate amount of time.
4. There are many legal and political issues that surround employment searches of this nature.
5. There is a desire to recruit a large number of outstanding applications.
6. There is reason to believe that the applicant pool will be unusually small unless a concerted effort is made to advertise the position and solicit applications.

Consultants may provide the following services:

- Helping the board to reach consensus on selection criteria
- Helping the board to devise a master plan for the search
- Preparing promotional materials including vacancy announcements and brochures

- Contacting qualified applicants
- Answering questions posed by applicants
- Communicating with potential applicants
- Assessing and screening applicants
- Checking on credentials and references
- Conducting or assisting with initial interviews
- Advising the board on contract negotiations
- Advising the board on procedural matters

More generally, consultant duties can be placed in three primary categories: (1) helping to secure candidates, (2) helping to screen candidates, and (3) helping to employ the right candidate.

Because a primary responsibility of search consultants is to identify potential candidates, it can be a major advantage for those aspiring to the superintendency to become acquainted with such consultants. Often these individuals attend state and national meetings for school administrators expressly for the purpose of meeting individuals who want to become superintendents.

The cost for consultant services can range from the reimbursement of expenses to well over $50,000. Many communities balk at higher fees because there is a common perception that there are a large number of qualified candidates chomping at the bit to become superintendents (a perception that is increasingly untrue in many parts of the country). Cost often reflects the complexity and size of a school district as well as the consultant's established record (Zakariya, 1987). Consultants often build their reputation on their ability to place impressive, highly qualified candidates before a school board. Thus, a consultant's networks and reputation within the profession are critical issues.

Consultant services can be obtained from universities, private firms, or from associations. Within the university category, two types of consultant services for superintendent searches may be available. The first involves professors who function as independent consultants. These providers compete directly with private consultants; in some instances, professors may be affiliated with private search firms. The second entails assistance provided by university employees as part of a general service to school systems. In Indiana and Michigan, for example, several state universities have made consultants available either at a very low cost or on an expenses-only basis. This type of assistance has come under increased scrutiny because of concerns for potential conflicts (e.g., Will a university promote the interests of its graduates while at the same time assisting school districts with recruitment and screening?).

The use of private search firms has escalated markedly over the past several decades. Many are operated by retired superintendents who have established a national network of contacts. More recently two of the nation's largest executive recruiting firms—Korn/Ferry International and Heidrick and Struggles—have become active in this segment of the market ("Meet the Power Brokers," 1994). Private firms usually operate on a national basis, and for school boards seeking a large pool of candidates with varied experiences, this is often seen as a distinct advantage.

Search consultants are also provided through associations, with the most common provider being state school board associations. In the early 1990s, 39 state school board associations were offering consultant services in this area ("Meet the Power Brokers," 1994). There are several variations on the kinds of services provided by these associations. In many instances, a single consultant is assigned to work with a school district; in other instances, a team of consultants is provided. The Illinois School Board Association, for example, has mostly used the latter approach (e.g., a team of consultants consisting of a superintendent from another school district, a school board member from another school district, a professor, and an association staff member).

PURSUING ONE'S FIRST SUPERINTENDENCY

Long-time superintendent, Peter Negroni (1992), observed, " . . . landing that first superintendency takes special job-search and interviewing skills, and effectively launching it requires some clear-headed strategies" (p. 21). However, as noted earlier, many who reach this point in their careers have not been adequately prepared for the challenge. As such, they enter the process with limited insights—or even worse, with incorrect information. This is unfortunate, because substantial risk is involved. For example, many applicants are successful assistant superintendents or principals, and they should not blindly accept a superintendency that offers little opportunity for success or personal growth. Risk is reduced when they seek accurate information and make efforts to plan at each stage of the application and selection process.

Before Applying

Deciding to apply for a superintendency can be an anxiety-producing experience. At first glance, many jobs are attractive. However, the cautious individual seeks to gather information prior to making application. Both the location of the school district and its prevailing needs and problems become fundamental considerations. Being impetuous can result in several different types of problems. One problem is wasting time and energy. The applicant's references and officials in the employing district may needlessly spend time and resources if the applicant withdraws from the search. Another issue involves the individual's reputation. The behavior of administrators who continuously withdraw applications does not go unobserved. University personnel, references, and search consultants may become reluctant to take a person with this reputation seriously when he or she applies for jobs in the future.

The decision to make an application should be based on an objective analysis of prevailing conditions. Among the questions that potential applicants should ask and answer are the following:

- *Am I ready?* Completing academic work and receiving a license do not ensure that a person feels confident about entering the superintendency. The entire scope of one's education and professional experiences needs to be weighed. Readiness is an issue that every individual should thoroughly assess before making an application.

- *Do I have sufficient information about the job?* It is imprudent to apply for a superintendency without having any background information about the community, the school district, and the position. This includes knowing the types of personal and professional characteristics the board may be seeking, the potential salary range for the job, and the strengths and weaknesses of the district. All too often, school boards use boilerplate announcements rather than providing specific information. Thus, candidates should not assume that vacancy announcements provide accurate or sufficient data.

- *Are there personal or family considerations that prevent me from accepting the position?* On occasion, individuals apply for positions without having considered how accepting the job would affect their personal or family life. In situations where family relocation is a potential problem, the location of the school district can be a significant factor in decisions about applying.

- *Will being an applicant affect my current position?* In some instances, employers react negatively when they discover that a person is seeking to move. Today the chances of keeping an application completely confidential are minimal. Thus, an individual needs to consider prior to making an application the potential ramifications if his or her employer learns about the job search.

- *Do I have sufficient information about the search and selection processes?* Before making an application, a person should know how the search will be conducted. For example, the applicant should know precisely what materials must be forwarded; the applicant should know whether references may be contacted without his or her being specifically informed.

- *Can I be competitive?* Self-confidence is extremely important. When a candidate feels that there is no chance of being successful, he or she is apt to behave accordingly. On the other hand, a false sense of confidence also can be troublesome. For example, a person applies for a superintendency, even though he or she does not meet the specified criteria; the belief is that other assets, such as personality or political contacts, will compensate for lack of qualifications.

- *Do personal strengths match school district needs?* In most school districts, the issues of the day play an influential role in superintendent selection decisions (Johnson, 1996). Knowing these issues allows an applicant to determine if personal strengths match the needs of the district. For example, a person who is very good at promoting change probably should not apply for a position in a district where the board is seeking stability.

- *How can I get additional information?* If there are information gaps, the applicant should know how to secure answers to relevant questions. Typically this can be accomplished by communicating with the official contact person (e.g., consultant or board member). If a contact person is not designated, the inquiries should be directed to the school board president.

At an early stage in a superintendent search, the applicant needs to answer all these questions. In certain situations, the applicant may not be able to cover all of these matters prior to making an application (e.g., time lines may prevent extensive data gathering). However, personally and professionally, it is best for an applicant to have as much information as possible as soon as possible.

The decision to become an applicant becomes clearer when data about the school district are related to personal information. Studying first-year superintendents, Susan Moore Johnson (1996) identified key issues that often guide selection committee decisions:

- How a candidate makes the members of the search committee feel about themselves
- The sufficiency of a candidate's intelligence, knowledge, and experience
- The candidate's personal appearance and communication skills
- The candidate's human relations skills
- The candidate's other personal attributes (e.g., health, toughness, stamina, courage, compassion)

In essence, making the decision to apply involves introspection to determine if the school district's needs and wants and the general conditions of the job are consistent with one's strengths and interests.

Making an Application

The importance of application materials is obvious. Unless the applicant is well known to the persons who complete the paper screening (that is, the review of written application materials), he or she could be eliminated quickly if the application materials submitted are sloppy, inaccurate, or incomplete. A vita and letters of application provide a first impression; they are indicators of one's organizational abilities and communication skills (Cummings, 1994). Likewise, skilled screeners can usually detect boilerplate letters of application. It is best to give careful thought to personalize materials to a specific vacancy; this shows one's enthusiasm for pursuing the position.

The vita should be concise, yet provide the necessary information about one's education and professional experiences. Most of all, it should be accurate and neat. If a reviewer finds an error or incorrect statement, it can totally destroy an applicant's credibility; a vita with a coffee stain may cause the reader to have an immediate negative reaction. While most search committees probably do not want to read 40-page documents filled with rather insignificant information, the vita should be comprehensive enough to exhibit the applicant's readiness for the position. Especially those seeking a first superintendency should be prepared to demonstrate how personal experiences and educational background constitute sufficient qualifications (Negroni, 1992).

Selecting references is also an important decision. It is generally best to choose persons in the profession because they are most able to comment on a person's ability to become a superintendent. This might include present or former professors, professional peers, past and present supervisors, or school board members. A person should never be listed as a reference unless he or she has agreed to provide this service. Search committees almost always become concerned if there are no references from individuals with whom a candidate currently works. If such references are not included (e.g., for reasons of confidentiality), it is beneficial to explain the omission. Search committee members also become suspicious if all or most of the references are from persons outside the profession (e.g., character references from ministers, elected officials, family members). Also, it is necessary to provide accurate information that allows those reviewing the vita to contact references (telephone numbers, addresses). If applicants are instructed to obtain letters of reference, it may be necessary to ask one's references to write original letters. Search committees are likely to be unimpressed with generic letters that begin "To Whom It May Concern."

After Applying

In some situations, especially those involving search consultants, preliminary interviews may be conducted with as many as 10 to 15 applicants. These encounters are usually conducted via telephone, but some are done face to face. Several search firms, for instance, tend to hold these interviews at airport hotels, allowing candidates to fly in and out in the same day. Preliminary interviews are often conducted because the consultant does not know the candidate. Other purposes may include (1) clarifying information supplied by the applicant; (2) getting additional information from the applicant; (3) evaluating communication skills; (4) checking on personal characteristics (e.g., sense of humor); (5) determining the extent of commitment with respect to the job in question; and (6) discussing specific problems or needs to determine if the candidate feels up to the task.

As part of the paper screening process, members of the search committee are likely to contact references. Information pertaining to the search process may not clearly state whether this will be done automatically or whether the candidates will be notified prior to such action. In the absence of this information, one should assume that it will be done. If a school board promises confidentiality, this message is usually overtly stated in search materials. In situations where this assurance exists, search committee members have an ethical obligation to seek the applicant's permission before contacting references. In some instances, contacts may be made with persons who are not listed as references (e.g., a school board member in the district where an applicant currently works). This may occur and the candidate never discovers that fact. Misunderstandings over such situations are best avoided by inquiring initially if the search committee or consultant intends to pursue information from persons other than references.

In addition to preliminary interviews, face-to-face encounters with school board members and search committees often occur in two stages. The first interviews are held with a select number of semifinalists, maybe as many as 7 or 8 applicants. After these sessions, the field of applicants is narrowed to several finalists. These finalists are then invited to have a second interview. In some school districts, however, the school board may decide to have only one round of interviews with a select number of finalists.

Every semifinalist has some qualities that are attractive to the school district. Hence, the purpose of the interview is to gain information not available through the written application materials. Personal appearance, poise, confidence, and personality are scrutinized. The following are helpful guidelines in preparing for an interview:

- *Look and act like a professional.* While community standards obviously vary, most board members recognize that a superintendent serves as the official representative of the school system. Dress, mannerisms, and social skills will be closely observed (Pigford, 1995).

- *Arrive on time.* Being late for an interview can be devastating because it can be interpreted in many ways—all of which are detrimental to the candidate (Davis & Brown, 1992). It is advisable to arrive for an interview 10 or 15 minutes before the scheduled time.

- *Be informed about the school district and the community.* Most school board members will be impressed by candidates who have taken the time to learn about the school district and community prior to the interview. Comments and questions should reflect the candidate's interest in studying relevant educational and management issues (Cummings, 1994).

- *Exhibit your communication skills.* Interviewer perceptions are influenced by both verbal and nonverbal behaviors. Here are some good rules: maintain eye contact when speaking or listening; avoid using jargon that may not be understood. Provide concise answers to questions, and do not attempt to dominate the discussion (Davis & Brown, 1992).

- *Be prepared to ask questions.* Almost always, candidates are given an opportunity to ask questions. The time to think about this is before the interview. Not asking questions or asking irrelevant questions may detract from overall performance (Steele & Morgan, 1991). The best questions are genuine, reflecting a need or desire to obtain certain information.

- *Show respect for the interviewers.* The candidate is a guest, and proper respect should be given to the school board members or other persons who are a part of the interview process. Candidates should be courteous and polite at all times (Pigford, 1995).

- *Think before you answer questions.* Simply shooting from the hip is not a good idea. Candidates need to think about the message they want to give and the impression they want to leave. Answers should be "long enough to cover the subject, but short enough to hold interest" (Cummings, 1994, p. 35).

- *Follow directions.* Most interviewers do not expect the interviewee to control the encounter. Rather, they may be observing the degree to which the person is able to listen and follow instructions (Davis & Brown, 1992).

- *Be prepared to discuss your strengths.* In many interviews, the interviewee is asked to identify his or her strengths and weaknesses. This too is an issue that should be considered prior to the interview. While discussing special talents and accomplishments is advantageous, some veteran superintendents believe that it is self-defeating to list one's own shortcomings (e.g., Cattanach, 1996). Simply ignoring a request to cite one's weaknesses, however, is not judicious; some candidates gracefully avoid answering the question by suggesting that others may be more objective sources of information.

- *Seek to determine if the board's philosophy is compatible with your personal philosophy.* The interview should be a two-way communication experience. It is possibly the only time during which the candidate can assess the compatibility of his or her values and beliefs with those of the board.

- *Attempt to evaluate the school board's performance.* The interview also is an opportunity for the candidate to assess the board's behavior. Most administrators do not want to work for a board that is (1) consistently divided, (2) close-minded, and (3) indifferent to distinctions between policy making and administration (Freund, 1987).

Regardless of the final outcome, it is advisable for an applicant to seek feedback on his or her performance during the interview. This often is easier to do when a search consultant is involved. Without this information, it is difficult for the applicant to benefit from the experience (Underwood, 1994).

If a candidate becomes a finalist, he or she can expect that the school board will look even more closely at current job performance. In many instances, board members visit the community in which the applicant is currently working. At this point, confidentiality is virtually impossible. This is the time when the applicant should also be engaging in information gathering. More precise information about the community, school district needs, financial conditions, and so on allows the person to make an enlightened decision if the position is offered.

Negotiating a Contract

Standardized contracts are the norm for teachers and most administrators, but not for superintendents. Individually designed and negotiated agreements between a school board and superintendent take many different forms and reflect substantial variance with regard to scope.

Superintendents' contracts differ from teacher contracts in that they typically span 3 or more years as length of employment and address issues that are not standard for other school district employees (e.g., a unique fringe benefit package). The document may also include provisions for evaluation, renewal, and dismissal. Many individuals who are about to enter their first superintendency have probably never had to negotiate specific terms of employment. For these individuals, the prospect of having to bargain with the board president or board's attorney can be intimidating; some simply accept what is offered. Veteran superintendent Robert Freeman (1985) believes that superintendents simply cannot afford to be timid when it comes to their own contracts—the stakes are too high. The initial contract is especially crucial because it is likely to have limiting implications on future contracts (O'Hara, 1994).

Some superintendents approach contract negotiations by retaining an attorney or consultant to act on their behalf. This allows the superintendent to influence decisions without risking face-to-face disagreements with school board members. If a superintendent is contemplating this alternative, he or she should consider several essential questions:

1. *How will the school board react?* Not all communities are likely to look favorably on a superintendent having an agent—especially if the superintendent is a neophyte who has yet to establish a record of successful practice in the position.

2. *What specific objectives will be served by having an agent?* Since there is cost involved, the administrator should know the potential gains—and a cost-benefit analysis should be completed.

3. *Is the agent the right person for the job?* While attorneys understand the legalities of structuring a written contract, not all are familiar with conditions in the superintendency. If an agent does not have this background, the administrator needs to spend considerable time discussing issues with this person prior to the negotiating process.

In most situations, though, the administrator negotiates his or her own contract. And when this is done, two errors should be avoided. First, it is not prudent for an administrator to accept what is offered on the spot. A person may be so anxious to become a superintendent that he or she immediately agrees to the school board's offer. Even if the package is extremely favorable, the contract may not address critical issues such as performance evaluation and dismissal. Or the board's offer may be composed of inflexible or unreasonable provisions. A board that is rigid and inconsiderate with respect to the employment contract may be conveying an important message about its philosophy. Some superintendents fail to heed such obvious warning signs, believing that the board will change over time (O'Hara, 1994). Second, it is not prudent to begin discussions about a contract without having done some preliminary planning. There are too many issues that can be overlooked—issues such as the salaries of other employees or common provisions in superintendent contracts in that state. The process of arriving at the contract is a significant starting point in the relationship between a school board and superintendent (O'Hara, 1994).

Scope

Standardized superintendent contracts or contracts from neighboring school districts often provide a good starting point for planning a specific document (Clark, 1983). In several states, superintendents and all other administrators are required to have a standard teacher's contract, but this does not mean that a contract addendum cannot be negotiated. Table 14–1 contains a list of possible clauses that may become subjects for negotiation in a superintendent's contract. All provisions of a contract must be in compliance with federal and state laws. State statutes usually affect the possible length of a contract, tenure, provisions for dismissal, licensing, and general responsibilities. In some states, laws also address ceilings on compensation and permissible fringe benefits.

Fringe benefit clauses may include many different items. In some districts, school boards may insist that superintendents only receive the benefits given to all other professional employees. From a national perspective, this practice is the exception. There are many possible fringe benefits that end up being placed in contracts. They are shown in Figure 14–1. Typically, superintendents attempt to negotiate as many of them as possible. Since boards may not be willing to agree to all of these benefits, it is advisable for an administrator to have a priority list when negotiating a contract.

Performance Evaluation

School boards have the challenge of evaluating both the superintendent's competence and his or her job performance (Genck & Klingenberg, 1991). It is difficult to meet this responsibility without a formal evaluation plan (Candoli, Cullen, & Stufflebeam, 1994). Ideally, all performance evaluations in education should serve both a formative and summative purpose. In addition to the obvious objective of assessing job performance and identifying possible areas of improvement, performance evaluation often opens communications between the board and superintendent. In some states, boards are required to complete an annual evaluation of the superintendent.

The most opportune time to discuss performance evaluation is at the time the board is attempting to employ a superintendent (Redfern, 1980). Why? There are several reasons.

First, studies conducted in various states show that somewhere between one third and one tenth of the superintendents do not receive any type of annual evaluation. Given that many problems that occur between superintendents and boards are political, having a performance evaluation is generally in the best interests of the administrator. Board members are more likely to focus on actual behaviors rather than biases, personal dislikes, or interpersonal conflict.

Table 14–1
Possible provisions in a superintendent's contract

Provision	Purpose
Term	Identifies the beginning and ending dates of the contract. (Superintendent contracts vary from 1 year to as many as 10 years; state laws may restrict this provision.)
Licensure and certification	Identifies the required license or certification that must be held by the superintendent for the contract to be valid.
Renewal	Specifies the terms under which the contract may be or must be renewed. (Some multi-year contracts contain provisions for automatic renewal each year. For example, a superintendent's 3-year contract is automatically extended for an additional year if the board does not vote to do otherwise by a specified date; hence, without board action, the superintendent always has a 3-year contract. This type of provision is often called a "rollover clause" or "evergreen clause.")
Salary	Establishes actual amount of compensation and method of payment—does not include fringe benefits.
Responsibilities	Details the specific responsibilities of the superintendency in that school district.
Contract termination	Specifies the conditions under which the contract may be terminated. (In some instances, school boards insist on language that specifies how either party may terminate the contract.)
Termination compensation	Specifies whether a superintendent is entitled to special compensation if he or she is terminated. (Such provisions provide severance pay; they are often called "golden parachutes.")
Professional growth	Identifies expectations and support for professional growth (e.g., attending workshops, national conferences).
Outside activities	Specifies conditions under which a superintendent may assume responsibilities not directly related to employment with the school district (e.g., working as a consultant, teaching a university class, serving on a board of directors).
Fringe benefits	Identifies benefits in addition to base salary. (Both vacation days and provisions for reimbursing the superintendent for job-related expenses may be placed in this clause.)
Personal protection	Relates to issues of protection in areas of professional and civil liability. (Comprehensive liability coverage does not include errors and omissions, and such protection is advisable [Clark, 1983].)
Retirement	Specifies conditions pertaining to the superintendent retiring (e.g., amount of notice that must be given). (Many superintendents have retirement provisions that exceed those granted to other district employees. This matter may be addressed in a retirement clause or under fringe benefits.)
Evaluation	Identifies the process for formally evaluating the superintendent and time lines for completing this responsibility.
Savings	Protects the contract from being invalidated if one clause or provision is found to be in violation of federal or state law.

Indirect Compensation

- Annuities, tax shelters (deferred income)
- Automobile (either unrestricted use or business only)
- Expense allowance (either reimbursement rates or an annual or monthly allowance)
- Professional dues/memberships
- Relocation costs (reimbursement for costs associated with relocating to accept the job)
- Retirement payments (includes state programs and other special provisions)

Insurance (any provisions beyond the regular employee program)

- Disability
- Health
- Liability
- Life

Leaves

- Bereavement
- Illness-related (days per year, accumulation provisions)
- Personal (days per year, accumulation provisions)
- Professional (sabbatical, consulting time)
- Vacation (days per year, accumulation provisions)

Figure 14–1
Common fringe benefits for superintendents

Second, performance evaluation can be conducted in many different ways. A superintendent ought to be more knowledgeable than board members about the process. By negotiating the procedures into the employment contract (or as an addendum to the contract), the superintendent exercises some control over this critical process. Among the issues that may be addressed are the following:

- Frequency of evaluations
- Instrumentation
- Relationship of job description to performance evaluation
- Purpose and philosophy
- Identification of the evaluators (that is, who will actually evaluate the superintendent)
- General procedures for completing the evaluation

- Procedures for the evaluation conference (e.g., Will it be done in executive session?)
- Relationship of evaluation outcomes to contract renewal

Third, each school district is unique and school board members develop criteria based on priorities, local conditions, and individual perceptions of effective performance. The evaluation clause can help to divide roles and responsibilities (McCurdy, 1992). Therefore, not only can overly vague and ambiguous contracts be a negative factor for the superintendent, they also can detract from quality operations in the school district.

PERSONAL CAREER PLANNING

While it is true that some individuals become superintendents purely by accident, many others have ascended to this position because of careful planning, skillful positioning, and hard work. In essence, they tailored their educational experiences and professional education toward a single career goal. More important, they took the time to reflect systematically on their personal and professional growth—and they connected this knowledge with their career goals. Career planning is an individual activity and a continuous process; it helps individuals determine what they want to do with their lives and to map a strategy for reaching those goals (Steele & Morgan, 1991).

Why Some Do Not Plan

Unfortunately, many aspiring administrators are not very organized when it comes to thinking about their future. They forego career planning because they conclude that the costs (time, energy) outweigh the potential benefit (the career plan produces a significant advantage). Rather, they accept the notion that being in the right place at the right time may allow them to grab the brass ring. Howard Figler (1979) described three categories of behavior in this regard, and they are presented below with explanations of how they apply to aspiring superintendents:

- *The divine calling.* These individuals argue that they knew they wanted to be a superintendent from a very early age. Thus, there is no need for them to consider alternatives.
- *Hang loose.* These individuals claim that one cannot plan what will happen in life. They argue that fate will largely determine whether they reach the superintendency.
- *Grocery store mentality.* These individuals believe that career decisions are like grocery shopping. A person buys a product off the shelf depending on the circumstances at the time the person is shopping. If a superintendency is available and if the timing is right, then a decision may be made to move in that direction.

People in all three categories share the experience of allowing others to dictate a career agenda.

An indifference toward career planning has been particularly noticeable among school administrators. Teachers often obtain licensing as principals or superintendents while commenting, "I don't know if I will ever become an administrator, but having the license might give me more choices." This attitude may be problematic for two reasons. Individuals who truly want to be a superintendent should not sit back and rely on kismet to determine their future. Even worse, an individual may become a superintendent by virtue of being in the right place at the right time, even though he or she is truly unprepared to assume the responsibilities of the position.

Mismatches of individual abilities, needs, and aspirations on the one hand and job opportunities or requirements on the other do occur in educational administration. Since careers in education typically span periods of more than 30 years, it is tragic to discover how few give attention to or understand the rudiments of career planning (Orlosky, McCleary, Shapiro, & Webb, 1984, p. 22). Apathy is particularly disheartening in light of the fact that highly successful executives in all fields are prone to taking responsibility for developing and managing their personal plans (Graen, 1989).

Advantages of Career Planning

One primary advantage of career planning is that it causes the person to gain a better understanding of his or her personal strengths and weaknesses. Introspection is a powerful tool for understanding oneself and one's dispositions toward work. An individual could have a very good grasp of school administration theory without having an objective picture of his or her personal interests and abilities. Self-assessment entails looking objectively at a range of conditions such as personality, academic preparation, professional experience, personal interests, physical and mental health, special skills and abilities, and leadership capabilities. Accurate information in these areas allows the person to correctly answer questions such as these: Do I have the skill and stamina to be effective in this position? Will I be happy doing this job? Am I really ready to assume so much responsibility?

Career planning encourages reflecting on the relationship between one's personal life and work life. So in addition to providing a better understanding of oneself, career planning helps an individual reach a more complete understanding of the profession. The individual is better able to weigh the differences between being a principal and being a superintendent; he or she is better able to anticipate and cope with obstacles that may interfere with one's journey toward the top job. Everyday experiences are analyzed in the context of short-term and long-term goals. Many of the potential benefits associated with career planning are listed in Table 14–2.

It is unlikely that individuals will be able to take charge of their professional futures unless they know themselves and what is required to become a superintendent, know the potential pitfalls, and integrate this information into an ongoing plan.

Table 14–2
Positive attributes of career planning

Attribute	Implications
Understanding of needs and wants related to work	The individual seeks linkages between personal life and work life.
Understanding of opportunities	Planning requires information about the superintendency, state laws, employment processes, and so on.
Likelihood of mentoring, sponsorship, and networking	The value of having support mechanisms becomes more apparent.
Examination of motivations	The individual considers intrinsic and extrinsic motivations and gains a better understanding of why the superintendency is a career goal.
Examination of potential barriers	The individual considers possible obstacles to reaching the superintendency.
Framework for difficult career decisions	Answering questions such as Should I get a doctorate? becomes easier in the context of a career plan.
Periodic assessment of performance	Career plans require periodic assessment; the individual becomes aware of personal and professional growth.
Prevention of complacency	The goal of reaching the superintendency reminds the individual of what is to be accomplished.
Understanding of individuality	Over time, the individual becomes aware of personal differences with respect to other educators who aspire to be superintendents.
Preparation for uncertainty	Many aspects of career are unexpected; career planning lessens the trauma and facilitates appropriate responses.

Elements of an Individual Plan

Too often aspiring administrators mistakenly believe that there is one best path to the superintendency. And when some barrier on that path cannot be scaled, they may completely relinquish their goal. In truth, people reach the superintendency in many different ways. Gender, ethnicity, age, academic degrees, and geographic location are possible variables that can influence the ideal approach for an individual. This is why building a career plan is so challenging: to be effective, it must be individualized.

An individual career plan can take many forms. More effective approaches are characterized by four qualities:

1. *Perenniality.* The process is continuous.
2. *Flexibility.* The process allows for periodic adjustments without losing overall value.
3. *Veracity.* The process is erected on a foundation of honest and objective information.

4. *Influenceability.* The process actually makes a difference in career behavior (Kowalski & Reitzug, 1993).

The challenge is to weave common components into a plan while maintaining a necessary degree of individuality. Examples of these common components are illustrated in Figure 14–2.

- The first is a *vision of life.* Here quality-of-life issues such as income, prestige, family life, and security are considered. Essentially, the person mentally answers the question, "What do I want out of life?"
- *Assessment of self* entails knowing one's own strengths and weaknesses. This information can come from several different sources, such as reflection and undergoing an assessment at a special center (e.g., an administrative assessment center).
- *Career needs statements* identify one's personal needs with respect to work. They are similar to quality-of-life needs, but framed in the context of work and profession. They might include needs related to status, social interactions, and professional challenges.
- *Long-term goals* are self-explanatory. However, a person may have multiple goals that specify what he or she hopes to accomplish at various stages of his or her career. For instance, obtaining a large-district superintendency may be the ultimate goal, whereas obtaining the first superintendency is an intermediate goal.
- Goals are of limited value unless they are accompanied by *strategies for goal attainment.* These are contingencies for achieving one's objectives, and they

Figure 14–2
Elements of a career plan

include short-term goals that allow a person to judge whether he or she is making satisfactory progress.

- Finally, all plans should include an *evaluation* component. This process should be ongoing and lead to periodic adjustments or fine tuning of strategies (and short-term goals). Evaluation provides a process for measuring progress, and over several years, it also helps a person to determine whether his or her initial long-term goal (becoming a superintendent) is realistic.

Special Challenges for Women and Minorities

The process of career planning is especially crucial for those who do not have social or political advantages for reaching the superintendency. White males, for example, have often benefited from being sponsored by the "good ole boys" network (Hord & Estes, 1993). While every aspiring superintendent faces career barriers, women and minorities usually encounter unique and more complex obstacles. These impediments are commonly classified as internal and external. In the former category are issues such as socialization, personality, aspiration level, personal beliefs, attitudes, motivation, and self-image. The latter category includes environmental circumstances such as stereotyping, discrimination, and family responsibilities (Leonard & Papalewis, 1987; Shakeshaft, 1981). Because of these disadvantages, it is particularly important that women and minority educators engage early in career planning (Dopp & Sloan, 1986).

One example of how a career plan can be especially helpful relates to mentoring, sponsorship, and networking. Even though mentoring has been widely advocated (e.g., Edson, 1988), several studies have shown that female administrators often lack this form of support (e.g., Angulo, 1995; Sharratt & Derrington, 1993)—a situation that almost always places them at a disadvantage. Women and minorities usually exhibit career paths to reaching the superintendency that are different from those of males (Mertz & McNeely, 1988)—another factor that illustrates the need to build a personal plan. And because of more and unique potential barriers, women often exhibit a greater range of strategies than do males in seeking the superintendency (Pavan, 1988, 1995).

The underrepresentation of women and minorities in the superintendency has raised questions about the extent to which society and the gatekeepers to this position are responsible (Richards, 1988). Linda Chion-Kenney (1994), for example, asked if search consultants helped or hindered the advancement of minority candidates; she decided that the answer was yes and no, depending on who was asked. Many key decision makers in superintendent selection are prone to concentrate on individual qualities, while ignoring or not understanding external barriers faced by women and minorities (Chase & Bell, 1994). Charol Shakeshaft (1989) noted the following:

> No matter how qualified, how competent, or how psychologically and emotionally ready women are to assume administrative positions in schools, they are still living and working in a society and school organization that is both sexist and racist. (p. 144)

This condition suggests that minority and female candidates need to give special attention to emphasizing their individual qualifications, while recognizing that they have to cope with external barriers such as stereotyping and discrimination. For instance, minority and female candidates are often expected to be better educated and more experienced than others—a situation pointing to the value of earning advanced degrees and gaining experience in a wide variety of settings (Valverde & Brown, 1988). A study of school boards that hired female superintendents revealed that board members were likely to be better educated and to be of a higher social class (Marietti, & Stout, 1994), at least suggesting that they are more aware of external barriers in our society. Not only does career planning help women and minorities to assess individual qualities and societal conditions objectively, it makes it more likely that they will understand that some school boards and some consultants are more aware of stereotyping and discrimination. This insight can be valuable when determining whether to apply for certain positions.

Focusing on Opportunities

Many graduate students who seek superintendent credentials do not intend to occupy this top position; rather, their primary career goal is to serve as assistant or associate superintendents. These positions usually allow practitioners to focus on specific areas of administration, such as instructional supervision, curriculum, personnel, or business management. In some states, a superintendent's license is necessary for such jobs. All central office leadership roles offer administrators the opportunity to touch thousands of young lives, contribute to the professional growth of other educators, and to make lasting contributions to entire communities. A study of urban superintendents, for instance, revealed that the greatest perceived rewards of the position were the ability to influence the lives of students and the ability to influence critical decisions about the future of the school districts (Kowalski, 1995). Current efforts to improve schools and to make their governance more professional and democratic enhance opportunities for superintendents and their assistants to achieve these goals.

While there are only a limited number of superintendencies across the United States (between 14,000 and 15,000), about half of the current holders are expected to retire during the 1990s. In addition, many other positions will become vacant for reasons other than retirement. Many in the profession fear, however, that the number of qualified applicants to fill these vacancies will decline (e.g., Murphy, 1991). This is true even though the extrinsic rewards associated with the position (e.g., salary, fringe benefits, and visibility) remain relatively high. And it is true even though the opportunities to truly make a difference are becoming greater.

Opportunities in the superintendency are appropriately considered in the context of current role expectations. Behaviors that constituted success in the past may not be effective in the future. Increasingly, the work of superintendents is taking them from the isolation of their offices where they once were able to focus almost exclusively on management tasks. Leadership responsibilities, by comparison, are more centered on interactions with other people; and as a result, social skills have become a critical aspect of successful practice (Henkin, 1993). A study of 90 Ohio superintendents participating in an institute for effective leadership, for example, revealed that these practitioners valued communication skills and interpersonal skills above all else (Mahoney, 1996).

While the superintendency is typically discussed in the context of problems and challenges, no one should lose sight of the fact that the position continues to offer a high potential for both intrinsic and extrinsic rewards. The four role conceptions examined in chapter 7 remain valid; however, expectations for professionalism and leadership in a democratic setting are becoming increasingly prominent in this age of reform. Leadership, service to others and to the profession, and the quality of human relationships are becoming inextricably intertwined in contemporary practice. Attributes such as loyalty, empathy, credibility, risk taking, creativity, and professionalism are rapidly becoming the hallmarks of successful practice. Opportunities are greatest for those educators who (1) understand the transitions that are occurring in society and in schools, (2) accept emerging role expectations, and (3) possess the knowledge and skills necessary to fulfill these expectations. The days of the steely-eyed, all-knowing superintendent are over. Ordering and supervising are being replaced by leadership and collaboration. Contemporary superintendents must learn to subordinate themselves to a shared purpose. If they do not, no one will follow—and selfishness and anarchy are likely to rule (Kouzes & Posner, 1993). Jerome T. Murphy (1991) offered the following suggestion for recruiting able young people to the superintendency, "One way, I think, is to portray education as a way of getting rich—the richness of spirit that comes from helping children get a start, from providing a service to society" (p. 510).

FOR FURTHER REFLECTION

This chapter examined several practical issues that relate to how one actually becomes a school superintendent. The search process, which is less than uniform among and within states, was discussed; special attention was given to the emerging practice of school boards to retain consultants to assist with the process. The second primary topic focused on personal decisions and behavior associated with applying for, and accepting, a superintendency. Tasks such as making an application, interviewing, and negotiating a contract were reviewed. The last two parts of the chapter addressed the critical issues of career planning and opportunities. Often overlooked by administrators, planning can be an asset in personal career management. Too often administrators focus solely on the problems and challenges commonly associated with the superintendency while overlooking the transitions that create novel opportunities.

As you consider what you read in this chapter, answer the following questions:

1. Are you aware of how school boards typically conduct superintendent searches in your area? What do you see as the positives and negatives of their approaches?

2. What conditions may have contributed to the growing interest of school boards in retaining search consultants?

3. If a school board is using a search consultant, should you contact the consultant or the school board president if you have questions about the position?

4. What questions should you ask yourself before you decide to apply for a superintendency?

5. Why are mentoring and networking possible advantages to reaching the superintendency?

6. What is the "good ole boys" network? How has it worked to the disadvantage of some who want to become superintendents?

7. What is introspection? Why is it an important element of career planning?

8. In what ways can a career plan help you to stay on track?

9. What role does evaluation play in a career plan?

10. What are the differences between internal and external barriers to the superintendency?

11. Why is it important to get feedback on your performance in an interview?

CASE STUDY

Although it was Saturday evening, Lucy Harrison was sitting in her office, trying to sift through 3 days of telephone messages and mail. She had returned that morning from a second interview for a superintendency in another state. Even though she tried to keep her mind on the paperwork piled on her desk, her thoughts kept drifting to the major decision she had to make in the next 5 days.

Lucy was raised in Georgia, the second of 11 children in her family. Her outstanding accomplishments as a high school student resulted in an academic scholarship to a college in a neighboring state. There she earned a bachelor's degree in elementary education, graduating with honors. Lucy's parents, neither of whom had graduated from high school, were extremely proud of their daughter. After college, she accepted a position teaching second grade in one of the large districts in the Atlanta area.

Lucy loved being a teacher. Students at her school came from a variety of social, economic, and ethnic backgrounds, and she felt that this environment made her work even more fulfilling. During the first 6 years of teaching, Lucy married Marcus Harrison, a young lawyer; had her first child; and completed her master's degree by attending night classes and a few classes during the summer months. Even though she had never considered being an administrator, her principal convinced her to return to school to take several more classes so she could get her principal's license. At first, she rejected the notion because she liked teaching and she liked having time in the summer to spend with her son. However, she followed the advice, deciding that some day she might want to be a principal.

Lucy's opportunity to become a principal came unexpectedly. Her principal was forced to retire in the middle of the school year because of poor health. He convinced the assistant superintendent for elementary education that Lucy was the person who should replace him. At the age of 32, she found herself as an interim principal, and the following fall she was appointed to the position permanently. The next 5 years passed quickly. Lucy had her second child, and her husband became a full partner in his law firm. Lucy was initially apprehensive about being an administrator. She was confident that she could do well, but she thought that the job would be less rewarding than teaching. However, she discovered this to be an unfounded concern.

After spending 8 years in the principalship, Lucy had an opportunity to accept another challenge. The assistant superintendent for elementary education was retiring, and she decided to apply for that job. Though she did not have a doctorate, a desired qualification for the position, she pledged to pursue the degree if selected.

Now 5 years later, Lucy had her earned her doctorate and was faced with the opportunity to become a superintendent. Things had happened rather quickly and unexpectedly. She had been contacted by a search consultant who thought she was ideal for the job in a small suburban district in a neighboring state. Initially, she indicated that she had no interest in the position; she enjoyed her current job, and her husband's work did not allow him to just pick up and move. However, the consultant convinced her to at least meet the school board.

The community and superintendency were almost too good to be true. The area is considered to be one of the finest places to live in the South. The school board was offering her substantially more money than she was currently earning, and there was every indication that the school district was in excellent condition. There were no major financial or facility problems, and the previous superintendent was resigning after being in the position for 18 years. Lucy could not imagine a better career opportunity.

As she sat in her office mulling over 3 days of communications, she knew that she had to make a major decision in no less than 5 days. Her husband did not hide his feelings—he did not want her to accept the job. At best, it would mean that they would live apart a good bit of the time; they did not need the income; and the superintendency would likely mean that she would have even less time to spend with the children. Questions kept running through her mind, and she could not concentrate on the papers piled in front of her. Finally at about 9:00 P.M. she decided to go home. She had not gotten through much of the work—and she still did not know what she would do about her future.

Issues for Discussion

1. Judging from your own experiences, do administrators often find themselves agonizing over taking a new position? Explain your answer.

2. To what extent would Lucy's situation be different if she had developed a career plan that set the superintendency as a career goal?

3. To what extent would Lucy's situation be different if she were a male?

4. What considerations should Lucy have made prior to applying for the superintendency?

5. Do you believe that Lucy is ready to become a superintendent? Why or why not?

6. Is it ethical for search consultants to persuade persons to become applicants?

7. Identify factors that appear to attract Lucy to the superintendency; identify factors that may cause her to reject the job offer.

8. Did Lucy's career pattern contribute to her uncertainty about accepting the superintendency?

9. Assume you attended graduate school with Lucy. She respects your opinion. What advice would you give her?

10. Is it common for superintendents to have conflicts between their personal lives and work lives? What evidence do you have to support your response?

11. Assume that Lucy does not accept the job. Do you think this will have negative repercussions for her career?

REFERENCES

Anderson, R. E., & Lavid, J. S. (1985). Factors school boards use when selecting a superintendent. *Spectrum*, *3*(3), 21–24.

Angulo, M. E. (1995). *Women superintendents of Illinois*. (ERIC Document Reproduction Service No. ED 381 855)

Candoli, C., Cullen, K., & Stufflebeam, D. (1994). *Superintendent performance evaluation: Current practice and directions for improvement*. (ERIC Document Reproduction Service No. ED 376 584)

Cattanach, D. L. (1996). *The school leader in action: Discovering the golden mean*. Lancaster, PA: Technomic.

Chase, S. E., & Bell, C. S. (1994). How search consultants talk about female superintendents. *School Administrator*, *51*(2), 36–38, 40, 42.

Chion-Kenney, L. (1994). Search consultants: Boon or bane to non-traditional candidates for the superintendency? *School Administrator*, *51*(2), 8–9, 12–15, 17–18.

Clark, J. F. (1983). Drafting the superintendent's contract. *American School Board Journal*, *170*(5), 29–31.

Cummings, J. R. (1994). Becoming the successful candidate. *School Administrator*, *51*(2), 28–30, 35.

Davis, B. I., & Brown, G. (1992). Your interview image. *Executive Educator*, *14*(6), 22–23.

Dopp, B. K., & Sloan, C. A. (1986). Career development and succession of women to the superintendency. *Clearing House*, *60*(3), 120–126.

Edson, S. K. (1988). *Pushing the limits: The female administrative aspirant*. Albany, NY: State University of New York Press.

Figler, H. E. (1979). *PATH: A career workbook for liberal arts students*. Cranston, RI: The Carroll Press.

Freeman, R. R. (1985). Don't be timid: Negotiate a decent superintendent contract. *Executive Educator*, *7*(11), 14–15.

Freund, S. A. (1987). Looking at superintendent candidates? They're checking you out, too. *American School Board Journal*, *173*(1), 37.

Genck, F. H., & Klingenberg, A. J. (1991). *Effective schools through effective management* (Revised Edition). Springfield, IL: Illinois Association of School Boards.

Graen, G. B. (1989). *Unwritten rules for your career*. New York: John Wiley & Sons.

Henkin, A. B. (1993). Social skills of superintendents: A leadership requisite in restructured schools. *Educational Research Quarterly*, *16*(4), 15–30.

Hess, F. (1989). Job seekers say you have a lot to learn about superintendent searches. *American School Board Journal*, *176*(5), 39.

Hord, S. M., & Estes, N. (1993). Superintendent selection and success. In D. Carter, T. Glass, & S. Hord (Eds.), *Selecting, preparing, and developing the school district superintendent* (pp. 71–84). Washington, DC: Falmer Press.

Johnson, S. M. (1996). *Leading to change: The challenge of the new superintendency*. San Francisco: Jossey-Bass.

Kouzes, J. M., & Posner, B. Z. (1993). *Credibility: How leaders gain and lose it, why people demand it*. San Francisco: Jossey-Bass.

Kowalski, T. J. (1993). *Keepers of the flame: Contemporary urban* superintendents. Thousand Oaks, CA: Corwin Press.

Kowalski, T. J., & Reitzug, U. C. (1993). *Contemporary school administration: An introduction*. New York: Longman.

Leonard, P. Y., & Papalewis, R. (1987). The underrepresentation of women and minorities in educational administration: Patterns, issues, and recommendations. *Journal of Educational Equity and Leadership*, *7*(3), 188–207.

Mahoney, J. (1996). The secrets of their success. *Executive Educator*, *18*(7), 33–34.

Marietti, M., & Stout, R. T. (1994). School boards that hire women superintendents. *Urban Education*, *28*(4), 373–385.

McCurdy, J. (1992). *Building better board and administrator relations*. Arlington, VA: American Association of School Administrators.

Meet the power brokers (1994). *School Administrator*, *51*(2), 20–23.

Mertz, N. T., & McNeely, S. R. (1988). *Career path of school superintendents*. (ERIC Document Reproduction Service No. ED 305 716)

Miklos, E. (1988). Administrator selection, career patterns, succession, and socialization. In N. Boyan (Ed.), *Handbook of research on educational administration* (pp. 53–76). New York: Longman.

Murphy, J. T. (1991). Superintendents as saviors: From the Terminator to Pogo. *Phi Delta Kappan*, *72*(7), 507–513.

Negroni, P. J. (1992). Landing the big one. *Executive Educator*, *14*(12), 21–23.

O'Hara, D. G. (1994). The superintendent's first contract. *School Administrator*, *51*(7), 19–21.

Orlosky, D. E., McCleary, L. E., Shapiro, A., & Webb, L. D. (1984). *Educational administration today*. Columbus, OH: Charles E. Merrill.

Pavan, B. N. (1988). *Job search strategies utilized by certified aspiring and incumbent female and male public school administrators*. (ERIC Document Reproduction Service No. ED 302 879)

Pavan, B. N. (1995). *First year district superintendents: Women reflect on contradictions between education and politics*. (ERIC Document Reproduction Service No. ED 389 077)

Pigford, A. B. (1995). The interview: What candidates for administrative positions should know and do. *NASSP Bulletin, 79*(569), 54–58.

Redfern, G. B. (1980). *Evaluating the superintendent*. Arlington, VA: American Association of School Administrators.

Richards, C. (1988). The search for equity in educational administration. In N. Boyan (Ed.), *Handbook of research on educational administration* (pp. 159–168). New York: Longman.

Shakeshaft, C. (1981). Women in educational administration: A descriptive analysis of dissertation research and paradigm for future research. In P. Schmuck, W. Charters, & R. Carlson (Eds.), *Educational policy and management of sex differentials* (pp. 403–416). Berkeley, CA: McCutchan.

Shakeshaft, C. (1989). *Women in educational administration* (2nd ed.). Newbury Park, CA: Sage.

Sharratt, G., & Derrington, M. L. (1993). *Female superintendents: Attributes that attract and barriers that discourage their successful applications*. (ERIC Document Reproduction Service No. ED 362 941)

Steele, J. E., & Morgan, M. S. (1991). *Career planning and development*. Lincolnwood, IL: VGM Career Horizons.

Underwood, K. (1994). The search consultant's obligations. *School Administrator, 51*(2), 24–25, 27.

Valverde, L. A., & Brown, F. (1988). Influences on leadership development among racial and ethnic minorities. In N. Boyan (Ed.), *Handbook of research on educational administration* (pp. 143–157). New York: Longman.

Zakariya, S. B. (1987). What you get (and what you pay) when you hire a superintendent search service. *American School Board Journal, 174*(11), 35, 37–38.

Name Index

Subject Index